THE BRETTON WOODS AGREEMENTS

Basic Documents in World Politics

Basic Documents in World Politics reproduces foundational documents that have had a major impact on the character and course of world politics, together with interpretive essays by major scholars. The essays, all previously unpublished, range over the historical context within which the documents were written and their evolving influence in shaping the contemporary world. The goal is to make the documents and controversies they have spawned accessible to newcomers, while contributing to scholarly debates about their meaning and significance.

Previous volumes in the series:

Charter of the United Nations, edited by Ian Shapiro and Joseph Lampert (2014)

Charter of the North Atlantic Treaty Organization, edited by Ian Shapiro and Adam Tooze (2018)

THE BRETTON WOODS AGREEMENTS

Together with Scholarly Commentaries
and Essential Historical Documents

Edited and with an Introduction by

NAOMI LAMOREAUX AND IAN SHAPIRO

Yale UNIVERSITY PRESS/NEW HAVEN & LONDON

Yale University Press books may be purchased in quantity for educational, business, or promotional use. For information, please e-mail sales.press@yale.edu (U.S. office) or sales@yaleup.co.uk (U.K. office).

Designed by Mary Valencia.
Set in Joanna and Eureka Sans type by Westchester Publishing Services.
Printed in the United States of America.

Library of Congress Control Number: 2018962180

ISBN 978-0-300-23679-8 (paperback : alk. paper)

A catalogue record for this book is available from the British Library.

This paper meets the requirements of ANSI/NISO Z39.48-1992 (Permanence of Paper).

10 9 8 7 6 5 4 3 2 1

Contents

Introduction

Naomi Lamoreaux and Ian Shapiro

On July 1, 1944, less than a month after the D-Day landings in Normandy, delegates from forty-four nations gathered at a sprawling hotel near the base of Mount Washington in Bretton Woods, New Hampshire, to plan the postwar financial order. As the delegates debated the arcane details of a system of fixed but flexible exchange rates, Allied troops fought their way through France and battled island by island across the Pacific. US forces were sustaining heavy casualties on Guam when the conference ended three weeks later with agreement on two accords. One accord created the International Monetary Fund (IMF), and the other the International Bank for Reconstruction and Development (IBRD), progenitor of the World Bank.

The contrast between the life-and-death struggles of the war and the esoteric debates at the conference could not have been starker. At stake in both, however, was the kind of world that would take shape in the aftermath of the fighting. The battles determined which side would get the chance to remake the world, and by July of 1944 it was clear that victory would go to the Allies. But what the postwar world would look like was yet to be determined. The Bretton Woods accords, reproduced at the end of this volume, were part of the answer. The essays we have collected here revisit the accords, dry and opaque as they might seem at first glance to be, with the aim of recapturing the fears and tensions that shaped their provisions. The essays also examine alternative proposals that the assembly might have adopted, ideas whose time had passed or were yet to come. Dominated by the United States, the conference left many problems unresolved, many countries' needs unmet, and these omissions would lead to the eventual collapse of the system. The fate of the Bretton Woods accords, the essays show, was as much bound up with what was not accomplished as with what was.

Dubbed the United Nations Monetary and Financial Conference, the gathering at Bretton Woods was the product of a series of planning conferences that began in Hot Springs, Virginia, in 1943 and culminated with a preconference meeting in Atlantic City, New Jersey, in June of 1944. Over the course of those meetings the scope of the discussion was increasingly narrowed. Although the initial Hot Springs conference addressed a broad set of development issues, by Bretton Woods the focus was on a single, core problem: designing a set of institutions to regulate the rates at which one nation's currency could be exchanged for another's.

However limiting the focus on exchange rates seemed to delegates interested in broader issues of development, the topic cut to the heart of how the world economy functioned. When people in Country A bought goods from Country B, they had to pay for them in B's currency and effectively had to change their own money into B's in order to do so. But what was a unit of A's money worth in B units? One way of finding out was to let the market determine the exchange rate. If Country A's currency was overvalued relative to B's, producers in B would increase their exports to A, and consumers in B would decrease their imports from A, causing the value of A's currency to fall. If Country A's currency was undervalued, the reverse would happen. Unfortunately, this simple market solution was not always sufficient in practice because people did not only (or even mainly) buy goods on the spot. More often they bought goods on credit, for which payment came due sometime in the future. When transactions involved payments in the future, people needed to know what the exchange rate would be when their debts came due, not just in the present. The problem, however, was that governments could intervene in the market and take actions that affected the value of their currencies. Most obviously, they could inflate their money by printing more of it. Moreover, it was possible they would deliberately take such actions with the aim of reducing the burden of debt on their citizens (or themselves).

Historically, countries sought credibly to commit not to change the value of their currencies by pegging them to a particular amount of precious metals—either gold or silver or a combination of the two. As the volume of global trade increased in the late nineteenth century, more and more countries joined the club of advanced nations that fixed their currencies to a given quantity of gold.[1] When they did so, they effectively promised to maintain reserves of gold (or of currencies like the British pound that were considered as good as gold) and allow holders of their currencies to redeem the bills at will at the fixed exchange rate. The only circumstances under which a country could break that promise without being ostracized from the club were major financial crises or wars. Then the country might suspend the convertibility of its currency, but only for the duration of the emergency.

During the heyday of the gold standard in the late nineteenth and early twentieth centuries, there was no international coordinating mechanism to enable countries to adjust the value of their currencies in response to trade imbalances. As a result, the system was characterized by a potentially dangerous asymmetry. On the one hand, nations whose currencies were undervalued ran trade surpluses that caused gold to flow in their direction. They had no incentive to revalue their exchange rates, because that would only make their exports more expensive. On the other hand, nations whose currencies were overvalued ran trade deficits and experienced gold outflows. In a pure market setting, countries with trade deficits would have experienced a fall in the value of their currencies, but under the international gold standard that could not easily happen. For the value of a nation's currency to fall, the government had to change the peg—that is, it had to announce it was going to inflate its currency. Such a policy change was difficult to effect politically because creditors in the domestic economy stood to lose money. It was also tantamount to going off the gold standard and so would hurt the citizens' ability to borrow internationally and hence to trade. To avoid one bad outcome, however, countries had to choose another—to inflict pain on their economies by, for example, raising interest rates to stem the outflow of gold—and that was what they most often decided to do.[2]

The international gold standard worked reasonably well until the First World War. When the fighting broke out, the belligerent nations suspended the convertibility of their currencies. That was to be expected, but it was also to be expected that they would return to gold as soon as possible when the war ended. The serious financial turbulence that followed the peace, especially the disastrous postwar inflation that afflicted many countries on the European Continent, made a return to the gold standard both more difficult and more imperative. Although the return was largely accomplished by 1926, the world had changed, and the gold values of the major currencies were no longer appropriate to their countries' altered positions in the world economy. As a result, the gold standard never worked the way it had before the war. It was now a drag on the economies of the countries that sustained it, particularly Britain's, whose currency was now overvalued, and it came crashing down in the early years of the Great Depression.[3] And as the gold standard collapsed, so did international trade.

These catastrophic events formed the intellectual backdrop for the Bretton Woods Conference. As the delegates convened in New Hampshire in the summer of 1944, the goal that was uppermost in their minds was to create a new kind of world financial order capable of withstanding the stresses that everyone expected would resume with the peace.

PART I: THE WEIGHT OF THE PAST

"The war to end all wars," as Woodrow Wilson dubbed it with unintended irony, was as catastrophic as it was unexpected. The European powers might have stumbled into the conflict in Sarajevo in June of 1914, but by the time it was over, seventeen million Europeans were dead and another twenty million were wounded. The devastation reached well beyond traditional battlefields into cities, towns, farms, and families. Countless millions lost homes and livelihoods. Streams of refugees wandered central and southern Europe. It was the world's first total war.

Unsurprisingly, the end of the conflict was marked by a widespread desire to turn back the clock. The major powers had been at peace for the better part of a century before 1914, apart from the Crimean War in the mid-1850s and the ten-month Franco-Prussian War of 1870–1871. Most European countries had enjoyed astonishing levels of economic prosperity in the decades leading up to 1914—the fruits of industrialization and empire. As Jeffry Frieden notes in the first essay, "The Political Economy of the Bretton Woods Agreements," the historically unparalleled rates of economic growth that fed this prosperity had been sustained by an open international economic order. Most of the participants at the Versailles peace talks in January of 1919 wanted and expected to restore it.

But the world, and the nations composing it, had changed irreversibly, and there was no going back. The United States had emerged from the fighting as the world's dominant economy, as well as the largest creditor nation. Woodrow Wilson's American-led global agenda did not include re-creating the prewar international economic environment that Britain had dominated. The United Kingdom's diminished economic position would in any case have doomed its effort to maintain the gold standard at its prewar peg. The remnants of the Ottoman and Austro-Hungarian Empires were emerging as new nations, with new demands and subject to new imperatives. And it was far from clear how the old European powers would relate to one another as they reconstituted themselves on a world stage that bore scant resemblance to the one that had existed in 1914.

A central feature of the prewar world had been that national economies were price-takers. Countries were bound, as Frieden says, to "adapt themselves to the state of their international economic relations rather than the other way round." Stability depended on the gold standard, the basic unit of value that backed national currencies and was the benchmark for setting their relative rates of exchange. Sustaining a country's commitment to gold meant that when its balance of payments came under stress, domestic wages and prices would adjust—not unlike the "internal devaluations" that have been forced on Eurozone countries like Greece since the 2008 financial crisis. This kind of internal adjustment had been feasible in the late nineteenth century because most countries had highly competitive economies in which labor was not organized and capital consisted mostly of small family farms and firms. People had little choice but to accept downward pressure on wages and prices when needed to keep their currency's gold value intact. Even with the expanding franchise in some European countries after the 1860s, neither workers nor employers had the power to force other policies on their governments.

All this had changed by the 1920s. By then the major industrial economies featured large firms—many of them monopolies or oligopolies with considerable market power—and unionized workforces. Now business and labor could, and did, resist pressure on prices and wages, causing "massive macroeconomic dislocations, including massive unemployment," according to Frieden. Semiauthoritarian political systems in which there had been few or no labor rights, and in which socialist movements were illegal or suppressed, had been replaced by democracies that "brought workers, farmers, and the middle classes into the center of politics." Gone were the days when elites could make them bear the costs of macroeconomic adjustment.

It was in this changed context that John Maynard Keynes declared the gold standard to be a "barbarous relic."[4] Keynes was one of the few people who understood that the prewar economic order could not be reconstituted. Most of Europe's leaders disagreed. Rejecting Keynes's advice, they returned the world to a rigid system centered on the gold standard, a system that was bound to bring latent economic and social conflicts to the fore.

The resulting turmoil was most obvious from the perspective of the vanquished powers whose empires were disintegrating and who faced ongoing conflict in the form of insurrections and civil wars that killed another four million people in the five years after the war.[5] The victorious powers initially seemed more secure, but the postwar international arrangements were too inflexible and too fragile to contain the industrial dynamics that now dominated their internal politics. In retrospect their leaders' confidence in their return to the prewar order was a bit like that which had prevailed in the staterooms of the Titanic in April of 1912. They were steaming toward the Great Depression, collapse of the gold standard, rising protectionism, and, eventually, German rearmament and resumption of the war that had never really ended.[6]

The victorious powers were determined not to repeat these mistakes at the end of World War II. Once victory was in sight, they set out to design an international trade and financial system that would allow for the relatively free flow of goods and capital that had prevailed before 1914. It would need to be flexible enough to allow nations to manage capital flows and currencies so they would be able to respond to the changing international economic landscape and to demands for growth, employment, and security from their domestic populations.

These twin goals led the negotiators at Bretton Woods to build on a middle ground between gold-standard orthodoxy and more radical forms of heterodoxy. The core of the agreement was a system of fixed but adjustable exchange rates. Each country's currency would be pegged relative to the dollar, which would be backed by gold at a price set at $35 an ounce. This arrangement would be overseen by a new international institution—the International Monetary Fund (IMF)—which would police the system of stable exchange rates called for in the agreement and provide the liquidity countries needed to withstand temporary imbalances. Bretton Woods also created a second financial institution, the World Bank, which would help finance the reconstruction of the war-torn economies and support economic development projects around the globe.

The Bretton Woods system worked well enough initially because the United States held most of the world's gold reserves and was able to supply enough dollars to meet international liquidity demands without compromising its domestic economy. But the gold standard was a ticking time bomb. As the European and Japanese economies reconstituted themselves and growth began to accelerate in the developing world, what would come to be known as the Triffin Dilemma emerged. Economist Robert Triffin testified before Congress in 1960 that as central banks and investors bought increasing numbers of dollars to hold as foreign exchange reserves, the United States would be forced to run ever-increasing trade deficits. The deficits would sustain cheap imports at home, but at the price of diminishing confidence in the dollar once it became obvious that the United States lacked the gold reserves to maintain convertibility at the stipulated rate. In effect, growing demands on the US dollar as the world's reserve currency would undermine its capacity to function as a reserve asset.[7] Eventually, as subsequent chapters detail, something would have to give.

In retrospect, it might seem odd that the Bretton Woods negotiators kept the gold standard in any form. In some ways the agreement was a way station on the road to abandonment. As Barry Eichengreen notes in "The Monetary Role of Gold as the Original Sin of Bretton Woods," the challenge that an ongoing role for gold created was well understood long before Triffin explained it to Congress in 1960. Some economists had proposed severing the ties between gold and the world's reserve currencies at the time, and there had even been successful—if bounded—experiments in the 1930s suggesting that currencies could be stabilized against one another without an external anchor. Yet few people were willing to make that leap away from gold for the world economy. Even Keynes's proposal for a supranational currency managed by the IMF (the "bancor"), which would be used as the unit of account for international trade, retained a residual role for gold.

Why? Eichengreen offers a three-part answer. First, gold had been the benchmark for so long that few took the idea seriously that a reserve currency could operate without it. Second, it was widely believed that people would not accept the dollar as the world's reserve currency unless it was backed by gold. There was no way to test this belief empirically, because the United States owned most of the world's gold in the 1940s, rendering the counterfactual exercise impossible, but it would turn out later that there were alternatives to gold—such as inflation targeting and price stability—that no one had thought of in the 1940s. Finally, imagining an alternative regime required a major shift in mind-sets, away from "a system of stable exchange rates" toward "a stable system of exchange rates," which outstripped the imaginative capacities of economists and policy makers in the 1940s.

This imaginative deficit among the Bretton Woods architects is not surprising in light of their experience at the time. The idea that an unanchored system of exchange rates could find enough of an equilibrium to be feasible in an anarchic world order was difficult for people to imagine. That the IMF could supply stability required a substantial leap of faith. The IMF was an unprecedented institution, in the process of being cut from whole cloth. No one knew whether it would work any more than they knew that the United Nations that the victorious powers were designing at the same time would work. The fate of Woodrow Wilson's League of Nations after World War I was scarcely grounds for optimism about the prospects for international institutions. The IMF, like the UN, turned out to be an enduring, if only intermittently effective, source of international stability, but it would have verged on reckless to bet the future of the world's financial system on this in 1944.

Indeed, as Douglas Irwin notes in "The Missing Bretton Woods Debate over Flexible Exchange Rates," for the first decade after the war the consensus diagnosis of the interwar period remained that the floating exchange rates that had been instituted when the gold standard collapsed in the mid-1930s had been a disaster. Influential economists like Ragnar Nurkse reaffirmed the views of Friedrich Hayek and Lionel Robbins that flexible exchange rate regimes lacked any tendency toward equilibrium—that they invited currency speculation, competitive depreciation, and protectionism, which would undermine trade. This seemed to be the lesson of the interwar years. The early 1920s, before most countries had returned to the gold standard, had been marked by instability and hyperinflation in Germany and elsewhere, and after 1936, when no country remained on the gold standard, the widespread resort to competitive devaluations and protectionism had fueled the mutual national hostilities that would eventually result in the resumption of war. The idea that hitherto untested international institutions could contain dynamics of this power and magnitude would easily be dismissed as wishful thinking.

To be sure, Keynes and many others recognized that exchange controls, currency depreciation, and expansionist monetary policies had been essential to reviving growth and employment after the Depression. As a result, they recognized the need for enough exchange rate flexibility to permit policy makers to prioritize domestic equilibrium over exchange rate stability at least some of the time. Hence their support for a gold-based regime that would allow for revaluation from time to time through adjustable pegs. But it would not be until Milton Friedman published "The Case for Flexible Exchange Rates" almost a decade after the IMF's founding that mainstream opinion would begin turning in favor of a fully floating regime.[8]

PART II: THE DISAPPEARING ORDER

The conventional view of Keynes's negotiations with his American counterpart Harry Dexter White at Bretton Woods is that Keynes played a losing hand about as well as possible. The United States was the ascendant hegemon, likely to be the largest creditor nation in the world for many years to come. Britain, the biggest debtor nation, was in dire need of a massive rebuilding program and on the verge of losing the great bulk—if not all—of its most valuable imperial assets and much of its global influence. Keynes made concession after concession: on the bancor, on maintaining a system of imperial preferences, on the governance of the IMF and the terms for borrowing from it, and on much else besides. But this was inevitable. Even if White had been inclined to give more ground than absolutely necessary, his masters in Washington were not. The Americans were going to be the principal architects of the new international order, and they would do it with their national interests first, and firmly in mind.

If British interests were on the wane at Bretton Woods, Keynes's influence was not. Six years earlier he had ended his *General Theory of Employment, Interest, and Money* with the oft-quoted remark that "Practical men, who believe themselves to be quite exempt from any intellectual influence, are usually the slaves of some defunct economist." Keynes's own ideas were by no means defunct in the 1940s, but James Boughton makes the case in "The Universally Keynesian Vision of Bretton Woods" that his influence on the agreement was more profound than many realized at the time or since.

Boughton notes that both the IMF and the World Bank were designed to promote Keynesian ideals—sustainable economic growth with price stability—that were broadly shared around the world. More important, the new institutions were designed to work toward those goals by Keynesian means: enabling member countries to pursue active fiscal and monetary policies by alleviating constraints, such as inadequate savings, and by discouraging reliance on trade barriers and autarkic or mercantilist economic policies. Boughton argues that the fact that both of the main founding partners in the United Kingdom and the United States were pursuing the Keynesian goals by Keynesian means has been obscured in the scholarly literature, which has been overly concerned with differences in the technical details and nuances in emphasis. Boughton redresses this imbalance by spelling out the larger commitments that the agreement's architects shared. Attending to these commitments leads him to a discussion of the subsequent evolution of the Bretton Woods and post–Bretton Woods system wherein, again, he discerns the long shadow of Keynes's influence. The 1965 statement frequently attributed to Milton Friedman that "we are all Keynesians now" might partly have misrepresented Friedman's views, but on Boughton's telling, it is more right than wrong.[9]

In "Bretton Woods: The Parliamentary Debates in the United Kingdom," Andrew Bailey, Gordon Bannerman, and Cheryl Schonhardt-Bailey analyze the British government's response to their declining leverage during and after the Bretton Woods negotiations by looking at parliamentary debates between 1943 and 1945. In some ways, these debates call to mind the stages of grief for a recently deceased relative that range from denial to outrage and eventual acceptance. MPs struggled to come to grips with America's muscle in getting its way on key features of the agreement—not to mention the stiff terms of the American $3.75 billion loan at 2 percent interest to Britain that accompanied it in 1945. But the MPs also saw that the agreement and loan presented them with opportunities.

It might seem odd that in 1945 the newly elected Labour government would accept such exacting terms. After all, its leaders were deeply committed to democratic socialism, nationalization, and the construction of the welfare state on an unprecedented scale. Moreover, during the war, as ministers in Britain's wartime National Unity government, these leaders had become effective politicians who even managed to get partial Tory support for the 1942 Beveridge Report, which would become the blueprint for Labour's postwar welfare state. But as Bailey, Bannerman, and Schonhardt-Bailey note, wartime government experience also had a chastening influence on Labour ministers. It forced them to become more realistic and pragmatic about the constraints within which they would have to work. They recognized, however reluctantly, that the agreement and the loan would give Britain a degree of financial stability in the immediate postwar world, stability that would enable them to pursue their economic and social agenda with the Keynesian tools discussed by Boughton in the preceding chapter. In this they turned out to be right.

If the British had trouble letting go of their glorious past, the French had trouble letting go of gold. As Michael Graetz and Olivia Briffault explain in "A 'Barbarous Relic': The French, Gold, and the Demise of Bretton Woods," they too were concerned with ascendant American power in the global economy. In some ways the French attachment to gold was rooted in the past. Since the time of the French Revolution, when a gold standard saved the nation from hyperinflation, France had wanted gold to serve as the linchpin of international monetary arrangements. The French had retained this strong predilection for gold thereafter, reaffirming its importance as the best antidote to inflation of the 1920s. But their attachment to the gold standard at Bretton Woods and afterward was for a different, political, reason. The only viable alternative to gold was a system based on the dollar. Believing that this would enhance American power, the French proposed, instead, a system of mutually pegged currencies based on gold to try to forestall that result.

But like the British, the French were playing a weak hand at Bretton Woods. Their proposal was ignored at the conference, and afterward they fought a series of losing battles to prevent the system from drifting away from its indirect peg to gold and toward what for all practical purposes was the floating "dollar standard" that they had anticipated and feared. Graetz and Briffault unpack this hitherto untold story. They also explain that the French attachment to a fixed-rate system, tied to a gold standard, was motivated partly out of the belief that this would make it easier to transition to a European economic union with its own currency, the "ecu" (European Currency Union), that could compete with the dollar. They might have been right about this. A fully fledged European currency did not come into operation until almost three decades after Richard Nixon suspended the dollar's convertibility to gold at a fixed price. Its viability as an alternative to the dollar is a story that is still unfolding, though its prospects since the 2008 financial crisis have surely dimmed.

PART III: PATHS TAKEN AND NOT TAKEN

Britain and France were not the only countries to pursue separate agendas at Bretton Woods. All of the other advanced industrial nations at the conference, including Belgium, Denmark, and the Netherlands in Europe, as well as colonial offshoots such as Canada and Australia in other parts of the world, had somewhat different interests. Moreover, although most of what we would today call the Global South was still under colonial rule and, with the exception of India, not independently represented at the conference, a number of developing countries, ranging from the likes of Brazil, Cuba, and Mexico in Latin America, to Czechoslovakia, Poland, and Yugoslavia in eastern Europe, to China and to the Soviet Union, pushed pro-development plans. As Boughton shows in his essay in part II, the United States was at pains to perpetuate its wartime cooperation with the Soviet Union and, to this end, agreed to clauses that reassured the Soviets that the IMF would not interfere with its relations with nonmember states within its sphere of influence. Although these concessions were sufficient to secure the Soviet Union's signature on the accords, Stalin subsequently blocked the USSR's membership in the IMF. Most of the other countries in attendance both signed the agreement and joined the IMF, though often with significant reservations. The Venezuelan delegation even appended to the final document the statement that its signature did "not imply any recommendation to its Government as to the acceptance of the documents contained."[10]

Australia is particularly interesting because it had a substantial industrial sector (over a quarter of its labor force was employed in manufacturing by the beginning of the Second World War), but, like many developing countries, it was a major exporter of primary agricultural and mineral products. Although a rich country in terms of per capita income, it had suffered greatly from the economic turbulence of the early twentieth century. Somewhere between 20 and 30 percent of its workforce was unemployed during the Great Depression, and its primary-goods sector was buffeted by gyrating terms of trade and the collapse of aggregate demand in the economies of its trading partners.[11] As Selwyn Cornish and Kurt Schuler show in their chapter, "Australia's Full-Employment Proposals at Bretton Woods," policy makers in Australia understood the importance of fixed but adjustable exchange rates, but, heavily influenced by Keynes, they pushed in addition for a commitment to maintaining full employment by the participating countries. Australia's leaders intended to prioritize the health of their domestic economy over the maintenance of exchange rates, and they did not want to be punished by the IMF as a consequence. Their insistence on giving full employment precedence over trade might seem strange for a country so dependent on primary-goods exports, but it was precisely for this reason that Australia wanted the leading industrial countries to commit to maintaining full employment. Such a commitment would prevent a recurrence of the general collapse in aggregate demand that had devastated primary-goods producers around the world. It would in effect allow Australia to have its cake and eat it, too: primary producers would flourish so long as world demand for their output was strong, and the government could focus on keeping unemployment in the industrial sector low.

Australia did not get the commitment it wanted at Bretton Woods, primarily because the Americans were more concerned with trade than full employment and, in any event, could not be seen by the US Congress as allowing domestic economic policy to be dictated by an international agreement. However, the accord that created the IMF at least paid lip service to the Australian position by describing the organization's larger purpose as "to facilitate the expansion and balanced growth of international trade" with the aim of "promotion and maintenance of high levels of employment and real income. . . ." (Article I, ii). Moreover, the Australians obtained a clause that gave member nations some freedom to protect domestic priorities by allowing them unilaterally to increase or decrease the value of their currencies by up to 10 percent.[12] As Cornish and Schuler show, these concessions were enough for Australia to sign the accords, albeit grudgingly "for purposes of certification," and Australia ultimately joined the IMF in 1947.

Australia's proposals had support early on from a number of developing countries, but many of these nations lost interest as the conference progressed. For them, the commitment to full employment was part of a broader package of proposals related to economic development, and they were less interested in full employment per se than in the other parts of the package. Over the course of the conference these other elements came to loom increasingly larger, but at the beginning the idea of full employment was deeply entangled in the delegates' minds with another set of concerns involving food security. As Martin Daunton details in "Nutrition, Food, Agriculture, and the World Economy," many policy makers believed that high food prices were as much a source of unrest as unemployment and that the drive to obtain an adequate supply of foodstuffs had helped to fuel the Second World War.[13]

Not surprisingly, then, the first conference held to plan for postwar reconstruction was devoted to food and nutrition, or, as President Roosevelt put it in his invitation, to the "possibilities of progressively improving in each country the levels of consumption within the framework of an expansion of its general economic activity."[14] Held in Hot Springs, Virginia, in the spring of 1943, the conference addressed nutritional standards, improved methods of farming, and trade policy. The meeting's agenda was largely the work of the Australian delegate Frank McDougall, and in addition to a statement of "the close interdependence between the level of employment in all countries, the character and extent of industrial development, the management of currencies, the direction of national and international investment, and the policy adopted by the nationals toward foreign trade," it asserted the importance of achieving freedom from "want of food."[15] As Daunton shows, nothing much came of the proposals except another meeting in Quebec in 1945 to establish what became the United Nations Food and Agriculture Organization. The idea of food security, however, was an important part of the intellectual baggage that many delegates brought with them to New Hampshire, and this earlier forum explains why the Australian proposals had so much initial support.

At Bretton Woods, however, this earlier agenda for the postwar order took a back seat to planning the international system of exchange rates, which luminaries like Keynes thought more important than nutrition.[16] Concerns about economic development did not disappear from the agenda but rather followed a different trajectory as plans for what would become the World Bank took shape. In his chapter, "How the Bretton Woods Negotiations Helped to Pioneer International Development," Eric Helleiner traces the idea of a development bank to a proposal that Sun Yat-sen sent to the Paris Peace Conference in 1919. Although the proposal did not gain any traction at the time—indeed concerns for economic development were eclipsed by the specter of mass starvation—it resurfaced, Helleiner shows, at Bretton Woods through the efforts of the Chinese delegation. Helleiner also highlights the role that inter-American organizations played in laying the groundwork for the World Bank. During the 1930s, bilateral loans from the US government for development projects had spurred a series of broader multilateral schemes, some of which, such as the Inter-American Coffee Agreement, were actually realized, and others, such as the Inter-American Bank, remained on the drawing board. Helleiner makes the case that White, who had been involved in many of these initiatives, brought this experience into planning for the Bretton Woods Conference, though his most radical proposals did not make it into the final draft he circulated at the start of the conference.

At the meeting itself, representatives from developing countries voiced concern that the IMF and World Bank would devote too large a proportion of their resources to reconstructing the belligerents' economies and would neglect the rest of the world. They pushed successfully for explicit recognition of a development mission for both institutions. The agreement creating the World Bank stated that its purpose would include "the development of productive facilities and resources in less developed countries," and committed the institution to give "equitable consideration" to development, along with reconstruction, projects in allocating the bank's resources.[17] Similarly, the agreement creating the IMF promised to promote "the development of the productive resources of all members."[18] Perhaps more important, developing nations used the discussions at Bretton Woods to shape the interpretation of the accords. In a speech in support of the IMF, Carlos Lleras Restrepo of Colombia skillfully reinterpreted the accord as embracing trade protection for infant industries in developing countries. White implicitly endorsed this reinterpretation in a speech of his own, applauding Restrepo's "splendid statement in support of the recommendation."[19] After Roosevelt's death, the Truman administration undercut the development mission of the IMF and World Bank, but as Helleiner convincingly demonstrates, that was not the position of the United States at the conference itself.

PART IV: DENOUEMENT AND LEGACY

Because of the enormous amount of damage inflicted on the major European and Asian economies by the Great Depression and the Second World War, it took nearly a decade and a half for the Bretton Woods Agreements to become fully operational. By the time that member countries had finally restored the convertibility of their currencies, moreover, Bretton Woods had evolved into something quite different from what was originally intended, or at least from what the French had hoped it would be. As Michael Bordo shows in "The Operation and Demise of the Bretton Woods System, 1958–1971," the United States quickly came to play an oversized role in the system's operation. Because the United States was the only country that pegged its currency to gold, and because the United States had emerged from the war as the world's dominant economy, the dollar became the lynchpin of the world financial system. Not only did it provide traders with a unit of account and medium of exchange, but other nations came to hold their reserves primarily in dollars rather than in the broad basket of currencies that the French had pushed for. US influence over the international monetary system also eclipsed that of the IMF, which lacked sufficient resources to support the postwar expansion of trade and whose regulatory role proved ineffectual, as first France, then Britain, and then Canada revalued their currencies in defiance of the accords.

For a time it seemed as if this revised Bretton Woods system was working well. The 1960s were characterized by higher, more stable rates of economic growth than any preceding period of history. However, serious problems lurked beneath the surface. In particular, the same kinds of balance-of-payments asymmetries that had plagued the interwar gold standard threatened to destabilize the system. Bordo argues that the new international financial institutions put into place in the wake of Bretton Woods would have kept these problems manageable had the United States maintained fiscal discipline. But the United States did not. The growing influence of Keynesian economic policy within the Johnson administration, coupled with administration pressure on the Federal Reserve System to accommodate borrowing for the Vietnam War, led to rising inflation in the United States, which spread to other countries and undermined faith in the dollar as a reserve currency.

The main transmission mechanism for this inflation was the growing balance-of-payments deficit between the United States and the rest of the world, especially West Germany and Japan. Prostrate after the war, these two former Axis powers had experienced healthy economic recoveries, and by the 1960s were beginning to run trade surpluses with the United States. Between 1961 and 1971 West Germany raised the value of its currency three times to reduce its trade imbalance with the United States, but Japan refused to take similar action. Frances McCall Rosenbluth and James Sundquist detail the growing tensions between Japan and the United States in "Japan and the Collapse of Bretton Woods." Although US policy generally supported the principle of free trade, the inroads that Japanese exports of textiles and steel were making in the US domestic market awakened powerful protectionist interests. US demands that the Japanese "voluntarily" limit textile shipments to the United States were met with resistance. Nor was Japan willing to revalue its currency. In the end, the US president, Richard M. Nixon, took unilateral action. In August of 1971 he imposed a 10 percent surcharge on imports to the United States to force Japan to raise the value of its currency. He simultaneously suspended the convertibility of the dollar into gold, effectively killing the Bretton Woods system.

Why this drastic step? Why not simply take action against the Japanese? As Bordo argues, inflation in the United States meant that there were too many dollars in foreign hands relative to the stock of gold in the United States, creating fears of a run on the dollar. Central banks in Europe had been cooperating with the Federal Reserve Board in the United States to maintain the value of the dollar, but there were limits to what they were willing to do. Increasing pressure on the dollar and reports that Britain and France were about to start exchanging their stock of dollars for gold had as much to do with Nixon's decision to close the gold window as did perceived Japanese intransigence. The immediate result of the US announcement was another international meeting to rescue the system by devaluing the dollar, among other things, but the reform was too little too late. By early 1973 all the major currencies were floating against the dollar.

The United States and its allies had held a number of international conferences in the mid-1940s to plan the postwar order, but Bretton Woods is the only one whose name resonates in the popular imagination. As Harold James points out in the volume's concluding essay, "The Multiple Contexts of Bretton Woods," not even the 1945 San Francisco conference that gave birth to the United Nations has gained as much name recognition from the general public. What James calls the "myth" of Bretton Woods had much to do with the "godlike" aura of Keynes, whose influence, we have seen, permeated the conference. But it was also a result of the long period of prosperity that followed. The delegates who gathered in New Hampshire had feared that the world economy would sink back into a depression once the warring powers were able to cut military spending and move to put their own fiscal houses in order. Not only did these fears prove unfounded, but the more than two decades of expansion that ensued were remarkably free from the kinds of financial turbulence that had buffeted the interwar economy. Keynes, it seemed, had come down from Mount Olympus and guided the delegates toward a system of fixed but flexible exchange rates that had saved capitalism from itself.

Keynes's ideas might have influenced the views of the participants, but as James underscores, Bretton Woods was the product of American hegemony. The British had wanted the postwar order to be shaped by Anglo-American agreement, but Roosevelt insisted that it must be the product of multilateral negotiations involving the Soviets, the Chinese, and developing nations around the world, as well as Britain and the other European powers. In fact, however, it was US priorities that dominated the proceedings and determined the final structure of the accords. That Bretton Woods was an American show from start to finish was not necessarily a bad thing, James suggests. No previous attempt at multilateral agreement had succeeded. Bretton Woods worked because the Americans knew what they wanted and had the power both to get their way and make their vision operational. What the Americans wanted, James shows, was to take the kinds of trade issues that had previously stymied attempts at international agreement (and that would also raise hackles in Congress) off the table and substitute monetary solutions in their stead. The Bretton Woods system, in James's words, was "the intellectual sugar covering" that masked "the bitter taste" both of Realpolitik dollar hegemony in the international context and of internationalism in the domestic. It worked until the Triffin Dilemma brought the system's internal tensions to the surface, after which it was no longer in the US interest to maintain it. Yet Bretton Woods left indelible marks on the global financial and political landscape. Although trade issues have once again come to the fore, the institutions Bretton Woods spawned—the IMF, the World Bank, and the dollar as the world's reserve currency—continue to structure the global political economy half a century after the agreements' formal demise. They show few signs of disappearing anytime soon.

Notes

1. Michael D. Bordo and Hugh Rockoff, "The Gold Standard as a 'Good Housekeeping Seal of Approval,'" *Journal of Economic History* 56 (June 1996): 389–428; and Barry Eichengreen, *Globalizing Capital: A History of the International Monetary System*, 2nd ed., (Princeton, NJ: Princeton University Press, 2008), chap. 2.

2. Peter Temin, "Transmission of the Great Depression," *Journal of Economic Perspectives* 7 (Spring 1993): 87–102.

3. The best accounts are Barry Eichengreen, *Golden Fetters: The Gold Standard and the Great Depression, 1919–1939* (New York: Oxford University Press, 1992); and Peter Temin, *Lessons from the Great Depression* (Cambridge, MA: MIT Press, 1989).

4. John Maynard Keynes, *A Tract on Monetary Reform* (London: Macmillan, 1923), 187.

5. Robert Gerwarth, *The Vanquished: Why the First World War Failed to End, 1917–1923* (New York: Farrar, Straus & Giroux, 2016), 7.

6. Adam Tooze, *The Wages of Destruction: The Making and Breaking of the Nazi Economy* (London: Allen Lane, 2006).

7. Triffin had forecast problems with the Bretton Woods system as early as 1947. See "National Central Banking and the International Economy," *Postwar Economic Studies* 7 (September 1947): 46–81.

8. Milton Friedman, "The Case for Flexible Exchange Rates," was written in 1950 and published in Milton Friedman, *Essays in Positive Economics* (Chicago: University of Chicago Press, 1953), 157–203.

9. Friedman actually said, "In one sense, we are all Keynesians now; in another, nobody is any longer a Keynesian." See "The Economy: We Are All Keynesians Now," *Time*, December 31, 1965.

10. See "Final Act (22 July 1944)," in the "Historical Documents" section of this book.

11. Ian W. McLean, *Why Australia Prospered: The Shifting Sources of Economic Growth* (Princeton, NJ: Princeton University Press, 2013), 162, 181, 189.

12. Australia also obtained an increase in its IMF quota.

13. For a recent version of this argument, see Timothy Snyder, *Black Earth: The Holocaust as History and Warning* (New York: Crown, 2015).

14. As quoted in Martin Daunton, "Nutrition, Food, Agriculture, and the World Economy," chap. 7 in this book.

15. As quoted in Selwyn Cornish and Kurt Schuler, "Australia's Full-Employment Proposals at Bretton Woods," chap. 8 in this book.

16. Daunton quotes a letter Keynes wrote to the American ambassador in London, scoffing at the idea for the Hot Springs conference: "What you are saying is that your President with his great political insight has decided that the best strategy for post-war reconstruction is to start with vitamins and then by a circuitous route work round to the international balance of payments!" (As reported by Ernest F. Penrose, *Economic Planning for the Peace* [Princeton, NJ: Princeton University Press, 1953], 120.)

17. See "Articles of Agreement of the International Bank for Reconstruction and Development, July 22, 1944," Article I (i) and Article III (i).

18. "Articles of Agreement for the International Monetary Fund, July 22, 1944," Article I (ii).

19. Quoted in Helleiner, "How the Bretton Woods Negotiations Helped to Pioneer International Development," chap. 9 in this book.

Part I

THE WEIGHT OF THE PAST

Chapter 1

The Political Economy of the
Bretton Woods Agreements

Jeffry Frieden

The Allied representatives who met at Bretton Woods in July 1944 undertook an unprecedented endeavor: to plan the international economic order. To be sure, an international economy has existed as long as there have been nations, and there had been recognizable international economic orders in the recent past—such as the classical era of the late nineteenth and early twentieth centuries. However, these had emerged organically from the interaction of technological, economic, and political developments. By the same token, there had long been international conferences and agreements on economic issues. Nonetheless, there had never been an attempt to design the very structure of the international economy; indeed, it is unlikely that anybody had ever dreamed of trying such a thing. The stakes at Bretton Woods could not have been higher.

This essay analyzes the sources of the Bretton Woods Agreements and the system they created. The system grew out of the international economic experiences of the previous century, as understood through the lens of both history and theory. It was profoundly influenced by the domestic politics of the countries that created the system, in particular by the United States and the United Kingdom. It was molded by the conflicts and compromises among the signatories to the agreements, as they bargained their way up to and through the Bretton Woods Conference. The results of those complex domestic and international interactions have shaped the world economy for the past seventy-five years.

THE HISTORICAL SETTING

The negotiators at Bretton Woods could look back on recent history to help guide their efforts. This history included both general successes and remarkable failures. The most relevant general success was the open international economy that prevailed from the 1870s until World War I broke out in 1914. During that first age of globalization, the movement of goods and capital across borders was quite free, and the movement of people—particularly Europeans—was even freer. In addition, the world's economies were tied together by the gold standard, which eventually came to cover virtually every significant economy (the only exceptions were Persia and China).[1]

This classical era saw the most rapid economic growth that the world had ever known: the world economy grew more in 75 years than it had in the previous 750. There was a substantial amount of convergence, with many poor countries catching up to middle-income countries, and many middle-income countries becoming rich. In addition, macroeconomic conditions were generally stable. There were periodic recessions and financial crises, and a lengthy period of gradually declining prices, but overall both growth and macroeconomic conditions were quite steady. To be sure, all was not sweetness and light: this was the age of colonial imperialism in Africa and Asia, of agrarian crisis in Europe, of grinding poverty in the industrializing cities. Nonetheless, in broad historical perspective, the classical world economy of the gold-standard era was a success, associated with economic growth, convergence, and macroeconomic stability.

However, the Bretton Woods negotiators could also look back on a stunning failure, one that was undoubtedly uppermost in their minds: the striking inability of the major powers to reconstitute the pre–World War I economic order in the aftermath of the war. There was no mystery about why the world economy had closed up during the war, but the widespread expectation after the war had been that something resembling the prewar system would be restored. The participants in the post–World War I Versailles conference largely took for granted that the world economy would return to a semblance of its prewar conditions.

Yet the open world economy of the pre-1914 era could not be restored. There was a brief period, for five years after 1924, when trade and capital movements—but not immigration—moved back toward prewar levels. But nothing was as it had been, and when trouble began in 1929 it turned into the most devastating economic catastrophe in modern history. The collapse was nearly complete: international trade, finance, and investment dried up, economic growth stopped, unemployment soared. And the political effects were, if anything, more disastrous than the economic failures: the Depression led more or less directly to the rise of Nazism in Germany, and of fascism elsewhere, and thence to World War II.[2]

The failure to reconstitute an open world economy after World War I was not for lack of trying. There was a multitude of conferences, agreements, treaties, and international institutions. And when the Depression began, there were many attempts to arrest the downward spiral. But nothing worked. And it seemed clear that it would be impossible simply to re-create the world economy as it had been constituted before 1914.

As the Bretton Woods Conference convened against this backdrop, it is worthwhile to review what had gone wrong. The architects of Bretton Woods had clear views on the causes of these catastrophic experiences, views that are largely in line with the current consensus among scholars on the causes of the interwar collapse.[3] The central point is that domestic and international economic and political conditions had changed fundamentally between the Victorian era and the interwar years.

Economically, circumstances had altered in ways that called into question the practicability of the gold-standard open economy. The central requirement of the classical era, to simplify wildly, was that national economies adapt themselves to the state of their international economic relations rather than the other way round. This can be seen most clearly in the balance-of-payments adjustment mechanism of the gold standard itself. To sustain a country's commitment to the gold standard required that when the balance of payments came under stress, domestic wages and prices would adjust. It was not uncommon for this adjustment to involve wage and price reductions that were so substantial as to be unthinkable today—sometimes of 25 percent or more in a couple of years. This was possible in part because nineteenth-century economies came close to the picture of competitive markets painted in textbooks. These economies were made up almost exclusively of small family firms and small family farms; labor was rarely organized. The fact that most markets were competitive and labor was unorganized meant that wages and prices were very flexible, including flexible downward. So when economic distress hit, wages and prices could drop precipitously to carry out the necessary macroeconomic adjustments, leaving the currency's gold value intact.[4]

By the 1920s, the major industrial economies had changed dramatically. Now they were characterized by large oligopolistic or monopolistic firms with substantial market power. As an example, by the late 1920s, in most leading economies the automotive sector dominated the industrial structure, and this sector was in turn dominated by a few large companies. At the same time, labor unionization grew rapidly after 1900 and skyrocketed during and after World War I. Between oligopolistic industries and organized labor movements, neither wages nor prices were very flexible. Attempts to fit the national economy—and specifically wages and prices—to a country's currency value ran up against wage and price rigidity and caused massive macroeconomic dislocations, including massive unemployment.[5]

Politically, conditions had changed just as utterly. The modal industrial country in the 1890s was semiauthoritarian, with limited suffrage, few or no labor rights, and an illegal or suppressed socialist movement. In the 1890s fewer than a dozen countries could be considered democracies, most of them only marginally so. Workers, farmers, and in many instances even the middle classes were represented only poorly, if at all, in prewar political systems. For example, Socialist parties were small or illegal in most countries before World War I. This was particularly relevant to the international economic order of the day. While there was elite consensus on the desirability of fitting the national economy to its international economic conditions, typically the costs of doing so were not borne by the elites. It was workers, farmers, and the middle classes who suffered most from the adjustment processes of the gold-standard era. But they had little or no voice, and so adjustment was politically as well as economically feasible.

Dramatic political changes during and after World War I fundamentally changed this political picture. By 1920 the number of democracies had risen to around twenty-five; virtually every advanced industrial nation had a civilian electoral democracy with universal or nearly universal suffrage. Perhaps most important, democratization had brought workers, farmers, and the middle classes into the center of politics, including electoral politics. By the 1920s, Socialist parties were important almost everywhere. Indeed, at one point or another in the interwar years, Socialist parties were in government in every western European country, and in many cases they were the largest party.[6]

The enfranchisement and empowerment of labor, farmers, and the middle classes meant that governments could no longer impose major adjustment costs on these groups without facing political opposition—in many cases, opposition that could not be overcome in a democracy. Adjustment by way of downward wage flexibility may have been desirable from a purely macroeconomic standpoint (although even that point was debatable in the new economic conditions), but it was almost certainly, and almost everywhere, politically impractical.

An embryonic variant of this interpretation of the changed conditions of the interwar political economy was common at the time.[7] Economists had come to understand that economies dominated by price-makers rather than price-takers could not be expected to behave in the same way as the simpler, more competitive, prewar economies. This was the background to John Maynard Keynes's frequent plea that policy makers not attempt to impose Victorian principles on utterly changed conditions. Calling the gold standard a "barbarous relic," Keynes railed against those who would apply "the principles of an economics, which was worked out on the hypothesis of *laissez-faire* and free competition, to a society which is rapidly abandoning these hypotheses." Throughout the interwar years, Keynes accused those in authority of "attacking the problems of the changed post-war world with . . . unmodified pre-war views and ideas," arguing that their insistence on this would "sow the seeds of the downfall of individualistic capitalism."[8]

Similarly, the interwar experience demonstrated that democratic societies were going to have a substantially increased range of social programs. These included such forms of social insurance as unemployment and disability insurance, publicly funded pensions (such as Social Security), and in many countries publicly funded health systems. Big business and big labor were going to have to live with—had, in the eyes of some, made necessary—big government. Whatever shape the international economic order was going to take, it had to be able to accommodate new notions of the appropriate role of government, and in particular the emerging welfare state.

In addition to the evolution of domestic political economies, the delegates at Bretton Woods also had a wealth of *international* experiences to draw from as they contemplated the new order. Whatever the benefits of the classical age may have been, it was undeniable that it had ended in the two most devastating wars in modern history. Whether features of the classical era had played a part in causing those wars was another matter; but it would be prudent to pay close attention to any possible international political lessons that could be drawn from the fact that the prewar global political order collapsed just as completely as did the prewar global economic order.

Two features of the pre–World War I international system were most striking. The first was cooperation among the monetary authorities of the principal financial centers, so as to avoid the transmission of crises that might have destabilized the international financial system. The second was the tendency for the principal countries engaged in international finance and investment to become embroiled in bitter political, diplomatic, and even military disputes over their foreign investment interests. Both issues had drawn both scholarly and popular attention and were well known to the delegates at Bretton Woods.

Regarding international monetary cooperation, by the 1940s policy makers and scholars had come to understand the fallacies of an earlier, naive, belief that the international monetary and financial order of the late nineteenth and early twentieth centuries had been self-regulating. Two powerful interpretations of both the gold standard and the interwar crisis strongly influenced contemporary views. The first was a monumental study by W. A. Brown published by the National Bureau for Economic Research in 1940; the other was an authoritative summary of the interwar period by a highly respected League of Nations economist, Ragnar Nurkse.[9] Their conclusion was that the pre–World War I international monetary and financial system's solidity depended in large part upon the willingness and ability of the major monetary authorities to support each other in times of difficulty. Central-bank cooperation was in fact quite common during the gold-standard era, especially when the system, or members of it, came under stress. Periodic crises, even panics, required collaboration among the main national authorities, and this collaboration was typically forthcoming.

International cooperation among the major financial centers fell apart in the interwar years. One cause was the continued conflicts between France and Germany, in particular; another was the unwillingness of the American government to participate in most attempts at international economic cooperation, despite the overwhelming dominance of the United States in interwar economic activity. Between American abdication and Franco-German rivalry, cooperation collapsed. It began to be rebuilt slowly in 1936, with the Tripartite Agreement, which eventually linked the United States, the United Kingdom, France, Belgium, the Netherlands, Luxembourg, and Switzerland in an accord to stabilize currencies. But these early attempts were overtaken by World War II.[10] Nonetheless, it was clear that some form of cooperation among the principal financial centers would be essential to the creation of a stable international monetary and financial order.

The second international issue that had attracted attention in the interwar years was the process by which international finance and investment became embroiled in interstate conflicts. Lenin was not the only observer to believe that competition among investors could drive their home countries toward political, even military, clashes. After all, the developing world was largely divided into competing empires, and it was only natural for imperial powers to protect the interests of their investors.

Many policy makers and observers came to see this intertwining of international investment and international politics as an impediment to the smooth functioning of international investment itself. Studies by Herbert Feis and Eugene Staley, for example, argued famously, and prominently, that the association of investments with their home-country governments was a major source of international conflict, including military conflict.[11] This dovetailed with a strongly held American view that imperial exclusions and preferences were both a threat to American interests and a threat to peace.

The governments represented at the Bretton Woods Conference, and their representatives, had important historical experiences to draw upon. Focusing, as is natural, upon the dominant British and American government views, we can summarize the historically grounded views of the leading participants. They believed that the classical economy of the late nineteenth and early twentieth centuries had many positive features, especially its openness to trade and investment. However, they also saw flaws in the classical economy. One was that the gold standard forced countries to undertake macroeconomic adjustments that were no longer economically or politically feasible. Another was that a commitment to openness could conflict with legitimate social-policy goals. Finally, international investment too often drew countries into interstate disputes.

To reconstruct some semblance of an open international economy, then, required an act of synthesis.[12] The openness of the pre–World War I system was desirable, but it needed to be managed so as to allow for national macroeconomic-policy flexibility, and for socially and politically desirable national policies. International investment should be encouraged but should not be connected to national interests in such a way as to spur interstate conflict. With these goals in mind, a varied array of diplomats and economists—led by Keynes at the head of the British delegation and Harry Dexter White at the head of the American one—met at Bretton Woods to create a blueprint for a new international economic order. But they did so within the constraints created by their respective nations' expected interests in whatever order did emerge.

THE CENTRAL PROPOSALS

The conference addressed two related problems, each of which gave birth to one of the Bretton Woods institutions.[13] The first, and the less politically contentious of them, was to prepare the way to rebuild a shattered Europe. In their deliberations, this goal was combined with that of encouraging the development of the poor countries of Asia, Africa, and Latin America. The institution responsible for both sets of tasks was to be the International Bank for Reconstruction and Development, or World Bank.

As it turned out, the Marshall Plan rendered the World Bank's reconstruction mandate irrelevant, and it ended up focused on development. But this was intended to be at least half of its purpose from the start.[14] The development-banking focus of the World Bank was based on a number of interrelated concerns. First was the widespread belief that private investment in the developing regions was hampered by the inadequacies of their basic economic infrastructure—ports, roads, railroads, electric power—and that the private sector was unable or unwilling to finance the development of this infrastructure. In this context, a public development bank could act—much as some of the public-spending countries like the United States had undertaken in the 1930s—to facilitate and stimulate private investment, including foreign investment. The World Bank's mission, in other words, was to ease the way for international private investment. There had in fact been some experience with initiatives of this sort in the 1920s, under the auspices of the League of Nations.[15] In any event, both developed and developing countries could agree on the goal of providing multilateral assistance to smooth the path for private investment, although of course they disagreed on how much money should be involved and on how stringent the conditions attached to World Bank loans should be.

Another rationale for the World Bank was more political. It is important to keep in mind that outside Latin America, much of the developing world was still colonial, and not expected to be postcolonial for quite some time. Whether they had in mind Latin America or the colonial world, the architects of the World Bank tended to believe that making at least some foreign lending multilateral might reduce the likelihood of the kinds of conflicts that had erupted previously among national investors. Where rich countries cooperated to provide common funding to infrastructure projects in the developing world, it was unlikely that they would clash with one another over these projects.

The World Bank was almost universally popular. Rich nations saw it as stimulating private investment by their citizens. Poor nations saw it as providing needed capital on favorable terms for important infrastructural projects. Private international financial institutions and international corporations regarded the bank's expected activities as complementary to their interests: public projects to improve the economic infrastructure could only be good for private foreign investors. Neither international bankers, international investors, nor multinational corporations felt the World Bank was in competition with them: most felt it was likely to facilitate their operations.[16]

The World Bank would fund its work by floating bonds in the major financial markets, with the relevant national government guaranteeing the bonds. This would provide the bank with low-cost funds, which it could then turn around and relend to developing-country governments at interest rates they would not have been able to obtain on their own. World Bank loans were expected to finance specific, defined projects to develop economic infrastructure.

The one area of controversy had to do with how stringent the bank's conditions would be on the borrowing country governments. Unsurprisingly, governments of countries that expected to be providing the funds believed that the bank needed to make sure that the projects funded were economically sound. There was no objection to this in principle, but in practice the countries that expected to be borrowers were anxious to secure favorable conditions. Ultimately, the extent of fiscal stringency of the World Bank's requirements was left undecided. It would take years after the bank began operations before its American presidents were able to establish the expectation that World Bank loans would come with quite stringent conditions—in some ways, more explicit than those that had traditionally been imposed on sovereign borrowers by private lenders. Of course, the terms offered were very favorable, and borrowers got access to funds they could not have borrowed on private markets, at low interest rates. By the same token, World Bank borrowing was typically for such very specific projects as power plants. In this context, agreement on the desirability of World Bank lending was virtually universal, with disagreements only around the edges.

There was much more controversy over proposals for the International Monetary Fund. Governments could agree on the general shape of the reconstituted international monetary order, as Keynes and White had worked it out over many months of discussions. National governments would tie their currencies to gold, but the precious metal would only serve as a nominal anchor rather than as an actual base for international currency relations. Even more important, governments would maintain the right to change their exchange rates should national conditions warrant such a change. The fact that currency values would be fixed against each other would provide some of the stability of the classical gold standard, which was seen as a stimulus to cross-border trade and investment. At the same time, the ability of governments to change their currencies' values would provide the macroeconomic flexibility whose absence had undermined both the gold standard and sociopolitical stability in the interwar period.

It was understood that the commitment among developed countries to maintain stable exchange rates presupposed some international institution to provide balance-of-payments financing for countries facing difficulties, and also perhaps to monitor the behavior of national governments. But agreement largely stopped with this general principle. Fixed but adjustable exchange rates, and a fund to oversee them, left open exactly how the system was expected to work, and this was not a trivial issue.

The balance-of-payments adjustment mechanism is the central, and most potentially controversial, component of any international monetary system. It was the central problem of the gold standard, and a hope of something different was the central attraction of a more flexible system. The issue is straightforward. A country in payments deficit has effectively two choices. It can adjust its domestic economic activity so as to restore balance, for example by decreasing consumption to reduce imports and by cutting wages to increase exports. The gold standard's collapse in the interwar years grew out of the requirement that it imposed on national economies to undertake such austere adjustment measures, especially when national populations were unwilling. It involved, in essence, forcing the domestic economy to conform to its international economic conditions.

The alternative would be to adjust the country's exchange rate. A country in payments deficit can devalue. This makes foreign goods more expensive at home and makes home goods cheaper abroad. A devaluation often reduces imports and increases exports quite quickly, as imports are less attractive to domestic residents and exports are more attractive to foreigners. A devaluation also has a domestic impact, making foreign goods more expensive and effectively reducing consumers' purchasing power. Nonetheless, changing the currency's value has a more gradual and muted impact on national consumption and wages than imposing major domestic austerity measures, softening the blow of the balance-of-payments adjustment somewhat. Unlike austerity measures, a devaluation does not force a direct reduction in consumption or wages. Nonetheless, it accomplishes a similar goal, typically with a less immediate social cost and typically over a longer time period.

However, the Bretton Woods negotiations presupposed a limited use of the devaluation option. This meant that countries with payments imbalances—surpluses or deficits—would have to adjust. Yet this requirement was exactly what the new system was supposed to avoid, given its political toxicity in the gold-standard era. The compromise that was worked out was that the system would rely on an international institution to smooth the path of adjustment so that governments could avoid the most severe social and political costs. To facilitate adjustment, the IMF would provide balance-of-payments financing to countries in difficulty. The fund would lend money to a government in difficulty so that it could avoid a devaluation and use the borrowed funds to cushion the impact of whatever adjustment measures might be adopted. IMF financing could therefore allow for a more gradual adjustment process; or even, if the shock was short-lived, it could simply get the country over a temporary difficulty.

Once there was a plan for an international institution that would lend money to countries facing payments difficulties, the obvious questions were on what terms it would lend and what it would require of the borrowers. It is commonly observed that the burden of adjustment is asymmetric. Countries in surplus can run surpluses indefinitely, simply holding on to their earnings; but countries in deficit cannot run deficits indefinitely unless they can borrow indefinitely, which few can. This means that they either must adjust—by imposing domestic austerity or by devaluing—or find a source of financing. And the financing source has the whip hand in imposing conditions on the lending, whether in terms of the interest rate and maturity, or in broader terms of the actions expected of the borrower.

The implication is that the way in which the IMF would provide its balance-of-payments financing could make all the difference to the functioning of the system—and especially to the measures expected of potential deficit countries. And it set up a major potential source of disagreement between countries that expected to be in surplus, thus providing funds to the IMF, and those in deficit, thus needing to borrow from it. The most prominent expected surplus nation was the United States; the most prominent expected deficit nation was the United Kingdom. And so the two principal architects of the system had powerfully different interests in how it might work.

AMERICANS AND BRITONS UNITE AND FIGHT

Keynes and White, and the governments they represented, agreed on a great deal: the need for a World Bank, the importance of an open international economy, the desirability of policy flexibility for democratically elected governments. But they had many reasons to disagree about exactly how the new international monetary order would work—and, in particular, on how much the IMF would be able to ask of countries that turned to it for financial assistance.

The central debate was between the British and American representatives, led by Keynes and White.[17] The terms of the debate were predictable. The United Kingdom expected to run current account deficits for the foreseeable future and to have difficulties restoring some semblance of international confidence to the pound sterling; as a result, it anticipated being a borrower from the fund. As a prospective borrower, it had every reason to want the fund to be relatively free with its resources and to attach as few strings as possible to them.

The United States, on the other hand, anticipated being in surplus and being a major international lender. The dollar was also the one currency that remained reliable and that was expected to return quickly to some relationship with gold. As a prospective lender, the United States had powerful incentives to limit other countries' access to the resources the United States would be providing, and to provide them only upon assurance that they would be carefully marshaled. In other words, the British wanted to avoid the burden of adjustment being placed on deficit, borrowing countries—like the United Kingdom—while the Americans wanted to make sure that the burden was not borne by the surplus, lending countries—like the United States.

This fundamental conflict of interest, and of opinion, drove the difficult Anglo-American negotiations. The British, led by Keynes, wanted a fund that would create an international currency, which Keynes called "bancor," that could be used by all countries. The Americans saw this as a license for the IMF to print money and dole it out to profligate nations and allow them to buy valuable American goods with unreliable "funny money." White and the Americans insisted on a "contributory" IMF, one that every member state would pay into with gold and major currencies, so that every country would be required to help underwrite the fund. Not surprisingly, given the unique status of the US dollar, this would place the dollar—not an artificially created international currency like bancor—at the center of the international monetary system.

By the same token, the British wanted the IMF to impose few or no conditions on countries borrowing from it. In Keynes's words, it should be "entirely passive in all normal circumstances, the right of initiative being reserved to the central banks of the member countries." Even more pointedly, the British cabinet instructed its representatives to oppose anything that might force borrowers to adopt "a deflationary policy, enforced by dear money and similar measures, having the effect of causing unemployment; for this would amount to restoring, subject to insufficient safeguards, the evils of the old automatic gold standard."[18]

The Americans were insistent that the fund had to exercise relatively tight control over the economic policies of countries that had access to its resources. After all, the United States would be the principal contributor to the fund. Keynes deplored the American view, which he accurately characterized as believing that the IMF "should have wide discretionary and policing powers and should exercise something of the same measure of grandmotherly influence and control over the central banks of the member countries, that these central banks in turn are accustomed to exercise over the other banks within their own countries."[19]

It was clear from the start that the United States had most of the bargaining chips at Bretton Woods and would maintain them in the new postwar world. And so while the conference itself left somewhat vague just how rigorous IMF conditionality would be, it surprised nobody that over the subsequent decade or so the fund evolved in the direction desired by the Americans.[20] Keynes and most of the other non-American delegates were not enthusiastic about the way the idea for the fund had developed since its inception, but they realized that there was little choice in the matter. The United States was the principal shareholder of the new organization, the dollar was the foundation stone of the new international economic order, and American preferences were bound to prevail.

THE BATTLE IS JOINED—AT HOME

While the non-American delegations grudgingly accepted an IMF that they regarded as likely to be too harsh in its insistence on restrictive economic policies, the situation in the United States was very different. The battle for Bretton Woods within the United States was bitter and primarily because some of the most powerful American political forces thought the fund was likely to be so lax as to be irresponsible. The Bretton Woods Agreements faced substantial opposition in the United Kingdom for precisely the opposite reasons—that it would be too stringent.

In the United States, opposition to Bretton Woods focused on the International Monetary Fund. Given the subsequent evolution of the fund, it is somewhat surprising that it was New York's international bankers who led the charge against the IMF. They saw the institution as a continuation of New Deal–era interventionism by meddlesome governments. The financial community believed that postwar monetary stability required a return to orthodox principles. As Winthrop Aldrich of the Chase National Bank put it, what was required was simple: "the checking of domestic inflationary forces, the resumption of gold payments, and the removal of all foreign exchange controls." *The New York Times*, close to the financial community, argued against the need for any elaborate international agreements: "The greatest contribution that America can make to international cooperation is to . . . balance the budget as soon as possible after the war, and . . . to stabilize the dollar in terms of a fixed quantity of gold."[21]

There was even more rabid opposition from those Americans who remained sympathetic to interwar isolationism. The Hearst newspaper chain led the charge, accusing Keynes of wanting to "preside at the liquidation of the American Republic," and calling the Bretton Woods institutions "a planned and controlled world state."[22] The battle continued in Congress, where the most common charge was that the IMF was a scheme to dole out American money to undeserving foreigners. As one opponent told a congressional hearing, "They put in lei, lits, lats, and rubles, and they take out dollars."[23]

The American administration, first that of Franklin Roosevelt and, after his death, that of Harry Truman, worked hard to win over both the public and Congress to support of the Bretton Woods Agreements. The task was simplified by the general view that they were part of a postwar settlement to avoid the catastrophic failures of the interwar period. Dean Acheson, who had headed the State Department's team at Bretton Woods and had worked on the monetary portions of the agreements, told Congress: "We cannot go through another ten years like the ten years at the end of the Twenties and the beginning of the Thirties, without having the most far-reaching consequences upon our economic and social system."[24] The administration insisted on the argument that the agreements were part and parcel of securing the peace and avoiding the disasters of the interwar years.[25] On July 19, 1945, the Senate passed the enabling legislation by a wide margin, and on July 31 President Truman signed it into law.

In the United Kingdom, the new institutions also excited opposition. British hostility to the Bretton Woods Agreements had two sources. The first was the predictable concern that the IMF's demands on a country in persistent deficit, such as the United Kingdom, would severely impinge on its sovereignty. This fear was compounded by the fact that many in Britain believed that the Bretton Woods Agreements would weaken the imperial ties between the United Kingdom and its colonies. This was in part because the agreements foresaw an early return of the pound sterling to general convertibility. A return to sterling convertibility would effectively end the system of "sterling balances" that the United Kingdom had instituted in the empire in the interwar period, which tied the colonies monetarily to the mother country. The threat to colonial monetary relations was especially sensitive in the United Kingdom, for there was a widespread feeling in Britain that the United States was openly hostile to the maintenance of the British Empire as a viable entity. The feeling was of course well-founded.

Nonetheless, Keynes and other supporters of the agreements made the case strongly to Parliament and public opinion that the system was the best Britain could obtain in a world economy dominated by the United States.[26] As a member of the House of Lords said during the debate, "We fought at Dunkirk, but to-day we are surrendering what I conceive to be our just rights. We are surrendering them to the power of the dollar. . . ."[27] After bitter debates, with strong opposition from members of both the Labour and Conservative Parties, the treaty was eventually ratified.[28] The Bretton Woods system was in place.

CONCLUSION

American economic leadership was crucial both to the design and implementation of the Bretton Woods institutions, which at some level reflect the overwhelming economic and diplomatic power of the United States in the aftermath of World War II. However, it is an exaggeration to argue that the United States imposed the Bretton Woods system; American and British policy makers consulted and compromised over all aspects of the agreements, and other countries contributed as well. The aura of international collaboration that began at Bretton Woods and prevailed for decades afterward undoubtedly helped establish the pattern of institutionalized multilateral cooperation that is one of the hallmarks of the post–World War II international political economy.

International cooperation at Bretton Woods was all the more remarkable inasmuch as it required a leap of faith in the workability of institutions that had been designed *de novo* by professional economists. To be sure, the designs relied upon an understanding of how previous international monetary and financial relations had worked—or failed. Nonetheless, it still seems extraordinary that the relatively abstract principles upheld by John Maynard Keynes and Harry Dexter White were able to translate into an international order whose broad outlines have defined the world economy for seventy-five years.

Notes

1. An outstanding summary of the history of modern international monetary relations is Barry Eichengreen, *Globalizing Capital: A History of the International Monetary System*, 2nd ed. (Princeton, NJ: Princeton University Press, 2008). Two excellent volumes of essays on the gold standard are Tamim Bayoumi, Barry Eichengreen, and Mark Taylor, eds., *Modern Perspectives on the Gold Standard* (Cambridge: Cambridge University Press, 1997); and Barry Eichengreen and Marc Flandreau, eds., *Gold Standard in Theory and History*, 2nd ed. (London: Routledge, 1997).

2. For a summary of the interwar experience, see Jeffry Frieden, *Global Capitalism: Its Fall and Rise in the Twentieth Century* (New York: W. W. Norton, 2006), chaps. 6–10. A classic study of interwar attempts at stabilization and their failure is Charles Maier, *Recasting Bourgeois Europe: Stabilization in France, Germany, and Italy in the Decade after World War I* (Princeton, NJ: Princeton University Press, 1975). Barry Eichengreen, *Golden Fetters: The Gold Standard and the Great Depression, 1919–1939* (New York: Oxford University Press, 1992) is a masterful and definitive study of the collapse of the interwar monetary order.

3. The canonical statement of the current consensus is Eichengreen, *Golden Fetters*, which also provides great detail on the views of policy makers at the time.

4. Today countries in and around the Eurozone that undertake this form of adjustment process are said, aptly, to be carrying out an "internal devaluation," i.e., to be reducing domestic wages, prices, and income while keeping the exchange rate constant. Then as now, the economic costs can be very high.

5. Two important summaries of analyses of the process are Ben Bernanke and Harold James, "The Gold Standard, Deflation, and Financial Crisis in the Great Depression: An International Comparison," in *Financial Markets and Financial Crises*, ed. R. Glenn Hubbard (Chicago: University of Chicago Press, 1991), 33–68; and Robert Margo, "Employment and Unemployment in the 1930s," *Journal of Economic Perspectives* 7 (1993): 41–59.

6. Donald Sassoon, *One Hundred Years of Socialism: The West European Left in the Twentieth Century* (New York: New Press, 1996) is the definitive study of the rise of the socialist movement.

7. Marriner Eccles, appointed by Franklin Roosevelt as chairman of the Federal Reserve in 1934, was a prominent and early proponent of the newer perspectives. He served as Fed chair until 1948. There were others in Roosevelt's "Brain Trust." See, e.g., William Barber, *Designs within Disorder: Franklin D. Roosevelt, the Economists, and the Shaping of American Economic Policy, 1933–1945* (Cambridge: Cambridge University Press, 1996).

8. As quoted in Frieden, *Global Capitalism*, 152–54.

9. W. A. Brown, *The International Gold Standard Reinterpreted, 1914–1934* (New York: National Bureau of Economic Research, 1940); and Ragnar Nurkse, *International Currency Experience: Lessons of the Inter-War*

Period (Geneva: League of Nations, 1944). Their view of the sources of stability of the prewar system and instability in the interwar period remains predominant. For the canonical presentation of a modernized version, see Eichengreen, *Golden Fetters*.

10. Frieden, *Global Capitalism*, 249.

11. Herbert Feis, *Europe the World's Banker 1870–1914* (New Haven, CT: Yale University Press, 1930); and Eugene Staley, *War and the Private Investor* (Garden City, NY: Doubleday, Doran, 1935).

12. John Ruggie has dubbed the synthesis that emerged "embedded liberalism," meaning that it was a commitment to a welfare state embedded in something approaching a liberal economic order. John Ruggie, "International Regimes, Transactions, and Change: Embedded Liberalism in the Postwar Economic Order," *International Organization* 36, no. 2.

13. For recent analyses of the Bretton Woods Conference, see, among many others, Ed Conway, *The Summit: Bretton Woods, 1944* (New York: Pegasus Books, 2014); Eric Rauchway, *The Money Makers: How Roosevelt and Keynes Ended the Depression, Defeated Fascism, and Secured a Prosperous Peace* (New York: Basic Books, 2015); and Benn Steil, *The Battle of Bretton Woods: John Maynard Keynes, Harry Dexter White, and the Making of a New World Order* (Princeton, NJ: Princeton University Press, 2013).

14. See Eric Helleiner, *Forgotten Foundations of Bretton Woods: International Development and the Making of the Postwar Order* (Ithaca, NY: Cornell University Press, 2014) for a detailed analysis of the emergence of plans for the World Bank at Bretton Woods.

15. See, for example, Juan Flores Zendejas and Yann Decorzant, "Going Multilateral? Financial Markets' Access and the League of Nations Loans, 1923–8," *Economic History Review* 69, no. 2 (2016): 653–78.

16. Armand Van Dormael, *Bretton Woods: Birth of a Monetary System* (London: Macmillan, 1978) covers both the controversial and uncontroversial aspects of the proposals.

17. Conway, *The Summit*; Steil, *Battle of Bretton Woods*; and Van Dormael, *Bretton Woods*, cover the preparations and debates in detail. For historical documents, see "The White Plan" and "The Keynes Plan," in the "Historical Documents" section of this book.

18. Quoted in Sidney Dell, *On Being Grandmotherly: The Evolution of IMF Conditionality* (Princeton, NJ: International Finance Section, Department of Economics, Princeton University, 1981), 2–3.

19. Ibid., 1.

20. Dell, *On Being Grandmotherly* is the classic analysis.

21. As quoted in Rauchway, *Money Makers*, 205 and 207.

22. As quoted in ibid., 206.

23. Conway, *The Summit*, 296.

24. Quoted in Fred Block, *The Origins of International Economic Disorder* (Berkeley: University of California Press, 1977), 40. On the more general attempts to convince Americans of the desirability of international economic engagement in the aftermath of World War II, see Frieden, *Global Capitalism*, chap. 11.

25. See Henry Morgenthau, "Bretton Woods and International Cooperation," in the "Historical Documents" section of this book.

26. See "Speech by Lord Keynes on the International Monetary Fund Debate," in the "Historical Documents" section of this book.

27. Quoted in Steil, *The Battle of Bretton Woods*, 285.

28. For more, see Andrew Bailey, Gordon Bannerman, and Cheryl Schonhardt-Bailey, "Bretton Woods: The Parliamentary Debates in the United Kingdom," in the "Historical Documents" section of this book.

Chapter 2

The Monetary Role of Gold as the Original Sin of Bretton Woods

Barry Eichengreen

The architects of the Bretton Woods system sought to avoid replicating the weaknesses and instability of the interwar gold standard. They therefore designed a system of pegged but adjustable exchange rates, pegged to foster the growth of international trade and investment, adjustable to avoid the rigidities of the 1920s system. While current account convertibility, defined as freedom to transact in currencies for purposes related to trade in goods and services, was made an obligation of members under the Articles of Agreement of the International Monetary Fund, countries were permitted to maintain restrictions on transactions on capital account (those related to cross-border investment) to give them additional space to pursue other goals, notably high growth and full employment. The dollar, the unit of the principal financial center, the United States, was explicitly recognized as a key currency to which other countries would peg and that they could accumulate as an elastic form of international reserves. The capstone of these efforts was of course the creation of the IMF to monitor the compliance of members with their obligations under the Articles of Agreement, to provide emergency financial assistance as necessary to assist with that compliance, and to discourage them from engaging in destabilizing beggar-thy-neighbor policies.

But the fatal flaw of Bretton Woods—the original sin of the founders, if you will—was that it retained a monetary role for gold. Under Article IV of the Articles of Agreement, members were obliged to declare par values for their currencies in terms of US dollars or gold and to keep their currencies within +/− 1 percent of those values. The United States, for its part, committed to maintaining the convertibility of the dollar and to providing gold on demand, in exchange for dollars, to foreign central banks and governments at the price of $35 an ounce established in 1934 and maintained subsequently. The United States would hold its reserves in gold. Other countries would then choose whether to hold their reserves in gold, dollars, or other subsidiary national reserve currencies to the extent that their issuers also had liquid financial markets open to the rest of the world. They had the choice of what proportions to hold them in. National currencies—meaning, in the main, the dollar—would become an increasingly important constituent of the stock of international reserves over time, given the relative inelasticity of global gold supplies and the confidence problems that would arise if the price of gold was raised (if countries agreed to a uniform change in par values). But in practice nothing prevented countries that preferred to hold their reserves mainly or exclusively in gold, like France, from seeking to do so.

This residual role of gold was what gave rise to the Triffin Dilemma, the tension between the growing foreign liabilities of the reserve-currency country and its limited gold reserves.[1] With the world economy and international commercial and financial transactions growing robustly in the third quarter of the twentieth century, the demand for international reserves rose strongly. Because the new flow supply of gold, provided mainly through mining in South Africa and the Soviet Union, was relatively insensitive to demand, and because the dollar price of the metal was fixed, the largest share of the increase in reserves necessarily took the form of foreign exchange reserves, in practice, dollars, the currency of the country with the largest, most liquid, most open financial market.[2] Over time, this meant that foreign dollar holdings rose relative to US gold reserves.

The crossover point where the foreign currency obligations of the United States exceeded US gold reserves in value occurred already in 1960, theoretically exposing the United States to a run on its reserves.[3] The imbalance between these two variables then continued to widen, heightening the danger. Understandably, this excess of foreign dollar holdings over US monetary gold reserves created doubts about the adequacy of the latter and about the ability of the United States to honor its commitment to convert dollars into gold at the fixed price of $35 an ounce. This was the so-called "confidence problem" at the heart of Bretton Woods.[4]

The Triffin Dilemma and the confidence problem are well known. The point is that what gave rise to this fatal flaw in the system was the residual role of gold. After 1971–1973—after the collapse of Bretton Woods—gold no longer played a residual role in the operation of the international monetary system. Convertibility of national currencies like the dollar into gold at a fixed price was no longer provided in official transactions between governments, although central banks and governments could continue to hold gold, like other reserve and balance-sheet assets, if they wished. Yet, to a surprising extent, the other elements of the Bretton Woods system remained intact. Aside from the elimination of the international monetary role of gold, a process that was completed by the adoption of the Second Amendment to the IMF's Articles of Agreement in 1978, there was much less change in the structure of the system than contemporaries anticipated.[5]

Specifically, other countries—developing countries in the main—continued to peg their currencies to the dollar, though now with wider fluctuation margins and more frequent parity adjustments. Restrictions on transactions on capital account were still widespread. There was strikingly little change in the level or composition of the international reserves of central banks and governments with the official demise of the Bretton Woods system.[6] The largest share of those reserves—an even larger share than under Bretton Woods—was still held in the form of dollars, gold being in relatively inelastic supply and accounting for a progressively smaller share of central-bank portfolios over time. The International Monetary Fund, rather than riding off into the sunset now that it no longer had a set of par values to superintend, came to play an even more prominent role in surveillance of the international monetary system, especially once the Second Amendment to the Articles of Agreement changed its mandate from overseeing a "system of stable exchange rates" to overseeing a "stable system of exchange rates."

This new set of arrangements, sometimes known as the post–Bretton Woods "nonsystem," is thus striking for its family resemblance to the Bretton Woods system that preceded it, aside from the diminished role of gold. This post–Bretton Woods nonsystem persisted for a long time—for longer than Bretton Woods itself, by some measures. Pointing to the continuing reserve role of the dollar, the existence of capital controls in countries like China, and the prominence of the IMF, some would say that this immediate successor to Bretton Woods persists even today.[7] It may not be a perfect system (although detailing its defects would take us far beyond our charge). But, arguably, it has been a more robust system than Bretton Woods itself.

The question, then, is why the architects of Bretton Woods committed the mortal sin of retaining a monetary role for gold, something that subsequent experience suggests could have been readily dispatched and whose retention rendered their construct intrinsically unstable. It is not as if contemporaries were unaware of the instability of a system in which both gold and national currencies were used as reserves while governments attempted to fix their relative price. Feliks Mlynarski, a Polish banker and finance ministry official who went on to work at the League of Nations, pointed to the existence of the equivalent of the Triffin Dilemma already in a 1929 book.[8] Ragnar Nurkse pointed to the instability of a system in which both gold and national currencies were used as international reserves in his 1944 book written for the League of Nations.[9] James Meade in his *Economic Surveys* for the League similarly alluded to these problems. John Maynard Keynes addressed the weaknesses of what is sometimes called the "gold-dollar system" in the negotiations leading up to the Bretton Woods Conference by famously proposing the creation of a synthetic reserve unit, dubbed "bancor," to supplement and substitute for both dollars and gold.

One answer to the question of why, despite all this, the architects of the Bretton Woods system retained a role for gold is that the international monetary system—in the interwar years, under the international gold standard of 1870–1913, and even before—had always been organized around gold or, in some periods, gold and silver, and that governments had always attempted to define the value of their currencies in terms of units of precious metal.[10] This history cast a long shadow; it gave rise to presumptions; specifically, once a role for gold, always a role for gold. This history made it hard for even experienced observers to imagine otherwise. As we will see below, there is something to this answer, although language like "had always been organized around gold" is overstrong, which in turn points to the limits of the argument.

A second answer is that the link between gold and the US dollar, the one national currency certain to be at the center of any post–World War II system, was particularly strong. By the time of World War II, the United States held the largest gold reserves of any country.[11] Franklin Delano Roosevelt's decision to take the United States off the gold standard in the spring of 1933 created great controversy. Partly in response, FDR had restored a fixed domestic currency price of gold, $35 an ounce, in 1934 after only nine months when that price had been allowed to fluctuate, and it remained there for the duration of the decade. The dollar, convertible into gold at that price for official foreign holders, became the closest thing the international monetary system had to a lodestar in the second half of the 1930s. There was the belief, albeit incorrect, as subsequent events would reveal, that the willingness of other countries to hold even a currency as strong as the dollar as international reserves depended on the maintenance of this fixed relationship between gold and the dollar and hence on a residual monetary role for the latter.

Third, and perhaps most importantly, there was the inability of contemporaries to adequately conceptualize an alternative along the lines of the post–Bretton Woods nonsystem. Post-1973 experience suggests that the "nth-country problem"—that in a system of n countries only n-1 of them can manage their exchange rates—can be solved by letting the nth country, in practice the largest country and therefore the one that is least sensitive economically to changes in its exchange rate, float its currency subject only to occasional interventions and intermittent cooperation among governments.[12] But for this system to work well, the nth country has to possess an alternative to the exchange rate as a nominal anchor. Over time the United States developed just that, where the alternative acquired the name "inflation targeting," a regime in which central banks commit to an explicit target for inflation and articulate a strategy for achieving it. Other countries not wishing to follow US monetary policy, or that were compelled to adopt more flexible exchange rates by the development of their financial markets and spontaneous opening of their capital accounts, could similarly adopt inflation targets as a nominal anchor and give their central banks the independence required to pursue them.

But inflation targeting as a concept was not well understood in 1944. Not being able to fully conceptualize an alternative, even countries like Sweden that had given lip service to conceptually similar arrangements in the 1930s—historians refer to the Sveriges Riksbank's "price level target"—pegged their exchange rates at least loosely to a foreign currency (in Sweden's case to sterling) in practice.[13] This conceptual lacuna was what gave rise to the continuing role of gold. History suggested that if the currency of the nth country (the United States) could not be anchored by pegging it to other currencies (by pegging the exchange rate), then it could only be anchored by pegging it to gold.

The remainder of this chapter will develop these ideas as follows. I first discuss the role of gold and foreign exchange reserves under the classical gold standard and then the reconstructed gold standard of the 1920s. The next section will describe the partial and uneven movement away from a gold-based system in the 1930s. The sterling area (where countries pegged to the pound rather than gold) and the Tripartite Agreement of 1936 (where currencies were stabilized not against gold but against one another) will be discussed as examples of "proto-gold-free" international monetary arrangements, while the continuing heavy weight of gold in foreign reserves (especially after the liquidation of sterling and dollar reserves in the early 1930s and approach of World War II later in the decade) and US maintenance of the $35 gold price from 1934 will be analyzed as countercurrents. The section following this will describe the Keynes and White Plans and the decision to provide for a continuing monetary role for gold under Bretton Woods. Finally, I will analyze the consequences: the 1950s "dollar shortage" followed by the 1960s "dollar glut"; the Gold Pool and negotiations over Special Drawing Rights as efforts to finesse the Triffin Dilemma; and finally the development of the confidence problem culminating in the advent of the two-tier gold market and the collapse of Bretton Woods. The conclusion will then summarize post–Bretton Woods developments and draw out the implications.

GOLD AND RESERVE CURRENCIES BEFORE BRETTON WOODS

The gold-based system that commentators portray as the normal international monetary state of affairs prior to 1914 was in fact short in life, limited in scope, and special in operation—which is not to say that rarified portraits had no impact on the negotiations leading up to the Bretton Woods Agreement.[14] Silver and not gold was the dominant commodity money used in financial transactions for much of the nineteenth century, as had similarly been the case before. Silver was less valuable and therefore more practical, especially in poor countries like China and India but also more generally; the use of gold coin was largely limited to high-value, long-distance trade. Countries with bimetallic systems, like the United States and France, struggled to keep both metals in circulation but saw the one that was undervalued at the mint repeatedly driven out of circulation.[15] Only Great Britain, largely as a matter of historical happenstance, had gone onto the gold standard in 1717, 1774, or 1821 (depending on how precisely one defines that regime).

Britain's industrial and commercial preeminence, rising incomes worldwide, falling silver prices due to increased mining in the New World and elsewhere, and the capacity to produce uniform token coins for low-value transactions, once steam-powered machinery came to the mint, then conspired to drive countries onto the gold standard starting in the 1870s.[16] Even then, however, the reign of gold was less than universal. Important parts of the world, notably China, continued to base their monetary circulation on silver. Others wracked by political and economic problems were unable to maintain the convertibility of their currencies into any precious metal for extended periods. Increasingly, countries concentrated their gold stocks at the central bank or government treasury, so that what circulated hand-to-hand was paper money and token coin convertible into gold rather than gold itself. Central banks and governments could then supplement their gold with foreign exchange reserves, that is, with foreign bills of and bank deposits in countries whose currencies were themselves freely and reliably convertible into gold, taking advantage of the fact that these alternative reserve assets paid interest.

Peter Lindert traced the rise of foreign exchange reserves—primarily British pounds, French francs, and German marks—in the two final decades of the nineteenth century and the first fourteen years of the twentieth.[17] Lindert estimates that the ratio of monetary reserves held in foreign exchange relative to gold rose from roughly 10 percent in 1880 and 1890 to 17 percent in 1913. We can thus see in this period the emergence of a gold-exchange standard in which both gold and one or more leading national currencies played a role as international unit of account, means of payment, and store of value.

The dual roles of gold and reserve currencies were then solidified in the 1920s by the reconstruction of the international monetary system as a gold-exchange standard. Prices had risen during World War I, while global gold stocks failed to keep pace. Deflation being painful, there was resistance following the war to pushing prices back down to 1914 levels. Ensuring that foreign reserves were adequate to back money supplies and settle international transactions thus required further encouraging firms, banks and governments around the world to hold and accept foreign exchange as well as gold reserves. In practice this meant holding and accepting sterling and US dollars, the former long since having emerged as the leading reserve currency, as befit London's status as the leading international financial center, and the latter having risen to prominence once the United States acquired a lender and liquidity provider of last resort with the adoption of the Federal Reserve Act in 1913.[18]

Resolutions adopted at the Genoa Conference in 1922 therefore endorsed a system made up of reserve centers—effectively New York and London— whose central banks would hold their reserves entirely in gold, while other countries would then hold their reserves in a combination of gold and foreign bills and balances in the reserve centers in question. Although countries declared parities (values for their currencies) in terms of gold, other countries de facto pegged their currencies to sterling and the dollar, while the United States and United Kingdom pegged their currencies to gold. With impetus from this agreement and technical assistance from the Bank of England and the Federal Reserve Bank of New York (the Federal Reserve System's de facto international branch), a growing number of countries embraced the practice of holding foreign exchange reserves. The ratio of foreign exchange to gold reserves rose further, to 58 percent in 1929.[19] In a sense, some of the outlines of Bretton Woods were already apparent fifteen and more years before the conference at Bretton Woods.

LESSONS OF THE 1930s

The lessons drawn from the unhappy international monetary experience of the 1930s are well known. International capital flows could be destabilizing, justifying resort to capital controls. More frequent changes in exchange rates to accommodate domestic economic conditions than had been permitted under the gold-exchange standard were necessary. Since those exchange-rate changes could be beggar-thy-neighbor depending on how they were implemented, there was the need for a multilateral entity to monitor national policies and oversee the operation of the post–World War II international monetary system.[20]

All of this may be conventional wisdom, but it does not explain the residual role of gold in that post–World War II international monetary system. In the course of the 1930s a growing number of countries had moved off the gold standard. They allowed their currencies to float or attempted to manage their value in terms of the pound or the dollar, either way diminishing the role of gold. The sterling area, made up of the United Kingdom, the British Commonwealth and Empire, and countries that traded heavily with the United Kingdom, was an example of an arrangement where the center country did not manage its currency with reference to gold but other countries still held a significant fraction of reserves in its currency. Starting in 1932, with the establishment of the Exchange Equalisation Account (EEA), the British Treasury assumed effective control of British monetary policy.[21] Under Neville Chamberlain, the EEA intervened in the foreign exchange market, expanding and contracting the money supply with the goal of ensuring that the pound remained relatively stable at competitive levels against the US dollar.

In other words, no longer was British monetary policy conducted with an eye toward maintaining a stable ratio of gold stocks to monetary liabilities. No longer was the monetary authority required to stabilize the domestic price of gold. Rather, British monetary policy aimed at keeping sterling at appropriate levels against the dollar, while the policies of the other members of the sterling area were aimed at keeping their currencies stable against sterling. There was general acceptance and satisfaction with the operation of this regime; advocates of a return to a gold standard of the pre-1932 variety were few and far between. This, then, was a monetary arrangement of stable exchange rates organized around a key currency with a minimal role for gold. The question it points up is why similar arrangements were not contemplated at Bretton Woods.

A second case in point was the Tripartite Agreement of 1936.[22] This was an agreement between the French, British, and American governments to ensure the orderly realignment of currencies at a time when the French, still on the gold standard and suffering from an increasingly overvalued exchange rate, were coming under pressure to devalue. On entering negotiations, the goal of the French government was to devalue by a sufficient amount to restore the country's competitiveness but also to ensure that the devaluation would stick; French officials were concerned that the shock to confidence from a first devaluation would not simply lead to another. They wanted to ensure that the British and Americans wouldn't retaliate, devaluing their own currencies competitively and neutralizing France's gains. French policy makers also wanted to dress up their devaluation as an international agreement so that it could be presented as an act of diplomacy rather than a surrender to the markets. The British and Americans, for their part, were concerned that the French devaluation not be so large as to significantly undercut their own competitiveness. They too desired the maintenance of a reasonably stable exchange rate system.

The French pushed for an agreement specifying central rates for exchange rates surrounded by fluctuation bands and commitments of bilateral support between participating exchange equalization funds. But this was more than the American and British governments were prepared to accept: both now saw the exchange rate as subordinate to domestic price stability and were not willing to tie their policies to France. As a result, the French got not a joint declaration but three separate, loosely harmonized statements. The three statements implicitly recognized the newly established exchange rates of 105 francs and $5 to the pound as broadly appropriate.[23] French officials would have preferred a more formal commitment but were forced to settle for what they could get.

This, then, was another arrangement designed to stabilize exchange rates between major currencies, but without a central role for gold. Again the question is why analogous arrangements were not contemplated at Bretton Woods. A hint of the answer may lie in the role of gold in the United States. After taking the dollar off the gold standard in March 1933 and pushing the dollar price of gold up from $20.67 to $35 an ounce, FDR stabilized the gold price in January 1934, as noted above. From this point the United States stood ready to purchase and sell gold to official foreign holders at that price. This constraint placed limits on the discretionary conduct of US monetary policy. Specifically, it limited how expansionary that policy could be. To be sure, those limits were not always binding. America was on the receiving end of substantial gold inflows in the second half of the 1930s, as European investors, seeing war clouds gather over the European Continent, sought a safe haven in the United States. The US Treasury sterilized gold inflows: it neutralized their impact on the money supply when that impact was seen as undesirable.[24]

Still, the currency of the single largest country, and the country that was destined to be the leading economic and financial power after World War II, retained a monetary role for gold. US legislators, by passing the Thomas Amendment and then the Gold Standard Act of 1934, preferred to constrain executive discretion at least to this limited extent. Foreign officials and investors, insofar as they willingly conceded to the United States an increasingly prominent role in the international monetary and financial system, clearly preferred this as well.

GOLD AND RESERVE CURRENCIES AT BRETTON WOODS AND AFTER

The Keynes and White Plans for the post–World War II international monetary order both attached a premium to domestic policy space—to measures giving governments room for maneuver to pursue full employment and economic growth. As recounted elsewhere in this volume, both plans envisaged greater exchange rate flexibility than had characterized the gold-exchange standard. Both made provision for capital controls. Strikingly, however, neither plan eliminated the international monetary role of gold, not even the plan authored by Keynes, who some two decades earlier had already dismissed gold as "a barbarous relic."[25] Formalizing a continued role of gold was important in order to enlist the support of countries like France, whose experience with a system not anchored by gold in the first half of the 1920s had been unhappy. It was a way of imposing discipline on the key currency country at the center of the system. Above all, it was seen as important for the credibility of the new regime. As White put it, "Any foreign country is willing to accept dollars in payment of gold or services today [only] because it is certain that it would convert those dollars in terms of gold at a fixed price."[26] White, it will be recalled, had written as his PhD dissertation a broadly favorable assessment of the operation of the pre–World War I gold standard.[27] Gold, he now wrote, "is the best medium of international exchange yet devised."[28] Under his plan, a minimum of half of each government's initial cash contribution to the institution that became the International Monetary Fund would be required to be made in gold, implying that when lending, the institution would similarly utilize the yellow metal.

Even the Keynes Plan, despite spilling much ink over "bancor" (supranational credits that governments would agree to accept in balance-of-payments settlement), retained this monetary role for gold. In the words of point 4 of the British proposal for an International Clearing Union (the final version of the Keynes Plan), "The proposal is to establish a Currency Union, here designated an *International Clearing Union*, based on international bank-money, called (let us say) *bancor*, fixed (but not unalterably) in terms of gold and accepted as the equivalent of gold by the British Commonwealth and the United States and all other members of the Union for the purpose of settling international balances."[29]

More strikingly still, the same presumptions infected the views of those who advocated more radical alternatives to the pre–World War II international monetary order. The Harvard economist John Williams, for example, criticized the Bretton Woods Agreement as a one-size-fits-all solution and advanced a "key currency plan" to accommodate the different circumstances of different countries. In Williams's plan, each country would have the option of stabilizing its currency at a time and manner suited to the extent and nature of the imbalances bequeathed it by the war. Order would be restored by having the two countries with the deepest financial markets and most widely accepted international currencies—the United States and the United Kingdom—first stabilize their bilateral exchange rate; other countries could then stabilize against the dollar and sterling at a time and in a manner of their choosing.

Williams's plan thus provided for even more domestic policy autonomy than the White Plan and even the Keynes Plan, notably during what might be a very lengthy reconstruction period. It is striking therefore that even Williams's key currency plan did not eliminate the international monetary role of gold. Gold was still relevant, in Williams's view, as an anchor for the key currencies around which the new order would be organized. It was important because "a lot of people believe[d]" in it.[30] In testimony to the Senate Committee on Banking and Currency in 1945, Williams acknowledged that gold convertibility was likely to become something of an anachronism in the postwar world and that he could envisage a future in which gold's monetary role fell away. But he was not prepared to suggest abolishing that role in 1944.[31]

Similarly, Robert Triffin was consistently critical of the Bretton Woods Agreement, notably in his now-famous 1947 study, but also more generally.[32] Triffin emphasized already at this early date the instability of a system in which the key currency or currencies were convertible into gold at a fixed price, while other countries held their reserves in a combination of gold and key currencies. But, revealingly, Triffin was not able to articulate a coherent alternative—a system in which gold was demonetized and reserve assets, what came to be known as Special Drawing Rights, were issued by the International Monetary Fund—until much later, in the 1960s. Again this is indicative of the influence of the historical role of gold in shaping and limiting the views of even relatively freethinking contemporaries.

The Cambridge and Oxford economist Roy Harrod, whom Keynes had commissioned in the 1930s to write a handbook of international economics, and who served with his Cambridge colleague in the British government during World War II, similarly pointed to the contradiction in the Bretton Woods system that eventually became known as the Triffin Dilemma. But instead of suggesting that the reserve role of gold simply be abolished, Harrod proposed periodically raising the price of gold in order to restore an appropriate balance between dollar and gold reserves. Whether Harrod's solution was in fact a solution is dubious; repegging gold at a higher dollar price after raising that price might only foster expectations of more of the same. Doing so would create a one-way bet for speculators, deepening the confidence problem and inciting a run on the dollar. It is striking that Harrod saw so clearly the problem with a continuing monetary role for gold but nevertheless hesitated to propose demonetizing the metal.

A final example is that of the Princeton economist Frank Graham. Graham was an especially vigorous critic of the gold and gold-exchange standards. The supply of newly mined gold, he emphasized, was relatively unresponsive to changes in its price and subject to unpredictable shocks. A system in which currencies were linked to gold could be destabilized by speculative attacks in which investors rushed to convert their growing currency reserves into the key-currency country's limited stock of gold. Since the price of gold in terms of other commodities could vary across a wide range, as it had after 1929, the gold standard was an engine of instability.[33]

The Bretton Woods Agreement, in Graham's critical assessment, thus re-introduced all the worst features of the interwar gold-exchange standard. But Graham's radical alternative was not to abandon commodity backing for currencies, but rather to replace gold with a basket of commodities, not just gold but also rubber, copper, wheat, and other storable commodities or, equivalently, warehouse receipts for the constituents of that commodity basket. With this link, national currencies would be stable in terms of that basket of commodities; equivalently, and more meaningful from a welfare standpoint, the price of that basket of commodities would be stable when expressed in domestic currencies.

In principle, Graham's plan would have addressed the problem that pegging the domestic currency price of gold created scope for the domestic currency prices of other commodities to vary in uncomfortable ways. But the proposal had practical drawbacks, such as the real resource cost of producing and storing the commodities providing the backing for internationally accepted currencies. Ultimately, Graham's scheme was a generalization of the gold-exchange standard, not a rejection of it. It proposed replacing the link between gold and currencies with a link between gold and other commodities, on the one hand, and currencies, on the other. It is no surprise that when Graham's proposal met with skepticism, negotiators fell back to a system with a monetary role for gold.

FROM DOLLAR SHORTAGE TO DOLLAR GLUT

In the aftermath of World War II the dollar shortage was acute, reflecting the voracious appetite of European countries for American-made machinery and merchandise and their difficulty in ramping up their exports. America's gold reserves, already high at the end of the war, rose further in the first five postwar years. US gold then declined gradually over the course of the 1950s, as other countries rebuilt first their capacity to export and then their international reserves.

American gold holdings then began falling more rapidly in the 1960s, as the dollar shortage gave way to the dollar glut and doubts developed about the convertibility of dollars into gold. There was a "gold rush" in 1960, when traders concerned about measures likely to be taken by the then Democratic presidential candidate John F. Kennedy to "get America moving again" pushed the free-market price of gold in London up to $40, significantly above the US Treasury's official buying price. The spike in the London market price sparked fears that governments, seeing the writing on the wall, might demand wholesale conversion of their dollars into gold. In response, the US Treasury provided the Bank of England with gold to be used to bring the price of gold on the London gold market, where the metal was bought and sold by private investors (some would say "speculators"), back down to $35, and the governments of the principal industrial countries agreed to refrain from buying gold at a higher price.

This agreement was then formalized as the Gold Pool in November 1961. Eight central banks, including the Federal Reserve, committed to buying and selling gold only at the official $35 price, and the other seven agreed to supply roughly half the gold needed to stabilize the market price at that level with the ostensible goal of limiting US gold losses. At the same time, however, they neutralized this effort to defend US gold reserves by continuously replenishing their gold stocks outside the pool, separately converting their dollar balances at the US Treasury. What the left hand gave, the right hand taketh away, in other words, in a classic instance of a collective-action problem. As a result, the Gold Pool did little to resolve the internal contradictions of what was now referred to as the Bretton Woods gold-dollar system. The US government responded to continuing gold losses with a variety of ad hoc measures, the Interest Rate Equalization Tax of 1963, for example, which was designed to strengthen the country's balance of payments by making it less attractive for residents to invest abroad. These delayed the day of reckoning by slowing US gold and reserve losses but did not resolve any of the underlying contradictions.

Meanwhile, furious negotiations were taking place behind the scenes to create an international reserve asset, along the lines of Keynes's bancor, to provide an alternative to additional dollar accumulation. Agreement to create this new asset, Special Drawing Rights, was reached in 1968 but activated only in 1970—too late to significantly delay the collapse of the gold-dollar system. Those negotiations had been underway since the mid-1960s; they were lent new urgency by the devaluation of the pound sterling, still the second most important reserve currency, in late 1967 in an event that pointed to the possibility that the dollar might be next. In the wake of sterling's devaluation, the Gold Pool hemorrhaged gold, leading to collapse of that arrangement in early 1968. Its members responded with a series of awkward expedients. They created a two-tier gold market, in which the monetary authorities of the Gold Pool countries agreed to transact only among themselves at the official price while now allowing the market price of gold to float freely, ignoring the reality that leakages between the official and private markets were certain to be extensive. The United States removed the requirement for Federal Reserve notes to be backed 25 percent in gold and pressured foreign governments not to convert their existing dollar holdings at the US Treasury. Governments formally agreed to abide by these requests, but continued to surreptitiously convert their dollars into gold.

These, then, were the de facto steps breaking the gold-dollar link and inaugurating the move from the Bretton Woods gold-dollar system to the post–Bretton Woods dollar system (or "nonsystem" as it is sometimes called). But the temptation to convert dollars into gold proved irresistible, and governments increasingly succumbed to it in 1970. The result forced President Richard Nixon to "close the gold window" (to suspend the convertibility of dollars into gold for official foreign holders in August 1971). It then led to the Smithsonian Agreement in December 1971, under which exchange rates were realigned but the dollar could no longer be converted into gold by official foreign holders at a fixed price. From this point the Bretton Woods gold-dollar system was no more.

CONCLUSION

The Bretton Woods system was fragile. It survived through 1971 only with the help of ad hoc measures not anticipated by its founders. These included the Gold Pool in 1961, the Interest Equalization Tax in 1963, and US pressure on friendly governments, like that of Germany, not to convert their dollar balances into gold. Even so, the system endured for at most a quarter of a century, if one dates its advent as the mid-1940s, and for barely half that long, if one regards it as having come into full operation only in 1958 when the principal European countries restored the convertibility of their currencies on current account (that is, when they authorized their free use for trade-related transactions).

A leading source of this fragility was the monetary role of gold. Rather than simply organizing the system around a key currency (the dollar), or a pair of key currencies (the dollar and sterling), or an international reserve unit (like Keynes's bancor or the IMF's Special Drawing Rights), delegates to the Bretton Woods Conference agreed to a system in which gold and convertible currencies like the dollar would both serve as international reserves and in which the currencies in question could be converted into gold at a fixed price. Predictably this gave rise to what was variously called the Triffin Dilemma and the confidence problem. Ultimately, it brought the system down.

Subsequent experience suggests that it would have been possible to dispense with this monetary role for gold. Post-1971 international monetary arrangements still centered on the US dollar, to which a majority of developing countries pegged their exchange rates, and in which some two-thirds of global foreign-exchange reserves were held. The level of reserves was not much different. The prevalence of capital controls, which had buttressed the operation of the Bretton Woods system, remained little changed. The International Monetary Fund merely altered its Articles of Agreement to refer its mandate to superintend not "a system of stable exchange rates" but now "a stable system of exchange rates."

Negotiations at Bretton Woods in 1944 were not informed by this subsequent experience. Instead, the outlook of the delegates and the governments they represented was heavily influenced by earlier international monetary arrangements in which gold had played a central role. A continuing monetary role for gold was viewed as important as a way of inspiring confidence in the new system. It was seen as disciplining the policies of countries, like the United States, whose currencies were destined to play a disproportionately important role in the new system. Finally, there was an inability to fully conceptualize a workable alternative in which monetary policy was anchored to something other than the yellow metal.

For all these reasons, the system that emerged from Bretton Woods was flawed and not destined to last.

Notes

1. Noted as early as 1947. See Robert Triffin, "National Central Banking and the International Economy," *Postwar Economic Studies* 7 (1947): 46–81.

2. A corollary was that the real price of gold fell steadily over the Bretton Woods period (since other prices were rising). The market price of gold in London, which for historical reasons was where gold was most actively traded, hardly diverged at all from the official $35 price until March 1968, when, faced with accelerating gold losses, the monetary authorities of the principal countries agreed to no longer sell (or buy) gold on the market but to transact only among themselves at the $35 gold price. At this point the London market price rose sharply relative to the official ($35) price, and incentives changed.

3. The other crossover point, where US external-dollar liabilities to foreign monetary authorities, as opposed to total external-dollar liabilities, exceeded US monetary gold reserves, came slightly later, in 1964.

4. The "confidence problem" has become part of the lingua franca of the literature on Bretton Woods; it is due to the Princeton University economist Fritz Machlup, who emphasized it in various publications. For discussion, see Carol Connell, "Fritz Machlup and the Bellagio Group: Solutions to Liquidity, Adjustment and Confidence Problems and their Opportunity Costs," *Quarterly Journal of Austrian Economics* 16 (2013): 255–98.

5. The Second Amendment changed the role of gold in the international monetary system by officially eliminating its function as numeraire for par values and as the basis for valuing the IMF's own reserve unit, Special Drawing Rights, and abolishing the obligatory use of gold in transactions between the fund and its members.

6. For evidence, see Jacob Frenkel, "The Demand for International Reserves by Developed and Less-Developed Countries," *Economica* 41 (1974): 14–24; Jacob Frenkel, "International Reserves: Pegged Exchange Rates and Managed Float," in *Economic Policies in Open Economies*, ed. Karl Brunner and Allan Meltzer (Amsterdam: North Holland, 1978), 111–40.

7. See, for example, Michael Dooley, David Folkerts-Landau, and Peter Garber, "Bretton Woods II Still Defines the International Monetary System" (NBER Working Paper no. 1473, February 2009).

8. Feliks Mlynarski, *Gold and Central Banks* (New York: Macmillan, 1929).

9. See Ragnar Nurkse, *International Currency Experience* (Geneva: League of Nations, 1944).

10. Before 1870, more often silver than gold, but no matter. See Jurgen Osterhammel, *The Transformation of the World: A Global History of the Nineteenth Century* (Princeton, NJ: Princeton University Press, 2014).

11. Counting, of course, gold *above* ground.

12. Like that which occurred under the Plaza Agreement in 1985 and the Louvre Accord in 1987. On these post–Bretton Woods episodes of foreign exchange market intervention, see Barry Eichengreen, "Before the Plaza: The Exchange Rate Stabilization Negotiations of 1925, 1933, 1936, and 1971," in *International Monetary Cooperation: Lessons from the Plaza Accord after Thirty Years*, ed. C. Fred Bergsten and Russell Green (Washington, DC: Peterson Institute for International Economics, 2016), 173–90.

13. See Claes Berg and Lars Jonung, "Pioneering Price Level Targeting: The Swedish Experience 1931–1937" (Stockholm School of Economics/EFI Working Paper in Economics and Finance no. 290, December 1998); Benny Carlson, "From the Gold Standard to Price Level Targeting: Swedish Monetary Policy in the Daily Press during the 1930s," *Sveriges Riksbank Economic Review* 1 (2011): 29–64.

14. A fuller treatment, on which the present text draws, is Barry Eichengreen and Marc Flandreau, "Editors' Introduction," in *The Gold Standard in Theory and History*, ed. Eichengreen and Flandreau (London: Routledge, 1997), 1–29.

15. Meaning that if the mint price of one metal was lower than its market price, arbitragers would obtain and export coins made of that metal, while importing and flooding the mint with the other metal (whose mint price was higher than its market price).

16. See Christopher Meissner, "A New World Order: Explaining the International Diffusion of the Gold Standard, 1870–1913," *Journal of International Economics* 66 (2005): 385–406.

17. Peter Lindert, "Key Currencies and Gold 1900–1913," Princeton Studies in International Finance no. 24, International Finance Section, Department of Economics, Princeton University (August 1969).

18. The French franc and German mark essentially lost their earlier roles as reserve currencies as a result of wartime disruptions and financial instability in the 1920s. See Barry Eichengreen and Marc Flandreau, "The Rise and Fall of the Dollar, Or When Did the Dollar Replace Sterling as the Leading International Currency?" *European Review of Economic History* 13 (2009): 377–411.

19. This according to Nurkse, *International Currency Experience*, 235.

20. These lessons were clearly drawn in Nurkse's book, *International Currency Experience*. It is not irrelevant that the book was published in 1944 or that a draft was circulated to the delegates at the Bretton Woods Conference.

21. A good introduction to the EEA is Susan Howson, "Sterling's Managed Float: The Operations of the Exchange Equalisation Account," Princeton Studies in International Finance no. 46, International Finance Section, Department of Economics, Princeton University (November 1980). On the sterling area, see Arthur Conan, *The Problem of Sterling* (London: Macmillan, 1966).

22. For details on the background, see S. V. O. Clarke, "Exchange Rate Stabilization in the Mid-1930s: Negotiating the Tripartite Agreement," Princeton Studies in International Finance no. 41, International Finance Section, Department of Economics, Princeton University (September 1977).

23. In fact, the statements contained no numbers, instead speaking in general terms of "consultation" and "cooperation."

24. See Douglas Irwin, "Gold Sterilization and the Recession of 1937–38," *Financial History Review* 19 (2012): 249–67.

25. In John Maynard Keynes, *A Tract on Monetary Reform* (London: Macmillan, 1923).

26. Quoted in Benn Steil, *The Battle of Bretton Woods: John Maynard Keynes, Harry Dexter White, and the Making of a New World Order* (Princeton, NJ: Princeton University Press 2013), 131.

27. Harry Dexter White, *The French International Accounts 1880–1913* (Cambridge, MA: Harvard University Press, 1933).

28. Steil, *Battle of Bretton Woods*, 129.

29. As reprinted in Keith Horsefield, *The International Monetary Fund, 1945–1965: Twenty Years of International Monetary Cooperation, Volume III: Documents* (Washington, DC: IMF, 1969), 3. As a key passage then elaborated, "The two founder States will agree between themselves the initial values of their own currencies in terms of bancor and the value of bancor in terms of gold; and the initial values of the currencies of other members will be fixed on their joining the system in agreement with them." Horsefield, ibid., 6.

30. Cited in Anthony Endres, *Great Architects of International Finance: The Bretton Woods Era* (London: Routledge, 2005), 54.

31. John Williams, "Testimony before Senate Committee on the Bretton Woods Agreements Act," repr. in John Williams, *Postwar Monetary Plans and Other Essays* (Oxford: Blackwell, 1949), 352.

32. Endres, *Great Architects of International Finance*, devotes a chapter to Triffin's views.

33. See Frank Graham, "The Primary Functions of Money and Their Consummation in Monetary Policy," *American Economic Review* 30 (1940): 1–16; Frank Graham, "Achilles' Heels of Monetary Standards," *American Economic Review* 30 (1940): 16–32.

Chapter 3

The Missing Bretton Woods Debate over Flexible Exchange Rates

Douglas A. Irwin

In his 1923 book *A Tract on Monetary Reform*, John Maynard Keynes argued that a country's central bank could stabilize the domestic price level or fix the exchange rate, but not necessarily do both at the same time. While the two objectives were compatible in some circumstances, a country would have to choose one over the other if they were incompatible. The potential conflict between internal and external policy objectives was forcefully demonstrated in the Great Depression of the early 1930s. Countries could either maintain fixed exchange rates by staying on the gold standard and enduring a painful deflation, or they could maintain stable prices by leaving the gold standard and allowing their currencies to depreciate. One by one countries opted for domestic price stability over exchange rate stability. By 1936 no major country was on the gold standard.

The collapse of the gold standard sparked a debate over international monetary arrangements that culminated in the Bretton Woods Conference in 1944. Given the disastrous experience of the 1930s, one might have thought that economists and government officials would have given sympathetic consideration to a system of flexible exchange rates that would allow central banks to focus on domestic economic stability and full employment. In fact, there was relatively little debate about the postwar exchange rate system and virtually no such debate at the Bretton Woods Conference itself. While there was no interest in returning to the gold standard or having rigidly fixed exchange rates, there was also no apparent interest in adopting floating exchange rates either. Instead, most economists advocated, and the participants at Bretton Woods endorsed, the halfway house of "fixed but adjustable" exchange rates. Exchange rate stability was desired, but it was also recognized that rates would have to be changed in the case of "fundamental disequilibrium."

Why were flexible exchange rates not seriously considered in the debate over the postwar international monetary system? Flexible exchange rates were dismissed because they were equated with monetary instability and trade protectionism. For most economists, the main lesson taken from the 1930s was not just that the gold standard had failed, but that flexible exchange rates had failed, too. That was the view of Ragnar Nurkse, whose influential *International Currency Experience* was published by the League of Nations in 1944. According to Nurkse: "If there is anything that interwar experience has clearly demonstrated, it is that paper currency exchanges cannot be left free to fluctuate from day to day under the influence of market supply and demand" because speculation would "play havoc" with them.[1] The professional consensus among economists ran against flexible exchange rates, at least until Milton Friedman published his famous essay "The Case for Flexible Exchange Rates" in 1953.[2]

This chapter examines why the case for floating exchange rates was not taken seriously in the discussions about the international monetary system in the late 1930s and 1940s. After looking at the debate about the exchange rate regime after the collapse of the gold standard, we turn to the reaction of economists to the Keynes and White Plans that formed the basis for the Bretton Woods Agreements. Finally, we look at the early postwar discussion of exchange rates after the International Monetary Fund (IMF) had been established and the Bretton Woods system was in place.

LESSONS FROM THE GOLD-STANDARD COLLAPSE

In 1923, Keynes argued that countries—specifically, their central banks—faced a dilemma in choosing between internal objectives (stable domestic prices) and external objectives (stable exchange rates). If a country chose external stability through a fixed exchange rate, it would give up control over internal prices; if it chose to stabilize internal prices, it might have to sacrifice stable exchange rates. Because the late-nineteenth-century gold standard was unique in delivering both external and internal stability, Keynes noted, "the choice between stable exchanges and stable prices had not presented itself as an acute dilemma." But if there were "violent shocks" to the world price level, the gold standard was "likely to break down in practice" because internal prices could not adjust quickly enough to avoid a painful transition to domestic production and employment. Therefore, he concluded, "when stability of the internal price level and stability of the external exchanges are incompatible, the former is generally preferable; and that on occasions when the dilemma is acute, the preservation of the former at the expense of the latter is, fortunately perhaps, the line of least resistance."[3]

Following this logic, Keynes dismissed any return to the gold standard after World War I. The gold standard would allow "the tides of gold to play what tricks they like with the internal price level," preventing governments from ensuring stable prices and full employment. Keynes also rejected a central-bank-managed gold standard "in the pious hope that international cooperation will keep it in order." At the same time, Keynes rejected an exclusive focus on domestic price stability, doubting "the wisdom and the practicability of a system so cut and dry" as Irving Fisher's compensated-dollar scheme.[4]

Instead, Keynes recommended a blended system in which the central bank would focus on stabilizing domestic prices as well as the exchange rate: "my scheme would require that they [the Bank of England] should adopt the stability of sterling prices as their *primary* objective—though this would not prevent their aiming at exchange stability also as a secondary objective by co-operating with the Federal Reserve Board in a common policy." Such a policy, he wrote, would ensure that exchange rates "would not move with every breath of wind but only when the Bank had come to a considered judgement that a change was required for the sake of stability of sterling prices."[5]

Though writing in 1923, Keynes was prophetic about the potential problems with the interwar gold standard and the possible conflict between internal and external policy objectives.[6] When the managed gold standard started to malfunction around 1929 and countries began to experience deflation, they began to abandon the gold standard, opting for stable domestic prices rather than stable exchange rates, just as Keynes suggested.[7] However, rather than simply choosing between staying with a fixed exchange rate under the gold standard or letting the exchange rate go to maintain internal price stability, some countries opted to impose exchange and capital controls in an effort to have both a fixed exchange rate and monetary independence.

Thus, Keynes's policy dilemma became a policy trilemma. Countries had to choose two of three policies: a fixed exchange rate, an independent monetary policy, and a convertible currency free from exchange controls.[8] Different countries with different historical experiences chose different paths, but the gold standard ceased to exist by 1936.

As is now well known, the countries that left the gold standard were able to pursue more expansionary monetary policies that helped stimulate economic recovery; the countries that prolonged their stay on the gold standard continued to suffer through the slump.[9] This lesson was recognized by international organizations at the time. In 1936, the League of Nations reported that the turning point from depression to recovery in every country was "characterized by an increase in the supply of money" and that "in those few countries which did not either depreciate their currency or use the protection afforded by exchange control to pursue an expansionist monetary policy, no considerable measure of economic improvement had taken place by the end of 1935." Similarly, the International Labour Office (ILO) concluded in 1937 that "one of the clearest teachings of the depression is that the maintenance of the domestic equilibrium must be the primary objective of monetary policy, even if it entails lowering the external value of the currency. . . . If the depression has shown one thing more clearly than anything else it is that economic prosperity and social security depend more on monetary policy than on any other single factor," the ILO continued. "The demonstration that in one country after another the upturn in business and employment coincided not with the reduction of wage-rates, the cutting of costs or the deterioration of working conditions but with the abandonment of deflation and the adoption of monetary expansion has made a deep impression on the world."[10]

WHAT COMES AFTER GOLD?

Yet apparently the impression was not all that deep because, in the wake of the gold standard's collapse, most policy makers and economists wanted a quick return to exchange rate stability rather than continuing with monetary policies that would provide for domestic economic stability and growth. Policy makers in the United States, Britain, and France reached the Tripartite Agreement in 1936 to restore relatively fixed exchange rates. Most economists were deeply suspicious of leaving exchange rates to be determined by the market. This suspicion came from their perception of recent historical experience. The two recent periods of floating exchange rates had been in the early 1920s, before most countries had returned to the gold standard, and in the mid-1930s, after Britain and others abandoned the gold standard. The first period was marked by monetary instability and hyperinflation in Germany and elsewhere and wide exchange rate fluctuations that were attributed to destabilizing speculative capital flows. The second period was described as a period of "competitive devaluations," which were thought to constitute "beggar thy neighbor" policies and result in protectionist trade policies.[11]

Keynes managed to negotiate all of these considerations in proposing a way forward. In *The General Theory of Employment, Interest, and Money*, Keynes argued against permanently fixed exchange rates as a "most dangerous" threat to the use of monetary policy (interpreted as changes in domestic interest rates) to maintain full employment. As he stated, "I am now of the opinion that the maintenance of a stable general level of money-wages is, on the balance of considerations, the most advisable policy for a closed [economic] system; whilst the same conclusion will hold good for an open [economic] system, provided that equilibrium with the rest of the world can be secured by means of fluctuating exchanges."[12]

Keynes seemed to be proposing that each country should pursue its own independent monetary policy based on its own domestic economic conditions with exchange rates left free to adjust. And yet he never actually embraced flexible exchange rates. When someone inquired about his position on exchange rates shortly after the publication of *The General Theory*, Keynes stated, "In general I remain in favour of independent national systems with fluctuating exchange rates" but "there need be no reason why the exchange rate should in practice be constantly fluctuating." Instead, he was "entirely in favour of practical measures towards *de facto* stability so long as there are no fundamental grounds for a different policy."[13] By the late 1930s, Keynes's position could be described as favoring fixed but adjustable exchange rates with exchange controls, just like he had in 1923.[14]

Keynes's preference for some exchange rate flexibility to pursue domestic economic policy objectives was considered heresy by many economists. At the London School of Economics, Friedrich Hayek and Lionel Robbins lamented the loss of security and dependability that came with the demise of the gold standard. They associated fixed exchange rates with stability and certainty, and adjustable exchange rates with instability and uncertainty. They disparaged Keynes's "monetary nationalism"—which implied managed, fiat currencies—on the grounds that it would bring monetary turmoil and economic chaos. Instead, they advocated "monetary internationalism" in which multilateral cooperation would permit a return to some type of gold standard. For example, Hayek believed that "a really rationale monetary policy could be carried out only by an international monetary authority" and would require reestablishing fixed exchange rates. Hayek thought this was "a demand for reforms in exactly the opposite direction from those advocated by Monetary Nationalists. Instead of flexible parities or a widening of the 'gold points,' absolute fixity of the exchange rates should be secured by a system of international par clearance."[15]

Hayek leveled three main criticisms against flexible exchange rates, all of which were frequently repeated during this period. First, flexible exchange rates would give rise to speculative capital flows that would be destabilizing; specifically, capital movements would reinforce exchange rate shifts arising from payments imbalances, thereby magnifying volatility and "turn what originally might have been a minor inconvenience into a major disturbance." Second, flexible exchange rates would lead to competitive depreciations, the flexible rate counterpart to competitive devaluations, which would encourage a return to mercantilism and an increase in trade barriers. "Without stability of exchange rates it is vain to hope for any reduction of trade barriers," he concluded. Third, exchange rate instability would create risks that would discourage international trade and deter long-term foreign investment.[16]

Echoing these arguments, Robbins held that "of all the forms of economic nationalism, monetary nationalism is the worst" and warned of the "dangers of a regime of free exchanges." Like Hayek, he believed that flexible exchange rates would lead to "cumulative financial chaos" and the disintegration of the world economy. Furthermore, Robbins found it "necessary to challenge directly" the assumption that flexible exchange rates will lead to equilibrium adjustments: "For there is no reason to believe that it is in any way justified. On the contrary, both theory and experience suggest that . . . the fluctuations of the exchanges have an actively disequilibrating tendency." Without a tendency to reach an equilibrium, the system would result in "just a vicious circle of inflation or deflation." Robbins also attacked Keynes and his followers for endorsing the intermediate position of fixed but adjustable exchange rates.[17]

However, because the British economic recovery occurred once the country had left the gold standard and the Bank of England was able to ease monetary conditions, other academic economists expressed some sympathy for the idea of floating exchange rates. For example, James Meade and Roy Harrod made positive statements about the merits of flexible rates but did not offer an unconditional endorsement.

Meanwhile, in comparison to their European counterparts, fewer American economists were wedded to the gold standard or even the goal of exchange rate stability. The dollar already played a central role in the international monetary system. From the American perspective, as long as the purchasing power of the dollar was relatively stable, that would help promote the stability of the world economy. Many economists held a position similar to that of Keynes, believing that exchange rate stability was desirable but absolute rigidity was not. For example, as early as 1934, Harry Dexter White at the US Treasury was writing in favor of a managed currency standard that would somehow combine the stability of the gold or a dollar standard with national monetary autonomy.[18]

This position was widely held. John H. Williams of Harvard University and the Federal Reserve Bank of New York, one of the most prolific international economists of the period, wanted a compromise between the extremes of rigidly fixed exchange rates and completely flexible exchange rates. Williams believed "there can be no general answer" to the question of whether fixed or flexible exchange rates were preferable and that it was "unduly simple" to pose the stark choice as "the difference between stable exchanges and stable prices, or as offering, or even compelling, a choice between external and internal monetary stability." At the same time, he recognized that "the case for flexible exchange rates . . . has appeared to receive further powerful support from the world's experiences in the depression. Looking back, we have to recognize that recovery in every country where it has occurred has been accompanied by monetary expansion, and this expansion occurred after the internal economy had been freed from external pressure, either by currency depreciation or exchange control." And yet he noted that no government actually wanted to have flexible exchange rates. Therefore, Williams put forward the compromise position of having the "largest measure of internal monetary protection and control which is consistent with exchange stability," with the proviso that "exchange variation, while not excluded, should be resorted to only when other means of control have been exhausted."[19]

By contrast, Frank Graham and Charles Whittlesey at Princeton University were among the few American economists who insisted that countries should have complete monetary independence and that flexible exchange rates were necessary to make such a system work. Graham and Whittlesey stated that "unchanging exchange rates are one of the least important forms of stability and they may give rise to more problems than they solve." They argued that no country should be asked to sacrifice internal stability for external stability, since fixed exchange rates required that adjustment be achieved "through the painful and disrupting alternation of the whole [domestic] price structure, some parts of which are flexible and some parts rigid."[20]

Graham and Whittlesey also took on the critics of flexible exchange rates. First, they argued that such rates were highly variable in the past because the underlying policies were highly variable.[21] Whittlesey believed that recent economic history had been widely misinterpreted: "the view that stable exchange rates are a means of achieving stable general prices is grounded in a tendency to associate any freedom of the exchange rates with wild inflation. The fact that exchange movements under conditions of extreme inflation were much more result than cause is usually forgotten."[22] Second, they suggested that speculative capital flows were not destabilizing if underlying policies were stable. Graham argued that speculators would be deterred from betting against floating rates since future currency values were uncertain. By contrast, a fixed rate would be subject to speculative attacks since the direction of a future exchange rate change was known with greater certainty. Third, they argued that historical experience had demonstrated that the deleterious effect of exchange rate fluctuations on trade were "greatly exaggerated." In fact, futures markets could be used to protect those engaged in trade against unanticipated exchange rate movements.[23]

Finally, Graham and Whittlesey dismissed the idea that fluctuating exchange rates would hamper the process of reducing trade barriers. Again, on the basis of historical experience, they argued that many import restrictions were imposed because of the payments imbalances that were the result of misaligned fixed exchange rates. Whittlesey stated that import restrictions were "merely the logical consequence of the desire to maintain a quotation for the currency out of line with the equilibrium rate." Moving to an equilibrium exchange rate, as determined by the market, would allow trade barriers to be reduced. "Just as controls are introduced only because of a situation where the exchange rate is out of line with the equilibrium rate, so they become superfluous if the exchange rate is brought into an equilibrium position," Whittlesey pointed out.[24]

Thus, the collapse of the gold standard sparked a debate with a broad spectrum of views being expressed about the type of international monetary regime that ought to replace it. However, despite the opinions of Graham and Whittlesey, the mainstream consensus was that exchange rate stability was desirable, although rates might have to be adjusted on occasion, whereas floating exchange rates would be unstable and therefore undesirable.

THE DEBATE OVER THE 1943 KEYNES AND WHITE PLANS

The US and UK governments began making plans for the postwar international monetary system after the outbreak of World War II. In 1943, the White and Keynes proposals were published. While they differed on matters such as the structure of international lending facilities and the burden of adjustment between surplus and deficit countries, they did not differ significantly on the exchange rate regime itself. Both plans saw fixed exchange rates as desirable, while admitting that exchange rate changes would be necessary from time to time to correct for chronic payments imbalances. As Benn Steil notes:

> Both plans aimed at stability in exchange rates. However, Keynes's plan set up a mechanistic approach for determining when and by how much a member state could, or would have to, devalue or revalue, whereas White's plan was less accommodative of exchange rate changes, requiring member states to secure fund approval for any changes in parity. White's harder line on fixed exchange rates reflected American preoccupation with stopping others from devaluing against the dollar. On the flip side, Keynes's softer line reflected a British preoccupation with avoiding further bouts of a persistently overvalued pound.[25]

While economists debated the various elements of the Keynes and White proposals, plans for a "fixed but adjustable" exchange rate system generated some discussion but little objection. Jacob Viner of the University of Chicago noted that "economists are still divided on these issues, but I believe a large majority of them would agree that exchange stability is desirable per se, for any country and still more for the world at large, provided it can be established without involving helpless submission to undesired inflation or deflation."[26] John Williams also applauded the compromise position—in which exchange rates would be fixed with "resort to currency variation only sparing and when other means had failed"—as one he had long championed. Furthermore, Williams noted that "among economists this debate over fixed versus flexible exchanges seems now to have almost entirely faded out, and to have been followed by a general recognition that international currency stability must be one of our main objectives for the post-war period."[27]

By contrast, Graham was critical of the White and Keynes proposals on the grounds that it was easy to agree on fixed-exchange-rate parities but that no provision had been made on the underlying monetary policies to be pursued. "The international financial collapse of the early thirties is very largely attributable to the effort, in preceding years, to keep exchange rates fixed in a regime of divergent monetary policies," he argued. "But, in complete disregard of this evidence of the folly of seeking stable rates . . . we seem bent on repeating the errors of the later thirties."[28] Graham insisted that domestic price stability be given first priority and exchange rate stability was a secondary objective, if one at all. Elsewhere, Graham was critical of the "quasi-official proposals of Lord Keynes and Dr. White" because they did "make a clean-cut choice of any of these alternatives." The problem with the Keynes and White Plans is that "They straddle [the trilemma alternatives] and will either fall between stools or will issue in the comprehensive controls of foreign trade that it is the primary purpose of both authors to avoid."[29]

Graham tried to defend flexible exchange rates on grounds of both theory and historical experience, but Ragnar Nurkse's influential League of Nations report, International Currency Experience, gave indirect support for the White and Keynes Plans by reinforcing the negative view of the historical experience with flexible exchange rates. "If there is anything that interwar experience has clearly demonstrated," he wrote, "it is that paper currency exchanges cannot be left free to fluctuate from day to day under the influence of market supply and demand." Nurkse warned that "if currencies are left free to fluctuate, 'speculation' in the widest sense is likely to play havoc" with them. To think that flexible exchange rates would help promote both external and internal stability was "quite unrealistic." Even with forward markets, exchange rate fluctuations would "inevitably tend to discourage international trade" and even result in "chaos."[30]

Nurkse asserted that flexible exchange rates had three serious disadvantages: they create an element of risk that discourages international trade, they create costly shifts of resources from traded to nontraded goods, and they cannot be relied on to promote adjustment. Hence, "stability of exchange rates has proved essential not only for international economic intercourse, but for domestic stability as well," pointing to France's experience in the 1920s.[31] At the same time, absolute rigidity of exchange rates was also undesirable: "While exchange variations are certainly an unsuitable and undesirable means of dealing with short-term discrepancies in the balance of payments, an absolute rigidity of exchange rate in the face of drastic changes in other factors at home or abroad may thus be equally harmful," Nurkse noted.[32]

Nurkse's widely lauded book became the accepted view on the matter. Joan Robinson commended him for producing "strong evidence to show that the notions of 'free' exchanges and of the 'automatic' gold standard are both equally chimerical. There is no escaping the fact that exchanges must be controlled by conscious policy." While "there are great advantages in exchange stability," she also noted that Nurkse "brings forward strong evidence of the impossibility of a return to a system of completely rigid exchange rates," which once again supported the halfway house of fixed but adjustable rates.[33]

Even Gottfried Haberler of Harvard University, a later advocate of flexible exchange rates, was at this point much more in line with the Austrian tradition and rejected flexible rates. Haberler wrote that "it is certain that a system of 'free exchanges' would lead to extremely undesirable results. It would incite capital flight and violent fluctuations. There are very few instances of really free exchanges in monetary history and none that could be called successful. . . . The upshot of this whole discussion is that a system of freely fluctuating exchanges is hardly acceptable."[34]

While Graham did not review Nurkse's book, Lloyd Mints of the University of Chicago was one of the few who rejected Nurkse's analysis. Mints wanted the monetary authority to pursue price stability and allow the exchange rate to seek its own level.[35] Mints wondered why this option was not sought and questioned why there was a prejudice against flexible exchange rates.[36]

THE BRETTON WOODS AGREEMENTS

Given the agreement between White and Keynes on the matter, the "fixed but adjustable" exchange rate system was soon enshrined in the Bretton Woods system. Other provisions of the IMF, such as the burden of adjustment between surplus and deficit countries and the role of international reserves, generated some debate at the Bretton Woods Conference. Yet there was almost no discussion about exchange rates. According to Article I of the IMF's Articles of Agreement, the goal of the system was "to promote exchange stability, to maintain orderly exchange arrangements among members, and to avoid competitive exchange depreciation." In addition, in Article IV, "a member shall not propose a change in the par value of its currency except to correct a fundamental disequilibrium," a concept that was left undefined.[37]

After the 1944 conference, most economists thought the debate over exchange rate policy was settled.[38] In a survey of work in international economics published shortly thereafter, Lloyd Metzler noted that "from the point of view of economic analysis, one of the most important results of the experience with fluctuating exchange rates during the 'thirties was a profound skepticism concerning the effectiveness of exchange-rate adjustments in rectifying a balance of payments discrepancy." He stated that "both the interwar experience with fluctuating exchange rates and the theory of exchange stability which emerged during the interwar years have clearly shown that adjustments of exchange rates are not likely, in the short run, to be an efficient or effective means of eliminating a deficit or a surplus from a country's balance of payments."[39]

Whatever economists thought about the new system in theory, the transition to the new system did not go smoothly in practice. In accepting a large loan from the United States, Britain was required to make the pound convertible in 1947, which resulted in a massive run on the currency. Rather than devalue, Britain suspended convertibility (after spending much of the American loan in supporting its currency) and reimposed exchange controls. The initial Bretton Woods exchange rates had severely overvalued the pound, just as it had been in 1925 when Britain returned to the gold standard. This time, however, instead of enduring deflation as a way of solving the trilemma, the British authorities used exchange controls to insulate the economy from the pressure to deflate, although this constricted imports and created a shortage economy. Britain was not alone: the "dollar shortage"—the excess demand for dollars at the parity exchange rates—meant that many European countries were forced to ration foreign exchange to restrain spending on imports if they were unwilling to adjust their exchange rate from their initial postwar setting.

The dollar shortage also generated a large debate about whether import restrictions or devaluation would be the best way of achieving external balance. In Ragnar Nurkse's view, exchange rate adjustment was "far preferable" to import restrictions as a means of ensuring external balance. Yet he was still skeptical of whether exchange rate changes would help achieve balance-of-payments equilibrium in the short run. Therefore, Nurkse continued to reject a regime of flexible exchange rates:

> Some liberal-minded economists are so impressed with the restrictive dangers of commercial policy that they would rather leave the maintenance of external equilibrium entirely to the care of fluctuations in exchange rates. This view may be attractive theoretically, but it places too much reliance on exchange-rate variations. Owing to the speculative tendencies which they provoke in commodity as well as capital flows, such variations are likely to be disruptive of internal stability. Experience has shown that the distinction between exchange stability and domestic stability may become quite unreal when exchange rates

are left free to fluctuate under the influence of speculative anticipations creating excessive and "nonfunctional" disturbances, not only in foreign trade, but also in domestic prices and production. This, at any rate, is apt to be the case when exchange variations are uncontrolled.[40]

Meanwhile, Frank Graham called fixed rates "a vicious anachronism" and argued that the objections to flexible rates were "largely sophistical." To Graham, the dollar shortage simply meant that the dollar was undervalued and European currencies were overvalued. Fixed rates increased speculation, as seen in the British case, because investors knew that existing rates were unsustainable. As he stated, "We should know that we must either forgo fixed exchange rates or national monetary sovereignty if we are to avoid the disruption of equilibrium in freely conducted international trade or the systems of controls and inhibitions which is the only alternative when the internal values of independent currencies deviate—as they always tend to do—from what was, perhaps, a correct relationship when the fixed rates of exchange were set up."[41]

British economists came to share this view. In particular, James Meade believed that maintaining unrealistically high and fixed exchange rates led to direct controls on import spending and posed an obstacle to the expansion of trade. In the choice between exchange rate adjustment and direct trade controls, he was decidedly in favor of the former.[42] Posed this way, his view gained currency. "The idea that variations in foreign exchange-rates can serve as an efficient regulator of a freely working international economic system has gained an astonishing vogue among British academic economists," Hubert Henderson observed. "This, it is worth noting at the outset, implies a remarkable change of view. It is not very long since the extremists of economic liberalism were disposed to stress, and even to exaggerate, the advantages of fixed exchange-rates." Yet Henderson himself concluded, "The idea that exchange-rate variations might be used systematically to correct maladjustments in the balance of payments is . . . fundamentally impracticable."[43]

The pressure on the system was finally relieved when Britain announced a 30 percent devaluation of the pound in 1949, an action followed by nearly a dozen other countries. By this time, criticisms of the Bretton Woods approach were becoming more common. Robert Triffin complained that "the elaborate provisions of the Fund's agreement designed to ward off the danger of *competitive devaluations* were found powerless, and indeed somewhat paradoxical, in the face of the actual, and reverse, threat of *currency overvaluation,* propped up by quantitative restrictions, exchange controls, bilateralism and discrimination."[44] Evidence accumulated that the emphasis on maintaining existing parities was making it difficult to remove trade and exchange controls.[45]

This was the context in which Milton Friedman visited Europe in 1950, where he drafted his famous essay "The Case for Flexible Exchange Rates," published in 1953.[46] The publication of Friedman's essay was followed by Friedrich Lutz's "The Case for Flexible Exchange Rates" in 1954 and Meade's "The Case for Variable Exchange Rates" in 1955.[47] By this time, Canada had adopted a flexible exchange rate regime, and more and more economists were moving to support floating rates. The debate over the exchange rate regime simmered for another two decades before the Bretton Woods system collapsed in the early 1970s.

CONCLUSION

While many features of the international monetary system were debated extensively prior to and during the 1944 Bretton Woods Conference, there was surprisingly little debate among officials about the exchange rate regime. The preference for fixed exchange rates was derived in part from the consensus view that recent history had shown floating rates to have been a failure. A small minority of economists disputed that history and warned that putting priority on fixed exchange rates might detract from other desirable policy objectives, such as domestic monetary autonomy and freer trade and capital flows. They criticized the Bretton Woods Agreements for not confronting the dilemmas and trilemmas involved in reconstructing the international monetary system, problems that eventually played a role in the system's undoing.

Notes

Prepared for the Yale Conference on Bretton Woods, November 5–6, 2015. I am grateful to Michael Bordo, Eric Helleiner, and other participants for helpful feedback.

1. Ragnar Nurkse, *International Currency Experience* (Geneva: League of Nations, 1944), 137.

2. Milton Friedman, "The Case for Flexible Exchange Rates," in *Essays in Positive Economics* (Chicago: University of Chicago Press, 1953).

3. John Maynard Keynes, *Tract on Monetary Reform* (London: Macmillan, 1923), 158.

4. Ibid., 172.

5. Ibid., 186, 190.

6. Bordo and Schwartz show how conflicts between internal and external stability have led to numerous currency crises throughout history. See Michael D. Bordo and Anna J. Schwartz, "Why Clashes Between Internal and External Stability Goals Result in Currency Crises," *Open Economies Review* 7 (1986): 437–68.

7. The desire of central banks to accumulate gold reserves contributed to a worldwide shortage of gold and strong deflationary pressure starting in 1929; see Barry Eichengreen, *Golden Fetters: The Gold Standard and the Great Depression, 1919–1939* (New York: Oxford University Press, 1992); H. Clark Johnson, *Gold, France, and the Great Depression, 1919–1932* (New Haven, CT: Yale University Press, 1997); Douglas A. Irwin, "The French Gold Sink and the Great Deflation, 1928–1932," *Cato Papers on Public Policy* 2 (2013): 1–47; Sandeep Mazumder and John H. Wood, "The Great Deflation of 1929–33: It (Almost) Had to Happen," *Economic History Review* 66 (2013): 156–77; and Scott Sumner, *The Midas Paradox: Financial Markets, Government Policy Shocks, and the Great Depression* (Oakland: Independent Institute, 2015). A large literature seeks to explain the reasons for the timing of a country's exit from the gold standard; see Kirsten Wandschneider, "The Stability of the Interwar Gold Standard: Did Politics Matter?" *Journal of Economic History* 68 (2008): 151–81; Nikolaus Wolf, "Scylla and Charybdis: Explaining Europe's Exit from Gold, January 1928–December 1936," *Explorations in Economic History* 45 (2008): 383–401.

8. Maurice Obstfeld, Jay C. Shambaugh, and Alan M. Taylor, "Monetary Sovereignty, Exchange Rates, and Capital Controls: The Trilemma in the Interwar Period," *IMF Staff Papers* 51 (2014): 75–108; Douglas A. Irwin, *Trade Policy Disaster: Lessons from the 1930s* (Cambridge: MIT Press, 2012).

9. Eichengreen's *Golden Fetters* is a classic reference. The countries that imposed exchange controls had some scope for monetary expansion but failed to use it; see Kris Mitchner and Kirsten Wandschneider, "Capital Controls and Recovery from Financial Crises: Evidence from the 1930s," *Journal of International Economics* 95 (2015): 188–201.

10. For the quotes in this paragraph, see Richard A. Lester, *Monetary Experiments* (Princeton, NJ: Princeton University Press, 1939), 297–98.

11. For an excellent account of economic thinking during this period, see Filippo Cesarano, *Monetary Theory and Bretton Woods: The Construction of an International Monetary Order* (New York: Cambridge University Press, 2006).

12. John Maynard Keynes, *The General Theory of Employment, Interest, and Money* (New York: Macmillan, 1936), 270.

13. John Maynard Keynes, *Collected Writings of John Maynard Keynes*, vol. 21 (London: Macmillan, 1980), 501.

14. As Moggridge points out, "By the time Keynes came to draft his proposals for the post–World War II monetary system, he had at one time or another recommended almost every exchange rate regime known to modern analysts except completely freely floating exchange rates." See Donald E. Moggridge, "Keynes and the International Monetary System 1909–46," in *International Monetary Problems and Supply Side Economics: Essays in Honour of Loris Tarshis*, ed. J. Cohen and G. C. Harcourt (London: Macmillan, 1986), 66–67.

15. Friedrich Hayek, *Monetary Nationalism and International Stability* (London: Longman, Green, 1937), 93, 84.

16. Ibid., 64, 74n.

17. Lionel Robbins, *Economic Planning and International Order* (London: Macmillan, 1937), 290–91, 287–89.

18. See Benn Steil, *The Battle of Bretton Woods: John Maynard Keynes, Harry Dexter White, and the Making of a New World Order* (Princeton, NJ: Princeton University Press, 2013), 22–23.

19. John H. Williams, "The Adequacy of Existing Currency Mechanisms under Varying Circumstances," *American Economic Review* 27 (1937): 151, 156, 163. See also John H. Williams, "The World's Monetary Dilemma: Internal versus External Monetary Stability," *Proceedings of the Academy of Political Science* 16 (1934): 62–68.

20. Frank D. Graham and Charles R. Whittlesey, "Fluctuating Exchange Rates, Foreign Trade, and the Price Level," *American Economic Review* 24 (1934): 401.

21. This point is also made in Frank D. Graham, "Self-Limiting and Self-Inflammatory Movements in Exchange Rates: Germany," *Quarterly Journal of Economics* 43 (1929): 221–49. For a discussion of Graham's

advocacy of flexible exchange rates, see Anthony M. Endres, "Frank Graham's Case for Flexible Exchange Rates: A Doctrinal Perspective," *History of Political Economy* 40 (2008): 133–62.

22. Charles R. Whittlesey, *International Monetary Issues* (New York: McGraw-Hill, 1937), 66.

23. Frank D. Graham, "Achilles' Heels in Monetary Standards," *American Economic Review* 30 (1940): 27.

24. Whittlesey, *International Monetary Issues*, 74, 95.

25. Steil, *Battle of Bretton Woods*, 150. White defended the plan saying "We cannot hope for sound recovery in international economic life so long as the germs of monetary instability infect a large part of the world. . . . Only an intelligent adjustment of exchange rates to the new international economic position in the postwar period can provide a firm foundation on which to build a high level of world trade and prosperity." Harry D. White, "Postwar Currency Stabilization," *American Economic Review* 33 (1943): 382.

26. Jacob Viner, "The International Economic Organization of the Future," in *Toward International Organization* (New York: Harper & Bros., 1942), 129–30.

27. John H. Williams, "Problems of Post-War International Monetary Stabilization," *Proceedings of the American Philosophical Society* 87 (1943): 134. For other reactions, see Joan Robinson, "The International Currency Proposals," *Economic Journal* 53 (1943): 161–75; Jacob Viner, "Two Plans for International Monetary Stabilization," *Yale Review* 33 (1943): 77–107, repr. in Jacob Viner, *International Economics* (Glencoe, NY: Free Press, 1951); and John H. Williams, "Currency Stabilization: American and British Attitudes," *Foreign Affairs* 22 (1944): 233–47.

28. Frank D. Graham, "Discussion," *American Economic Review* (Papers and Proceedings) 34 (1944): 401.

29. Frank D. Graham, "Fundamentals of International Monetary Policy," in *Essays in International Finance*, no. 2 (International Finance Section, Department of Economics, Princeton University, 1943), 22.

30. Nurkse, *International Currency Experience*, 137.

31. According to Nurkse, ibid., 118ff: "The dangers of such cumulative and self-aggravating movements under a regime of freely fluctuating exchanges are clearly demonstrated by the French experience of 1922–26" when exchange rates became highly unstable and speculation rampant. "The experience of the French franc from 1922 to 1926 and of such interludes of uncontrolled fluctuation as occurred in certain currencies in the 'thirties demonstrates not only the difficulty of maintaining a freely floating exchange on an even keel, any movement in one direction being liable to create expectations of a further movement in that direction; it also shows how difficult it may be for a country's trade balance to adjust itself to wide and violent exchange variations." Subsequent economic historians have examined whether the French experience was one of destabilizing speculation or not. See also S. C. Tsiang, "Fluctuating Exchange Rates in Countries with Relatively Stable Economies: Some European Experiences after World War I," *IMF Staff Papers* 7 (1959): 244–73; Robert Z. Aliber, "Speculation in the Foreign Exchanges: The European Experience," *Yale Economic Essays* 2 (1962): 171–245; Johan Myhrman, "Experiences of Flexible Exchange Rates in Earlier Periods: Theories, Evidence and a New View," *Scandinavian Journal of Economics* 78 (1976): 169–96; Barry Eichengreen, "Did Speculation Destabilize the Franc in the 1920s?" *Explorations in Economic History* 19 (1982): 71–100.

32. Nurkse, *International Currency Experience*, 211.

33. Joan Robinson, review of *International Currency Experience* by Ragnar Nurkse, *Economic Journal* 55 (1945): 406–7.

34. Gottfried Haberler, "The Choice of Exchange Rates after the War," *American Economic Review* 35 (1945): 309, 311. He did concede that "if it were possible to prevent speculative capital movements, one of the most serious disadvantages of frequently changing exchange rates would be removed."

35. Drawing from the experience of the 1930s, Mints argued, "The essential thing is that the monetary agency of the government be not hamstrung in dealing with domestic deflation because of the loss of reserves. It would be far better if there is this danger simply to leave the gold standard, allowing the exchanges to seek their equilibrium level, and to increase the stock of currency to any level required to maintain the price level. This action would create no such restraint of trade as exchange rationing,

and it does not involve a deliberate depreciation of the currency to which other nations may reasonably object." Lloyd Mints, review of *The International Currency Experience: Lessons of the Inter-War Period*, by Ragnar Nurkse, *American Economic Review* 35 (1945): 193.

36. Mints argued that "This opposition seems to be founded in very large part upon a belief that the difficulties of the 1930's are inherent in any system of free exchanges. It is one thing to condemn, as one must, exchange fluctuations which are the consequence of widespread internal instability, and of consequent speculation in, and flights from, particular currencies; and it is quite a different thing to condemn, as one need not, such exchange fluctuations as would occur under conditions of internal stability. It is more than a little anomalous to condemn fluctuating exchange rates under conditions which a system of fixed exchanges could not survive. It is doubtful that fluctuating exchanges, under conditions of internal monetary stability, would create an undue discouragement to trade; or that they would be disequilibrating under the same conditions." Mints, ibid.

37. See Filippo Cesarano, "Defining Fundamental Disequilibrium: Keynes's Unheeded Contribution," *Journal of Economic Studies* 30 (2003): 474–92.

38. A paper argued that "the controversy a decade ago over fixed versus variable exchange rates, of little interest today, has been settled in favor of fixed rates with infrequent adjustments." John Parke Young, "Exchange Rate Determination," *American Economic Review* 37 (1947): 589.

39. Lloyd Metzler, "The Theory of International Trade," in *A Survey of Contemporary Economics*, ed. Howard S. Ellis (Philadelphia: Blakiston, 1948), 223, 232.

40. Ragnar Nurkse, "International Monetary Policy and the Search for Economic Stability," *American Economic Review* 37 (1947): 574.

41. Frank D. Graham, "Exchange Rates: Bound or Free?" *Journal of Finance* 4 (1949): 21, 18.

42. James E. Meade, "Financial Policy and the Balance of Payments," *Economica* 15 (1948): 101–15. "Indeed, it becomes daily clearer that perhaps the main conflict in international economic policy—at least in so far as normal peace time arrangements are concerned—is the choice between quantitative controls and fluctuating exchange rates as the means of achieving and maintaining external balance. Those who seek for an extensive removal of trade barriers must logically work for fluctuating exchange rates." J. E. Meade, "The Removal of Trade Barriers: The Regional versus the Universal Approach," *Economica* 18 (1951): 198.

43. Hubert Henderson, "The Function of Exchange Rates," *Oxford Economic Papers* 1 (1949): 1, 15, 17.

44. In 1949, Triffin noted, "Exchange stability, without substantial exchange freedom, is a meaningless objective to pursue. Our greatest danger is not competitive devaluation, but rather currency overvaluation buttressed by increasing controls, bilateralism, and discrimination. We must, therefore, *facilitate* rather than hamper exchange adjustments, insofar as they are conducive to an exchange rate-pattern which will hasten the dismantlement of quantitative restrictions." Robert Triffin, *Maintaining and Restoring Balance in International Payments* (Princeton, NJ: Princeton University Press, 1966), 180.

45. Mints was also critical of the Bretton Woods trade-off: "It seems evident that the American delegates to the Bretton Woods conference were chiefly interested in promoting multilateral trade, a consummation greatly to be desired, and that they believed stability of exchange rates would operate powerfully in this direction. While they by no means completely ignored the necessity of providing for international equilibrium, they nevertheless apparently either underestimated the importance of this problem or overestimated the efficacy of the very awkward means that the International Monetary Agreement provides. The result is that the government of the United States has been an important influence in support of the system of pegged exchange rates, and this system has compelled various nations to resort to direct controls of imports and bilateral agreements of precisely the kinds that the government of the United States was hopeful of avoiding." Lloyd Mints, "Discussion," *American Economic Review* 43 (1953): 55.

46. Lloyd Mints, Friedman's colleague at the University of Chicago, devoted a chapter of his 1950 book *Monetary Policy for a Competitive Society* to "fixed versus flexible exchange rates." He pointed out the "irrec-

oncilable conflict between the requirements for international equilibrium and for domestic stability. . . . This dilemma has long been recognized and many able writers have sought without success some way of escape from it." See Lloyd W. Mints, *Monetary Policy for a Competitive Economy* (Chicago: University of Chicago Press, 1950), 90.

47. See Friedrich A. Lutz, "The Case for Flexible Exchange Rates," *Banca Nazionale del Lavoro Quarterly Review* 7 (1954): 175–85; James E. Meade, "The Case for Variable Exchange Rates," *Three Banks Review* 27 (1955): 3–27.

Part II

THE DISAPPEARING ORDER

Chapter 4

The Universally Keynesian Vision of Bretton Woods

James M. Boughton

The extensive literature on the Bretton Woods Conference almost invariably focuses on the differences between the British and American visions and goals.[1] Not only did the two leading countries come to the table with opposite needs and interests; the task of reconciling those interests fell to two men with strikingly different natures and backgrounds: the aristocratic and iconically brilliant and cosmopolitan Baron of Tilton, Lord John Maynard Keynes; and the scrappy little first-generation American from the poorer side of Boston, Harry Dexter White. The temptation to portray the whole process as a battle between competing visions and purposes has proved to be irresistible. A partial corrective is in order, as both of their plans were essentially Keynesian.

An examination of underlying interests and motives is important, because a superficial review of the British and American plans for Bretton Woods makes them seem almost diametrically opposed. The Keynes Plan emphasized the provision of enough financing to enable deficit countries to restore economic growth after the war while constraining surplus countries from accumulating limitless reserves. The White Plan emphasized the restoration of multilateral trade and finance in ways that would constrain Britain from using restrictive practices in the sterling area to secure trade advantages. In the debates leading to Bretton Woods, Keynes was (in Robert

Skidelsky's phrasing) "fighting for Britain" against the contrary aims of the US Treasury.[2]

The deeper question that these differences imply is whether the IMF was designed to promote employment and growth or to promote fiscal probity and price stability. A complete answer requires attention to both goals and to their prioritization and timing. Gradually through its first half century, the IMF acquired a reputation for focusing excessively on fiscal austerity. Although that reputation is not unfounded, it tends to ignore the underlying philosophy, in which strengthening a country's finances is a necessary step toward achieving sustainable growth. The question here is how clearly the founders at Bretton Woods understood this fundamental relationship and built it into the institutional charter.

THE FOUNDING PHILOSOPHY

That Keynes was a Keynesian needs no justification, although a definition is essential. For this purpose, Keynesian economics may be defined in both normative and positive terms. Normatively, it is a conviction that, because the invisible hand will not maintain macroeconomic balance on its own, national governments have a responsibility and should accept as a primary goal to promote full employment and price stability. Positively, it is the hypothesis that fiscal and monetary policies are effective tools for managing aggregate demand to achieve that goal. This definition distinguishes Keynesianism from other schools of thought that were in play in the 1930s and 1940s: the laissez-faire economics of the classicists, the heavy statist interventionism of the various socialist schools, and the atheoretical economic policies exemplified by Nazi Germany.[3] It assigns a major economic role to the state and asks it to guide but not replace or undermine private markets.

The historical record shows that White was also a Keynesian. His differences with his British counterparts were partly technical and partly derived from their different national interests. The two economists developed their plans for postwar monetary cooperation independently, roughly from mid-1941 to mid-1942.

The financial facet of the Keynes Plan was based on the British banking system and aimed to provide automatic credits (overdrafts) to deficit countries on an as-needed basis. Credits would be provided in the form of an international currency (bancor) that could be used only to settle official imbalances between central banks and other monetary authorities. Excessive borrowing would be discouraged through interest charges that would increase with the relative size of an outstanding debit balance.

The White Plan was based on the US banking system and on the practices of the US Exchange Stabilization Fund (ESF). (The US government established the ESF in 1934 as a fund for the Treasury to use to stabilize the exchange value of the US dollar. One means of doing so was for the ESF to exchange dollars for other currencies under repurchase agreements. That practice was the prototype for the credit arrangements made by the IMF starting in 1947.) His plan aimed to provide loans to member countries in limited amounts upon approval by a board of executive directors, using gold and reserve assets deposited by member countries.

In the course of two years leading up to the Bretton Woods Conference, the United States and Great Britain, in conjunction with other invited countries, negotiated a compromise structure. On most technical issues and on the scale of the institution's lending capacity, the differences were resolved largely in the direction of the American plan.

These technical differences should not overshadow the fact that the purposes toward which Keynes and White were working were essentially similar. Both aimed at growth and prosperity through international cooperation and active governmental oversight. Keynes made his purpose plain and simple: "The plan aims at the substitution of an expansionist, in place of a contractionist, pressure on world trade." White, in contrast, was never one to express himself either simply or plainly. His plan listed eleven purposes, all of which were variations on the theme of promoting "intelligent international collaboration" and reducing "barriers to foreign trade." Such obstacles, he argued "are serious barriers to recovery and maintenance of a high level of economic activity among countries. . . . Each of the objectives . . . , if achieved, would help in some degree to restore and maintain world prosperity."[4]

Lest there be any doubt, White's background demonstrates the depth of his commitment to the ideas that we now think of as Keynesian. A few examples will illustrate the point.

In 1932, while White was still studying toward his PhD at Harvard, he and two fellow graduate students—Lauchlin Currie and Paul T. Ellsworth—wrote a paper extolling the use of monetary and fiscal policy in combination to combat the Depression. This unpublished paper anticipated the New Deal by a year and prefigured the analysis of Keynes's *General Theory* by four years.[5]

In 1934, Jacob Viner recruited White to join his "brain trust" in the US Treasury as an analyst of the use of monetary and exchange rate policy in service of the New Deal. For the next decade, White argued (mostly internally in the Treasury) that the United States should adhere to the gold standard as an anchor for monetary policy but should also be open to changing the dollar price of gold in "periods of stress," so as to prevent shortages of gold from dragging down the economy.[6] Throughout the 1930s, Keynes and White both evolved toward what ultimately became the "fixed but adjustable" standard for setting exchange rates, enshrined in the original Articles of Agreement of the IMF.

As early as 1935, but especially in 1937 and 1938 after the recovery from the Depression had stalled, White argued for a combination of increased spending on New Deal programs and a loosening of monetary policy to restart economic growth. In 1938, he was instrumental in persuading the Treasury to stop sterilizing gold inflows so that the gold could support an increase in the money supply and to encourage the Federal Reserve to reverse the disastrous increase in reserve requirements of 1936.[7]

Internationally, White focused consistently throughout the 1930s on promoting monetary cooperation as an antidote to the autarkic policies that had aggravated the global Depression. He was the Treasury's point man for organizing the Tripartite Agreement of 1936, in which France, the United Kingdom, and the United States agreed to cooperate and consult before changing exchange rates. Through the ESF and purchases of gold and silver, he helped provide financial support for many developing countries. And he tried, without success, to establish a multilateral development bank for Latin America.

All this activity was in a direction of which Keynes would have approved. Moreover, Keynes—though frequently annoyed by White's crudely American abrupt style, and prone to a condescending anti-Semitism—admired him and worked well with him. During a visit to Washington in October 1943, Keynes wrote to a colleague in London that White was "over-bearing, a bad colleague . . . but I have a very great respect and even liking for him. In many respects he is the best man here."[8]

SOURCES OF CONFUSION

For several reasons, analysts of Bretton Woods have generally focused more on the differences between Keynes and White than on their similar visions. The record has been obscured by three interrelated misconceptions about White's motivations at Bretton Woods. The first is that he was opposed to

Keynes's conception of the IMF and worked actively to undermine it. The second, more generally, is that he was anti-British and was trying to weaken the British economy. The third is that he was sympathetic to the Soviet economic system and was trying to establish a US-Soviet condominium for the postwar world. Recent examples of these arguments may be found in bestselling books.[9]

The first misconception arises because of all the technical disputes between Keynes and White. White insisted on including all the Allied countries in the planning; he insisted on scaling down the resources available for the new institutions; he rejected Keynes's desire for a new international currency; he rejected the idea of funding the IMF through overdrafts instead of subscriptions; he insisted on having a resident executive board to oversee policies and lending decisions; and he insisted on having both the IMF and the World Bank headquartered in Washington instead of London. Keynes lost all those battles, but they were fights over details, not over purposes. On purposes and objectives, they were largely in agreement.

Were the American negotiators anti-British? White shared and was instrumental in implementing the views of the Roosevelt administration that Britain was no longer a major economic power, that it was exaggerating the extent of its financial needs during the war, and that its requests for assistance provided an opportunity for the United States to force an end to British imperialism and the associated restrictive economic policies. Those policies included promoting trade between Britain and its colonies by linking currencies together in the bloc known as the sterling area and controlling the use of sterling-denominated accounts by colonies and other countries in the British Commonwealth. Whether those views were anti-British or anti-imperialist and whether they were motivated by a desire to promote American over British interests or by a desire to establish a broad multilateral system of international trade and finance is essentially a matter of perspective. The effect was both anti-imperial and broadly multilateral, but it also served American interests.

If Britain was a fading world power, the Soviet Union was on the rise both economically and politically. Of the four members of the Grand Alliance, Great Britain and China were less powerful (though no less important in the war effort) than either the United States or the Soviet Union. The Roosevelt administration viewed the Soviets as an essential bulwark against a resurgence of German militarism. The Treasury secretary, Henry Morgenthau, Jr., with help from White, went further than others in the administration by proposing to de-industrialize Germany to render it incapable of threatening its neighbors, as it had already done twice in the past thirty years. Critics interpreted this Morgenthau Plan as an indirect way to clear the path for Soviet expansionism, but Morgenthau was just naively assuming that the Soviets would be so preoccupied with rebuilding their own economy that they would have neither the interest nor the ability to take over additional territory. After some hesitation, Roosevelt rejected the Morgenthau Plan as impractical.[10]

What was important to White was to foster a good relationship with the Soviet Union: to perpetuate the Grand Alliance in peacetime. As he put it in the White Plan of April 1942: ". . . to exclude a country such as Russia [from IMF membership] would be an egregious error. Russia, despite her socialist economy, could both contribute and profit by participation. To deny her the privileges of joining in this cooperative effort to improve world economic relations would be to repeat the tragic errors of the last generation and introduce a very discordant note in the new era millions everywhere are hoping for."[11]

White pursued this theme throughout his preparations for Bretton Woods. He held an extensive series of meetings with the Soviet delegation in the first half of 1944, in a successful effort to persuade them to participate in the conference and sign the Final Act establishing the IMF and the World Bank. In this effort, he and his American colleagues were far more enthusiastic and optimistic than were Keynes and his team.

In the early planning for Bretton Woods, Keynes accepted a major role for the Soviet Union only with great reluctance. To maximize British influence, he proposed that the United Kingdom and the United States jointly develop a plan for the postwar financial institutions, in which the two countries would be the "founder-States." If that suggestion did not prevail, then "Russia, which might be a third founder, if she can be a party to so capitalist-looking an institution, would need special consideration," he wrote in 1942.[12] Clearly Keynes and White had different conceptions of the process for developing postwar institutions and for governing them once they were created. White was more multilateralist than Keynes and was more committed to sharing responsibility widely across the alliance. It would, however, be a stretch of logic to construe that difference as opposition to Britain's legitimate interests.

White's interest in promoting cooperation with the Soviet Union requires a bit more elaboration. After Bretton Woods, apparently to overcome domestic US opposition to the creation of the Security Council as part of the proposed United Nations organization, White drafted a more explicit appeal to the continuation of the Grand Alliance as a means of preventing a resurgence of militarism in Germany or Japan. In a handwritten rough draft of a speech (apparently never finished nor delivered), White wrote, "With U.S., U.K., U.S.S.R., and China combined in a tight military alliance designed to uphold [international] law, no [combination] of powers outside these four would have the slightest chance of victory against them."[13]

White's belief in the importance of cooperation with the Soviet Union has led some critics to conclude that he was trying to promote Soviet interests over those of the United States or the United Kingdom. Robert Skidelsky was particularly imaginative, asserting that White "envisaged a 'new course' leading to the eventual convergence of the United States and Soviet Union in a single social democratic world system."[14] This view of Bretton Woods as a communist plot was taken even further by Benn Steil, who wrote that White "was far more interested in locking the United States and Russia into political alliance than in the creation of a system to revive trade among private enterprises."[15] These conclusions are based on a misreading of White's drafts and taking his words out of context.[16] The United Kingdom was as much a part of the Grand Alliance—and of White's vision—as was the Soviet Union.

What parts of the Bretton Woods Agreements were aimed at promoting the interests of the Soviet Union? Four elements in the original IMF Articles[17] were relevant, none of which was fundamental to the design or operation of the IMF. None undermined the key role of the United Kingdom, and none interfered with the underlying Keynesian purpose and structure of the IMF. Rather, each one was designed simply to reassure Soviet officials that membership would not impede or conflict with their economic and political system. Among the major countries involved in the preparations for Bretton Woods, the Soviet Union was the only one that expected to do much of its trade and finance within a bloc of nonparticipants using nonmarket prices and exchange rates. It thus had a special interest in avoiding making commitments inconsistent with its economic system.

First, Article IV, Section 5 (e), specified that a "member may change the par value of its currency without the concurrence of the Fund if the change does not affect the international transactions of members of the Fund." This provision implied that a member country that had bilateral trading arrangements with nonmember countries could modify the exchange rate for those bilateral arrangements without needing the concurrence of the IMF.

Second, Article IV, Section 5 (f), specified that the IMF "shall not object to a proposed change [in a par value for a member's exchange rate] because of the domestic social or political policies of the member proposing the change."

Third, Article VIII, Section 5, specified a limited list of data that each member had to provide to the IMF. That list reassured potential members that they would not be required to provide other data, such as the amount or currency composition of foreign exchange reserves.

Fourth, Article XI, Section 2, gave member countries the right "to impose restrictions on exchange transactions with non-members or with persons in their territories unless the Fund finds that such restrictions prejudice the interests of members and are contrary to the purposes of the Fund." The effect of this provision was similar to that of the one in Article IV, Section 5 (e).

Although the inclusion of these provisions succeeded to the point of persuading the Soviet delegation at Bretton Woods to sign the Articles *ad referendum*, it appears that Joseph Stalin perceived (correctly, as became evident) that the IMF would be dominated by the United States and Western Europe. Stalin personally intervened at the last hour to block the Soviet Union from joining.[18] Over the rest of its existence (until it was dissolved in 1991), the country never did become a member of the IMF.[19]

CONFLICTS IN THE DESIGN OF THE IMF

Although White and Keynes both had a fundamentally Keynesian conception of the goals of the IMF, they differed substantially on both the structure and the scope of the proposed institution. Keynes was representing the country that was destined for many years to be the IMF's largest borrower. He manifested that national interest by arguing for a large fund: ideally a true lender of last resort, with sufficient resources to stabilize international payments positions. To enable that structure, the IMF would have to issue its own international currency and would have to extend loans virtually automatically to member countries facing payments deficits. Representing the United States as the IMF's only potential creditor, White's responsibility was to tone down those demands to manageable levels. Most of these conflicts were resolved several months before the Bretton Woods Conference, primarily in a series of bilateral meetings between the American and British negotiators—led personally by White and Keynes—in Washington from September 21 to October 9, 1943.

Keynes's conception of an international lender of last resort began with the idea that each member country could borrow whatever amounts it needed simply by being willing to pay an appropriate rate of interest. As he explained in a 1943 letter, his view was "very strongly that if countries are to be given sufficient confidence they must be able to rely in all normal circumstances on drawing a substantial part of their quota without policing or facing unforeseen obstacles."[20]

The two key references in Keynes's letter are to the country's "quota" and to the "policing" of borrowing. He envisaged an agency—he called it the International Clearing Union—in which each member country would be assigned a maximum borrowing quota based on the magnitude of its international trade. In the absence of large capital flows unrelated to trade (which was the situation at that time), a country's potential need for financing could be presumed to bear a close relationship to the volume of its trade. His plan paid lip service to the need to have some "means of restraining improvident borrowers."[21] Nonetheless, *ex ante*, each member could borrow within its quota without being subjected to specific conditions, such as required changes in economic policies.

Keynes seems to have had a remarkably naive belief in the efficacy of interest charges to keep his Clearing Union in financial balance. Both creditors and debtors would have to pay interest to the union (he suggested 1 percent per annum) whenever their balances exceeded 25 percent of quota, and would pay higher rates (another 1 percent) if balances exceeded 50 percent of quota. Thus, if the United States were to run a large payment surplus and the United Kingdom a corresponding deficit, both countries would have to pay interest on the outstanding balances on the Clearing Union's books. Keynes imagined that these charges would induce both creditor and debtor to mend their ways and shift policies voluntarily to restore equilibrium in their balance of international payments and thus end the obligation to keep paying interest.

The Clearing Union would extend these credits by creating its own currency, which Keynes called "bancor." Both a unit of account and a limited medium of exchange, bancor would have had a value fixed in relation to gold. Only the central banks of member countries would be authorized to hold bancor, which they could then use to settle deficits with other members. To settle a deficit with the United States, Britain (through its depository, the Bank of England) would draw bancor from the Clearing Union and transfer it to the US central bank, the Federal Reserve. Both countries would pay interest on the outstanding balance until it was repaid. While the amounts of bancor that the union could create in this way would not be unlimited, Keynes envisaged a set of quotas that would be large enough to accommodate all reasonable requests. If the ceilings proved to be too small, they could always be adjusted upward.

White objected both to Keynes's concept of the structure of the institution and to the proposal for unfettered access. The structure of Keynes's Clearing Union was based on the British banking system, where customers would borrow in the form of overdrafts on their deposit accounts. In US banking, overdrafts resulted from customer errors and were generally frowned upon. White therefore proposed a different structure based on US mutual savings banks and credit unions, which he called a stabilization fund. In this scheme, each member country would deposit a certain amount of gold plus a credit balance in its own currency. That stock would constitute a fund that the institution could lend to members on request. The British team agreed to this proposal but devoted some energy to trying to reduce the amount of gold that countries would have to deposit relative to the amounts that they could borrow. The Americans wanted 25 percent of quotas to be deposited in gold; the British fought for 12.5 percent but ultimately yielded.

A major sticking point concerned control over loan requests. White did not believe that a general goodwill and the price mechanism inherent in interest charges could prevent countries from abusing the privilege of borrowing from the stabilization fund. The fund's executive board, he argued, should have a responsibility to approve or disapprove loan requests and the ability to oversee how loans were being used. If borrowers were not using the opportunity afforded by the financing to correct their economic policies and restore balance in trade and payments, then the fund would not be doing its job.

White had a hard time selling that idea, even within the US team. During a heated argument in front of Keynes and the other British negotiators, Emanuel A. Goldenweiser—representing the Federal Reserve Board—suggested to White that "large countries would find this procedure [that is, fund oversight] intolerable." Adolf A. Berle, Jr.—representing the US State Department—agreed and added that "no great country would submit to this sort of scrutiny."[22]

The controversy was left unresolved. Article V, Section 3, of the IMF Articles of Agreement, on "Conditions Governing Use of the Fund's Resources," as adopted at Bretton Woods, specified that a member country could borrow up to 25 percent of its quota simply by representing to the IMF that it needed the money consistent with the purposes of the IMF. Beyond that, the IMF could lend "in its discretion." Moreover, if the IMF determined that a country was not using the proceeds properly, it could declare the country to be ineligible for further borrowing.

The vagueness of these rules proved to be troublesome in practice. Beginning in 1947, the IMF began interpreting the Articles in ways that gave it more control over the use of its resources. By the mid-1950s, it was granting standby arrangements conditional on borrowers undertaking specific policy commitments. Over the next half century, those conditional borrowing arrangements gradually became an increasingly greater portion of total lending, and the policy conditions gradually became more extensive and detailed. Because those conditions often included a tightening of monetary and fiscal policies, the IMF eventually gained a reputation as an arbiter of austerity rather than of economic recovery.

A related contentious issue concerned the size of the fund. Each member country would be required to deposit 25 percent of its assigned quota in gold, subject to a maximum requirement of 10 percent of its total holdings of gold and US dollars. That pool of resources would constitute a fund that the IMF could lend. If the pool was too large, countries might borrow excessively and contribute to global inflationary pressures. If too small, the IMF would be constrained in its ability to help countries meet legitimate financing needs. Keynes, representing borrowers' interests, saw his task as to argue for as large a fund as possible. White, representing creditors' interests, saw his task as to argue for an adequate fund. He wanted the IMF to be effective, but he also knew that persuading the US Congress to approve the plan and to permit the transfer of a large amount of US gold to a new multilateral institution would not be easy.

Keynes's initial proposal, in 1942, was for each country to have a quota equivalent to 75 percent of its prewar international trade. White's proposal was for "at least $5 billion" in total quotas.[23] The two plans had different conceptions about how quotas would translate into borrowing limits, but the Keynes Plan was roughly equal to a $12 billion fund under the White Plan. Over the next two years, the two teams worked out a joint plan for a total of $8 billion: roughly halfway between the two starting points.

These estimates of the necessary size of the fund were based on economic activity between the two world wars. The implicit goal was to prevent a recurrence of the disruptions caused by the wars and the Great Depression. The idea that the postwar world would see rapid and sustained economic growth and would need unprecedented amounts of official financing does not seem to have occurred to any of the participants at Bretton Woods.

By the time the IMF started lending in 1947, the potential for economic growth was becoming apparent, and price inflation was becoming a widespread problem. Keynes died of a heart attack in April 1946 and was unable to witness or comment on the increasing evidence of an impecunious IMF. White, however, had become the US executive director at the IMF (its number-two official, after the managing director) and was becoming concerned about his creation's ability to do its job once growth and inflation really took off. After White left the IMF in the middle of 1947, the beginnings of the Cold War necessitated a renewal of large military spending in many countries. It was now clear to White that he had been overly cautious in constraining the IMF's lending potential. "We cannot expect a boy to do a man's job," he lamented.[24]

In 1948, as a project for the government of Mexico (for which White was then working as a consultant), White sketched out a proposal for amending the IMF Articles of Agreement to overcome the IMF's shortage of resources. He too died of a heart attack before he could finalize the plan, but the essence of it was contained in a thirty-four-page draft that the Mexican authorities circulated posthumously to the IMF Executive Board.[25] The details of the plan are not what matters, and White most likely would have revised them had he lived to do so. What is interesting is that the proposal prefigures the creation of the SDR (Special Drawing Rights) as an international reserve asset by some twenty years.

In White's scheme, the IMF would create bookkeeping entries for each participating country in the form of credits to a "Trade Dollar" (TD) account. A participant wanting to increase its imports above a base-year level could use its TD balance to settle the corresponding payments deficit. Interest would be charged on the outstanding balance, and the debit would have to be repaid after a lengthy period (suggested to be twenty-five years). A complex set of constraints would ensure that no one participant would be called upon to accept more TD credits than was reasonable for its size. Because the credits could be used only to finance an increase in international trade, the TD accounts would be assured to be additional to, rather than replacements for, existing sources of official reserves (which were then effectively limited to gold and US dollars).

Partly because of the technical complexity of the scheme and partly because it was orphaned before it was circulated, White's proposal was not given any further consideration by the IMF. By the mid-1960s, however, the problem that it had sought to address—a serious shortage of dollar reserves and of lendable resources in the IMF—had become acute and had to be addressed. After some years of discussion, the membership of the IMF agreed in 1968 to amend the Articles by creating the SDR Department. Much as in White's conception, the IMF created SDRs as bookkeeping entries in the form of SDR "allocations," which participating countries could use to settle payments deficits with other participants. As with White's scheme, each SDR was equal in value to the gold content of the US dollar at the base year. (Only later was the SDR reconstituted as a basket of convertible currencies.) Both the TD scheme and the SDR functioned essentially as lines of credit and supplements to other forms of official reserves.

The lesson of these stories is that the structure of the IMF as conceived at Bretton Woods was fundamentally flawed, for two reasons. First, because the Articles of Agreement omitted any mention of policy conditions on borrowing, the structure lacked a viable mechanism for ensuring that borrowers would use loan proceeds appropriately and in ways that would contribute to a sustainable balance of international payments. Second, the system lacked a viable means to increase resources in line with a growing demand for international credit. The IMF could increase members' quotas, but only if countries had enough gold and dollars to deposit in the IMF. Only by developing a strategy for making its lending conditional on policy reforms and supplementing its resources through the SDR mechanism was the IMF able to continue to play a useful role as the world economy grew dramatically in the postwar era.

Another important issue that had to be settled at Bretton Woods concerned the central role of the US dollar. The Keynes Plan of 1943 obviated the need for any reference to specific currencies, because it was based on an international asset (bancor) to be issued by his proposed currency union. The White Plan of 1943 rejected that premise and was based primarily on gold. To create a fund of lendable resources, each country would deposit a portion of its quota in gold, up to a maximum determined by its holdings of gold and "free foreign exchange." The latter term was left undefined but was understood to mean the country's official foreign exchange reserves. At that time, the only major currency that was freely convertible and thus usable as reserves was the US dollar, but it seems that White was trying to allow for the inclusion of other currencies as various countries recovered financially from the war.

The plan that was jointly agreed to by the American and British teams in October 1943 and published in April 1944 retained most of the financial structure of the White Plan but replaced the phrase "free foreign exchange" with the slightly more concrete term "gold-convertible exchange." Again, it was obvious that the dollar was the only major currency that met this definition in 1944, but neither the Americans nor the British wanted to narrow the options to that extent. Nor did they want to elevate the dollar's role in a way that might attract criticism from other countries.

When the forty-four delegations at Bretton Woods began the serious work of agreeing on a draft for the IMF Articles of Agreement, they could no longer fall back on vague definitions. Finally, at a meeting of the commission that was charged with drafting the IMF Articles (Commission I, chaired by White) on July 13, 1944, the Indian delegate—A. D. Shroff—asked for a clarification. "Those words 'gold' and 'convertible exchange' are subject to definition, and I don't know if the US delegation is now prepared to give us a definition of gold and convertible exchange as used in this provision." Before anyone on the US side could respond, the British delegate—Dennis Robertson, since Keynes was off chairing the commission on the World Bank—intervened, apparently because he thought that his team was responsible for the ambiguity. "I think that it is not in any way [the Americans'] fault that the furnishing of this definition has been so long delayed." And Robertson had a solution readily at hand. "I would like to propose an amendment to the text which is before us, according to which the criteria of payment of official gold subscription should be expressed as official holdings of gold and United States dollars." The US delegate—Edward Bernstein, since White was chairing the meeting—demurred slightly but basically agreed. Bernstein noted that there were "a number of other currencies which can be used to purchase dollars without restriction . . . but the practical importance of holdings of the countries represented here is so small that it has been felt it would be easier for this purpose to regard the United States dollar as what was intended when we speak of gold convertible exchange."[26]

Bernstein's phrasing—"it has been felt"—suggests that he and Robertson had discussed the matter beforehand and had agreed between themselves on this practical solution. Perhaps they felt it was necessary and would be more palatable if it came from someone outside the US delegation. In any event, it was the only sensible answer, because defining convertibility is notoriously arbitrary, even today. The US dollar was always going to be the keystone of the postwar financial system, and Robertson was merely agreeing to describe the system as clearly as possible.[27]

IMPLICATIONS FOR THE FUTURE

Beyond the questions of White's motives and the balance of power between the United States and the United Kingdom, the issue of the purpose of the IMF remains important today. The IMF is commonly viewed as obsessed with imposing austerity on indebted countries without regard to the borrowers' growth prospects. Joseph Stiglitz put the argument more starkly than most, suggesting that the IMF "has taken on the pre-Keynesian position of fiscal austerity in the face of a downturn, doling out funds only if the borrowing country conforms to the IMF's views about appropriate economic policy, which almost always entail contractionary policies leading to recessions or worse."[28] If correct, this argument implies that the IMF now acts with a purpose that is totally contrary to that for which it was created at Bretton Woods.

In response to Stiglitz and other critics, the IMF's (then) chief economist, Kenneth Rogoff, defended the IMF's policy advice as no harsher than was required by the unfortunate circumstances in which the IMF's borrowers typically found themselves. "Blaming the IMF for the reality that every country must confront its budget constraints is like blaming the fund for gravity," he wrote.[29] In addition, for purposes of the present argument, it is important to explore whether insisting that borrowers must face budget restraints is "pre-Keynesian," as suggested by Stiglitz.

In *The General Theory*, Keynes clearly stated the case for austerity in the early stages of adjustment. In his model of the business cycle, recovery from a downturn had to be delayed until excess inventories ("stocks") could be eliminated. "Sometimes, indeed, the reduction of stocks may have to be virtually completed before any measurable degree of recovery can be detected." Keynes then proceeded to describe favorably the "earlier phases of America's 'New Deal,'" which "partly consisted in a strenuous attempt to reduce these stocks—by curtailment of current output and in all sorts of ways. The reduction of stocks to a normal level was a necessary process—a phase which had to be endured. . . . Only when it had been completed was the way prepared for substantial recovery."[30]

Austerity as a component of a program aimed at restoring growth and prosperity is not "pre-Keynesian." As the preceding paragraph shows, it is fully consistent with the Keynesianism of *The General Theory*. Nonetheless, the practical question remains: Does the IMF focus excessively on austerity while paying too little attention to the other requirements for restoring growth?

Examples are not hard to find, but they are never unambiguous. One that would seem to be an obvious case is Greece in the aftermath of the 2009 crisis. Greece was forced, as a condition for remaining in the euro area, to endure more than five years of crippling adjustment, with little recovery even in sight. Until 2015, the IMF was a mostly silent and willing partner in a program that was far from adequate as a path to recovery. What is now known, however, is that the IMF understood all along that the program was inadequate, that Greece could not restore growth without much more substantial external financial assistance, particularly in the form of debt relief.[31] Until the middle of 2015, the IMF hemmed itself in from making its views public, apparently because that was the price of being invited to participate with European institutions in the program.

The general issue throughout much of the seventy-year history of IMF lending is that the institution has not assumed responsibility for generating official financing for indebted countries, other than through its own lending. In a typical case, the IMF staff will first calculate the country's financing "need" as the amount required to produce balance in external payments. It will then estimate the amount of financing that is likely to be available from various sources, plus whatever amount the IMF can lend as determined by its own access limits. Those calculations yield a budget constraint, and all too often the only way the constraint can be met is through contractionary macroeconomic policies.

If the IMF is to be an agent of Keynesian economics in the full spirit of that term—if it is to live up to its founding purpose—it needs to be a proactive agent for *loosening* the budget constraint when a borrowing country is preparing to undertake policy reforms that are expected to reduce aggregate demand over the short or medium term. That is, the IMF should be an active proponent for increased financial assistance whenever—as is very often the case—its own resources will be insufficient to restore growth over a reasonable horizon. In most major capital-account crises over the past two decades, the IMF has helped assemble multilateral financing packages, though usually only after major creditor countries have taken the initiative. The IMF's belated rebellion against European austerity in the case of Greece, and its recent insistence on debt relief for Ukraine, might turn out to presage a more proactive and sustained movement in that direction.

Notes

1. The practice of emphasizing the differences rather than the similarities in the two main plans dates from the early literature on Bretton Woods. See, in particular, Richard N. Gardner, *Sterling-Dollar Diplomacy: Anglo-American Collaboration in the Reconstruction of Multilateral Trade* (Oxford: Oxford University Press, 1956); Alfred E. Eckes, Jr., *A Search for Solvency: Bretton Woods and the International Monetary System, 1941–1971* (Austin: University of Texas Press, 1975); and Armand Van Dormael, *Bretton Woods: Birth of a Monetary System* (London: Macmillan, 1978). Recent examples include Robert Skidelsky, *John Maynard Keynes: Fighting for Britain, 1937–1946* (London: Macmillan, 2000); Benn Steil, *The Battle of Bretton Woods: John Maynard Keynes, Harry Dexter White, and the Making of a New World Order* (Princeton, NJ: Princeton University Press, 2013); Ed Conway, *The Summit: The Biggest Battle of the Second World War—Fought Behind Closed Doors* (London: Little, Brown, 2014); and Eric Rauchway, *The Money Makers: How Roosevelt and Keynes Ended the Depression, Defeated Fascism, and Secured a Prosperous Peace* (New York: Basic Books, 2015). For a broader view of the negotiations that focuses instead on the role of developing countries in shaping the outcome, see Eric Helleiner, *The Forgotten Origins of Bretton Woods: International Development and the Making of the Postwar Order* (Ithaca, NY: Cornell University Press, 2014).

2. The phrase is the subtitle of Skidelsky's 2000 book. For the US edition of the book, the publisher changed it to *Fighting for Freedom*.

3. For a detailed discussion of these distinctions, see the essays in Peter A. Hall, ed., *The Political Power of Economic Ideas: Keynesianism Across Nations* (Princeton, NJ: Princeton University Press, 1989). In chap. 9, Harold James argues that German economic policies in the Nazi era were formulated in a "theoretical vacuum" (p. 243).

4. The Keynes and White Plans are in J. Keith Horsefield, ed., *The International Monetary Fund, 1945–1965, Volume III: Documents* (Washington, DC: International Monetary Fund, 1969). The quotation from the Keynes Plan is from p. 4, and the quotations from the White Plan are from pp. 41 and 46–48.

5. The paper is reproduced and exposited in David E. W. Laidler and Roger J. Sandilands, "An Early Harvard Memorandum on Anti-Depression Policies: Introductory Note," *History of Political Economy* 34, no. 3 (Summer 2002): 515–52.

6. Harry Dexter White, "Selection of a Monetary Standard for the United States," report submitted to Jacob Viner, US Treasury, on September 22, 1934 (Princeton, NJ: Harry Dexter White Papers, Seeley G. Mudd Manuscript Library, Princeton University), 232.

7. See Harry Dexter White, "Outline Analysis of Current Situation," memorandum of February 26, 1935, to George C. Haas (Princeton, NJ: Harry Dexter White Papers, Seeley G. Mudd Manuscript Library, Princeton University); "Effects of Increase in the Gold Price of the Dollar," note sent to George C. Haas on March 27, 1937 (College Park, MD: US National Archives and Records Administration, Records Group 56.12.3, entry 360P, box 1); "Shall Excess Reserves Be Increased, and If So, How?," memorandum of April 7, 1938, to Wayne C. Taylor (Hyde Park, NY: Franklin D. Roosevelt Presidential Library and Museum, *Diaries of Henry Morgenthau, Jr.*, Book 118:217–23); and "Does the Present Business Situation Call for a Program for Recovery, and If So, What Should the Program Be?," memorandum of April 8, 1938, to Henry Morgenthau, Jr. (*Diaries of Henry Morgenthau, Jr.*, Book 118:235–39). Less than two weeks after White circulated the memoranda in April 1938, the Treasury closed the account it had been using to sterilize (or hoard) the gold inflows.

8. Letter to Sir Wilfried Eady (October 3, 1943), in John Maynard Keynes, *The Collected Writings of John Maynard Keynes, Volume XXV. Activities 1940–1944: Shaping the Post-War World: The Clearing Union*, ed. Donald Moggridge (London: Macmillan, 1980), 356. Keynes's anti-Semitism during the Bretton Woods negotiations was directed more pointedly at White's assistant, Edward M. Bernstein, whom Keynes described in another letter to Eady on the same date as "a regular little rabbi, a reader out of the Talmud, to Harry's grand political high rabbidom. He . . . knows every rat run in his local ghetto . . ."; ibid., 364.

9. See Liaquat Ahamed, *Lords of Finance: The Bankers Who Broke the World* (London: Penguin Press, 2009); Skidelsky, *John Maynard Keynes*; and Steil, *Battle of Bretton Woods*.

10. Henry Morgenthau, Jr., *Germany Is Our Problem: A Plan for Germany* (New York: Harper & Brothers, 1945). The origins of and reactions to the plan have been much debated. For some diverse examples that include discussions of White's role, see John Lewis Gaddis, *The United States and the Origins of the Cold War, 1941–1947* (New York: Columbia University Press, 2000); Michael Beschloss, *The Conquerors: Roosevelt, Truman, and the Destruction of Hitler's Germany, 1941–1945* (New York: Simon & Schuster, 2002); and Bruce Craig, *Treasonable Doubt: The Harry Dexter White Spy Case* (Lawrence, KS: University Press of Kansas, 2004).

11. Horsefield, *International Monetary Fund*, 72–73.

12. Ibid., 6 and 15.

13. Undated manuscript in the Seeley G. Mudd Manuscript Library at Princeton University, p. 4. The bracketed terms in this quotation are expansions of White's shorthand ("int." and "comb."). Although the manuscript was undated, the approximate timing (probably late 1944) can be inferred because it was linked implicitly to the proposed UN Security Council and because it mentioned "Walter Lipmann's recent book": *U.S. Foreign Policy: Shield of the Republic* (New York: Little, Brown, 1943).

14. Skidelsky, *John Maynard Keynes*, 242.

15. Steil, *Battle of Bretton Woods*, 136.

16. The error was heavily inspired by a conviction that White was secretly a Soviet agent. For a debunking of that story, see James M. Boughton and Roger J. Sandilands, "Politics and the Attack on FDR's Economists: From the Grand Alliance to the Cold War," *Intelligence and National Security* 18, no. 3 (Autumn 2003): 73–99.

17. See "Articles of Agreement of the International Monetary Fund, July 22, 1944," in the "Historical Documents" section of this book.

18. Harold James and Marzenna James, "The Origins of the Cold War: Some New Documents," *Historical Journal* 37, no. 3 (1994): 615–22.

19. For the history of relations between the Soviet Union and the IMF, see James M. Boughton, *Tearing Down Walls: The International Monetary Fund 1990–1999* (Washington, DC: International Monetary Fund, 2012), 57–66.

20. Letter to Jacob Viner (October 17, 1943), in Keynes, *Collected Writings*, 333.

21. See Keynes's "Proposals for an International Clearing Union (April 1943)," in the "Historical Documents" section of this book.

22. British minutes of a meeting at the US Treasury, September 24, 1943; in Keynes, *Collected Writings*, 345–46. Goldenweiser was the director of the Division of Research and Statistics at the Federal Reserve Board. Berle was assistant secretary of state.

23. See Horsefield (1969), pp. 23 (Keynes) and 44 (White).

24. Harry Dexter White, "Proposal for an Amendment to the International Monetary Fund Charter to Increase the Level of World Trade," Executive Board Document EBD/48/347, October 14, 1948 (Washington, DC: IMF Archives), 1.

25. White, "Proposal for an Amendment."

26. This exchange was transcribed by one of the official stenographers at Bretton Woods. The (partial) transcripts were recently compiled and published in Kurt Schuler and Andrew Rosenberg, eds., *The Bretton Woods Transcripts* (New York: Center for Financial Stability, 2012); this exchange is on pp. 68–69.

27. Steil, *Battle of Bretton Woods*, 196, depicts White as scheming to switch from "convertible exchange" to dollars "on the sly" at Bretton Woods. For a more accurate account, see Conway, *The Summit*, 243–45.

28. Joseph E. Stiglitz, *Globalization and Its Discontents* (New York: W. W. Norton, 2002), 38.

29. Kenneth S. Rogoff, "The IMF Strikes Back," *Foreign Policy* 134 (January/February 2003): 41.

30. John Maynard Keynes, *The General Theory of Employment, Interest, and Money* (London: Macmillan, 1936), 331–32.

31. See James M. Boughton, "*The IMF As Just One Creditor: Who's In Charge When a Country Can't Pay?,*" CIGI Research Paper no. 66 (April 27, 2015) and references therein.

Chapter 5

Bretton Woods: The Parliamentary Debates in the United Kingdom

Andrew Bailey, Gordon Bannerman,
and Cheryl Schonhardt-Bailey

Our interest in Bretton Woods lies in seeking to identify the nature of contemporary deliberation in the British Parliament relative to the proposed postwar monetary and financial organizations. Britain is the focus of the study because, along with the United States, it was the main designer of the Bretton Woods system, starting with the so called Keynes and White Plans, which formed the basis for negotiations for each country.[1]

The United States, as the foremost creditor among the wartime Allies, and Britain, whose debt to the rest of the world had increased during the war both substantially and rapidly, played out their designated roles in a way that reflected their respective global positions. But British acceptance of Bretton Woods was fraught with difficulties, for the terms of the agreements were a stark and formal indication of British decline. From at least 1942 onward, it was clear to many observers that though Britain would emerge from the war victorious, she would also be depleted of resources, financially prostrate, with her colonial empire in disarray, and highly dependent on the benevolence of wartime allies, most notably the United States.

Prior to Bretton Woods, the international monetary system had evolved incrementally and at times accidentally. All previous efforts to modify by design had failed. A change of this magnitude inevitably required the United States to engage internationally, which it had not done in the institutional structure created after the First World War, and for Britain to overcome its historical and ideological attachment to empire. As a means of understanding this engagement by Britain and the United States, we examine the debates in the British Parliament between 1943 and 1945 in order to understand how Britain came to accept Bretton Woods when there were so many ideological obstacles to such acceptance.

We interpret the parliamentary debates by reference to Britain's financial position and the British party system. The latter was not unimportant, for while a Conservative-led coalition government was in power for most of the war, between May 1940 and May 1945, it was succeeded for two months by an interim "caretaker government" pending the result of the 1945 election. This ministry was then succeeded by the first majority Labour government, whose peacetime socialist agenda, propelled by a huge victory at the polls, was different from the approach of the wartime ministry. Thus, while monetary and financial negotiations were ongoing throughout the period, and there was a select cadre of officials who had come to the fore in wartime, there was a degree of discontinuity in government as well as the more pronounced economic dislocation.[2]

Throughout the negotiations leading to the Bretton Woods Agreements, it was fully apparent that any international agreement would involve striking a balance between establishing, on the one hand, multinational and multilateral rules and institutions, and, on the other hand, maintaining nation-state discretion in the postwar international system.[3] At Bretton Woods, there was a tension involving the rights of nations to revise their exchange rates without International Monetary Fund (IMF) agreement. Determining boundaries and rules and appropriate multilateral institutional structures involved the thorny issue of agreeing on limits to national sovereignty in shaping domestic policies, with the tension between international adjustment needs and domestic political requirements forming a central dilemma of international monetary relations.

Important to understanding Bretton Woods are two roles that the institutions that were created there would fulfil. First was the role of an international reserve currency and its part as a credible anchor for domestic monetary policy. The two principal architects of Bretton Woods, John Maynard Keynes and Harry White, began the process by outlining plans for the postwar system from respectively British and American positions. The Keynes Plan envisaged a supranational currency, whereas the White Plan had the dollar playing the anchor role, though formally tied to gold.

Second was the role of an institution to solve international collective-action problems and thus achieve adjustment of national imbalances, which were misaligned with fixed exchange rates, and whether this action was to be symmetric or asymmetric, and thus on all countries or just debtors, and to prevent competitive currency devaluations as well as tariffs.[4] Such a system required limiting national discretion in macroeconomic policy making, and giving force to this constraint required an enhanced role for national governments operating through international institutions. The international monetary system, as it had evolved in the nineteenth and twentieth centuries, had meant that national governments, by linking their currencies to gold, were de facto linking their currencies to each other. While providing a kind of spontaneous order to the international monetary system, ultimately, the system had proved to be too much of a constraint.[5]

Keynes and White acknowledged that the gold standard had proved excessively rigid, as had been painfully evident in the interwar period, when nations had been required to impose domestic recessions to maintain the international standard. International macroeconomic policy was led more by central banks than national governments, but it had failed to provide a stable institutional framework. With the benefit of hindsight, this was a failure in the conception of central-bank independence—that is, central banks not operating under transparently delegated parliamentary authority with clear objectives set in national statute. Beyond this observation on the appropriate setting for central-bank independence, tackling international macroeconomic policy making required an institution that embodied the authority of national governments alongside the remit of central banks.[6]

A further important change was to require a clearer, but by no means absolute, separation of public and private interests in financing external government deficits. The interwar system had depended largely on private, mainly New York banks, providing lending facilities to debtor governments. These same banks stood accused of benefiting from currency speculation alongside debtor-government financing. Bretton Woods therefore sought to separate a public-good function from a private good. It was therefore viewed by the New York banks as challenging their interests, specifically by allowing capital controls between nations and by promoting the IMF as substitute lender to indebted nations. In doing so, it was considered a radical departure from sound banking principles, in giving debtors a voice in determining the policies of creditors.[7]

While these features represented the broad prospective financial architecture, the evolution of the respective plans and the progress of the war led to heightened debate on the postwar monetary and international order, which was inseparable from the growing awareness of changes in global politics and leadership.

THE 1943 DEBATE: THE WHITE AND KEYNES PLANS

Amid increasing wartime cooperation between Britain and the United States, plans for the postwar financial world were advanced in the respective countries with the White and Keynes Plans.[8] In 1943, Parliament debated the Keynes Plan, in the following year it debated a White Paper summarizing the "combined" White and Keynes Plans (which formed the basis of the Bretton Woods Conference), and in 1945 debated and accepted the agreements. Across these years, the circumstances were very different.[9] The debates in 1943 and 1944, in considering postwar plans, took place while the war was continuing. They were therefore aspirational and somewhat removed from the reality of the postwar world. In contrast, the 1945 debates were precisely focused on approving a bill to put in place the necessary technicalities for Britain to approve the Bretton Woods Agreements and join the new institutions.[10]

As previously stated, the question of national discretion in economic policy making was at the heart of the economic issues surrounding the debates. For Britain, this assumed the form of whether Bretton Woods could impose domestic deflation as the interwar gold standard had, and whether it would limit or end Britain's development of imperial trade preference and the sterling area (broadly but not exactly Commonwealth countries). The concern with national interests and economic and political freedom informed the legislative scrutiny and debate in Britain, and these concerns were framed within the context of the financial crisis enveloping the country at the end of the war, but which had been apparent much earlier. The postwar world was going to be a very difficult place for Britain, and politicians of all parties were aware of it.

In May 1943, the respective plans of Keynes and White for postwar international monetary reform were debated in Parliament. The schemes were presented "as a basis for discussion, criticism and constructive amendment."[11] At this stage, debate primarily concerned seeking approval for new monetary institutions and mechanisms facilitating international trade and full employment. In his 1930 *Treatise on Money*, Keynes had projected the idea of an international currency issued by a supernational bank, which would supplant gold as the ultimate reserve asset. Keynes refurbished this idea in the 1940s, naming the currency "bancor" with the aim not just of supplanting gold but of preventing the global hegemony of the dollar.[12]

Keynes defined his plan's broad purpose as to "provide that money earned by selling goods to one country can be spent on purchasing the products of any other country."[13] Awareness that Britain would be highly indebted after the war led to praise for Keynes's requirement that creditor countries should restore trade imbalances by accepting payment in goods and not merely in specie. The US plan was notably silent on creditor nations, and a few speakers argued that global trade could not recover by placing the onus on debtors.[14] The White Plan, as it developed and became the blueprint for Bretton Woods, made the dollar, backed by gold, the dominant postwar currency, which White viewed as essential for the success of the proposed institutions.[15] Another view of US motives, often associated with Treasury secretary Henry Morgenthau, involved the United States intentionally acting as benevolent guide, in the sense that what would be good for the United States would be good for the rest of the world—an attitude redolent of nineteenth-century British free-trade imperialism. A further element in the US approach to negotiations was the "Congress won't agree" position when resisting unpalatable proposals. Keynes himself perhaps underestimated the legitimacy of congressional and popular resistance to his plan, often described as a "credit scheme," the bill for which Congress was unlikely to accept.[16]

The configuration of national interests explains why the Keynes Plan involved the IMF being able to impose symmetric adjustment responsibilities for deficit and surplus nations, whereas in White's Plan (the eventual outcome), the adjustment fell on debtor nations. The US objection to the Keynes Plan was that it involved too much discipline falling on the United States as the creditor nation, as well as exposing the United States to almost unlimited extensions of credit to other countries; on this issue the United States strongly played the congressional-objection card. Thus, the White Plan envisaged a smaller IMF in terms of balance-sheet capacity, with more constraints on nations using it, and preserving gold standard–type discipline but adding the modern concept of required economic adjustment or conditionality for IMF lending.[17]

Both plans had grown out of the same intellectual climate and possessed an identical purpose—to establish new global monetary institutions aimed at exchange-rate stability.[18] White's fund would bring about a world congenial to American economic interests, where US exports would be protected by the commitment of other countries not to raise tariffs or engage in competitive devaluation—stipulations underpinned by fund penalties. Keynes insisted on a system that left more discretion to national policy-making, but his clearing bank incorporated corrective action on balance of payments by debtors and creditors. British concern with creditor obligations led to suggestions that the United States should reduce their credit balances, in the interest of pursuing a genuinely multilateral system, and the United States appeared to comply, with a scarce currency clause allowing debtor countries to limit imports from persistent creditor countries. Under White's plan, a creditor country's currency could become scarce owing to fixed exchange rates and by demand exceeding supply. However, it was not long before White reneged by implying the burden of adjustment lay with debtors.

At this early stage, British aims were defensive: to seek the survival of as much of the prewar imperial preference system as possible, to create a postwar system with some measure of protection from a sudden outflow of cash, and to prevent exporters being outcompeted by overseas rivals. Britain was opposed to the presumed effect of the White Plan that the IMF could prevent a country devaluing its exchange rate. These defensive aims were reflected in the parliamentary debate on the plans, with support being cautious and lukewarm and opposition or concern being forthright and stridently expressed. Government support for Keynes was signaled by the Chancellor, Kingsley Wood, who contrasted the Clearing Union proposal and the attempt at international financial organization with the economic instability and political extremism of the interwar period.[19] Further government support came from Ralph Assheton, Financial Secretary to the Treasury, who sought to allay fears of the magnitude of the proposed changes by stating: "The essence of the plan is that no change should be made in the exchange rate between countries except under well-defined conditions . . . the marriage with gold, so far as the British plan is concerned, is more in the nature of a companionate marriage than an indissoluble union."[20]

Further support came from Conservatives such as Henry Brooke, who welcomed further discussion on monetary planning without committing to specific measures. While these sentiments were the main tenor of the debate, unanimity was unlikely, and anticipating his opposition to the final Bretton Woods Agreement, the Conservative MP Robert Boothby considered the White Plan a return to the gold standard, accompanied by a cycle of falling prices, profits, and purchasing power, with competitive tariffs, subsidies, and devaluation.[21] At this stage, Boothby was positive toward the expansionist effects of the Keynes Plan but warned that there must be no compromise on full convertibility or interference with the right to impose exchange restrictions. Boothby was uncompromising: "If we do this again, it will be the end. The end of all our hopes of an expansionist policy, and of social advance. It will be the end of the Beveridge plan, of improved education, of housing reconstruction, the end of the new Britain that we are fighting to rebuild. It will lead once again to world depression, to chaos, and, ultimately, to war."[22]

Comparing the merits of the two plans, Sir A. Lambert-Ward (Conservative) saw fundamental differences, most pertinently, the role of gold in the US plan. The accumulation and hoarding of gold indicated that the United States "do not appear to have realized the responsibility which attaches to a creditor nation." Frederick Pethick-Lawrence (Labour) saw more rigidity in the American plan, which was "in fact a full return to the gold standard" and appeared to ignore the lesson that "shackles of gold" had damaged international trade in the interwar period, but he thought the British scheme was more expansionist compared to the deflationary aspects of the American plan.[23] Despite concerns and criticisms, plans continued apace for further discussion on the shape of the postwar monetary world.

NEGOTIATIONS ON THE KEYNES AND WHITE PLANS

Negotiations for a joint statement between the United States and the United Kingdom took place in Washington between September 15 and October 9, 1943. Though the British government had supported the proposals made by Keynes, by late 1943 the government had abandoned hope of the Clearing Union being accepted by the United States, but now "sought to secure changes in the White plan that they believed were essential for Britain's welfare and for acceptance by the British Parliament."[24]

For the duration of the war, Churchill had little to say about monetary and economic issues but trusted the judgment and expertise of the legion of economic advisers now attached to the government. Keynes was brought into the Treasury as a special adviser in 1940, and many academic economists, especially in the Economic Section, were closely associated with Keynes in Anglo-American and international negotiations and in postwar planning.[25] Lionel Robbins recounted how the Americans appreciated the size of the British delegation as an indication of how seriously Britain was taking the talks. Robbins recorded how domestic political considerations had influenced discussions, for the experience of 1925 and the overvaluation wrought by the gold standard "had so burnt itself into the memory of the public that it was safe to say that no British government could commit itself to a settlement which ever appeared to involve inflexibility. The Americans seemed to be impressed by this."[26]

With sufficient modifications between the schemes, Robbins remained convinced a settlement could be reached, and British optimism was buttressed by recognition of a clear shift in US policy from bilateralism to multilateralism by 1943. Both Britain and the United States had reached the same conclusion, that the world needed a multilateral trading system, tariff reductions, and multilateral inclusion and input into the design and operation of the system's rules and guidelines facilitated by an international financial organization.[27]

THE 1944 DEBATE: THE PLAN FOR BRETTON WOODS

Before the Bretton Woods proceedings, Lionel Robbins recorded how *The New York Times* launched "an almost continuous barrage of hostile and, for the most part, ignorant criticism" of the prospective arrangements.[28] Much of the disagreement at Bretton Woods between the two countries was framed by the United States' desire to reform the prewar international system while assuring US control, which effectively limited the discretion of other nations. While accepting the need for change, Britain's immediate desire was to secure a path of adjustment that did not destabilize the British economy and that preserved some national discretion for exchange rate adjustment. We can aptly characterize US objectives as seeking to impose macroeconomic adjustment obligations onto debtor and not creditor nations while limiting the scope for national discretion on exchange rate revaluation by empowering the IMF, in which there was a built-in US veto.[29] British objectives were constrained by the immediate need to deal with its difficult postwar legacy, while favoring an international system with more symmetric adjustment by debtors and creditors, consistent with Britain's new position as a net debtor.

Above all, Britain sought a reduction of the wartime national debt to the United States and the means to set its own terms in resolving the problem of sterling balances. Those objectives required tariffs and capital controls, ostensibly to enable the British economy to adjust, with the intention that balances should be used only to buy British goods.[30] Britain had purchased goods to support the war effort from countries within the sterling area paying for goods in sterling. Consequent of exchange controls in the sterling area, balances were not convertible into other currencies, thus creating significant short-term indebtedness for Britain, which persisted after the war. While mobilizing the economic resources of the Commonwealth countries to support the war effort, it left liabilities far exceeding British gold and foreign exchange reserves and led to the continuation of capital controls, notwithstanding the objective of Bretton Woods to end controls and establish currency convertibility.

Rejecting the idea of alternative financing, in the form of a loan from private New York bankers, Keynes continued dealing with Morgenthau and White, in the hope of blending the Keynes and White Plans.[31] The result was the "Joint Statement by Experts on the Establishment of an International Monetary Fund."[32] The "Joint Statement" was only an agreement of principles by technical experts and not approved by national governments. The British government was in no way committed to the IMF, and Parliament only considered the statement as "a suitable foundation for further international consultation with a view to improved monetary co-operation after the war."[33] The plans provided for establishing and maintaining exchange rate stability based on free convertibility, while proposing an orderly process for exchange rate adjustment. Moreover, the external value of the domestic currency would conform to the internal value, not the reverse, leaving countries in full control of domestic monetary policy.

At a War Cabinet meeting on December 17, 1943, Herbert Morrison, along with other Labour ministers, did not allow fond imperial sentiment to cloud his judgment in stating: "On sentimental grounds we should all of us favour Empire Trade. But this country could not live solely on it, nor could the Dominions live on trade merely with the United Kingdom and the other Dominions."[34]

Divided counsels became more apparent on February 23, 1944, with Hugh Dalton recording Lord Beaverbrook's opinion that "We are giving up our economic Empire."[35] The winter of 1943–1944 had seen a combined effort between Bank of England officials and Beaverbrook to thwart moves toward a liberal, international order. Keynes castigated what he saw as old arrangements and old-fashioned ideas, and he informed Beaverbrook, "it is only under the aegis of an international scheme that we can hope to preserve the sterling area" though it remained unclear whether a genuinely multilateral system could coexist alongside imperial preference.[36]

In the House of Commons debate of May 1944, left and right attacked the notion of nonreciprocal trade, that is, where preferences, typically lower tariffs on imports from developing countries, were given to particular countries.

The chancellor of the exchequer, Sir John Anderson, denied there was anything in the monetary plan prohibiting reciprocal commercial agreements. A key issue was whether countries in balance-of-payments disequilibrium could restore their position through the system's mechanism. Keynes argued the plan placed an appropriate share of responsibility for adjustment on creditor countries, and not overreliance on debtors as the gold standard had.[37] The survival of imperial preference and the sterling area were concerns for many MPs, but Anderson preempted Keynes in stating there was "nothing in the proposed scheme to preclude continuance of sterling area arrangements."[38] Moreover, free convertibility of sterling within an international system was deemed necessary for Britain to maintain imperial preference, otherwise, Commonwealth countries would realize they were better off in another arrangement. Yet many peers and MPs voiced concern over the uncertainty of the future arrangements and the survival of Britain's monetary infrastructure.[39]

In debating the proposed new monetary institutions, specifically the IMF, allusions to past mistakes of central banks in the interwar period surfaced. However, Keynes stressed the primacy of national sovereignty and political authority in describing the IMF as "an organisation between Governments, in which Central Banks only appear as the instrument and agent of their Government."[40]

For many members, protecting Britain's "vital interests" was a paramount consideration, and the sense of dictation was a concern and a blow to national prestige and pride. Trying to assuage these fears, Viscount Simon, the lord chancellor, despite acknowledging that achieving approximately equal voting strength to the United States was important, argued that the new body was "a forum for consultation," which could not "impose its will on every country."[41]

The debates drew on the contrast between the flawed interwar gold standard, whereby the United States had stockpiled gold, the result of her trading surplus, and the classical nineteenth-century gold standard, whereby Britain recycled her trade surplus into productive overseas investment rather than gold stockpiling. In the Commons, Pethick-Lawrence, leader of the opposition to the coalition government, thought the scheme went some way toward returning to a "gold basis" though not the historical gold standard. The Liberal MP Graham White supported the proposal and held that the United States realized that the days of isolationism were over and that they would cooperate for the sake of global prosperity. However, pessimism over

US intentions and objectives were not hard to find, with the socialist Emanuel Shinwell arguing there was not the "remotest prospect" of the United States reducing tariffs to allow British goods to enter the market. In another vein, the Liberal MP George Schuster doubted tariff reductions would lead to a great increase in imports because the economic position of the two countries was not complementary. Richard Stokes, an independent-minded Labour MP, argued that the scheme was "a cunning way of re-introducing into the European monetary system the hoards of gold at present locked in America." Predictably, Boothby, a persistent critic of international monetary organization, argued there was no assurance that the United States intended to pursue a policy of deliberate expansion in the postwar world.[42]

In the House of Lords, Keynes made a robust case that there must be no return to the 1930s, when the huge trade surplus of the United States led to stockpiling gold as the countervailing asset on its capital account.[43] He found substantial support across the political spectrum. Referring to Keynes's long-standing opposition to the gold standard, the Conservative Lord Melchett argued Keynes "has spent a lifetime fighting the restrictive effects of the gold standard, and it is quite amazing to hear people coming forward at this stage to accuse him of trying to tie us to the gold standard system." Another Conservative, Lord Balfour of Burleigh, stated that Keynes had proved the new arrangements did not anchor Britain's economy "to other people's conditions through the medium of gold" but provided for domestic adjustment, thus retaining economic sovereignty. Viscount Simon (Liberal), reflecting the government position, viewed gold as a convenient "measuring stick" for the "comparative relations of currencies" and "nothing to do with going back to the gold standard or anything of that kind."[44]

The parliamentary exchanges of 1944 reveal that few were ready to accept the full implications of Britain's decline. To cushion the effects of change it was anticipated that the proposed transition period would be lengthy, with some continuation of the Lend-Lease agreement to avoid dislocation, something some speakers mistakenly assumed the United States would feel obliged to do as recompense for Britain's wartime sacrifices.[45] Keynes's supranational reserve currency idea had been jettisoned, and the dollar assumed the role of anchor currency tied to gold. While currencies would set their value against the dollar and gold, Keynes stipulated this relationship merely expressed the relative value of currencies, not a return to a gold standard.[46] As we have seen, most speakers, while acknowledging superficial similarities, recognized the substantive differences.[47]

Overall, the tone of the 1944 debates was one of slight pessimism and considerable uncertainty, though with a few exceptions criticism was primarily focused on the absence of specificity.[48] Party divisions were largely though not completely blurred in debate by wartime bipartisanship, for normal party politics was suspended for the duration of the coalition government between 1940 and 1945. Nevertheless, there were grounds for criticism and anxiety, primarily over IMF powers, the survival of the sterling area and imperial preference, and fears of a return to a gold standard. Yet hope remained that the new international system would be underpinned by symmetrical adjustment between creditors and debtors, and that domestic policy would not be constrained by the IMF.

THE 1945 PARLIAMENTARY DEBATES: THE BRETTON WOODS AGREEMENTS

Several points are relevant to understanding the 1945 debates. Firstly, they were not solely, or even mainly, focused on Bretton Woods. They also covered the end of Lend-Lease and conditions for a US loan designed to sustain a faster transition to the new international system than envisaged in 1944. Accepting the loan and faster transition was a condition placed on Britain by the new Truman administration. Secondly, the 1945 debates did not concern the design of Bretton Woods and whether it could be amended, and there was dissent at the circumscription of the role of Parliament. Thirdly, the debates also involved a request from the government to approve a negotiating position in a future international trade conference as part of the postwar shift toward international cooperation. The 1944 debates had been somewhat nebulous, for it was unclear what the specific proposals would be, when the war would end, and which countries would participate in the postwar financial institutions. The more informed sessions of 1945 were based on the greater clarity and substance of the Bretton Woods Agreements, which had superseded the aspirations of the 1944 "Joint Statement."[49]

Britain and the United States held fundamentally differing conceptions of the scope and nature of the IMF—reflecting their relative positions as debtor and creditor nations. Commensurate with debtor-nation status, Britain stressed national discretion, especially in adjusting exchange rates and a longer transition period, and while seeking a larger fund, was unhappy with the proposed national quota formula. As dominant creditor nation, the United States held an almost diametrically opposed position, emphasizing exchange rate stability, promoting the powers of a smaller fund with a short transition period, and with no change in the proposed quotas for borrowing capacity and voting power.[50]

In the event, the IMF agreement on July 22, 1944, formalized the shift toward the dollar becoming the dominant currency with a link to gold. White argued that the fund's special purpose was to prevent competitive devaluation of currencies, but the 10 percent devaluation permitted by the so-called "exchange clause" was accepted. Sterling was to be freely convertible after five years, when, as a founding member of the IMF and the International Bank for Reconstruction and Development, Britain would fully abide by IMF rules.[51]

After Bretton Woods, moves were made toward formal ratification of the agreements. In the policy document "Overseas Financial Policy in Stage III" of March 1945, and circulated to the cabinet on May 15, Keynes had warned of the high external debt, weakened export industries, and bloated overseas expenditure that Britain was now burdened with. Keynes starkly outlined Britain's choices and famously considered the views of economic nationalists and imperialists, and their advocacy of autarky and bilateral trade agreements, and opposition to an American loan, as leading to extreme austerity and "Starvation Corner" for Britain. The bleak economic position was exemplified at the end of the war, with Britain having lost one-quarter of her wealth, with sterling debts of $14 billion, and her volume of exports reduced by 54 percent between 1938 and 1945.[52]

In August 1945, the United States terminated Lend-Lease. With its end, underlying tensions in Anglo-American relations surfaced, with both sides contending with domestic interests resistant to any agreement. There had been a change of government in Britain, with the Labour Party coming to power in July. In the United States, the new Truman administration appeared hostile to favorable deals, not least because of suspicions surrounding the financial prudence of a socialist government.[53] After the 1945 election victory, the composition of the Labour Party and the extent of its parliamentary majority became a crucial element in ratifying Bretton Woods. In the 1930s, Labour's economic policy had been based on a planned domestic economy alongside a foreign policy component termed "international planning." By 1945 this rather vague concept was rejected, replaced by a "theological maze" surrounding how to align subscription to a liberal international economic order with a domestic economy based on socialist planning.[54] It appeared contradictory to aim at controlling most aspects of one's own national economy while trying to abolish "economic nationalism" throughout the world.

During the war, international economic issues had been discussed to an unprecedented degree. Labour ministers had been privy to cabinet discussions on international affairs and had access to expert advice. Labour economists and politicians, including Hugh Gaitskell, Douglas Jay, and Evan Durbin, laid particular emphasis on extensive planning in the postwar world, and by 1943, many of them held government posts.[55] Labour was not primarily Atlanticist, and its somewhat paradoxical behavior after taking office in 1945 can be explained by the exceptionally tough conditions the government faced and the fundamental contradiction of the "planning paradox" in reconciling its socialist aspirations toward domestic planning with international capitalist institutions.[56] Labour's commitment to empire trading connections was also a difficult issue, and Labour's continued and undoubtedly genuine internationalist aspirations were called into question, not least by American opinion and by the party's defense of Britain's preferential trade privileges.

Britain's dire financial position had forced her to seek financial assistance, but negotiations in Washington in 1945 went badly, and Keynes, meeting American resistance to his calls for a grant reimbursement in recognition of wartime sacrifices, had to retreat. After proposals and counterproposals between the respective governments, including an American loan conditional on Britain dismantling imperial preference, making sterling freely convertible, and cooperating with the United States in establishing global free trade, Britain accepted a $3.75 billion loan at 2 percent interest, which represented a humiliation for Keynes, who also conceded free convertibility of sterling for current transactions one year after enactment of loan terms. The United States argued that the loan changed Britain's position and that the transition period, the five-year buffer for convertibility secured at Bretton Woods, should be adjusted accordingly.[57]

There were further shocks. Attlee's statement to Parliament on December 6 was accompanied by details of the financial agreement and joint statements on the preliminary Anglo-American trade agreement and the Lend-Lease settlement. The United States had warned that financial aid was conditional on Britain accepting Bretton Woods, and with ratification one of the few negotiating weapons Britain possessed, the new chancellor, Dalton, tied the parliamentary passage of Bretton Woods to the "even more strongly disliked, but scarcely escapable" loan proposal.[58] The loan was the keystone of the arch in Anglo-American relations for without it Parliament was unlikely to accept Bretton Woods. Equally, the British government was clearly not going to terminate the imperial preferential arrangements without recompense.[59]

The cabinet was sufficiently nervous of negative reaction as to allow very little parliamentary debate, and though the terms were not debatable by Parliament, the deadline for ratification—making Britain a founding member of the IMF and the World Bank—and for accepting the American loan was December 31, 1945. The 1945 debates were far less consensual than in 1944. The early end of the war had produced a set of unusually unfavorable circumstances for Britain. Debate focused on three main areas: firstly, the loan terms; secondly, the IMF's remit, terms of reference, and operational capability; and thirdly, the ramifications of new commercial arrangements. Additionally, there was disquiet over process, with members complaining Britain was being forced to hastily accept unfavorable terms under duress without proper parliamentary debate and scrutiny.[60]

Despite promoting the loan's positive features, Keynes was ashamed of the interest charges, and his speech has been characterized as partly "an apology," for he was angered by the unfavorable final terms, which, reflecting the dominance of the White Plan, veered heavily toward US interests.[61] Wartime sacrifices were not seen by the Americans as justification for special treatment, and Keynes's argument that US negotiators stressed "future mutual advantage rather than past history" provoked fury among many MPs. Sir John Anderson called for a "clean slate," and the Labour MP Rhys Davies thought the terms very hard. Lord Woolton stated that he could accept Bretton Woods but not the loan. For the government, the loan was presented as a means of minimizing austerity, a stance aimed at inducing loyalty among Labour MPs and peers, and one that was broadly accepted.[62]

Voicing the deep disquiet that characterized the debate, the Conservative MP Oliver Stanley likened it to a "vanquished people discussing the economic penalties of defeat."[63] For the government, Sir Stafford Cripps described the agreements as "inter-dependent" and "not quite independent" of the loan. Many MPs were disturbed by this connection, and even leading ministers possessed little enthusiasm for the loan. Dalton described it as "a strange and ironical reward" for Britain's wartime efforts, and conceded that the agreements fell short of what Britain had hoped for. For Boothby, onerous loan terms were of a nature "never hitherto imposed on a nation that has not been defeated in war." For the independent MP Denis Kendall, the loan was a "very bad bargain" that would cost Britain her "economic liberty and the development of our Empire."[64] Others argued that Britain should have sought a loan from the empire, or insisted that the United States provide a loan with fewer punitive conditions, but Cripps stated that other options had been carefully considered.[65]

Those supportive of the loan pointed to the proviso that Britain could cancel interest payments if exports in any year did not cover the prewar level of imports adjusted for inflation and if official reserves were inadequate to make payments. However, both opponents and abstainers questioned the value of this waiver clause because, on the assumption that trade levels would always be above prewar rates, they argued the bar was set in the wrong place for it to be meaningful.[66]

The Bretton Woods Agreements provided greater scope for debating the shape of the postwar world. For its supporters, an optimistic view prevailed that the IMF provided a balance between national discretion in policy-making, and reasonable domestic freedom to adjust exchange rates, while securing financial advantages of international cooperation. Despite a linkage to gold, the system was not a return to the gold standard. By establishing multilateral trade based on exchange rate stability it was hoped that competitive devaluation would be prevented. However, opponents held, as it turned out correctly, that the 10 percent permitted devaluation would be insufficient.

The scarce currency clause provided that if the IMF had low stocks of a currency, it could be deemed a "scarce currency" and members would be entitled and expected to discriminate against that country's goods by their commercial practices. Those supporting the clause claimed it allowed other countries to apply sanctions, like import restrictions, if the United States pursued a mercantilist-type policy. Opponents argued that the clause could not be invoked so long as the fund could borrow dollars from the United States, thus enabling that country to avoid changing its pattern of trade.[67] They had little confidence that concessions made over scarce currency were not easily evaded, and the one-year conversion was considered too short an interval for a change of this magnitude, though voting power in the IMF, with Commonwealth votes at 25 percent, including 13 percent for Britain, almost matching the 27 percent for the United States, provided some reassurance.[68] It was widely expected that after the war the dollar would become a scarce currency, but owing to the Marshall Plan and other aid programs, this did not in fact occur.

The loan and Bretton Woods arrangements were conflated most often in relation to imperial preference and the sterling area. The proposal to make sterling convertible for current payments and to terminate the wartime form of the sterling area was vigorously debated.[69] Point 4 of the 1941 Atlantic Charter had stated the desire of the United States and the United Kingdom for open trading conditions, and Article VII of the 1941 Mutual Aid Agreement, anticipating pressure from the United States for ending imperial preference, projected elimination of all forms of trade discrimination. This connection was known as "the Consideration" for American help with Lend-Lease.

It was acknowledged as early as 1941 that, despite the insertion of the words "with due respect to their existing obligations" at the behest of the War Cabinet, such a course might conflict with the 1932 Ottawa Agreements. Visiting Washington in May–July 1941, Keynes, as principal adviser to the chancellor, had acknowledged this could be a difficulty for Britain.[70] The Ottawa Agreements had significantly strengthened and extended preferential tariffs throughout the British Empire, with fifteen bilateral preferential agreements made representing an extension of imperial preference at the expense of non-empire countries, but divisions now arose over defending or even extending and strengthening imperial trade.

In 1943, the future Conservative politician Enoch Powell viewed the United States, not Japan or Germany, as the real enemy of the British Empire.[71] Roosevelt, for his part, deprecated past "artificial barriers created through senseless economic rivalries," and after the loan agreement, expectations ran high that the end of imperial preference was in sight.[72] Arguably, Churchill had not understood how costly American support would prove to be, for Lend-Lease was used by White and Morgenthau to secure the "grand principle" of nondiscriminatory, multilateral trade. Many MPs made the connection, broadly believing "loss of preferences was the price of the loan."[73] For the United States, arguments for equal access to Britain's export markets acquired more urgency from the accumulating sterling balances, which blocked the conversion of pounds into dollars. Those balances had grown during the war. In 1940, Britain was dangerously short of dollars, and currency transactions by British residents were subject to exchange controls, with imports only permitted under license. Inhabitants of sterling area countries could use sterling accumulated from exports within the area, but as British exports declined, so the sterling balances, that is, British debts, increased. By agreement, the dollars secured for exports were collated in London and drawn on only to pay for essential American exports. Regarding non-sterling countries, Britain negotiated agreements with neutrals in Europe and Latin America to pay for exports in "area pounds sterling," which could be used only for goods and services purchased within the sterling area. The overall effect was to keep the demand for American exports artificially low by blocking conversion of sterling into dollars and by controlling Dominion spending of directly earned dollars.[74]

The evolution of the sterling area led to divergent interpretations of its utility and value. Keynes warned that the sterling area would be destroyed if Britain rejected currency convertibility, but opponents argued otherwise, and Boothby went further in arguing that London's position as a financial center would be threatened by currency convertibility.[75] By 1945, Attlee's government, while indicating imperial preference was negotiable, nevertheless assured MPs that contracting preferences was contingent on compensation of US tariff reductions. Despite mutual professions of support for freer trade, the Americans suspected the British of wanting to maintain preferential tariffs, while the British were convinced the Americans wished to maintain high tariffs.[76] Both Sir John Anderson and Churchill maintained that wartime agreements did not compromise imperial preference, with Britain no more bound to remove preferences than the United States was to reduce tariffs. However, while viewing the IMF as no threat to the sterling area, Anderson was concerned at the unprecedented use of the word "elimination" entering the international vocabulary. The new foreign secretary, Ernest Bevin, dismissed such sentiments, stating that the price of American aid was the elimination of the discriminatory preferences of Article VII, "and we knew it."[77]

More positively, the government argued that without a multilateral agreement there could be a return to economic blocs, unstable currencies, and trade discrimination. Viscount Samuel (Liberal) praised the United States for seeking to facilitate free trade, while Keynes added that the US commitment to full employment indicated renunciation of high tariffs. Some members, such as the Labour MP Richard Stokes, doubted the legitimacy of the American conversion to free-trade internationalism, for while the pressure to export to promote domestic employment might be greater, it would not be uncontested, for Congress and public opinion also influenced policy-making, and following postwar demobilization, protectionism would just as likely reemerge as a solution to unemployment.[78]

Those who favored acceptance and abstention had different reasons for not rejecting the agreement. In the main, the former made a virtue of a necessity by placing, despite misgivings, the best possible construction on the deal. The acquiescence of the latter was underscored by general dissatisfaction with the terms. With a large Labour majority in the Commons, the bill passed by 345 to 98, but 24 Labour MPs, including future leaders James Callaghan and Michael Foot, voted against it, and some Labour speakers saw

Bretton Woods as sealing American economic hegemony and a surrender of economic sovereignty.[79] There was also some politicking by ministers. As leader of the Commons, Herbert Morrison informed the Parliamentary Labour Party the government would not discipline any member opposing ratification and the loan. Dalton even told Callaghan that he didn't mind if some MPs voted against it, as it would show the United States that the Labour government was not a pushover and had its own domestic problems and dissensions to deal with.[80]

Despite a two-line whip instructing Conservative MPs to abstain, forty-seven MPs voted against Bretton Woods. The Conservative opposition included mavericks like Max Aitken but also "coming men" including Oliver Stanley and two future chancellors, John Selwyn-Lloyd and Peter Thorneycroft. Boothby, a veteran empire free-trader, typically viewed the agreement as compromising the sterling zone and imperial preference, central pillars of economic sovereignty, while caustically reminding abstaining Conservatives of the party's imperial identity. Treading the line between accepting the need to approve new arrangements while deprecating the terms was difficult, but Churchill tried his best. Weakly stating that Conservative votes "could not affect the position," he maintained that abstention reflected refusal to accept responsibility for the proposals.[81]

Ultimately, possessing a large parliamentary majority, it was the Labour Party opinion that mattered. During the wartime political truce, there had been little in the way of partisan politics. MPs like Aneurln Bevan and Emanuel Shinwell had been critical of the wartime coalition but only once forced a division—on the Beveridge Report in February 1943, a vote closely associating Labour with social welfare reform.[82] In relation to Bretton Woods, there were multifaceted factors involved for Labour MPs, of ideology, party discipline and loyalty, national interest, and the blunt determination to reject any policy that might lead to a return to the economics of the 1930s. Indeed, the 1945 Labour Party Manifesto had described the interwar years in dramatic terms: "Great economic blizzards swept the world in those years. The great inter-war slumps were not acts of God or of blind forces. They were the sure and certain result of the concentration of too much economic power in the hands of too few men."[83]

While there was a tension in the Labour Party between Keynesian demand management and socialist planning, the 1945 manifesto broke with the coalition consensus, with an explicit commitment to strict economic controls, planning, and a socialized sector of the economy. These concerns seem at odds with accepting international institutions aimed at regulating international commerce and capital. The IMF and World Bank were hardly socialist organizations, yet Labour ministers, except (until 1945) Bevin, were strong supporters. Bevin's eventual conversion was important, for his authority and popularity in the Labour movement, especially in the trade unions, was considerable.[84] That Dalton, Gaitskell, and others fell in with what has been termed an Atlanticist approach to the postwar world should occasion little surprise, for it was no longer theoretical speculation but practical realities and difficulties of the postwar domestic economy that intruded.

Labour's course was a product of contradictions in previous thinking and the need to comply with Britain's powerful wartime ally. As Keynes predicted, most sceptics acquiesced when faced with the alternative of "trying to survive the post-war transition without United States aid."[85] Attlee and Dalton were ultimately pragmatists in recognizing that Britain badly needed the loan and that Anglo-American cooperation was essential to postwar reconstruction— an acknowledgment of the harsh realities of the postwar world. The extent to which Britain should accept restrictions on her freedom in return for claiming a more satisfactory international environment continued to be a dilemma for the Attlee government in the postwar period.[86]

It was never likely, despite the Conservative majority, that the House of Lords would reject the agreement, though it was less of a foregone conclusion than the Commons vote. While deprecating the government's handling of negotiations, Viscount Cranborne stated, "it is not our job to make their task impossible." That advice was heeded, for of ninety-eight votes cast, only eight votes were against the agreement, though there were many abstentions. Two-thirds of those who spoke against the agreement abstained, and of all who spoke, most were against the arrangement, yet the predominantly silent majority prevailed.[87] For those abstaining, the lack of a viable alternative explains their actions, but behind the decision not to reject the bill lay fears of a constitutional struggle with the Commons. Abstention attracted criticism, as it was (correctly) suspected that it would allow the Conservatives to make political capital from later austerity and privations.[88]

CONCLUSION

The changing tone of the parliamentary debates reflected the changing relationship of the United States and Britain based on their respective political and financial fortunes between 1943 and 1945. The debates reveal that by using the loan as a condition and a forcing-device to secure agreement to Bretton Woods, there remained several unresolved substantive points on the design of the postwar system. Arguably most important was the consequence of introducing the asymmetric adjustment obligation on debtor countries, which was raised but not resolved. As a feature of the White Plan, it was carried into the final agreement, and alone contradicted the argument advanced by proponents of Bretton Woods, more so in 1944 than 1945, that the new system protected national sovereignty, and that unlike the interwar gold standard, domestic economies would not be compelled to respond to international developments. In the event of structural disequilibrium, national solutions were expected, such as changes in currency values or improvement in a country's competitiveness, but discretion in national policy would be limited to what other governments believed necessary to maintain fixed exchange rates.[89]

Secondly, flaws in the scarce currency clause, projected as the bulwark against asymmetric adjustment, were raised but not adequately debated, though, as it turns out, the clause was never triggered. Thirdly, Britain was in no position to undertake a one-year transition to convertibility, a point made forcefully in the debates, and almost universally agreed, and fully demonstrated when the time arrived, with severe austerity, dollar scarcity, balance-of-payment difficulties, and ultimately devaluation.[90] Fourthly, the waiver clause on interest payments on the loan was rightly criticized for setting the bar in the wrong place, though ultimately it proved difficult to adjust the repayment burdens of countries to domestic economic performance.

The question posed at the beginning—as to whether political deliberation on Bretton Woods in the British legislature recognized the main issues relating to limits on national discretion in macroeconomic policy making against the operations of international financial institutions—can be answered affirmatively. There was broad awareness that past mistakes must not be repeated, and while most parliamentarians were prepared to make a leap in the dark, idealists, optimists, and visionaries were very much a minority. Hardheaded pragmatism and cynicism held sway, and few concurred with Keynes that Bretton Woods represented an attempt "to implement the wisdom of Adam Smith."[91] Among economists, however, there was great admiration for Keynes's contribution, for as Robbins recorded: "I think he may well feel that with all the faults of the agreement which has emerged, something has been accomplished in the way of constructive internationalism which, despite the vagaries of Parliaments and Congresses, will not easily be brushed on one side."[92]

Regardless of how the agreement was presented, the compelling nature of arguments for acceptance, of pressing financial necessity, and the need for international cooperation to promote stability and prosperity, reflected the divergent economic reality of the respective countries. Opposition to Bretton Woods and the loan was grounded on the fear of American economic dominance, with little hope or expectation that the United States would treat Britain favorably in the postwar world. An air of general disgruntlement characterized much debate, with regrets for a world now lost accompanied by fears for the future. Keynes was despondent that many politicians refused to accept clear evidence that Britain's resources were not what they once were.

While the urgency of securing an agreement was fully apparent, Britain's subordinate position created difficulties. Members of all parties appreciated that the United States could not be blamed for seeking to protect her own interests, though there was divergence over the justice of that stance, but the perceived harsh treatment meted out by a wartime ally cut deeply. Even if loss of economic sovereignty and termination of imperial preference did not immediately materialize, the blow to national and imperial prestige remained great.

Notes

1. See White's "Preliminary Draft Outline of a Proposal for an International Stabilization Fund for the United and Associated Nations (Revised July 10, 1943)," in the "Historical Documents" section of this book.

2. Alec Cairncross, "Economists in Wartime," *Contemporary European History* 4 (1995): 19–36.

3. Benn Steil, *The Battle of Bretton Woods: John Maynard Keynes, Harry Dexter White, and the Making of a New World Order* (Princeton, NJ: Princeton University Press, 2013), 2.

4. Ed Conway, *The Summit: The Biggest Battle of the Second World War—Fought Behind Closed Doors* (London: Abacus, 2014), 121–50.

5. Giulio Gallarotti, *The Anatomy of an International Monetary Regime: The Classical Gold Standard, 1880–1914* (Oxford: Oxford University Press, 1995), 227–35.

6. Conway, *Summit*, 70–72, 179.

7. Marc Allen Eisner, *The American Political Economy: Institutional Evolution of Market and State* (New York: Routledge, 2014), 94.

8. See White's "Preliminary Draft Outline of a Proposal for an International Stabilization Fund for the United and Associated Nations (Revised July 10, 1943)" and Keynes's "Proposals for an International Clearing Union (April 1943)," in the "Historical Documents" section of this book.

9. House of Commons Debate (henceforth abbreviated, HC Deb), 12 May 1943 [Postwar International Currency], vol. 389, cols. 645–745; House of Lords Debate (henceforth abbreviated HL Deb), 18 May 1943 [International Clearing Union], vol. 127, cols. 521–64; HC Deb, 10 May 1944 [Monetary Policy], vol. 399, cols. 1923–2046; HC Deb, 12 May 1944 [International Monetary Fund: Joint Statement], vol. 399, cols. 2268–74; HC Deb, 16 May 1944 [International Monetary Fund: Joint Statement], vol. 400, col. 3131; HC Deb, 18 May 1944 [Questions: International Monetary Arrangements: Sterling Area], vol. 400, cols. 330–

32; HL Deb, 16 May 1944 [Postwar Economic Policy], vol. 131, cols. 771–86; HL Deb, 23 May 1944 [International Monetary Fund], vol. 131, cols. 834–83.

10. HC Deb, 6 December 1945 [Anglo-American Economic and Financial Agreement], vol. 416, cols. 2662–84; HC Deb, 12 December 1945 [Anglo-American Financial and Economic Discussions], vol. 417, cols. 421–558; HC Deb, 13 December 1945 [Anglo-American Financial and Economic Discussions], vol. 417, cols. 641–739; HC Deb, 13 December 1945 [Bretton Woods Agreements Bill], vol. 417, cols. 739–48; HC Deb, 14 December 1945 [Bretton Woods Agreements Bill], vol. 417, cols. 804–14; HL Deb, 17 December 1945 [Anglo-American Financial Arrangements], vol. 138, cols. 677–776; HL Deb, 18 December 1945 [Anglo-American Financial Arrangements], vol. 138, cols. 777–897.

11. HC Deb, 12 May 1943, vol. 389, cols. 654–55, 662. See Keynes's "Proposals for an International Clearing Union (April 1943)," in the "Historical Documents" section of this book.

12. Peter Clarke, *Keynes: The Rise, Fall, and Return of the 20th Century's Most Influential Economist* (New York: Bloomsbury, 2009), 88.

13. HL Deb, 18 May 1943, vol. 127, col. 528.

14. HC Deb, 12 May 1943, vol. 389, cols. 668, 691, 694, 703; Steil, *Battle of Bretton Woods*, 165.

15. See White's "Preliminary Draft Outline of a Proposal for an International Stabilization Fund for the United and Associated Nations (Revised July 10, 1943)," in the "Historical Documents" section of this book.

16. Conway, *Summit*, 211, 269–70; Steil, *Battle of Bretton Woods*, 97–98.

17. See Keynes's "Proposals for an International Clearing Union (April 1943)," and White's "Preliminary Draft Outline of a Proposal for an International Stabilization Fund for the United and Associated Nations (Revised July 10, 1943)," both in the "Historical Documents" section of this book.

18. Clarke, *Keynes*, 88–89; Harry Blustein, *The Ascent of Globalisation* (Oxford: Oxford University Press, 2015), 46–48.

19. HC Deb, 12 May 1943, vol. 389, cols. 649–50 [Kingsley Wood].

20. HC Deb, 12 May 1943, vol. 389, cols. 741–42 [Assheton].

21. HC Deb, 12 May 1943, vol. 389, cols. 715–16 [Brooke]; cols. 689, 701–2 [Boothby].

22. HC Deb, 12 May 1943, vol. 389, col. 702 [Boothby].

23. HC Deb, 12 May 1943, vol. 389, cols. 675–76 [Lambert-Ward]; col. 666 [Pethick-Lawrence].

24. Raymond F. Mikesell, *The Bretton Woods Debates: A Memoir* (Princeton, NJ: Princeton University Press, 1994), 25.

25. Cairncross, "Economists in Wartime," 24–29.

26. Lionel Robbins, Hot Springs Conference Diary, June 22, 1943, British Library of Political and Economic Science, available at https://digital.library.lse.ac.uk/objects/lse:yak575lex.

27. Ibid.; Richard Toye, "The Attlee Government, the Imperial Preference System and the Creation of the Gatt," *English Historical Review* 118 (2003): 912–39 (915–16).

28. Lionel Robbins, Bretton Woods Diary, June 30, 1944, British Library of Political and Economic Science, available at http://digital.library.lse.ac.uk/objects/lse:pat524yab.

29. Kathleen Burk and Alex Cairncross, *"Goodbye, Great Britain": The 1976 IMF Crisis* (New Haven, CT, and London: Yale University Press, 1992), 6.

30. Conway, *Summit*, 117–18.

31. Steil, *Battle of Bretton Woods*, 135, 143–47, 153–54, 170–72.

32. See "Joint Statement by Experts on the Establishment of an International Monetary Fund (April 1944)," in the "Historical Documents" section of this book.

33. HC Deb, 10 May 1944, vol. 399, col. 1923.

34. Richard Toye, "The Labour Party's External Economic Policy in the 1940s," *Historical Journal* 43 (2000): 189–215 (202).

35. Richard Toye, *The Labour Party and the Planned Economy, 1931–1951* (London: Boydell Press, 2003), 169.

36. John Fforde, *The Bank of England and Public Policy, 1941–1958* (Cambridge: Cambridge University Press, 1992), 58–61; Steil, *Battle of Bretton Woods*, 80–81.

37. HC Deb, 10 May 1944, vol. 399, col. 1982 [Shinwell]; col. 2019 [Boothby]; col. 2045 [Anderson]. See "Speech by Lord Keynes on the International Monetary Fund Debate. House of Lords, May 23, 1944," in the "Historical Documents" section of this book.

38. HC Deb, 18 May 1944, vol. 400, col. 331 [Anderson]. See "Speech by Lord Keynes on the International Monetary Fund Debate. House of Lords, May 23, 1944," in the "Historical Documents" section of this book.

39. HC Deb, 10 May 1944, vol. 399, col. 1939 [Elliot]; col. 1984 [Shinwell]; col. 1991 [Schuster]; col. 2010 [George Strauss]; col. 2041 [Anderson]; HL Deb, 23 May 1944, vol. 131, col. 854 [Lord Nathan]; col. 869 [Lord Balfour of Burleigh].

40. See "Speech by Lord Keynes on the International Monetary Fund Debate. House of Lords, May 23, 1944," in the "Historical Documents" section of this book.

41. HL Deb, 23 May 1944, vol. 131, col. 882 [Simon].

42. HC Deb, 10 May 1944, vol. 399, col. 2030 [Pethick-Lawrence]; col. 1971 [White]; col. 1990 [Schuster]; col. 1960 [Stokes]; col. 2025 [Boothby].

43. See "Speech by Lord Keynes on the International Monetary Fund Debate. House of Lords, May 23, 1944," in the "Historical Documents" section of this book.

44. HL Deb, 23 May 1944, vol. 131, col. 858 [Melchett]; col. 867 [Balfour of Burleigh], col. 880 [Simon].

45. HC Deb, 10 May 1944, vol. 399, col. 1997 [Benson]; HL Deb, 23 May 1944, vol. 131, col. 821 [Balfour of Burleigh].

46. See "Speech by Lord Keynes on the International Monetary Fund Debate. House of Lords, May 23, 1944," in the "Historical Documents" section of this book.

47. For some examples, see HC Deb, 10 May 1944, vol. 399, cols. 1960, 1964, 1969–70, 1997, 2002, 2030–31, 2040; HL Deb, 23 May 1944, vol. 131, cols. 845–46, 858, 861–62, 867–68, 876–78, 880.

48. HC Deb, 10 May 1944, vol. 399, col. 1986 [Shinwell]; HL Deb, 23 May 1944, vol. 131, cols. 849–57 [Lord Nathan]; G. John Ikenberry, "The Political Origins of Bretton Woods," in *A Retrospective on the Bretton Woods System: Lessons for International Monetary Reform*, ed. B. Eichengreen and Michael D. Bordo (Chicago: University of Chicago Press, 2007): 155–200 (188).

49. See "Final Act (22 July 1944)," in the "Historical Documents" section of this book.

50. Steil, *Battle of Bretton Woods*, 193, 229–33.

51. See "Articles of Agreement of the International Monetary Fund, July 22, 1944," and "Articles of Agreement of the International Bank for Reconstruction and Development, July 22, 1944," in the "Historical Documents" section of this book.

52. G. C. Peden, ed., *Keynes and His Critics: Treasury Responses to the Keynesian Revolution, 1925–1946* (Oxford: Oxford University Press, 2004), 265–66; Richard Wevill, *Britain and America after World War II: Bilateral Relations and the Beginnings of the Cold War* (London & New York: I. B. Tauris, 2012), 55; Sidney Pollard, *The Development of the British Economy, 1914–1980*, 3rd ed. (London: Edward Arnold, 1983), 217.

53. Conway, *Summit*, 308, 315–18.

54. Toye, "Labour Party's External Economic Policy," 204.

55. Stephen Brooke, "Revisionists and Fundamentalists: The Labour Party and Economic Policy During the Second World War," *Historical Journal* 32 (1989): 157–75 (162–63).

56. Toye, "Labour Party's External Economic Policy," 215.

57. Alec Cairncross, *Years of Recovery: British Economic Policy 1945–51* (London and New York: Routledge, 2013), 105; Steil, *Battle of Bretton Woods*, 265, 277–79.

58. HC Deb, 12 December 1945, vol. 417, cols. 430–31; Ikenberry, "Political Origins," 188. See "Final Act (22 July 1944)," in the "Historical Documents" section of this book.

59. Mikesell, *Bretton Woods Debates*, 46.

60. Conway, *Summit*, 330–31.

61. Mikesell, *Bretton Woods Debates*, 51; Blustein, *Ascent of Globalisation*, 47–50; Steil, *Battle of Bretton Woods*, 218, 251–53.

62. HC Deb, 12 December 1945, vol. 417, cols. 446 [Anderson]; col. 520 [Rhys Davies]; HC Deb, 13 December 1945, vol. 417, cols. 644–45 [Sir Thomas Moore]; cols. 685–86 [Patrick Gordon-Walker]; HL Deb, 17 December 1945, vol. 138, cols. 689–90 [Viscount Simon]; col. 702 [Viscount Samuel]; cols. 717–18 [Woolton]; col. 725 [Balfour of Burleigh]; col. 727 [Lord Strabolgi]; HL Deb, 18 December 1945, vol. 138, cols. 788–90, 846 [Keynes]; cols. 852–54 [Lord Russell]; cols. 892–96 [Viscount Addison].

63. HC Deb, 13 December 1945, vol. 417, col. 653.

64. HC Deb, 12 December 1945, vol. 417, cols. 424, 440 [Dalton]; col. 457 [Boothby]; cols. 487–88 [Cripps]; col. 515 [Kendall]; Steil, *Battle of Bretton Woods*, 283–87.

65. HC Deb, 12 December 1945, vol. 417, col. 464 [Boothby]; col. 502 [Cripps]; col. 542 [Christopher Hollis].

66. HC Deb, 12 December 1945, vol. 417, cols. 428–29 [Dalton]; col. 447 [Anderson]; col. 458 [Boothby]; HC Deb, 13 December 1945, vol. 417, col. 646 [Sir Thomas Moore]; HL Deb, 17 December 1945, vol. 138, col. 678 [Pethick-Lawrence]; col. 786 [Keynes]; HL Deb, 18 December 1945, vol. 138, cols. 813–15 [Viscount Bennett].

67. HC Deb, 12 December 1945, vol. 417, col. 437 [Dalton]; cols. 459–60 [Boothby]; cols. 523–24 [Christopher Hollis]; HC Deb, 13 December 1945, vol. 417, cols. 648–49 [Evan Durbin]; cols. 656–57 [Oliver Stanley]; cols. 686–89 [Gordon-Walker]; HL Deb, 17 December 1945, vol. 138, cols. 679–81 [Pethick-Lawrence]; col. 806 [Lord Piercy].

68. HC Deb, 12 December 1945, vol. 417, col. 434 [Dalton]; col. 543 [Oliver Lyttelton]; F. McKenzie, *Redefining the Bonds of Commonwealth, 1939–48: The Politics of Preference* (Basingstoke, UK: Palgrave Macmillan, 2002), 153.

69. Mikesell, *Bretton Woods Debates*, 46.

70. L. S. Pressnell and Sheila V. Hopkins, "A Canard out of Time? Churchill, the War Cabinet, and the Atlantic Charter, August 1941," *Review of International Studies* 14 (1988): 223–35 (224); Steil, *Battle of Bretton Woods*, 121.

71. Camilla Schofield, *Enoch Powell and the Making of Postcolonial Britain* (Cambridge: Cambridge University Press, 2013), 50.

72. Steil, *Battle of Bretton Woods*, 13–14, 262–63.

73. Ibid., 107–8; McKenzie, *Redefining the Bonds*, 153.

74. Steil, *Battle of Bretton Woods*, 115.

75. HC Deb, 12 December 1945, vol. 417, col. 461 [Boothby]; HL Deb, 17 December 1945, vol. 138, cols. 701–2 [Samuel]; cols. 721, 724–25 [Balfour of Burleigh]; HL Deb, 18 December 1945, vol. 138, cols. 790–94 [Keynes].

76. HC Deb, 6 December 1945, vol. 416, cols. 2668–69 [Attlee]; HC Deb, 12 December 1945, vol. 417, col. 490 [Cripps]; McKenzie, *Redefining the Bonds*, 154; Clarke, *Keynes*, 88.

77. HC Deb, 12 December 1945, vol. 417, cols. 452–53 [Anderson]; HC Deb, 13 December 1945, vol. 417, col. 723 [Churchill]; col. 729 [Bevin].

78. HC Deb, 13 December 1945, vol. 417, col. 710 [Stokes]; HL Deb, 17 December 1945, vol. 138, col. 706 [Samuel]; HL Deb, 18 December 1945, vol. 138, col. 792 [Keynes]; Steil, *Battle of Bretton Woods*, 46, 88–89.

79. HC Deb, 12 December 1945, vol. 417, cols. 469–79 [Norman Smith]; HC Deb, 13 December 1945, vol. 417, col. 673 [Jennie Lee]; col. 707 [Stokes], cols. 728–29 [Bevin].

80. Toye, "Labour Party's External Economic Policy," 211.

81. HC Deb, 12 December 1945, vol. 417, cols. 461–62 [Boothby]; HC Deb, 13 December 1945, vol. 417, col. 663 [Stanley]; col. 720 [Churchill].

82. Andrew Thorpe, *A History of the British Labour Party*, 3rd ed. (Basingstoke, UK: Palgrave Macmillan, 2008), 110; Alfred F. Havinghurst, *Britain in Transition: The Twentieth Century*, 4th ed. (Chicago: University of Chicago Press, 1985), 331–32.

83. The Labour Party Manifesto, *Let Us Face the Future: A Declaration of Labour Policy for the Consideration of the Nation* (Labour Party, 1945), 2 (pdf).

84. Douglas Jay, *Change and Fortune: A Political Record* (London: Hutchison, 1980), 137.

85. Toye, "Labour Party's External Economic Policy," 208.

86. Toye, "Attlee Government," 916.

87. HL Deb, 18 December 1945, vol. 138, col. 877 [Cranborne]; cols. 896–97; Orin Kirshner, ed., *The Bretton Woods–GATT System: Retrospect and Prospect after Fifty Years* (Routledge: New York, 2015), 78.

88. HL Deb, 17 December 1945, vol. 138, col. 726.

89. Steil, *Battle of Bretton Woods*, 134.

90. Conway, *Summit*, 140–41, 170; Steil, *Battle of Bretton Woods*, 309–11.

91. HL Deb, 18 December 1945, vol. 138, col. 791.

92. Robbins, Bretton Woods Diary, 22 July 1944, available at http://digital.library.lse.ac.uk/objects /lse:pat524yab.

Chapter 6

A "Barbarous Relic": The French, Gold, and the Demise of Bretton Woods

Michael J. Graetz and Olivia Briffault

By the time 730 delegates from forty-four countries met at the Mount Washington Hotel in Bretton Woods, New Hampshire, in July 1944 to create a new postwar international financial order, two decades had passed since John Maynard Keynes had described the gold standard as a "barbarous relic." But the French were never convinced: to them, gold was the key to international monetary stability and an essential paving stone for their path to global political prominence.

The French attachment to gold dates back as far as the French Revolution. In 1789, the National Assembly began issuing "assignat" or paper money backed by the value of the properties that had been confiscated from the Catholic Church. Rampant inflation and illegal exchanges for old-regime coins caused the assignat to depreciate quickly. In an attempt to combat this hyperinflation, in 1803 Napoleon established a gold standard (albeit in bimetallic form) with the fixing of the ratio of silver to gold at 15.5:1, a rule that was successfully maintained for seventy-five years.[1] The history of the assignat and the first major hyperinflation instilled in French politicians a fear of hyperinflation and a preoccupation with the stability of gold.

By the end of the nineteenth century, not only France but also the United States and all the powers of Europe had adopted a gold standard that permitted people to convert their money into gold on demand. Gold served as the "nineteenth-century global monetary anchor."[2] Indeed, from the earliest use of bills and coins as money until August 1971, money was thought of as a claim on gold.[3]

On Sunday, August 15, 1971, at 9:00 p.m., Richard Nixon, the thirty-seventh president of the United States, announced what he called a "New Economic Policy."[4] Most of what he said described domestic economic policy changes designed to help ensure Nixon's reelection the following year: income tax cuts for the middle-class and for businesses, elimination of an excise tax on automobiles, and most dramatically, a ninety-day freeze on all US wages and prices along with a new government agency (the Cost of Living Council) to maintain price stability after the freeze expired. Nixon also announced a 10 percent surcharge on all imports. Finally, in a move that, along with the import surcharge, produced shock and dismay around the world, Nixon announced that the United States, which had long been willing to exchange dollars for gold at the rate of $35 per ounce, would no longer do so routinely at any price.[5]

Beyond understanding that this meant the US dollar would be devalued, especially against the Japanese yen and the German mark, no one knew exactly what Nixon's "closing the gold window" implied. But it soon became clear that in a few short paragraphs the president had dismantled the existing international monetary system and abrogated the agreements of Bretton Woods, a key plank of which had required each country to maintain the exchange rate of its currency within 1 percent of a specified value of gold. What would follow, however, was unknown.

The French knew what they wanted: a return to a gold standard with its price doubled. For the French—without denying the critical economic role of international currency relationships—international politics had long played a crucial role. To achieve its political and economic objectives, the French hungered for gold to be reinstated as the centerpiece of any worldwide monetary agreement.

BEFORE BRETTON WOODS

Richard Nixon was not the first US president to abandon the gold standard. In 1933, shortly after Franklin Roosevelt took office, the United States—faced with a growing imbalance of payments with imports exceeding exports despite large tariffs—dissolved the link between the dollar and gold. By executive order, Roosevelt required private citizens to turn their coins and bullion over to the Federal Reserve and prohibited any exports of gold. Congress then followed with a law overriding the gold payment requirements of public and private contracts, a decision that was ratified by a 5–4 vote in the Supreme Court two years later.[6] Roosevelt had become convinced that his only choice was between devaluation of the dollar or domestic deflation, and he preferred the former, a sentiment shared by the twenty-five other nations, including the United Kingdom, that had already devalued and de-linked their currencies from gold beginning in 1931.[7]

The French, however, stayed on the gold standard, and that produced serious imbalances between the value of the French currency and those of the US dollar and UK sterling. By going off the gold standard, the United States and United Kingdom had devalued their currencies—lowering export prices and raising import prices—while the French franc stayed strong and the French economy continued to stagnate.[8] This imbalance was further exacerbated by fears among owners of French assets following the formation in 1936 of a French socialist Popular Front government led by Léon Blum. In combination, these events induced major gold outflows from France and forced the French also to devalue their currency in 1936 but without abandoning the franc's relation to gold.[9]

In 1934, Roosevelt, using powers Congress had granted him, set the price of gold at $35 an ounce, devaluing the dollar by nearly 60 percent.[10] (Gold's previous price had been $20.67 an ounce.)[11] This sharp devaluation was intended to stabilize domestic prices, improve the US economy, and provide greater liquidity to the capital markets.

Instability in currency markets, which some labeled "currency wars," led in September of 1936 to what Roosevelt described as a "gentleman's agreement" (certainly not a treaty) among the United States, the United Kingdom, and France, under which the Americans and the British agreed not to contest a 30 percent devaluation of the franc.[12] The initial French draft of this "Tripartite Agreement" had proposed a system where the franc, the dollar, and sterling would fluctuate within narrow bounds, and the three countries would agree not to devalue except by mutual consent. The French aim was to stabilize the relationships among the currencies and to restore gold convertibility.[13] The Americans, however, refused to agree to bilateral rates or to return to a firm link between the dollar and gold, so the final Tripartite Agreement simply stated the three nations' desire to minimize exchange rate fluctuations (limit devaluations) and continue free trade.[14] The agreement, however, required subscribing nations to agree to avoid competitive depreciations of their currencies and to maintain currency values at existing levels (after the 30 percent French devaluation).[15]

The Tripartite Agreement, coupled with other economic measures in the United States, helped stabilize the currencies, at least in the short term, but by 1938, the French had to devalue again.[16] While the French held on to the gold standard in the interest of currency stability and urged a return to a proper international gold standard, Roosevelt was determined to achieve both monetary stabilization and the dominance of the US dollar by establishing the dollar price of gold as an essential monetary benchmark.[17]

Years later, at Bretton Woods, the stability of the dollar—not a link to gold—became the key to international monetary stability. And the same divergence in French and US attitudes toward the monetary role of gold would be repeated in the aftermath of Nixon's shattering of Bretton Woods.

BRETTON WOODS

A monetary and financial conference held in Bretton Woods, New Hampshire, to shape the postwar Western economic order and open international trade met in 1944. The most important questions at the conference were with respect to the governance and powers of the international institution that would become the International Monetary Fund (IMF), how to create international liquidity, and how countries could gain access to that liquidity.[18] Although 730 delegates from all forty-four allied countries met at Bretton Woods, the United States and United Kingdom dominated the accords and economic agreement.[19] The leading figures drafting and discussing how best to organize the postwar economic order were Harry White from the United States and John Maynard Keynes from the United Kingdom. Each drafted their version of an economic agreement, and much of the conference was devoted to arguing over their plans. The White Plan advocated a central status for the dollar as the world's sole surrogate for gold, but it conceded that the dollar should be backed by gold (reflecting the United States' large gold holdings).[20] Keynes, on the other hand, was repelled by the idea of a gold standard.[21] The two plans overlapped, however, in many other features: an end to the economic warfare of the 1930s; the need for an institutional forum for international cooperation on monetary matters; and fixed exchange rates. The governments agreed that, absent floating exchange rates, all states needed the assurance of liquidity through an adequate supply of monetary reserves.[22] The big disagreement was whether that assurance should be, as proposed by Keynes, provided by a world bank, which could create new reserves called "bancor," or a borrowing mechanism through what became the IMF, as preferred by White.[23] After bargaining for some concessions, the other countries at Bretton Woods largely agreed to American proposals for the IMF and World Bank in the expectation that most of them would be net borrowers and that the United States would be the largest creditor. So the final agreements ended up being closer to the White Plan, reflecting US preferences, with the dollar exchangeable for gold at the fixed price of $35 an ounce.

The French had also drafted an economic plan that they presented at the conference. Unlike the White and Keynes Plans, the French Plan was less theoretical and more pragmatic.[24] The French Plan of 1943, written by Hervé Alphand and André Istel, was designed to create balance and parity among participating countries—relying on a gold standard.[25] The French Plan would have had participating countries fix their official currency values by reference to the currencies of other countries—official values that must be maintained and could be changed only after consultation with all other participating countries.[26] The French Plan also would have required each member to hold each others countries' currencies to increase liquidity. The French, for example, would hold dollars and other currencies, especially those of European countries recovering from World War II. Pegging all international currencies with reference to the dollar meant that gold could be used as an international reserve asset and as a means of settlement.[27] The French hoped that the agreements would define currencies in terms of a fixed weight of gold.[28] The French also proposed a Monetary Stabilization Office to facilitate currency clearings, serve as a depository for collateral, and become the location of international consultation.[29] The French would have placed gold, not the US dollar, at the center of the world monetary system. That did not happen.

The French Plan had virtually no impact on the structure of the IMF or the World Bank. The Articles of Agreement at Bretton Woods, however, did define international currencies with reference to gold, and members agreed to declare a par value and maintain it within a 1 percent margin.[30] Members also agreed to make their currencies convertible for current account transactions. The United States pegged the price of gold at $35 an ounce.[31] Other members would then intervene in foreign exchange markets by either buying or selling dollars to maintain the value of their currency within the 1 percent margin.

The last attempt the French made to shape these international arrangements related to gold quotas. Each country's gold quota determined their position in the directorship, with the top three getting permanent seats. The French wanted a more important gold quota so they could hold a rank in the directorships of the IMF and World Bank. The first three ranks were the United States, the United Kingdom, and Russia. The French wanted the fourth rank out of pride, but the United States insisted it should be given to China, whose economy was growing more quickly.[32] Pierre Mendès France, the head of the French delegation, complained, "the Americans have taken key positions which are against the French." To placate the French and affirm the US commitment to France, Henry Morgenthau, the US Treasury secretary and president of the Bretton Woods Conference, added a fourth and fifth directorship (for China and for the French), up from the previously planned three. He responded to Mendès France: "I told you I would not go to bed until I tried to correct [the] impression that the American delegation was unfriendly to France."[33]

From its inception, the Bretton Woods system became an asymmetrical dollar-gold system.[34] Instead of turning dollars into gold and holding gold, countries held dollars, and the dollar became both the private and official international currency.[35] As the system moved farther away from a gold standard and closer to a "dollar standard," there was little the French, who so wanted a return to gold, could do. France's reconstruction problems—including chronic external and internal imbalances—limited its influence in the postwar monetary system. Because of its weak economy, France had to devalue the franc multiple times to comply with the Bretton Woods Agreements.[36] The United States—by far the wealthiest and most stable Western country—basically dominated international monetary arrangements. The Bretton Woods system, therefore, never actually became a convertible system of international currencies into gold, as the agreement seemed to imply, but instead was effectively a dollar standard, with the dollar pegged to a fixed price of gold.

"BANALISER LE DOLLAR"

If French policy makers had any policy priority in the period between Bretton Woods and when Nixon closed the gold window in 1971, it was to "*banaliser le dollar*" (dethrone the dollar).[37]

By 1947, postwar difficulties and domestic reconstruction needs, along with troubles for the British around the world (especially in India, Greece, and Palestine), had undone the British Empire and simultaneously any potential for sterling to compete with the dollar as an international reserve currency.[38] The French viewed the British as overly sympathetic to American needs. The beginning of the Marshall Plan the following year, coupled with large US military expenditures, provoked an unprecedented outflow of dollars from the United States. The French regarded the enormous power the United States held in the international community as an attempt to control the world economy for selfish purposes.[39]

Over the next decade, the fragility of the Bretton Woods arrangements became apparent. In 1959, the economist Robert Triffin told Congress that the use of "national currencies in international reserves" was a "built in" destabilizer to "world monetary arrangements."[40] Foreign governments that accumulated dollars as reserves could not use them at home, so they either lent any dollars in excess of the costs of the imports they purchased back to the United States or held them as reserves. The Triffin Dilemma, as it became known, is that there was no practical way for the United States to provide sufficient dollars to satisfy the world's liquidity needs for trade and international capital transactions and simultaneously limit the number of dollars to guarantee that they could be redeemed for gold at a fixed price.[41]

Jacques Rueff, a distinguished French economist and adviser to the French government committed to a gold standard, agreed. Here is how Rueff described the problem of deficits in the US balance of payments while the dollar serves as the international reserve currency:

> The United States . . . pays the creditor country dollars, which end up with its central bank. But the dollars are of no use in Bonn, or in Tokyo, or in Paris. The very same day, they are re-lent to the New York money market. . . . So the key currency country never feels the effect of a deficit in its balance of payments. And . . . there is no reason whatever for the deficit to disappear. . . . [I]f I had an agreement with my tailor that whatever money I pay him he returns to me the very same day as a loan, I would have no objection at all to ordering more suits from him.[42]

In theory, dollars could be converted into gold at $35 an ounce, but it did not take long for the number of dollars in circulation to overwhelm the capacity of the United States to redeem them in gold. In 1962, British Prime Minister Harold Macmillan told President Kennedy that most of the world's monetary difficulties would be solved if the United States doubled the price of gold to $70 an ounce, but Kennedy regarded such a devaluation as signaling US weakness and he refused.[43] Nor was Kennedy willing to accept austerity at home, so the United States kept expanding its money supply. By the mid-1960s, the dollar shortage of the early 1950s had turned into a dollar glut.[44] And the ratio of US gold reserves to the number of dollars circulating through the world had shrunk. The French, unsurprisingly, were unhappy. More than thirty countries around the world had devalued their currencies since the war. France, which had faced ongoing economic difficulties, including budget deficits and trade imbalances, had devalued its franc numerous times by 1958.

The rebellion of a division of the French Army in Algiers in May of 1958 revealed the weakness of the French Fourth Republic. This attempted coup led to the return of Charles de Gaulle to political power. De Gaulle blamed the constitution and the institutions of the Fourth Republic for France's economic and political weaknesses. He drafted a new constitution with Michel Debré that emphasized a strong executive in a presidential regime with bicameralism. This new constitution ushered in the French Fifth Republic. De Gaulle wanted to create a new image of France: politically unified, economically strong, and internationally powerful.[45]

De Gaulle addressed the country's ongoing deficits through tax increases, large cuts in government spending, and another devaluation of the franc in 1958.[46] This austerity, de Gaulle believed, was necessary to restore France to its rightful place at the center of world affairs and to offset the predominance of the United States. De Gaulle appointed Jacques Rueff to lead a commission to pave a path to economic expansion, which he believed to be the first step toward French domination. Rueff concluded that the major obstacle to French economic strength was that the United States blocked and manipulated interest rates.[47] Returning to a real gold standard and a strong French franc was a centerpiece of his plan to regain economic domination.

The Treaty of Rome, signed in 1957 by six countries—France, Germany, Italy, the Netherlands, Belgium, and Luxembourg—had liberalized and expanded trade, especially within Europe, and by the mid-1960s the European economies were enjoying robust postwar economic growth.[48] This was accompanied by growing European concerns with domination by the US government and by American multinationals. No one expressed this unease more forcefully than Charles de Gaulle. "The purpose of Europe," he said, "is to avoid domination by the Americans or Russians." "Europe," he added, "is the means by which France can once again become what she has not been since Waterloo, first in the world."[49]

At a press conference on February 4, 1965, de Gaulle urged major changes in international monetary arrangements.[50] He described a monetary system based on any single nation's currency as a danger to the world and sang praises to gold.[51] Gold, he said, "does not change to nature" and is "in all places and at all times, the immutable and fiduciary value par excellence."[52] In his memoir, de Gaulle was even more explicit. He described the countries of the West as having "no choice" but to accept the international monetary system of Bretton Woods in which "the dollar was automatically regarded as the equivalent of gold."[53] This, de Gaulle said, enhanced American hegemony, and the surplus dollars exported by the United States to France, he added, "put a strain on our currency" that benefited only the Americans. "[T]he monumentally over-privileged position that the world has conceded to the American currency since the two world wars," he said, "left [America] standing alone amid the ruins of others."[54] So, beginning in 1965, the French adopted as official policy the conversion of its dollar reserves into gold to induce the United States to begin reform of the international monetary system.[55] The United States and France were on a collision course over their differing visions of international monetary reform and over the role of gold.[56] France had become the principal antagonist of the United States in monetary affairs.

This was in sharp contrast to Germany, which relied heavily on the US military commitment. The German Bundesbank promised the United States that it would hold on to dollars. Given the inflation that the United States experienced in the 1960s and the accompanying influx of dollars to Germany, this was a decision the Germans came to regret. In a 1970 interview, Karl Blessing, president of the Bundesbank, said, "we should aggressively have converted the dollars into gold until [the Americans] were driven to despair."[57] The French were convinced that the Germans were being manipulated by American desires. The very different frustrations of the French and the Germans inspired both to seek a more coordinated international financial policy; this, in turn, would two decades later result in the creation of the euro, in part at least, as a counterweight to the dollar.[58]

In 1961, nine central banks from the United States and eight European countries created the London Gold Pool in an attempt to maintain fixed convertible values for their currencies and the $35 price for an ounce of gold.[59] Half the required supply of gold for the pool came from the United States. But by 1965, the pool could not stem the outflow of gold. The world gold supply had not increased to match the growing supply of dollars, the US deficit had ballooned, and US inflation was increasing as a result of spending on both social programs and the Vietnam War. By the late 1960s, the Bretton Woods Agreements had largely unraveled.

De Gaulle's attempts to control the international monetary system, however, did not stop at simply controlling imports and exports of gold. Beginning in 1965 de Gaulle began exchanging France's dollar reserves for gold. This was de Gaulle's attempt to punish the British, as he believed their economic policies were also being unduly influenced by the United States. In 1966 France stopped contributing to the international Gold Pool, forcing the United States to increase its contribution to the Gold Pool by the amount previously supplied by France. By 1966, gold accounted for more than 70 percent of French international holdings.[60] When the United States rebuffed France's pressure to devalue the dollar by increasing the price of gold, the French continued accumulating gold. President de Gaulle refused to devalue the franc, calling the idea, "the worst possible absurdity," a refusal that was widely criticized by the international community.[61] French economic and political difficulties then created large imbalances of payments for France that produced substantial reserve losses. After de Gaulle retired to his country home in April 1969, the newly elected Georges Pompidou was soon forced to devalue the franc. The *Chicago Tribune* called the decision a thankful "break with de Gaulle's monstrously absurd foreign exchange policy."[62]

By May 1968, the Gold Pool had completely fallen apart and had been replaced by a two-tier gold system with separate private and public gold markets. Governments traded gold only in the public market, while the private price of gold was set by supply and demand.[63] The next year, the Gold Pool nations stabilized the price of gold by agreeing to stop selling gold in private markets and by allowing the price of gold for nonmonetary transactions to fluctuate.[64]

In the meanwhile, private gold markets faced separate pressures. Economic sanctions against South Africa for its policy of apartheid and its relations with the Soviet Union made the Krugerrand—which accounted for close to 90 percent of the global gold coin market—an illegal import in many Western countries (including the United States). This limited the supply of gold, and contributed to anxiety about the status of gold in the international monetary system.[65] The reduced supply of gold from South Africa was accompanied by speculation about a potential devaluation of the dollar. In March 1968, the IMF abandoned a single fixed price for gold and reversed its policies regarding purchases of gold from South Africa.[66] By September 1969, Germany informed the IMF that it was unable to maintain values for the mark within the prescribed limits around par value and revalued the mark against the dollar.[67] A year and a half after that, in a contentious decision, especially upsetting to the French, Germany decided to float the mark to accommodate the growing demand for the mark on foreign exchange markets.[68]

French minister of finance Giscard D'Estaing then declared, "The world monetary system must be set in concentric circles: the first one being gold, and then, the second, if necessary, recourse to deliberate and concerted creation of either reserve assets or credit facilities. The inner circle is gold. Experience in recent years has shown us that, aside from any theoretical preference, gold remains the essential basis of the world payments system."[69] According to D'Estaing (in a speech to the National Assembly in May 1971), the French government had three main concerns: to protect the French economy from the international upheaval in currency markets; to fix the roots of international monetary problems; and to ensure that any measures taken in response to international monetary difficulties not compromise the French desire to create a monetary and economic union in Europe.[70] D'Estaing criticized Germany's decision to float their currency—complaining that it was not a European community decision and would not help in creating a European economic monetary union.[71] D'Estaing was willing instead to accept a collective revaluation of international currencies.[72] In such a case, the European countries would compensate for the United States' monetary inflation by deflation in Europe.[73] But D'Estaing would accept this sacrifice only if it meant continuing the gold standard.

By the late 1960s, it was unmistakable that US gold reserves, which had been falling relative to US dollars since 1957, were inadequate to fund convertibility of dollars into gold at the fixed price of $35 an ounce.[74] In 1968, riots in both France and the United States essentially took international monetary reform off the agenda. In 1969, Georges Pompidou succeeded Charles de Gaulle as president of France, and Richard Nixon succeeded Lyndon Johnson in the United States. Domestic disorder on both sides of the Atlantic was a harbinger of the next decades' social, economic, and international upheavals. In the period leading up to Richard Nixon's August 1971 policy shift, the US balance of payments deteriorated substantially: the $3.2 billion deficit in the second quarter of 1971 exceeded the deficit for all of 1970. In the third quarter, the deficit was $3.1 billion, hardly better. One of the few constants, however, was the continuing divergence of American and French views concerning the proper role of gold in international monetary affairs.

AFTER THE "NIXON SHOCK"

In August 1971, French president Pompidou sent a battleship to New York Harbor to remove France's gold from the vault of the New York Federal Reserve Bank and to transport it to the Banque de France in Paris. Soon thereafter, gold accounted for 92 percent of French reserves. On August 11, the British requested that the Treasury remove the $3 billion of gold from the US depository of Fort Knox to the New York Federal Reserve vault, where the gold of foreign governments was stored. As Paul Volcker, who was then Treasury's undersecretary for monetary affairs, has put it: "If the British, who had founded the system with us, and who had fought so hard to defend their own currency, were going to take gold for their dollars, it was clear the game was indeed over."[75] When Nixon spoke on August 15, 1971, the United States held less than ten thousand metric tons of gold, less than half of what it once had.[76]

Nixon's August 1971 decisions caught foreign governments by complete surprise. They also surprised most US policy makers and officials. Nixon's speech and the policies it announced had been suggested to him a few weeks earlier by his charismatic Treasury secretary, John Connally, and the details had been developed at a meeting of Nixon's economic advisers, who had been sequestered at Camp David the weekend before Nixon's Sunday-night address.[77] As Paul Volcker had told the group, billions might be made with advance knowledge of what the president was planning to do. The necessary secrecy, however, had meant that both technical and strategic planning for its aftermath could not happen until the new policies had been announced. In the weeks following Nixon's announcement, Connally, Volcker, and other administration officials spent much of their time traveling to foreign capitals attempting to assuage foreign leaders who were apoplectic about the import surcharge and insecure about the new US monetary policy—whatever that might be.

Within the US government, efforts to fashion a new international monetary agreement did not jell until mid-November 1971 in anticipation of a meeting of the G10 (the world's ten richest countries) in Rome later that month. The US position was heavily influenced by the need for the French—its principal antagonist—to agree. For economic reasons primarily having to do with trade, the United States wanted a substantial devaluation of the dollar vis-à-vis the German mark and the Japanese yen. For its trade policy, the

French needed to maintain the relationship between the franc and the mark, but because its trade with the United States was relatively small, France had little concern about the relationship of the franc and the dollar. The French government, however, cared deeply about the price of gold and, unsurprisingly, wanted to preserve an official relationship between the US dollar and gold. Not only did the French government hold the bulk of its official reserves in gold, but virtually every French resident also had a little gold stashed away.

On November 29, 1971, the arguments and discussions culminated in a meeting of the finance ministers of the G10 in Rome. At the Rome meeting, the chairmanship, which rotated, was held by the United States' John Connally, and he insisted, so that he could be "impartial," that Paul Volcker would present the US position. Volcker then announced that the United States—which had refused since the 1930s to change the official price of gold from $35 an ounce—would accept an upward revision of that price and would eliminate the import surcharge in exchange for an appreciation of other OECD currencies by a weighted average of 11 percent. This devaluation of the dollar was greater than the other G10 countries expected and not well received by the other finance ministers. The only real outcome of the meeting was to hold another meeting the next month in Washington, DC.[78]

In the interval between the two meetings, crucial negotiations took place between Nixon and Pompidou in the Azores. Pompidou began their meeting with a "Gaullist lecture on gold and the evils of the dollar standard."[79] Ultimately, however, Pompidou agreed to a rise in the price of gold from $35 to $38 an ounce, a rise of 8.5 percent, significantly less than the 11 percent the United States had wanted.

Soon thereafter, the G10 meeting took place at the Smithsonian Castle on the National Mall in Washington, DC. The negotiations, as in Rome, centered on trade agreements and tariffs, the need to devalue the dollar, future exchange rates, and the convertibility of the dollar into gold.[80] The United States was adamant about its desire to move away from gold. The French were equally adamant to the contrary.

The differences in French and US policies were neither new nor driven solely by the economics of the time. French policy was, to be sure, based upon the long-standing French position. By December 1971, the French held enormous gold reserves but had limited international economic power. The United States was in the opposite position: its gold reserves had dwindled, but it still had immense international economic sway. The United States was determined both to maintain its global economic dominance and to improve economic conditions at home.

The first issue discussed at the Smithsonian meeting was gold convertibility. The French insisted on maintaining gold convertibility, arguing that such convertibility was essential to a fixed currency parity system, and that under the IMF agreement the United States was required to maintain fixed currency relationships.[81] The French expressed their dismay that the United States had violated international law, and were determined not to reward the United States for breaking its international commitments.[82] For the French, Nixon's unilateral action was just one more example of how the US behavior transgressed the laws that all other countries had to obey.[83] The only way to force the United States to act like other countries, the French believed, was to force the United States to return to a gold standard.

The French argued that, although the dollar was clearly overvalued, the only proper way to devalue the dollar was to adjust the price of gold—otherwise the system would remain biased in the United States' favor.[84] When countries allow their currencies to stray too far from the price of gold, the French insisted, they must revalue their currency.[85] Georges Pompidou criticized the American approach: "I cannot conceive that the U.S. thinks it can make up the deficit in its balance of payments with exports to Europe. The U.S. balance-of-payments deficit is an American problem."[86] After Nixon suspended convertibility in August 1971, the French had urged Europe to make the United States pay.[87]

Paul Volcker, then undersecretary of the Treasury, said that the fundamental structure of the IMF would have to be changed for convertibility to be maintained.[88] Volcker believed that gold should no longer play a role in the international monetary system and, instead that SDRs (Special Drawing Rights issued by the IMF to play the role of an alternative reserve currency) should be extended.[89] Volcker proposed to increase liquidity, but without any link to gold, and he insisted that in order to maintain the necessary liquidity the United States must be free to adjust its own exchange rate. The French rejected Volcker's arguments, continuing to insist on a return to gold convertibility in order to limit the role of the US dollar in international economic arrangements. The United States, having consistently rejected French proposals for monetary reform since before the Tripartite Agreement, held firm.

It was difficult for the French to gather much support for their position. If gold remained at the center of the international monetary system and the United States doubled or even tripled the price of gold in dollars, other countries' exchange rates with the dollar would also have to change—many by a large amount.

Unsurprisingly, the discussion at the Smithsonian then turned to the question of fixed versus floating exchange rates. By the time of the Smithsonian meeting, not only Germany but also the United Kingdom, Canada, and several other nations had begun to float the value of their currencies against the dollar. Fixed exchange rates had been difficult to maintain with the ongoing decline in the value of the dollar. The United States had already decided to lift its import surcharge for nations that agreed to float their currencies against the dollar, and was also interested in floating the dollar.[90] But the French were adamantly opposed to floating rates. In the French view, floating exchange rates caused unnecessary instability and price uncertainty.[91] On the other hand, fixed exchange rates created a need for the United States to constantly adjust its domestic economic policies and increased the likelihood that the United States would erect and maintain significant trade barriers to solve its balance-of-payment deficit problems.[92] The French thought that a two-tier market for gold would solve this problem: governments would privately trade gold and francs at a fixed exchange price, but in the public market, supply and demand would determine the price of gold.[93]

According to the French, floating rates were highly selfish. A *Le Monde* article from September 1971, reflecting French government opinions on floating rates, compared floating exchange rates to a state of anarchy.[94] The article suggested that by floating a currency, a country is freer to pursue any policy it would like—as opposed to being constrained by the linkage of its currency to that of other countries.[95] Flexible rates allow countries to pursue autonomous economic and monetary policy. The French insisted that floating rates, free from fixed links to the currencies of other countries, would in the long run create even greater international disorder.

A central reason that the French wanted to maintain fixed exchange rates was that fixed rates would make the transition to a European economic union, which could compete against the United States, easier.[96] The French believed that Europe needed a common currency.[97] The French regarded a link to gold as helping to facilitate the monetary unification of Europe, and with monetary unification, the French expected greater political unification and enhanced French influence in world affairs.[98] An ECU (European Currency Unit) could be linked to gold and might replace the ubiquity of the dollar in international transactions.[99] Transition to the ECU would be made easier by maintaining fixed exchange rates. The French planned to have the ECU defined by its relationship to gold and guaranteed by a European reserve fund.[100] A European currency would then help France counterbalance the United States in international economic matters by providing the world an alternative currency that might compete with the dollar.

In a final attempt to salvage the Bretton Woods Agreements, the negotiations at the Smithsonian meeting concluded with the result that the Azores agreement between Nixon and Pompidou had preordained: the dollar was pegged to gold at $38 an ounce (up from the previous $35), and all currencies were pegged to the dollar—maintaining the "gold-exchange standard" but avoiding an actual gold standard (which would have allowed a fixed amount of dollars to be exchanged for gold). This resulted in an official devaluation of the dollar of 8.57 percent, less than the United States had proposed at Rome, but more than other countries had initially anticipated.[101] The G10 also set wider margins for currency fluctuations based on the new dollar value. The group agreed to help balance the world trading system through Special Drawing Rights (SDRs) issued by the International Monetary Fund.[102] The United States also agreed to eliminate its new 10 percent surtax on imports. President Nixon announced the agreement at the Smithsonian's National Air and Space Museum, then next door to the Castle where the meetings had been held.

The French were still not content. They continued to insist that the United States return to the gold standard, but the United States would not. For the next decade, the French would continue to blame any failures of the Smithsonian agreement on the US refusal to return to a gold standard.

The Smithsonian agreement did not long survive. The rather small margins of currency fluctuations that were agreed to proved impossible to maintain, and as the price of dollars in the free market fluctuated, this put pressure on its official price for exchange. As early as 1972, the French were again criticizing American monetary policy. The French continued to insist that the United States should buy surplus dollars from European nations with gold, but the United States no longer held enough gold to do that.[103] Nor did the United States have any intention to do so. The French said, "The dollar cannot be a truly international currency, why not make more use of gold, this fiduciary asset par excellence? The official price of the yellow metal, in order to be credible, must not vary too greatly from the market price. Since Washington insists on an excessive discrepancy between the two prices, let us, the Europeans, decide to fix a realistic price for gold for our own transactions."[104]

However, the rest of Europe did not support the French view. In June of 1972, the British decided to float the pound, a move that created even greater price discrepancy. The French complained and called the British move a political failure.[105]

On September 11, 1972, Paul Volcker, still undersecretary of the Treasury, testified before a subcommittee on international exchange of Congress's Joint Economic Committee. He described the British decision in July to float the pound as disrupting the "period of calm" following "the exchange of rate equilibrium so arduously worked out" at the Smithsonian. He also described the interventions in world currency markets undertaken by the Treasury and the Federal Reserve as necessary to keep the value of the dollar in an appropriate relation to other currencies, and he informed the committee that such interventions would continue at US discretion. Here is what he said about gold:

> With respect to gold, the United States has repeatedly expressed the view that the role of that metal in the international monetary system should and must continue to diminish. Such an evolution is, of course, fully consistent with the trend of monetary history over a period of many years. Governments around the world long ago reached the inevitable judgment that domestic monetary systems and policies could not safely be hostage to vagaries in gold demand and supply—the cost in terms of economic stability was simply too high. Internationally, gold 25 years ago accounted for about 70 percent of total national monetary reserves. By 1972, the ratio had declined to some 27 percent.
>
> There are irresistible geological, industrial, and economic facts behind these trends. The physical supply of gold is both limited and, in the Western World, virtually entirely under the control of one producing nation. . . . Gold is both an attractive and useful metal, but the residual supply is in no way related to the liquidity needs of the world community.
>
> . . . I suppose there are some who would argue that additional liquidity in a gold-based system can be provided by increasing from time to time the price at which gold is traded among monetary authorities. But surely such an approach would make a mockery of any presumed "discipline" from a gold centered monetary system—the virtue sometimes still attributed to the use of gold. A system relying on gold price increases to regulate liquidity would be both continuously destabilizing to the monetary system and capricious in whom it benefits and whom it hurts.[106]

Obviously referring to the French view, Volcker added, "I do not think it will be easy to resolve differences about what to do about the precise role of gold." That was an understatement.

The Smithsonian agreement continued to disintegrate. Rather than stabilize the dollar and produce a large US surplus to cure an adverse US balance of international payments, the agreement was followed by a weak dollar and similar problems as before. Early in 1973, the United States devalued the dollar to make US products more competitive in world markets and to improve the US balance of payments. This was followed by a dump of dollars into the market in a rush to exchange them for German marks and Japanese yen.[107] The combination of high rates of inflation and the first oil crisis in the fall of 1973 made the fixed rates agreed to at the Smithsonian untenable. By late 1973, the United States, Japan, and all the countries of the European treaty had decided to let their currencies float against the dollar.

In the fall of 1975, the principal antagonists, the United States and France, reached agreement on a few sentences of amendments to the IMF Articles of Agreement to provide a formal legal basis for floating exchange rates, and in 1976 the IMF Articles were formally amended to reflect the new reality. Both the 1944 agreements of Bretton Woods and the one reached just a few years earlier at the Smithsonian were officially dead.

CONCLUSION

The interment of gold as a monetary standard has not ended ongoing debates over its strengths and weaknesses. But despite the periodic calls for its renewal by some analysts and many politicians both in the United States and abroad, it is difficult to imagine gold's resurrection as the foundation of international monetary arrangements. Floating rates allow nations to reduce their exposure to the risks of any one currency by diversifying their holdings of foreign currencies. Intermittent national interventions that affect the valuation of domestic currencies to serve domestic economic and political interests remain inevitable. The Maastricht Treaty of February 1992, which led to the adoption of the euro, has, to be sure, reduced the international power of the dollar, but it has also produced some serious economic dislocations in the Eurozone. Some analysts are now looking to the currencies of large emerging countries, such as China, to add stability to the system. But it seems that all we can be sure of—more than seven decades after Bretton Woods and nearly half a century since its demise—is that the stability of the international monetary system rests primarily with judgments of the world's central bankers and of the international monetary institutions, especially the IMF. This state of affairs proved its mettle during the 2007–2010 financial crisis, but it hardly ensures confidence or monetary stability. The French failure in its efforts to return to a gold standard has not, so far at least, become a loss for everyone.

Notes

1. Michael Bordo and Finn Kydland, "The Gold Standard as a Rule" (Federal Reserve Bank of Cleveland Working Paper 9205, 1992), 24.

2. Ibid., 81–83.

3. Benn Steil and Manuel Hinds, *Money, Markets & Sovereignty* (New Haven, CT: Yale University Press, 2010), 88.

4. See "Address to the Nation by Richard Nixon Outlining a New Economic Policy: 'The Challenge of Peace.' August 15, 1971," in the "Historical Documents" section of this book.

5. Nixon's speech on going off the gold standard is available at http://www.presidency.ucsb.edu /ws/?pid=3115. Proclamation 4074—Supplemental Duty for Balance of Payments Purposes (August 15, 1971), is available at http://www.presidency.ucsb.edu/ws/index.php?pid=107023.

6. Benn Steil, *The Battle of Bretton Woods: John Maynard Keynes, Harry Dexter White, and the Making of a New World Order* (Princeton, NJ: Princeton University Press, 2013), 25.

7. Ibid.

8. Michael D. Bordo, Dominique Simard, and Eugene White, "France and the Bretton Woods International Monetary System: 1960 to 1968" (NBER Working Paper Series 4642, 1994).

9. Steil, *Battle of Bretton Woods*, 32.

10. Roosevelt's gold proclamation, "16 - Proclamation 2072—Fixing the Weight of the Gold Dollar," is available at http://www.presidency.ucsb.edu/ws/index.php?pid=14750.

11. Steil, *Battle of Bretton Woods*, 28.

12. Ibid., 32.

13. Bordo, Simard, and White, "France and the Bretton Woods International Monetary System," 5.

14. The Tripartite Monetary Agreement is available at http://www.bis.org/publ/arpdf/archive/ar1937 _en.pdf.

15. Ibid.

16. Steil, *Battle of Bretton Woods*, 33.

17. Ibid. The United States increasingly took control of the gold standard, as the US economy was nearly three times larger than that of either France or Germany. See also Robert A. Mundell, "A Reconsideration of the Twentieth Century" (Prize Lecture: Department of Economics, Columbia University, December 8, 1999).

18. Ibid., 233.

19. Ibid., 229.

20. See White's "Preliminary Draft Outline of a Proposal for an International Stabilization Fund of the United and Associated Nations (Revised July 10, 1943)," in the "Historical Documents" section of this book. Steil, *Battle of Bretton Woods*, 128.

21. Ibid., 138. See Keynes's "Proposals for an International Clearing Union (April 1943)," in the "Historical Documents" section of this book.

22. Steil, *Battle of Bretton Woods*, 148.

23. Comité pour l'histoire économique et financière de la France, *La France et les institutions de Bretton Woods, 1944–1994, Colloque tenu à [Paris]-Bercy les 30 Juin et 1er Juillet 1994* (Paris: CHEFF, 1998), 11.

24. Ibid.

25. Bordo, Simard, and White, "France and the Bretton Woods International Monetary System," 3.

26. Ibid.

27. Ibid.

28. Ibid.

29. Ibid.

30. See "Articles of Agreement of the International Monetary Fund, July 22, 1944," and "Articles of Agreement of the International Bank for Reconstruction and Development, July 22, 1944," in the "Historical Documents" section of this book. Steil, Battle of Bretton Woods.

31. Bordo, Simard, and White, "France and the Bretton Woods International Monetary System," 6.

32. La France et les institutions de Bretton Woods, 17–18.

33. Steil, Battle of Bretton Woods, 233.

34. Ibid.

35. Ibid.

36. Ibid., 6.

37. Harold James, "The Multiple Contexts of Bretton Woods," Oxford Review of Economics Policy 28, no. 3 (October 2012), 91.

38. Steil, Battle of Bretton Woods, 309–11.

39. Éric Monnet, "Une coopération à la française. La France, le dollar et le système de Bretton Woods, 1960–1965," Histoire@Politique 2013/1 (n19), 83–100. DOI 10.3917/hp.019007, 1.

40. Ibid., 333.

41. Steil, Battle of Bretton Woods, 333. See also Robert Triffin, Gold and the Dollar Crisis: The Future of Convertibility (New Haven, CT: Yale University Press, 1960).

42. Jacques Rueff and Fred Hirsh, "The Role and the Rule of Gold: An Argument," Princeton Essays on International Finances 47 (June 1965): 2–3. See also Jacques Rueff, The Monetary Sin of the West (New York: Macmillan, 1972), available at http://mises.org/library/monetary-sin-west.

43. Rueff, Monetary Sin, 334.

44. Benjamin J. Cohen, "Bretton Woods System," in Routledge Encyclopedia of International Political Economy, ed. R. J. Barry Jones (London and New York: Routledge, 2002).

45. Bordo, Simard, and White, "France and the Bretton Woods International Monetary System," 6–7.

46. Cohen, "Bretton Woods System."

47. Marc Flandreau, Money Doctors: The Experience of International Financial Advising 1850–2000 (New York: Routledge, 2003).

48. James, "The Multiple Contexts of Bretton Woods," 36–37.

49. Ibid., 37.

50. See "Press Conference by Charles de Gaulle, Seeking the Abolition of the Gold Exchange Standard and a Return to the Gold Standard, February 4, 1965," in the "Historical Documents" section of this book.

51. See "Charles de Gaulle, Monetary Crisis Ghost of 1965," available at https://www.youtube.com/watch?v=Q9r1NLMFixo.

52. Rueff and Hirsh, "Role and the Rule of Gold," preface.

53. Charles de Gaulle, Memoirs of Hope: Renewal and Endeavor, trans. Terrence Kilmartin (New York: Simon & Schuster, 1972), 371–72.

54. Ibid., 371.

55. Bordo, Simard, and White, "France and the International Monetary System," 12; James, "Multiple Contexts of Bretton Woods," 64.

56. Monnet, "Une coopération à la française," 12.

57. James, "Multiple Contexts of Bretton Woods," 64.

58. La France et les institutions de Bretton Woods, 101.

59. Peter M. Garber, "The Collapse of the Bretton Woods Fixed Exchange Rate System," in *A Retrospective on the Bretton Woods System: Lessons for International Monetary Reform*, ed. Michael D. Bordo and Barry Eichengreen (Chicago: University of Chicago Press, 1991), 464.

60. Bordo, Simard, and White, "France and the International Monetary System," 12.

61. "After the French Devaluation," *Chicago Tribune*, August 13, 1969, 24.

62. Ibid. The 1969 devaluation was particularly important as parity between the French franc and the German mark was an important topic in the 1969 German elections. Germany was debating whether it should revalue the mark upward. Germany welcomed the French devaluation because it removed the disparity of a key currency with the mark and suggested that an upward revaluation was "wholly unnecessary." Germany relied heavily on its relationship to the franc as it struggled between national pressures to maintain the mark's value and the American desire for the mark to be revalued upward.

63. Margaret de Vries, *The International Monetary Fund 1966–1971*, vol. 1 *Narrative* (Washington, DC: International Monetary Fund, 1976).

64. Ibid.

65. Ibid.

66. Ibid.

67. Garber, "Collapse of the Bretton Woods Fixed Exchange Rate System."

68. Ibid.

69. De Vries, *International Monetary Fund 1966–1971*, vol. 1 *Narrative*.

70. "La politique étrangère de la France: Textes et documents," Dir. de publ. ministère des Affaires étrangères (Paris: La Documentation Française, Octobre 1971); "Déclaration de Valéry Giscard d'Estaing à l'Assemblée nationale," 12 Mai 1971, 162–67.

71. De Vries, *International Monetary Fund 1966–1971*, vol. 1 *Narrative*.

72. Ibid.

73. Ibid.

74. Bordo, Simard, and White, "France and the International Monetary System," 18 and fig. 5.

75. Paul Volcker and Toyoo Gyohten, *Changing Fortunes: The World's Money and the Threat to American Leadership* (New York: Three Rivers Press, 1993), 77.

76. One metric ton of gold is composed of 32,150 troy ounces.

77. See "Address to the Nation by Richard Nixon Outlining a New Economic Policy: 'The Challenge of Peace.' August 15, 1971," in the "Historical Documents" section of this book.

78. These events were related in Edwin S. Cohen, *A Lawyer's Life Deep in the Heart of Taxes* (Falls Church, VA: Tax Analysts, 1994) and the collections of his papers at the University of Virginia Law Library, box 102, "Institutional Monetary Issues." Cohen's account is confirmed in Volcker and Gyohten, *Changing Fortunes*.

79. Volcker and Gyohten, *Changing Fortunes*, 88–89.

80. Garber, "Collapse of the Bretton Woods Fixed Exchange Rate System."

81. Jacques Amalric, "Les dirigeants américains paraissent résignés à la dévaluation du dollar," *Le Monde*, August 17, 1971, 1.

82. Ibid. By participating in and creating the fund, the United States had promised to tie the dollar to gold; by stopping dollar convertibility, the United States effectively broke its promise.

83. Monnet, "Une coopération à la française," 12

84. Jacques Rueff, "La réévaluation des monnais, faux problème," *Le Monde*, September 10, 1971, reporting the French insistence that the way to fix Bretton Woods would be to enlarge the margin of fluctuations and change the price of gold—not remove gold from the picture.

85. Ibid.

86. Clyde H. Farnsworth, "Europeans Re-Examine Goals," *New York Times*, January 14, 1973.

87. Rueff, "La réévaluation des monnais, faux problème."

88. Edwin S. Cohen, "The Highlights of the Group of Ten Deputies Meeting at the International Monetary Fund at 11:00 am, November 16, 1971," in *International Monetary Problems*, folder 202, Special Collections, University of Virginia Law School, December 16, 1971.

89. Ibid.

90. Department of the Treasury, "Memorandum: Preliminary Notes on International Monetary Problems," ed. Edwin S. Cohen (Washington, DC: University of Virginia Law School, September 16, 1971).

91. Ibid.

92. Ibid.

93. De Vries, *International Monetary Fund 1966–1971*, vol. 1 *Narrative*.

94. Paul Fabra, "La faillite du système monétaire," *Le Monde*, September 25, 1971

95. Ibid.

96. Léon Lambert, "Une monnaie Européen tout de suite," *Le Monde*, December 20, 1971.

97. Ibid.

98. Ibid.

99. Ibid.

100. Ibid.

101. Garber, "Collapse of the Bretton Woods Fixed Exchange Rate System."

102. Ibid.

103. Richard Janssen, "Connally Suggests New Monetary Rules Discipline Nations with Chronic Surpluses," *Wall Street Journal*, March 20, 1972.

104. Ibid.

105. Roman Eisenstein, "France Has to Back Dollar," *The Guardian*, August 5, 1972.

106. "Statement of the Honorable Paul A. Volcker, Under Secretary of the Treasury for Monetary Affairs, Before the Subcommittee on International Exchange and Payments of the Joint Economic Committee," September 11, 1972, available at https://www.jec.senate.gov/reports/92nd%20Congress/Gold%20and%20the%20Central%20Bank%20Swap%20Network%20(582).pdf.

107. Farnsworth, "Europeans Re-Examine Goals."

Part III

PATHS TAKEN AND NOT TAKEN

Chapter 7

Nutrition, Food, Agriculture, and the World Economy

Martin Daunton

The Bretton Woods Conference of July 1944 was not the first major international gathering during the Second World War to consider the nature of the postwar economic order. It was preceded by an earlier meeting, the first to be called under the auspices of the United Nations: the Conference on Food and Agriculture held at Hot Springs, Virginia, in May and June 1943. This conference—as well as the General Conference of the International Labour Organization at Philadelphia in April–May 1944—took a wider approach to distributive justice in the world economy, with a concern, respectively, for nutrition and full employment. Although the Bretton Woods Conference mainly focused on monetary issues, the initial proposals of Harry Dexter White were concerned more generally with development, particularly in Latin America. The agenda at Bretton Woods was narrowed for pragmatic reasons in order to secure an agreement on the shape of the postwar monetary order—but the wider ambitions were not entirely abandoned even during the conference, where representatives of less-developed or primary producing countries were anxious that their concerns were not overlooked.

In the opinion of the delegates from these countries, the crucial issues were not monetary or trade policy, but wider issues relating to distributive justice in the world economy. Their concern was shared by some voices within the developed industrial countries who did not consider that the problems that disrupted the international economy in the 1930s could be solved by multilateral trade or a stable monetary regime as advocated by Cordell Hull at the US State Department and by Henry Morgenthau and Harry Dexter White at the US Treasury. But there were other voices, above all the former secretary of agriculture and current vice president Henry Wallace, who stressed the need to deal with the problems of agriculture and food and to create full employment as means to restore prosperity. He drew on the work of John Boyd Orr, a leading British nutritional scientist, and Frank McDougall and Stanley Melbourne Bruce of Australia, who linked agriculture and nutrition to resolve the problems of depression in primary producing economies. These approaches went beyond the concerns of White and other New Dealers for Latin America, and connected with debates over nutrition in India, the solution of agrarian poverty in eastern Europe, and the depression of primary producers such as Australia—and the main forum for debates was the League of Nations.

The monetary solution to the problems facing the world economy was therefore contested both within the advanced industrial economies and from the less-developed and primary producing countries, with alternative approaches to the reconstruction of the world economy. These alternative visions did not disappear after Bretton Woods and continued to be advocated as a way of redressing the balance in the world economy between industrial economies and primary producers, rejecting the narrow vision of the International Monetary Fund and International Bank for Reconstruction and Development in favor of structural adjustment to the world economy. These alternative visions continued to evolve at the conference to negotiate a charter for an International Trade Organization in 1947–1948, in the Bandung Declaration of 1955, and in the United Nations Conference on Trade and Development, established in 1964. The Bretton Woods Conference must not be taken in isolation but placed within the context of other diagnoses of the problems of the 1930s and solutions to create a prosperous and just postwar economic order.

WHY DID ROOSEVELT CALL A CONFERENCE ON FOOD AND AGRICULTURE?

The United Nations Conference on Food and Agriculture was the result of an invitation issued by President Roosevelt to forty-three nations. He felt that the time had arrived "to begin joint consideration of certain fundamental economic questions" that would arise after the war, and in particular production and trade in food "in the light of possibilities of progressively improving in each country the levels of consumption within the framework of an expansion of its general economic activity." The conference would also consider "equitable" agricultural prices from the point of view of producers and consumers; and "the possibilities of international coordination and stimulation of national policies for the improvement of nutrition."[1] Roosevelt's decision to call a conference on food and agriculture puzzled John Maynard Keynes, who was deep in negotiations over monetary policy. In his view, it was a distraction from more important matters. Keynes wrote in sarcastic terms to E. F. Penrose, the economic adviser to the American ambassador in London who was to be a member of the secretariat at Hot Springs: "What you are saying is that your President with his great political insight has decided that the best strategy for post-war reconstruction is to start with vitamins and then by a circuitous route work round to the international balance of payments!"[2]

In fact, food and nutrition were, in the eyes of primary producers, less-developed economies, and nutritional scientists, more immediately pressing than technical issues of international currency, with more far-reaching implications in creating a prosperous, socially equitable world economy. The conference brought together two important considerations. One issue was inadequate dietary standards that had become an important theme in the work of the League of Nations and in national and imperial discourse, and entailed resolving problems of poverty and economic stability. The second concern was the economic difficulties faced by agricultural producers as a result of unstable or low prices and lack of demand. These two issues were both connected and in tension. Together, they offered a solution to the problems of economic development through structural change to the world economy. Better nutrition might increase the demand for food and thus create prosperity for farmers, in turn increasing demand for industrial goods. But there was also the possibility of tension, for the attempt to stabilize or increase the price of food might lead to commodity agreements that protected producers with a loss of welfare for consumers. These questions were fought between countries that were predominantly consumers of food (such as Britain) and predominantly producers (such as Australia), and also within countries that were both major producers and consumers—above all the United States.

A focus on food made sense given the immediate and pressing problems in 1943. Indeed, food was a central feature of the war, rather than a peripheral matter as Keynes implied. Bengal was in the early stages of a famine that resulted in perhaps three million deaths and cast serious doubts over the competence of the British government.[3] The situation in Europe was also alarming. In his book on starvation in Europe, G. H. Bourne remarked that "it is a pathetic story and the desire just to relieve this hideous by-product of war is in itself almost a sufficient war-aim at this moment."[4] Starvation was not only an unintended by-product of war, for it was a central element in the strategy of the Third Reich. Expansion to eastern Europe and clearing of the population—both Jewish and Slav—was part of a plan to secure food supplies. The Hunger Plan of 1941 aimed to starve thirty million inhabitants of the Soviet Union, thereby releasing the grain supply of the Ukraine for consumption in Germany.[5] For its part, Britain relied on imported food from the empire and other areas of the New World, and Germany tried to cut off supplies by submarine warfare. In June 1942, the British and Americans formed the Combined Food Board in Washington, DC, to coordinate transport and distribution between North America and Europe, which was linked with the London Food Committee that covered the empire. The management of food supplies and entitlements was therefore a central concern during the war, and serious issues would arise on the return to peace.[6]

The conference was not only about food but also agriculture—a major part of the world economy and population. Britain was an exception among the developed economies, with only 7.6 percent of its population in agriculture in 1930. In other major developed economies, the proportion remained much higher. In Germany, 29.9 percent of the workforce was employed in agriculture in 1935.[7] In the United States, the farm population was 24.8 percent of total population in 1930 and 21.1 percent in 1940.[8] The major agricultural sectors and regions of the United States faced the same problem of falling prices between the wars, as is clear in the data for wheat and cotton (see table 7.1). The needs of American agriculture could not be ignored, for the political influence of agricultural states was disproportionate to their population. Each was represented by two senators, and the South was vital to Democratic control of the Senate. Many advanced industrial economies turned to policies of protection and autarky in the 1930s to support their rural populations, with the result that domestic food prices were often above prices on world markets with deleterious effects for urban consumers at home and for primary producers who lost their markets.[9]

The major exporters of food—Australia, Canada, Argentina—suffered from a collapse in their exports, low prices, and balance-of-payments deficits, which made them look to import-substituting industrialization, or to

TABLE 7.1. PRICES OF WHEAT AND COTTON
IN THE UNITED STATES, 1909–1939

	Wheat (dollars per bushel)	Cotton (cents per pound)
1909	0.99	13.5
1919	2.16	35.3
1924	1.24	22.9
1929	1.03	16.8
1934	0.84	12.4
1939	0.69	9.1

Source: Historical Statistics of the United States, Millennial Edition Online, Da7192, Da757.

schemes to increase their exports of food and shift the terms of trade in their favor. In Australia, for example, two-way merchandise trade fell from 40.1 percent of GDP in 1901 to a trough of 25.7 percent in 1931–1932. By far the largest category of trade was wool, accounting for something under 40 percent of the total value. The price of a merino fleece from Australia fell from a peak in 1920 of 79⅞ pence a pound in the postwar boom to 37 pence in 1928, before falling to a trough of 15 pence in 1932.[10] Consequently, Australia suffered from a serious depression in the 1930s. Other parts of the world had a different problem: subsistence peasant agriculture made up the vast bulk of the population, often trapped in poverty, barely able to feed itself let alone secure sufficient income to buy industrial goods. This problem affected eastern and southeastern Europe, with its poverty-stricken peasantry suffering from deficiency diseases and low productivity. Paul Rosenstein-Rodan extended his work of 1943 on these regions to five "vast international depressed areas" containing 80–90 percent of the world's population in the Far East (India and China), the colonial empires (above all Africa), the Caribbean, and the Middle East. The economic development of these backward areas was, he argued, "the most important task facing us in the making of the peace." The basic problem was the existence of "agrarian excess population" and disguised unemployment.[11] The issue was a major concern in India, where agriculture accounted for more than three-quarters of the labor force in the 1930s and where deficiency diseases and poverty stood as a reproach to

British rule. These issues were brought together in the interwar period at the League of Nations to reach a new understanding of nutrition and its links with welfare and economic stability. Roosevelt's decision to call the conference at Hot Springs was an expression of these longer-term political and intellectual concerns.

There were also immediate, contingent reasons of political expediency for Roosevelt to call the conference. As he realized, the provision of adequate food might be politically appealing because it was more concrete and personal than discussions of abstruse matters of monetary policy. It connected with the grand statement of the Atlantic Charter of August 1941, with its commitment to the "fair and equitable distribution of essential produce" and "the fullest collaboration between all nations in the economic field with the object of securing, for all, improved labor standards, economic advancement and social security."[12] Emilio G. Collado, a monetary expert with expertise in Latin America who was an American delegate at Bretton Woods and the first American executive director of the International Bank for Reconstruction and Development, saw the point of focusing on food. In February 1943, he remarked that "For popular consumption the food and relief aspects, which have the greatest popular appeal, might be stressed, as the reasons warranting the more basic discussions." Roosevelt was anxious to contain domestic criticisms that America was too generous to the allies, and he wanted some way of taking policy in an internationalist direction. Food offered a way of convincing the public, for who could be in favor of starvation? In Collado's words, "a conference on food problems would have the greatest publicity value in the eyes of the American people and would be the least likely to involve controversial issues."[13]

Marvin Jones, the head of the American delegation and president of the conference, later recalled that Roosevelt "wanted to see if the representatives of the various nations could work together. This was an experiment in their sitting around a table. . . . A sort of pattern for other conferences that would follow." At the time, Walter Lippmann felt that the meeting was less about food than "testing out the machinery for the representation of all the United Nations." The successes and failures of Hot Springs did indeed provide lessons for the conference at Bretton Woods in 1944, but it was much more than a rehearsal.[14] Food, agriculture, and nutrition emerged as major issues for the international economy in the interwar period, within the European empires and at the League of Nations. Roosevelt's decision to call the conference in

1943 was the culmination of long-term debates over the nature of deficiency diseases and their impact on welfare and productivity.

DISCOVERING DEFICIENCY DISEASES

The League of Nations was involved with issues of food and nutrition from its inception. The prosecution of the First World War led to inter-Allied controls over food supplies, and some of the civil servants involved in this task joined the League after the war and looked to a new world order of planning and regulation.[15] More immediately, at the end of the war, central Europe faced a crisis of inflation and financial collapse, with scarcity of food as a result of the Allied blockage and lack of funds. Herbert Hoover, a member of the Supreme Economic Council set up by the Allied governments to handle reconstruction, established the American Relief Administration (ARA), which disposed of surplus American food in central Europe and Russia. Hoover took a different line from President Wilson, stressing that resolving the problems of hunger and unemployment were crucial for stability and that they "will not be cured at all by law or by legalistic processes."[16] Keynes's hostility to the Versailles settlement arose from the "hunger catastrophe" as well as from hostility to reparations. Starvation might, he pointed out, lead to helpless despair or to hysteria that could "submerge civilisation"—a point that he seems to have overlooked in 1943.[17] One solution was an organization to deal with global imbalances of food surpluses coexisting with famine. Fridtjof Nansen, the League's commissioner for refugees, pointed out in October 1921 that "Argentina is burning its grain surplus; America is letting its grain rot in silos; Canada has more than two billion tons of left over grain—and yet, in Russia, millions are dying of hunger." These concerns led the League to consider means of balancing the global supply of food, appropriating the techniques of international coordination that emerged during the war.[18]

A central element in this new understanding of the importance of food security and its wider links to agriculture and the world economy was nutritional science. Scientific approaches to hunger were changing from a thermodynamic model that treated food as a fuel for the human motor, based on measurements of the number of calories needed to sustain different forms of activity and work. An understanding of deficiency diseases started with studies in coercive conditions in "closed" communities of adult men in colonial prisons, asylums and work camps.[19] These findings were followed up in the metropolis in laboratory conditions, with a biochemical analysis of food quality and the discovery of "accessory food factors," or vitamins, and their role in deficiency diseases.[20] One of the central figures was Elmer McCollum, an American scientist who studied the impact of diets on rats, leading to the discovery of vitamin A in 1913 and vitamin B in 1915. He worked with Hoover and the ARA and went on to develop international standards for measuring vitamins, minerals, and amino acids.[21] Subsequently, Hazel Stiebeling, head of food economics at the US Department of Agriculture from 1930, produced quantitative dietary allowances of minerals and vitamins; she served as an American delegate to the League of Nations committees on food and nutrition.[22] Similar work was carried out in London at the Lister Institute of Preventive Medicine, where Harriette Chick was a member of the scientific staff from 1905. She was appointed secretary of the Accessory Food Factors Committee of the Medical Research Council in 1918, which sent her to Vienna to work on deficiency diseases during the hunger catastrophe. She became the head of a new division of nutrition at the Lister Institute and was secretary of the League of Nations committee on the physiological bases of nutrition between 1934 and 1937.[23]

The most important scientist in terms of impact on public policy was John Boyd Orr,[24] director of the Rowett Institute set up by the University of Aberdeen and the North of Scotland College of Agriculture. When Orr returned from war service in 1919, he developed the institute on more ambitious lines, moving from an initial focus on the nutrition of farm animals to human populations. His findings on the value of milk in the health and growth of children led the undersecretary of state for Scotland, Walter Elliot—a medically trained politician who continued to research at the Rowett Institute— to provide milk for schoolchildren. In 1925, heavy losses of livestock in South Africa and Kenya led the British government to appoint a committee on mineral deficiency of pastures, with Orr as the chief scientist. During his work in Kenya, he collaborated with the head of the medical department in analyzing the diets of two neighboring tribes. They found that the Maasai were healthier and stronger, with a diet of meat and dairy products; the Kikuyu, with their vegetarian diet, were less sturdy.[25]

This work on African nutrition led to a new committee to consider the dietary determinants of health and physique within Britain, and it reported in 1931. Orr's advocacy of a national food policy to raise the level of British health and nutrition was supported by Elliot, who was minister of agriculture from 1932 to 1936, and the leading civil servant in the department, E. H. M. Lloyd, who worked on the regulation of food supplies during the war and joined the League's economic and financial section between 1919 and 1921 before returning to the British civil service, where he advocated organized capitalism and internationalism to prevent price fluctuations and developed policy on food consumption and nutrition. Orr's research led to *Food, Health and Income: Report of a Survey of Adequacy of Diet in Relation to Income* (1936). He used biochemical understanding of the intake needed for health, drawing on the work of Stiebeling, and linked the data with social surveys of family budgets and diet at different income levels. He found that an adequate diet was achieved only by the upper 50 percent of incomes in Britain, with 4.5 million people deficient in every constituent and a further 9 million in all minerals and vitamins. Diet had a major influence on health, and he felt that the lesson should be applied so that "every member of the community may have a diet adequate for perfect health." The study raised major political issues, including agricultural protection during the Depression. As Orr remarked, "Everyone is agreed that, while it is economically desirable to make agriculture prosperous, it is equally desirable to ensure that the food supply of the nation is sufficient for health, and is available at a price within the reach of the poorest." The suggestion that workers in receipt of public relief were unable to maintain health caused outrage at the Ministry of Health, and the government refused to publish the report.[26]

Orr's findings were closely connected with the growing interest in nutrition in the empire and in the League of Nations. Earlier work on prison diets was taken further by Robert McCarrison, who used laboratory rats to show that a Sikh diet created healthy specimens, unlike a Bengali diet that meant a loss of vitality. He also found that a British working-class diet produced rats that were stunted, poorly proportioned, prone to pulmonary and gastrointestinal diseases, and unhappy in living together. His work at the Pasteur Institute of India at Coonoor on beriberi—a deficiency disease caused by a lack of vitamin B1—showed a link with consumption of mill-polished rice, which removed the husk from the grain. His research was expanded in 1925 as the Deficiency Disease Enquiry. McCarrison presented a memorandum on malnutrition to the Royal Commission on Agriculture in India, stressing that "of all the disabilities from which the masses in India suffer, malnutrition is perhaps the chief." Endemic and epidemic diseases killed thousands, but "malnutrition maims its millions, and is the means whereby the soil of the human body is made ready for the rank growth of the pathogenic agents of many of those diseases which afflict the Indian people." As he explained to the commission, malnutrition meant "the impairment of the normal physiological processes of the body consequent on the use of a food which is deficient in quality although it may be abundant in quantity."[27]

In 1935, McCarrison was succeeded as director of the Nutrition Research Laboratories, as the Coonoor institute had been renamed, by Wallace Aykroyd. He had worked on deficiency diseases at the Lister Institute, and from 1931 to 1935 carried out studies for the League of Nations on the impact of mass unemployment on public health, on malnutrition in the rural economy of Romania, and on a schedule of nutritional standards. At Coonoor, he brought these wider concerns to bear, moving away from studies of the diet of male prisoners to groups of the population, such as women, children, and workers in plantations and factories, analyzing their diets and stressing that poverty rather than culture or religion was the determinant of malnutrition. In his view, malnutrition halted colonial economic development. Aykroyd went on to represent India at Hot Springs, and to serve as a member of the commission to study the Bengal famine in 1944.[28]

This work at Coonoor informed nationalist critiques of British rule in India. Nagendranath Gangulee, professor of agriculture and social economics at the University of Calcutta and a member of the Royal Commission on Agriculture in India, was impressed by McCarrison's work, and in 1939 he published *Health and Nutrition in India* with a foreword by Orr and a dedication to Jawaharlal Nehru, the leader of the Congress Party. The book offered a dietary critique of colonial neglect, feudalism, and capitalism, rejecting Malthusianism for the "rational reconstruction" of agriculture. Analysis of deficiency disease could therefore lead to state planning as advocated by Nehru, who argued that "The prevalent under-nutrition and malnutrition shall be tackled by systematic crop planning." But it could also lead in a different direction. Gandhi had personal contacts with McCarrison and Aykroyd but was suspicious of their stress on meat and milk. Instead, he wished to create a new Indian diet, with a social obligation by those who were better off for those who were starving. He drew on Aykroyd's realization that the value of food given by the market was not the same as nutritional value, to argue against the consumption of commercially milled rice that led to deficiency diseases and undermined village communities. He favored communal preparation and cooking of food that preserved nutrients and gave employment, prioritizing the village as a site of ethical production and consumption.[29]

The analysis of nutrition and deficiency diseases therefore linked a concern for domestic welfare with the plight of the imperial population. Moreover, the new concern for nutrition was linked with proposals to bring about a radical change in world agriculture as a way of solving the problems of depression and instability, both in primary producing and in advanced industrial economies. This approach moved beyond a concern for monetary stability and multilateral trade, which were seen as secondary phenomena of less importance than removing economic instability caused by low primary-product prices and ensuring that trade led to prosperity rather than exploitation.

CREATING A PROSPEROUS WORLD ECONOMY

The connection between nutrition and establishing a prosperous world economy was drawn by two Australians: the former prime minister, Stanley Melbourne Bruce, and Frank McDougall, a fruit farmer who became Bruce's confidante, representing Australia in London and at international conferences. Both men started out as advocates of imperial economic integration based on large-scale loan-financed investment to attract more population to Australia in order to develop markets—the policy of men, money, and markets.[30] This program collapsed with the Depression in the 1930s, and they moved to a nutritionist approach that owed much to Orr and went beyond him. They played a major role at the League of Nations, which they turned into a platform for their policies: Bruce represented Australia in the League's Assembly from 1932, becoming president in 1936; McDougall was the Australian delegate to the Economic Committee of the Economic and Financial Organization from 1927 and substitute delegate to the Assembly. The provision of better food to remove deficiency diseases was linked to the restructuring of agriculture across the world in order to solve the problems of economic depression in the food-exporting countries, thereby allowing them to buy more industrial goods.

The achievement of McDougall and Bruce was to link nutritional science with an analysis of agriculture, poverty, and economic policy. In 1935, Bruce argued at the Assembly of the League that health and agriculture should be combined, and that nutrition was a "lever to lift agriculture and eventually the whole world economy out of depression." In particular, he referred to a report for the League's Health Committee on "nutrition and public health," which was written by Aykroyd and Étienne Burnet, a French bacteriologist who worked for the Health Committee between 1928 and 1936, and drew on the scientific work of Stiebling and McCollum.[31] Above all, McDougall presented his views in a series of memoranda that shaped the League's policy. He argued that restrictive policies on food imports led to high prices, shielding inefficient producers at the expense of the consumer and reducing the income of exporters by limiting markets. What was needed was a nutritional policy that would both end malnutrition and restore trade.

McDougall divided food into two categories. The first category was "protective foods," such as eggs, vegetables, fruit, dairy products, and meat, that contained vitamins and minerals. Many people suffered from malnutrition because they did not eat enough of these foods. The second category comprised "energy foods" that produced calories, such as wheat. In McDougall's view, the failure to consume sufficient protective foods was partly the result of shielding European farmers from imports of cheap energy foods, so that European consumers had less money to buy preventive foods. The problem could be solved if small farmers in Europe concentrated on growing protective foods, thus allowing efficient, low-cost, large-scale exporters (such as Australia) to supply energy foods, which would give them income to buy manufactures. By such means, the problem of overproduction and malnutrition could be resolved, and at the same time political stability would be reestablished by raising the standard of living. Further, nutrition should be linked with international action on pay and conditions by the International Labour Organization, which produced its own report titled *Workers' Nutrition and Social Policy* in 1936, and set up a permanent agricultural committee comprising workers, employers, experts, and international institutions. In addition, nutrition should be linked with redistributive national social policies on pensions, family allowances, and distribution of food to the poorest. The adoption of nutrition policies by advanced countries "could bring about an expanding need for the products of international trade in which all countries may find full outlets for their energies and full employment for their peoples." These methods would mainly help industrial countries; it was also vital to assist peasants in central and eastern Europe, where low productivity led to severe poverty, bare subsistence, and an inability to buy industrial goods. Better credit and cooperatives were needed to improve agriculture, thereby creating purchasing power that would in turn encourage industry. McDougall gave priority to these policies as the basis for economic recovery and stability. The agreement on currency alignment between Britain, France, and the United States in 1936 and the efforts of Cordell Hull on trade agreements were welcome, but he insisted that progress would only be possible if approached from the direction of the standard of living.[32]

Such an approach was not welcomed by the International Institute of Agriculture, which had been established in Rome in 1905. The IIA was increasingly influenced by fascism, and it represented European farmers who favored protection over the interests of consumers. Nevertheless, the IIA did have some sensible, pragmatic criticisms of McDougall's approach. Augé-Laribé, a French delegate to the IIA, felt that McDougall failed to realize that changes in diet were slow and that major adjustments to agricultural output would be complicated and expensive. Would new food habits really be more profitable for farmers? And was the optimal diet clearly defined? He feared that McDougall was guilty of bad faith: Europe would be left with perishable foods so that Australia and other countries would have a market for energy foods. His criticism had some force on practical grounds but also reflected an ideological split over policy. The fascist government in Italy was engaged in a "battle for wheat" to make the country self-sufficient, which ran directly counter to McDougall's policy of importing energy foods. Fascism rested on national regeneration, with employers coming together with nonunionized workers in corporations that would run the economy in the interests of the nation and under the guidance of the state.[33] This difference of approach surfaced within the League when it entered into an agreement to provide advice to China in 1931. The League's experts saw rural cooperation as a solution to peasant backwardness rather than Soviet collectivization. British officials with experience in India argued that cooperatives should consist of small farmers coming together to achieve more than they could as individuals. By contrast, Carlo Dragoni, the fascist head of the IIA, wanted local cooperatives to form part of a hierarchy of associations leading up to national bodies that would bring together the interests of farmers, workers, and capitalists in a corporatist system, working with the state.[34] The solution to the problems of peasant agriculture were therefore contested within the League.

The demand for better nutrition could rise above these ideological divides, and the League responded to Bruce's call to marry health and agriculture by passing a resolution that urged "Governments to examine the practical means of securing better nutrition." A mixed committee of the IIA, ILO, and Health Committee was established in 1936 to report on the relation of nutrition to health, agriculture, and economic policy, and it received a report from a technical commission on the physiological bases of nutrition. The fascist approach was soon rejected, for the League imposed sanctions on Italy in 1937 in response to the invasion of Abyssinia, and Mussolini withdrew from the organization. As the world drifted toward conflict, the League needed to find a new purpose and to come up with policies to prevent war and re-create international harmony. Here was the attraction of "economic appeasement" advocated by McDougall in 1937. He was a vocal member and main author of the report that argued for a restructuring of agriculture to specialize in energy or protective foods, assisted by better credit and cooperatives, improved distribution and marketing, and redistributive social policies, with direct assistance to supplement diets, especially in childhood through school milk and meals. Malnutrition was linked with agricultural depression:

> Nutrition policy . . . must be directed towards achieving two distinct, though mutually dependent, aims. Its primary concern is with consumption: with bringing the foods which modern physiology has shown to be essential for health and physical development within the reach of all sections of the community. But, in addition, it must also concern itself with supply. Changes in demand involve changes in supply; increased demand, increased supply.[35]

Alexander Loveday, a senior official at the League, realized that the nutrition campaign led to an intellectual shift "on account of the influence it is likely to have on our whole economic outlook. Ever since the time of Adam Smith economic thought has centred around the art of production or the conditions of citizens as producers. The nutrition movement reflects the first serious endeavour, certainly on an international scale, to consider the economics not of production but of consumption."[36]

The United States was not a member of the League and did not play a role in these debates. However, the political importance of domestic agriculture, and its experience of deep depression, meant that policies were emerging in the United States that complemented the approach of McDougall, Bruce, and Orr. The central player was Henry Wallace, secretary of agriculture from 1933 to 1940 and vice president from 1941 to 1945. Unlike Cordell Hull's emphasis on multilateral trade as the foundation for recovery, or the secretary of the Treasury Henry Morgenthau's emphasis on monetary stability, Wallace gave priority to a radical program of full employment. To Wallace, the Bretton Woods scheme was only part—and not the most important part—of the program for postwar recovery.

AGRICULTURAL POLICIES IN THE UNITED STATES

In the United States, Wallace brought together the twin concerns for nutrition and markets for agricultural commodities. He had long advocated the idea of an "ever normal granary" to store basic commodities to balance demand and supply and create price stability. The Agricultural Adjustment

Act, 1933, introduced voluntary production controls to reduce output, with compensation for lost production. In addition, farmers were given "non-recourse" loans on the security of crops stored with the Commodity Credit Corporation. The farmer forfeited the commodities and kept the loan if the price fell below the support level, or reclaimed the crops for sale if the price rose. The programs were financed by a "processing tax" which was declared unconstitutional in 1936, but a new Agricultural Adjustment Act in 1938 introduced mandatory output controls and payments for wheat, corn, and cotton, with government storage of surplus crops. This attempt to raise prices benefited farmers, but Wallace was also concerned with distributing food to the poor. His advisers, Mordecai Ezekiel and Paul Appleby, made him realize that agricultural prosperity rested on industrial production, employment, and consumption. In May 1939, he introduced food stamps as a way of providing surplus food to the unemployed and workers on relief, thus helping both poor consumers and farmers.[37]

In 1941, Wallace pressed for the extension of the ever-normal granary to deal with conditions after the war. He realized that the problems faced by producers of primary products between the wars were a major source of instability, for excess production led to lower prices and a lack of purchasing power, which hit everyone. Hence a requirement after the war was "an economic arrangement to protect the raw-material producers of the world from such violent fluctuation in income as took place after World War I." Wallace hoped that the ever-normal granary could be extended to the world "with export quotas and with prices stabilized at a point to be fair to producers and consumers." Wallace also looked to an improvement in nutritional standards through food stamps, school meals, low-cost milk, and subsidies. He wanted an increase in the production of dairy products, poultry, meat, fruit, and vegetables, and a shift in European production away from wheat, which would help staple-producing countries elsewhere in the world—a direct reference to the ideas of McDougall and the League. Wallace linked this policy with the creation of "an economy of abundance" through full employment, lower trade barriers, productive investment, reduction of income inequality, and the application of technology to undeveloped areas.[38]

The British were willing to enter into discussions with the Americans in 1941 on the disposal of surpluses, for "If we should succeed in preventing sharp fluctuations in the prices of the chief primary materials, we should have gone a long way towards smoothing out the cyclical depressions of trade in manufacturing countries."[39] Keynes hoped that it would be possible to stabilize the price of internationally traded raw materials and even to create an international holding cartel based on the "ever normal granary," with international cooperation to distribute surpluses to deal with postwar relief in Europe.[40] Keynes turned to the issue as part of his initial thoughts on financial policy, producing a memorandum early in 1942 on international controls of buffer stocks to achieve "the internationalisation of Vice-President Wallace's 'ever-normal granary.'" He rejected restrictions on output and higher prices favored by producers, which would depress demand, freeze the existing distribution of production, and misallocate resources. Of course, many primary producers took a different line and wanted higher prices for their commodities through controls and quotas. Indeed, negotiation of an international wheat agreement in Washington, DC, in 1941 threatened to impose export quotas and to exclude low-cost producers.[41] Britain was a major importer of food and clearly did not want higher prices. Rather, Keynes's concern was to end "truly frightful *price* fluctuations" by holding stocks and keeping prices within a reasonable range around a basic price defined by the long-term equilibrium cost of the most efficient producer. The basic price would fall as production moved to more-efficient areas of the world and high-cost producers lost market share. "Thus we should aim at combining a short-period stabilisation of prices with a long-period price policy which balances supply and demand and allows a steady rate of expansion to the cheaper-cost producers." A version of Keynes's paper went to the British War Cabinet and was approved in May 1943 for use at Hot Springs and discussions with the US State Department.[42]

The idea for a conference on production and trade in food therefore arose from a combination of nutritional science in the metropole and colonies, from thinking in the League about the links between agriculture and depressions, the policies of Wallace in the United States, and proposals on buffer stocks. These strands came together in 1940 and 1941. In February 1940, McDougall sent a memorandum to Anthony Eden, the secretary of state for Dominion Affairs in the British government, arguing for reconstruction on the lines of the nutrition approach under the supervision of a World Organization for Economic and Social Affairs. Eden rejected the scheme, but the prime minister (Neville Chamberlain) was more sympathetic. In March 1941, Bruce approached the new American ambassador to London, John Winant, who was enthusiastic and passed the proposal to Roosevelt. McDougall was in Washington for the international wheat conference in July 1941, where he met Wallace and explained his thinking to Dean Acheson and Sumner Welles at the State Department and to the secretary of the Treasury Morgenthau.[43] McDougall's advocacy was reinforced by Orr, who visited America in 1942. By this time, Orr was arguing that the possibilities of increased production offered by science were limited in order to preserve monopoly capitalism, and he now pressed for fundamental change. He urged the creation of a National Food Board for Britain, with commodity boards for individual foodstuffs to ensure that supplies were sufficient for everyone at a guaranteed price. Still more ambitiously, he called for the establishment of world government and planning to provide everyone with an adequate diet for health.[44]

The discussions of a wheat agreement led to the creation of the International Wheat Council, and McDougall returned to Washington in 1942 as the Australian representative. Wallace and Welles asked him to convene an informal group of officials from the Departments of Agriculture and State, to include the US surgeon general Thomas Parran. McDougall and Parran were largely responsible for the "memorandum on a UN programme for freedom from want of food," which called for an expansive economy with full employment, better labor conditions, and social security. They argued that better nutrition was not only an end in itself but would also prevent the resurgence of economic nationalism. The efficient production of protective and energy foods should be overseen by a new International Agricultural Authority. McDougall stressed that agriculture was an ideal issue for the United Nations, giving the new body something to do on a topic that was both important and noncontroversial.[45]

Such was the background to the conference at Hot Springs, which pulled together discussions of agriculture in the less-developed countries, the plight of primary producing countries, the Depression faced by American farmers, the concern over malnutrition, the development of domestic welfare policies, and the reshaping of world agricultural production. Despite McDougall's claim, these were controversial issues—not least given British interests in low prices as a major food importer, and the claim of food producers for higher prices. What would happen when the delegates assembled at Hot Springs?

THE HOT SPRINGS CONFERENCE

The conference at Hot Spring was a rehearsal for Bretton Woods—and not everything went according to plan. Both conferences were held at isolated resort hotels, which allowed the delegates to concentrate on the task at hand. But at Hot Springs, Roosevelt excluded the press and representatives of Congress, which undermined his wish to win over public opinion to the cause of internationalism. One Democratic senator expressed concern at the exclusion of the press, pointing out that "the American people want to know what is being done in the distribution and production of food during and after the war. No military secret is involved." The California State Assembly complained of "a breach of the American principle of freedom of the press, . . . a reversion to Star Chamber principles." Similarly, the Republican leader in the House argued that "This war is a people's war, and the peace must be a people's peace. The representatives of the Congress represent the people, and they should sit in at these . . . conferences." Paranoid members of Congress even feared that Roosevelt was becoming autocratic, and that the conference "was called primarily to begin the construction of the world super-state . . . along communistic lines." Eventually, Marvin Jones relaxed the ban on the press on his own initiative. A lesson was learned. As Walter Lippmann pointed out, it was impossible "to have a large mass meeting act as if it were a small executive committee," either in secret or in public. The answer was to have a small meeting in confidence to thrash out a deal prior to a large meeting that could be open to secure public consent. This was exactly what happened with the monetary talks, with a small, closed meeting in Atlantic City prior to the mass meeting at Bretton Woods with congressional representatives and a press presence.[46]

Although the Americans requested that Orr attend the Hot Springs conference as a British delegate, the British government refused for reasons that Orr understood: he could not represent his own government's preference for cheap imported food. Nevertheless, he was present in the form of the film *World of Plenty*—a powerful documentary made by Paul Rotha for the British Ministries of Food and Agriculture, which showed Americans the strictures of rationing, the virtues of vitamins, and the improved diet needed for health. It stressed the need to "win the other war" of freedom from want, providing food for everyone on the "new gold standard of health." Such an approach would also remove the glut of food that so badly affected farmers between the wars. The film urged the application of science to increase yields, particularly of protective foods, and the management of production, prices, and fair distribution on the lines developed during the war both nationally and internationally through the Combined Food Board. By such means, "every man, woman and child . . . shall have enough of the right kind of food to enable them to develop their full and inherited capacity for health and well-being." The delegates stood and cheered. It marked the integration of domestic rights and duties with an understanding of global needs, in what Frank Trentmann calls a "new symbiotic relationship between social citizenship and global coordination."[47]

The agenda for the conference was divided into four sections. The first section dealt with the character and extent of consumption deficiencies, the causes and consequences of malnutrition, and "reasonable national and international goals for improved consumption with sustained employment and expanded industrial activity." It pointed to the "widespread impairment of human efficiency" caused by malnutrition, and recommended national nutritional bodies to tackle these issues. The second section turned to the expansion of production and adaptation to consumption needs. The achievement of high nutritional standards meant not only the expansion of output but also a reorientation of agriculture to maintain soil fertility, reduce pests, and cope with drought. Above all, it meant a change in the composition of output by producing foods needed for better nutrition closer to the point of consumption, and allowing other areas to produce energy foods. Agricultural production meant better provision of credit and might be encouraged by cooperatives and by changes in land tenure. The third section turned to distribution, considering the relation of national and international economic policies in expanding international trade, improving agricultural marketing, raising consumption by low-income groups, disposing of surpluses, and creating buffer stocks to ensure equitable prices. The final section dealt with proposals for carrying the work of the conference forward. The agenda for the conference clearly reflected the thinking of McDougall and the League.[48]

Much of the discussion at Hot Springs was idealistic and impractical, but there was one concrete issue that provoked deep disagreement: commodity policy. William Clayton at the US Department of State was skeptical about the British approach. His experience of falling prices as a cotton merchant led him to wonder how a decision would be reached on the basic price for a commodity. In any case, he believed that the main cause of booms and slumps was the misuse of credit. Buffer stocks were irrelevant and "underrated the constructive aspect of private trade on the commodity exchanges in regulating market forces." Paul Appleby at the US Department of Agriculture took a different approach from Keynes, arguing for the regulation of production in order to raise the price of agricultural products and close the gap between the money incomes of farmers and industry. It was no wonder that Lionel Robbins, a British delegate at Bretton Woods, commented that it was easy to agree that people should have more food and that peace should be assured—but not to agree on practical issues such as buffer stocks.[49] Unsurprisingly, the conference declaration fell back on high-minded generalities.

The declaration made a link with Roosevelt's "four freedoms" speech of January 1941 and the Atlantic Charter by stressing the need after the war "to win and maintain freedom from fear and freedom from want." The supply of food could be increased by using knowledge, but that was not enough: it was necessary to achieve an "economy of abundance."

> The first cause of hunger and malnutrition is poverty. It is useless to produce more food unless men and nations provide the markets to absorb it. There must be an expansion of the whole world economy to provide the purchasing power sufficient to maintain an adequate diet for all. With full employment in all countries, enlarged industrial production, the absence of exploitation, an increasing flow of trade within and between countries, an orderly management of domestic and international investment and currencies, and sustained internal and international economic equilibrium, the food which is produced can be made available to all people.

The primary responsibility for providing its people with food lay with each nation, which should take responsibility for attaining the physiological requirement of health through adequate social security, by making protective foods available free or at low prices, and by assisting groups such as pregnant women, nursing mothers, children, the aged, invalids, and the low paid. National action was not enough: it was necessary to have "concerted action among all like-minded nations to expand and improve production, to increase employment, to raise levels of consumption, and to establish greater freedom in international commerce." Above all, it was necessary to create international security by ending policies of aggression that led to an "uneconomic employment of human and material resources, the development of uneconomic industries, the imposition of barriers to international trade, the introduction of discriminatory trade practices, and the expenditure of huge sums on armaments." The conference therefore affirmed "the principle of mutual responsibility and coordinated action to establish such conditions of international security as will make possible an expanding and balanced world economy." This ambition entailed "full employment of human and material resources, based on sound social and economic policies" to increase production and purchasing power, linked with the "sound expansion of industry in undeveloped and other areas," which would stimulate purchasing power for agriculture. Barriers to the production, distribution, and consumption of food and other commodities should be reduced by removing tariffs and restrictions to trade and by controlling fluctuations in exchange rates by "the orderly management of currencies and exchange"—a nod to Hull's case for multilateral trade and the US Treasury's case for monetary policy. International commodity arrangements should promote the expansion of an orderly world economy. Robbins was dismissive of these grand statements, remarking that "it is very easy to be friendly in a luxury hotel with all expenses paid and no binding commitments on the agenda."[50] Essentially, the declaration was a statement of McDougall's approach—allied with the growing interest in full employment, which formed another element of the thinking of the Australians and Wallace that was presented at the ILO conference in Philadelphia in 1944. Would the declaration lead to any practical outcome?

CREATING THE FOOD AND AGRICULTURE ORGANIZATION

Although the conference agreed to create a permanent body for food and agriculture, there was disagreement on its character. McDougall wanted a strong organization that would increase production and stabilize prices in line with Australia's international economic policy of full employment. Latin American countries, especially Argentina and Brazil, took the same approach. By contrast, the United States preferred a weak consultative body. The interim commission, with McDougall as a member, decided to limit itself to collecting statistics, promoting research, and providing technical assistance. Orr was frustrated by this breach of the Atlantic Charter's promise of "freedom from want for all men in all lands." In his view, "the old men had crept back into power determined to resist any economic change which threatened their financial interests."[51] Would the new permanent organization be able to take a wider role, alongside the new International Monetary Fund and International Bank of Reconstruction and Development, which had recently been created at Bretton Woods?

In 1945, a conference was held in Quebec to establish the Food and Agriculture Organization, and Orr was invited to join the British delegation. He was reluctant, fearing that the meeting would be futile given that the Labour government opposed any executive power for the FAO. Orr pressed for a more active policy and, at the behest of McDougall, reluctantly accepted the post of director general of the FAO, where he was joined by other advocates of a nutritional approach, such as Lloyd and Aykroyd.[52] Would they be able to press their more radical approach to postwar reconstruction? Orr was fatalistic, pointing out that what seemed "like a victorious end to the long struggle for international cooperation in a food policy" was in reality "a sterile victory because the organisation had neither the authority nor the funds to initiate a policy which would achieve the results hoped for." Orr appointed McDougall as assistant director and his prospective successor and pressed for a change in the constitution of the FAO to give it real power. He secured an International Emergency Food Council to respond to the postwar crisis, but his longer-term ambition was a World Food Board to purchase and stockpile surplus commodities when they were cheap, so helping to stabilize prices, with the surplus allocated to poor countries. A conference was called in Copenhagen in September 1946 to consider the issue.[53] The outlook was not propitious.

In the United States, Wallace's radical policies were in retreat, and the State Department feared that a World Food Board would raise prices at the expense of consumers, thus attracting more capital and labor into agriculture, leading to more output, including by less-efficient producers. The result would be the accumulation of larger stocks that would be sold to the board. Orr's plan simply allowed any surplus to be swallowed by the "bottomless pit of oriental hunger" so long as money was available. It also threatened market prices and private trading, handing funds to an international agency over which national governments had little control. The US Department of State was more interested in establishing an International Trade Organization and did not welcome Orr's initiative. He wanted food to be an exception to the ITO's drive for free, open markets, because, in his view, it was a public good like clean water. The Australians also preferred an activist FAO to the ITO, for it "would place emphasis on increasing consumption as objective and means to achieve stability." In their view, policies on food and full employment of the resources of the world were preconditions for accepting the Bretton Woods institutions. This approach was not welcomed by the British government, which feared higher prices for food imports and a heavy bill for distributing food to poorer countries. The Labour government instead emphasized the need for full employment in industrial countries to ensure that there was a demand for primary products. Although the leader of the American delegation, Norris Dodd, undersecretary of agriculture, was told to oppose Orr's scheme at Copenhagen, he realized that American farmers would benefit from disposal of their surpluses. He therefore proposed that a commission be set up to devise a program to stabilize agricultural prices "at levels which will be fair to producers and consumers and which will bring about the improvement of nutrition throughout the world." Against British opposition, the conference approved the principle of a World Food Board and appointed a commission under the chairmanship of Bruce. It seemed that the radical schemes of McDougall and Orr had triumphed against the odds.[54]

The victory was hollow. Dodd was obliged to withdraw support, and the Bruce commission and plans for a more ambitious policy came to nothing. Orr resigned from the FAO, complaining that America had turned its back on Roosevelt's plans at the Hot Springs conference as surely as it had turned its back on Wilson's plans for the League of Nations.[55] Orr's plans were blocked by divisions with other international organizations, by British concern about prices, and by American fears that it would have to pay. Plans were scaled back, and in the 1950s, the FAO moved to short-term food aid and technical assistance.[56]

CONCLUSION

On one level, the debate over food, nutrition, and agriculture came to nothing, forming no more than a footnote to the success of the Bretton Woods institutions of the IMF and IBRD, or the reduction of trade barriers through the General Agreement on Tariffs and Trade. Nevertheless, it would be wrong to dismiss these debates, for they show that the emphasis on monetary and tariff policy was contested by those who saw a neglect of the needs of a large part of the world's population. Hull's stress on multilateral trade and Morgenthau's on currency stability were challenged within the American administration by Wallace, both from a concern for domestic agriculture and a more ambitious program of full employment. The approaches of Hull and Morgenthau were also challenged by the proposals at the League of Nations for a reconstruction of world agriculture and nutrition that connected with the needs of primary producing and underdeveloped countries. Bretton Woods should not be taken in isolation, for it was only one part of a highly contested vision of the postwar international economic order.

Although the FAO proved a disappointment to Orr and McDougall, their criticism of the IMF and IBRD as agencies of advanced industrial countries did not disappear. Of course, issues of economic development were not entirely absent at Bretton Woods, and some of the delegates tried to keep these wider concerns on the agenda—not least the Australians, with their policy of full employment that was closely linked with food and nutrition.[57] The underdeveloped or primary producing countries had little practical success at Bretton Woods, but they returned to the offensive at the international conference to negotiate a charter of the ITO at Geneva in 1947 and Havana in 1947–1948. The Australians renewed their case for full employment of the resources of the world, which drew on the thinking of McDougall and Bruce; and the Indian and Latin American delegations demanded policies for economic development. Concessions made by the Americans at Havana to secure support for the charter led to a loss of support on Capitol Hill, so that the charter was not ratified and the ITO failed. In this sense, the wider claims of the primary producers and less-developed economies shaped the postwar institutions—and their claims for a more radical approach returned in the context of decolonization and the Cold War through the Bandung Declaration of 1955 and the creation of the United Nations Conference on Trade and Development in 1964, which developed a critique of the Bretton Woods institutions as narrow expressions of the interests of advanced industrial countries. The basic assumption of UNCTAD was that the needs of less-developed countries could only be met by a change in the terms of trade between industrial and primary products—a stress on the structure of world trade, rather than stable exchanges and open markets, which did nothing to overturn past experiences of exploitation. These wider debates challenged the legitimacy of the Bretton Woods institutions, and the concerns of Orr and others for malnutrition and poverty continue to resonate.

Notes

1. "The Acting Secretary of State (Welles) to the Chargé in the United Kingdom (Matthews)," in *Foreign Relations of the United States: Diplomatic Papers* [hereafter FRUS], 1943, General, vol. 1, doc. 729, Washington, March 8, 1943, https://history.state.gov/historicaldocuments/frus1943v01/d729, accessed July 4, 2016.

2. As reported by Ernest F. Penrose, *Economic Planning for the Peace* (Princeton, NJ: Princeton University Press, 1953), 120.

3. Amartya Sen, *Poverty and Famine: An Essay on Entitlement and Deprivation* (Oxford: Clarendon Press, 1981), chap. 6.

4. Geoffrey H. Bourne, *Starvation in Europe* (London: George Allen and Unwin, 1943), 35, 129–31; see also Ruth Jachertz and Alexander Nützenadel, "Coping with Hunger? Visions of a Global Food System, 1930–1960," *Journal of Global History* 6 (2011): 105–7.

5. Adam Tooze, *The Wages of Destruction: The Making and Breaking of the Nazi Economy* (London: Allen Lane, 2006), 476–85, 538–49.

6. For an overview, see Lizzie Collingham, *The Taste of War: World War Two and the Battle for Food* (London: Allen Lane, 2011).

7. S. N. Broadberry, *The Productivity Race: British Manufacturing in International Perspective, 1850–1990* (Cambridge: Cambridge University Press, 1997), table 5.1 (p. 64).

8. Historical Statistics of the United States, Millennial Edition Online, table Da15.

9. Michael Tracy, *Government and Agriculture in Western Europe, 1880–1988*, 3rd ed. (Hemel Hempstead, UK: Harvester Wheatsheaf, 1988).

10. Australian Government, Department of Foreign Affairs and Trade, "Australia's Trade since Federation," https://dfat.gov.au/about-us/publications/Documents/australias-trade-since-federation.pdf, accessed December 19, 2017; B. R. Mitchell, with the collaboration of Phyllis Deane, *Abstract of British Historical Statistics* (Cambridge: Cambridge University Press, 1962), Prices 13C, p. 496.

11. P. N. Rosenstein-Rodan, "Problems of Industrialisation of Eastern and South-Eastern Europe," *Economic Journal* 53 (1943): 202–11; "The Internal Development of Economically Backward Areas," *International Affairs* 20 (1944): 157–65.

12. Franklin D. Roosevelt, "Statement on the Atlantic Charter Meeting with Prime Minister Churchill," August 14, 1941, online at *The American Presidency Project*, by John Woolley and Gerhard Peters, http://www.presidency.ucsb.edu/ws/?pid=16154, accessed July 4, 2016.

13. Craig Alan Wilson, "Rehearsal for a United Nations: The Hot Springs Conference," *Diplomatic History* 4 (1980): 265, 267.

14. Ibid., 266.

15. Frank Trentmann, *Free Trade Nation: Commerce, Consumption and Civil Society in Britain* (Oxford: Oxford University Press, 2008), chap. 5.

16. Nick Cullather, "The Foreign Policy of the Calorie," *American Historical Review* 112 (2007): 350.

17. John Maynard Keynes, *The Economic Consequences of the Peace* (London: Macmillan, 1919), 212–16.

18. Patricia Clavin, "The Austrian Hunger Crisis and the Genesis of International Organization after the First World War," *International Affairs* 90 (2014): 265–78; Jachertz and Nützenadel, "Coping with Hunger?," 102–3; Frank Trentmann, "Coping with Shortage: The Problem of Food Security and Global Visions of Coordination, c. 1890s–1950," in *Food and Conflict in Europe in the Age of the Two World Wars*, ed. Frank Trentmann and Flemming Just (Basingstoke, UK: Palgrave Macmillan, 2006), 14, 27–28.

19. Dana Simmons, "Starvation Science: From Colonies to Metropolis," in *Food and Globalisation: Consumption, Markets and Politics in the Modern World*, ed. Alexander Nützenadel and Frank Trentmann (Oxford and New York: Berg, 2008), 173–79.

20. Cullather, "Foreign Policy of the Calorie," 338–40, 351–52, 355, 361–62; David F. Smith, "Nutrition Science and the Two World Wars," in *Nutrition in Britain: Science, Scientists and Politics in the Twentieth Century*, ed. David F. Smith (London and New York: Routledge, 1997), 153.

21. Cullather, "Foreign Policy of the Calorie," 354; Kenneth J. Carpenter, "The Nobel Prize and the Discovery of Vitamins," https://www.nobelprize.org/prizes/themes/the-nobel-prize-and-the-discovery-of-vitamins-2, accessed August 31, 2018.

22. Hazel K. Stiebeling, "Food Budgets for Nutrition and Production Programs," US Department of Agriculture Miscellaneous Publication no. 183, December 1933; Alfred E. Harper, "Contributions of Women Scientists in the US to the Development of Recommended Dietary Allowances," *Journal of Nutrition* 133 (2003): 3699; Alfred Harper, "Recommended Dietary Allowances and Dietary Guidance," in *Cambridge World History of Food*, vol. 2, ed. Kenneth F. Kiple and Kriemhild Coneè Ornelas (Cambridge: Cambridge University, 2008), 1610.

23. H. M. Sinclair, "Chick, Dame Harriette (1875–1977)," rev. by David F. Smith, in *Oxford Dictionary of National Biography* (Oxford: Oxford University Press, 2004), online ed., January 2008, http://www.oxforddnb.com/view/article/30924, accessed July 4, 2016.

24. K. L. Blaxter, "Orr, John Boyd, Baron Boyd Orr (1880–1971)," rev. by Michael Bevan, in *Oxford Dictionary of National Biography*, online ed., January 2008, http://www.oxforddnb.com/view/article/31519, accessed July 5, 2016.

25. Michael Worboys, "The Discovery of Colonial Malnutrition Between the Wars," in *Imperial Medicine and Indigenous Societies*, ed. David Arnold (Manchester, UK: Manchester University Press, 1988), 210–12; Gordon F. Millar, "Elliot, Walter Elliot (1888–1958)," in *Oxford Dictionary of National Biography*, online ed. January 2011, http://www.oxforddnb.com/view/article.33003, accessed July 21, 2016.

26. Frank Trentmann, "Lloyd, Edward Mayow Hastings (1889–1968)," *Oxford Dictionary of National Biography*, online ed., http://www.oxforddnb.com/view/article/34566, accessed July 15, 2016; John Boyd

Orr, *Food, Health and Income: Report of a Survey of Adequacy of Diet in Relation to Income* (London: Macmillan, 1936); Collingham, *Taste of War*, 350–53; James Vernon, *Hunger: A Modern History* (Cambridge, MA: Belknap Press of Harvard University Press, 2007), 124–39; Simmons, "Starvation Science," 181; Charles Webster, "Healthy or Hungry Thirties?," *History Workshop Journal* 13 (1982): 110–29; Jachertz and Nützenadel, "Coping with Hunger?," 104.

27. Vernon, *Hunger*, 106; David Arnold, "The 'Discovery' of Malnutrition and Diet in Colonial India," *Indian Economic and Social History* Review 31 (1994): 11–19; *Report of the Royal Commission on Agriculture in India*, Parliamentary Papers (PP) 1928, vol. VIII, 74, 656; "Memorandum on Malnutrition as a Cause of Physical Inefficiency and Ill-Health among the Races of India," in *Royal Commission on Agriculture in India*, vol. 1, pt. 2: *Evidence of Officers Serving under the Government of India* (Calcutta: Government of India Central Publication Branch, 1927), 95–116; Robert McCarrison, *Nutrition and National Health, Being the Cantor Lectures Delivered Before the Royal Society of Arts, 1936* (London: Faber and Faber, 1944); Worboys, "Discovery of Colonial Malnutrition," 213–14.

28. Patricia Clavin, *Securing the World Economy: The Reinvention of the League of Nations, 1920–1946* (Oxford: Oxford University Press, 2013), 165; Arnold, "'Discovery,'" 12–19; Kenneth J. Carpenter, "The Work of Wallace Aykroyd: International Nutritionist and Author," *Journal of Nutrition* 137 (2007): 873–78.

29. Arnold, "'Discovery,'" 22–25; Vernon, *Hunger*, 113–15, 144; Sunil Amrith, "Food and Welfare in India c. 1900–1950," *Comparative Studies in Society and History* 50 (2008): 1010–35; M. K. Gandhi, *Diet and Diet Reform* (Ahmedabad, India: Narajivan, 1949), repr. of his 1934 essay "Polished v. Unpolished." Gandhi also reported on the League's report on the physiological bases of nutrition in 1936: see Alison Bashford, *Global Population: History, Geopolitics, and Life on Earth* (New York: Columbia University Press, 2014), 413, 416.

30. Sean Turnell, "F. L. McDougall: Éminence Grise of Australia Economic Diplomacy," *Australian Economic History Review* 40 (2000): 52–57; John B. O'Brien, "F. L. McDougall and the Origins of the Food and Agricultural Organisation," *Australian Journal of Politics and History* 46 (2000): 165–66; F. L. McDougall, *Sheltered Markets: A Study in the Value of Empire Trade* (London: J. Murray, 1925).

31. Étienne Burnet (1873–1960), available at https://webext.pasteur.fr/archives/e_buro.html, accessed July 15, 2016; W. R. Aykroyd and Étienne Burnet, "Nutrition and Public Health," League of Nations, *Quarterly Bulletin of the Health Organisation* 4 (1935): 326–474; League of Nations, Health Organisation, *Report on the Physiological Bases of Nutrition by the Technical Commission Appointed by the Health Committee* (Geneva: League of Nations, 1935); R. Passmore, "Wallace Ruddell Aykroyd," *British Journal of Nutrition* 43 (1980): 246; Clavin, *Securing*, 171; Turnell, "F. L. McDougall: Éminence Grise," 51–70; O'Brien, "F. L. McDougall and the Origins of the Food and Agricultural Organisation," 169–70; speech by S. M. Bruce to Assembly of League of Nations, September 11, 1935, repr. in *The McDougall Memoranda: Some Documents Relating to the Origins of the Food and Agriculture Organisation and the Contribution Made by Frank L. McDougall* (Rome: FAO, 1956), 18–24, available at http://www.fao.org/fileadmin/templates/library/docs/mcdougall _memoranda.pdf, accessed July 21, 2016; Heather Radi, "Bruce, Stanley Melbourne (1883–1967)," in *Australian Dictionary of Biography*, National Centre of Biography, Australian National University, available at http://adb.anu.edu.au/biography/bruce-stanley-melbourne-5400/text9147, accessed July 21, 2016.

32. F. L. McDougall, "Remarks on the Present Phase of International Economic Relations (September 1937). The Carrying-Out of the Programme of the Tripartite Declaration of September 26th 1936. Report to the Council by the Economic Committee, 46th Session–Geneva, September 6th–10th 1937, Annex: Economic Appeasement, Memorandum by F. L. McDougall," *League of Nations Official Journal*, 98th and 99th Council Sessions, December 1937, Annex 1681, pp. 1222–29; F. L. McDougall, "The Agricultural and the Health Problems," in *McDougall Memoranda*, 2–17; League of Nations, *Nutrition: Final Report of the Mixed Committee of the League of Nations on the Relation of Nutrition to Health, Agriculture and Economic Policy* (Geneva: League of Nations, 1937); F. L. McDougall, *Food and Welfare: League of Nations' Studies of Nutrition and National Economic Policy* (Geneva: Geneva Research Centre, 1938); Amalia Ribi Forclaz, "A New Target

for International Social Reform: The International Labour Organization and Working and Living Conditions in the Interwar Years," *Contemporary European History* 20, special issue 3 (2011): 324–26; Turnell, "F. L. McDougall," 52, 57–64; O'Brien, "F. L. McDougall," 170–73.

33. Clavin, *Securing*, 85, 167–68; Ribi Forclaz, "New Target," 319, 321; Luciano Tosi, "The League of Nations, the International Institute of Agriculture and the Food Question," in *For Peace in Europe: Institutions and Civil Society between the World Wars*, ed. Marta Petricioli and Donatella Cherubini (Brussels: Peter Lang, 2007), 117–38.

34. M. Zanasi, "Exporting Development: The League of Nations and Republican China," *Comparative Studies in Society and History* 49 (2007): 143–69; J. Osterhammel, "Technical Cooperation Between the League of Nations and China," *Modern Asian Studies* 13 (1979): 661–80.

35. League of Nations, *The Problem of Nutrition*, vol. 2: *Report on the Physiological Bases of Nutrition* (Geneva: Technical Commission of the Health Committee of the League of Nations, 1936); League of Nations, *Nutrition: Final Report*, 34.

36. Quoted in Jachertz and Nützenadel, "Coping with Hunger?," 105.

37. Richard S. Kirkendall, "Commentary on the Thought of Henry A. Wallace," *Agricultural History* 41 (1967): 139–42; and R. S. Kirkendall, *Social Scientists and Farm Politics in the Age of Roosevelt* (Columbia: University of Missouri Press, 1966); Stanley L. Engerman and Robert E. Gallman, eds., *The Cambridge Economic History of the United States*, vol. 3: *The Twentieth Century* (Cambridge: Cambridge University Press, 2000), 324, 732–35.

38. Henry A. Wallace, "Foundations of the Peace," repr. in *Democracy Reborn: Selected from Public Papers, Edited with an Introduction and Notes by Russell Lord* (New York: Reynal and Hitchcock, 1944), 181, 183–85, 187–89.

39. "The Director General, British Ministry of Economic Warfare (Leith-Ross), to the Assistant Secretary of State (Acheson)," *FRUS, 1941*, vol. 3, London, February 14, 1941, doc. 65, https://history.state.gov/historicaldocuments/frus1941v03/d65, accessed July 21, 2016.

40. Donald Moggridge, ed., *The Collected Writings of John Maynard Keynes*, vol. 27: *Activities, 1940–1946: Shaping the Post-War World: Employment and Commodities* (London: Macmillan for the Royal Economic Society, 1980), 3–41, 105–99; "The Assistant Secretary of State (Acheson) to the Director General, British Ministry of Economic Warfare (Leith-Ross), *FRUS, 1941*, vol. 3, Washington, July 22, 1941, doc. 70, https://history.state.gov/historicaldocuments/frus1941v03/d70, accessed July 6, 2016.

41. "War Cabinet: Official Committee on Export Surpluses, Draft International Wheat Agreement, Memorandum by JMK, 18 Aug 1941," in Moggridge, *Collected Writings of John Maynard Keynes*, vol. 27, 32–36; "The Wheat Conference: JMK to R Hopkins and H Wilson Smith, 3 Sept 1941," in Moggridge, *Collected Writings*, vol. 27, 37–40.

42. Robert Skidelsky, *John Maynard Keynes*, vol. 3: *Fighting for Britain, 1937–1946* (London: Macmillan, 2000), 234–36; Moggridge, *Collected Writings of John Maynard Keynes*, vol. 27, 105–11, on correspondence on the first drafts; "The International Control of Raw Materials," April 14, 1942, in Moggridge, *Collected Writings*, vol. 27, 112–33; "War Cabinet Committee on Reconstruction Problems: The International Regulation of Primary Products," in Moggridge, *Collected Writings*, vol. 27, 168–94; on the outcome, see p. 196.

43. Sean Turnell, "Monetary Reformers, Amateur Idealists and Keynesian Crusaders: Australian Economists' International Advocacy, 1925–1950," PhD thesis, Macquarie University, 1999, 64.

44. John Orr, *Fighting for What? To "Billy Boy" and All the Other Boys Killed in the War* (London: Macmillan, 1942), v, ix, 1–2, 22, 26, 30–41, 49–53, 58.

45. Turnell, "Monetary Reformers," 140–41.

46. Wilson, "Rehearsal," 268–74, 278, 280.

47. Collingham, *Taste of War*, 482–83, available at https://media.dlib.indiana.edu/media_objects/avalon:3497, accessed December 21, 2017. See also Timothy Boon, "Agreement and Disagreement in the Making of World of Plenty," in Smith, ed., *Nutrition in Britain*, 166–89; Trentmann, "Coping with Shortage," 32.

48. "The Secretary of State to Certain Diplomatic and Consular Officers," *FRUS, 1943*, vol. 1, doc. 746, Washington, April 13, 1943, https://history.state.gov/historicaldocuments/frus1943v01/d746, accessed July 21, 2016.

49. National Archives and Records Administration, RG43, International Trade files, 698 ITO, box 18, folder: article VII–discussions with British–commodity policy; and box 25, folder: commodity documents: Special Committee on Commodity Agreements and Methods of Trade; Boris C. Swerling, "Buffer Stocks and International Commodity Problems," *Economic Journal* 63 (1953): 778–90; R. S. Porter, "Buffer Stocks and Economic Stability," *Oxford Economic Papers*, n.s. 2 (1950): 95–116; Susan Howson and Donald Moggridge, eds., *The Wartime Diaries of Lionel Robbins and James Meade, 1943–1945* (Basingstoke, UK: Macmillan, 1990), 52.

50. *United Nations Conference on Food and Agriculture, Hot Springs, Virginia, 18 May–3 June 1943. Final Act and Section Reports* (Washington, DC: Government Printing Office, 1943), 5–31; "3 - Annual Message to Congress on the State of the Union," January 6, 1941, online at *The American Presidency Project*, by John Woolley and Gerhard Peters, http://presidency.ucsb.edu/ws/index.php?pid=16092, accessed July 20, 2016; Wilson, "Rehearsal," 279; Howson and Moggridge, *Wartime Diaries*, 52.

51. *Documents on Australian Foreign Policy* [hereafter *DAFP*], 1944, vol. 7, doc. 199, "McDougall to Hodgson, Memorandum, Washington, June 19, 1944, Food and Agriculture," available at https://dfat.gov.au/about-us/publications/historical-documents/Pages/volume-07/199-mcdougall-to-hodgson.aspx; and doc. 272, "Full Cabinet submission by Evatt on FAO," September 6, 1944, at https://dfat.gov.au/about-us/publications/historical-documents/Pages/volume-07/272-full-cabinet-submission-by-evatt.aspx, accessed July 6, 2016; Turnell, "Monetary Reformers," 137–45; Jachertz and Nützenadel, "Coping with Hunger?," 107–8; John Boyd Orr, *As I Recall* (London: MacGibbon and Kee, 1966), 157–61.

52. Orr, *As I Recall*, 161–64.

53. Ibid., 166–71; Amy L. S. Staples, "To Win the Peace: The FAO, Sir John Boyd Orr, and the World Food Board Proposals," *Peace and Change* 28 (2003): 495–523; Collingham, *Taste of War*, 483; *DAFP*, 1946, vol. 9, doc. 267, "Legation in Washington to Department of External Affairs," May 23, 1946, at https://dfat.gov.au/about-us/publications/historical-documents/Pages/volume-09/267-legation-in-washington-to-department-of-external-affairs.aspx, accessed July 6, 2016.

54. Harry S. Truman Presidential Library, Joseph D. Coppock Papers, box 2, folder: World Food Board Proposal, "Proposals for a World Food Board," J. Coppock, August 26, 1946; Jachertz and Nützenadel, "Coping with Hunger?," 110–12; *DAFP*, 1946, vol. 10, doc. 248, "Burton to Coombs," November 26, 1946, at https://dfat.gov.au/about-us/publications/historical-documents/Pages/volume-10/248-burton-to-coombs.aspx, accessed July 6, 2016; Orr, *As I Recall*, 171–78; Collingham, *Taste of War*, 483–84; The National Archives, PREM8/195, CP(46)374, October 11, 1946: "Cabinet. International Commodity Policy. Memorandum by the President of the Board of Trade and the Minister of Food, 11 Oct 1946"; and "International Commodity Policy: Memorandum by the President of the Board of Trade and the Minister of Food, to Prime Minister, 14 Oct 1946"; and "International Commodity Policy: Memorandum by the President of the Board of Trade and the Minister of Food, J. M. Fleming, 14 Oct 1946."

55. Orr, *As I Recall*, 179, 191–95, 202–3, 205–6, 210–11.

56. Jachertz and Nützenadel, "Coping with Hunger?," 110–18; Mitchel B. Wallerstein, *Food for War, Food for Peace: United States Food Aid in a Global Context* (Cambridge, MA: MIT Press, 1980).

57. See Selwyn Cornish and Kurt Schuler, "Australia's Full-Employment Proposals at Bretton Woods: A Road Only Partly Taken," chap. 8 in this volume.

Chapter 8

Australia's Full-Employment Proposals at Bretton Woods: A Road Only Partly Taken

Selwyn Cornish and Kurt Schuler

At the Bretton Woods Conference, Australia advocated full employment as a goal of international economic cooperation. The second paragraph of the International Monetary Fund's Articles of Agreement listed as one of the organization's purposes "To facilitate the expansion and balanced growth of international trade, and to contribute thereby to the promotion and maintenance of high levels of employment and real income and to the development of the productive resources of all members as primary objectives of economic policy." However, the conference rejected Australia's proposals to give full employment priority as a goal in itself rather than as a consequence of expanded trade, and refused to be more specific about using international coordination to promote full employment. Australia's proposals remain worth thinking about today because of the connection between full employment, or at least high employment, and political stability as well as economic growth—a connection that the global financial crisis of 2007–2008 and its aftermath have made evident in country after country.

Australia's concern with full employment and the economic stability it implied arose from Australia's history and economic circumstances. In the half century preceding Bretton Woods, Australia experienced two world wars and great depressions in the 1890s and the 1930s. In the 1890s, real GDP fell nearly 20 percent, unemployment may have exceeded 25 percent, and the terms of trade deteriorated 20 percent as prices dropped in particular for wool, Australia's main export. In the 1930s, real GDP fell 8 percent, unemployment may have reached the same levels as in the 1890s, and the terms of trade deteriorated 37 percent. During the four decades preceding the 1890s, Australia experienced massive economic expansion. In the half century afterward, Australian economic policy aimed to promote employment by shielding Australians from the instability of market forces, especially those operating in the international economy. There were also fears, not limited to Australia, of postwar economic stagnation. Australia's manufacturing sector overtook agriculture in output and employment during World War II, but Australia's exports remained mainly agricultural, hence subject to the large swings in price typical of international commodity markets. With a population of about 7.3 million—less than New York City—Australia was too small to practice autarky without hurting its high standard of living. To achieve domestic economic stability it would therefore need substantial world economic stability.

That was the context in which Australia argued its case at international conferences in the 1940s. At Bretton Woods, Australia proposed that all participating nations—but especially the major economic powers—should declare their commitment to maintaining full employment after the war. Australia also wanted larger quotas (capital contributions, linked to voting power) and drawing (borrowing) rights at the International Monetary Fund for countries dependent on a narrow range of primary exports whose prices fluctuated widely, and argued for greater discretion to be given to countries that needed to adjust their exchange rates to maintain external balance.[1]

DEVELOPMENT OF AUSTRALIA'S "POSITIVE APPROACH"

The leading advocates of Australia's "positive approach" (full-employment approach) to post–World War II economic policy—Leslie G. Melville and H. C. "Nugget" Coombs—were heavily influenced by John Maynard Keynes's writings. Melville became the first professor of economics at the University of Adelaide in 1929 at age twenty-seven. In 1931 he was appointed chief economist of the Commonwealth Bank of Australia, the country's quasi central bank. He was an original member of the Financial and Economic (F & E) Committee, which the Australian government established to advise it as World War II loomed. Coombs completed a PhD at the London School of Economics in 1933 and joined the Commonwealth Bank as Melville's assistant.[2]

As early as 1936, Melville formulated a policy framework containing key elements of what later became known as the Bretton Woods system. Fixed but adjustable exchange rates would provide the anchor for monetary policy. In the event of excessive pressure on the exchange rate, deflationary or expansionary policies would be applied. In the case of an intractable disequilibrium, the exchange rate would be adjusted. Melville argued that "one factor in an economy must be fixed to make the monetary problem sufficiently simple to be capable of human regulation," but "fixing of the rate of exchange as an objective of monetary policy does not mean that the rate selected should be maintained at all costs."[3] The Great Depression had changed Melville's earlier commitment to highly rigid exchange rates, and he had moved closer to the position of Keynes, whom he had met in 1932 and 1933 at meetings in London.

While Australian politicians gave priority to full employment as a means of raising living standards, Coombs and Melville gave priority to full employment over trade liberalization on conceptual grounds. A state of full employment, they argued, was more likely to stimulate international trade than one where unemployment existed. In a paper titled "The Post-War Economy," Melville concluded that the benefits of any reallocation of resources from relaxing trade barriers would be meager compared to the waste of resources created by unemployment from increased exposure to the uncertainties of international trade. He also observed that the assumptions underlying the classical theory of international trade did not square with recent experience: full employment could scarcely be said to have existed in recent years, if at all; factors of production were not perfectly mobile within countries or between countries; perfect competition had never prevailed; and competing nations in world trade were never similar in terms of size or bargaining power; nor were countries at the same stage of economic development. While he admitted that "we must not underestimate the importance of international trade and freedom to export," Melville concluded that "countries, particularly small or under-developed countries, would be foolhardy to throw up their right to make use of protectionist devices to maintain employment, to give them time to adapt immobile factors of production to sudden developments abroad, and to safeguard their local industries from the power of external firms entrenched within large domestic markets."[4] The experience of the 1930s, in which employment and international trade had plummeted together, buttressed Coombs's and Melville's view.

The position Australia took at the conferences on postwar planning arose from its interpretation of Article VII of the Mutual Aid Agreement, signed by the United States and Britain on February 23, 1942, and by the United States and Australia on September 3, 1942. Article VII contained the so-called "Consideration" that countries were expected to honor after the war in return for US wartime assistance. They were to commit themselves to "agreed action . . . directed to the expansion, by appropriate international and domestic measures, of production, employment, and the exchange of goods . . . [and] . . . to the elimination of all forms of discriminatory treatment in international commerce, and to the reduction of tariffs and other trade barriers." Article VII also specified that at "an early convenient date conversations shall be begun between the two Governments with a view to determining, in the light of governing economic conditions, the best means of attaining the above-stated objectives by their own agreed action and of seeking the agreed action of other like-minded Governments."[5]

When deciding how to respond to Article VII, Britain had asked the self-governing British Dominions (Canada, Australia, New Zealand, and South Africa) and India (still a colony) for comments. In late 1941 the Australian government established an Interdepartmental Committee on External Relations (ICER) to advise on its response. Members included the prominent economists Lyndhurst F. Giblin and Douglas B. Copland.[6] A preliminary report of February 1942 recommended that Australia support Article VII subject to future negotiations over details. Given its generally pessimistic view about postwar economic prospects, the ICER recommended that Australia cooperate with international attempts to enhance postwar prosperity but also that cooperation be based on highlighting the "positive" aims of Article VII.[7]

The government accepted the ICER's recommendations and invited the Financial and Economic Committee to undertake further work. The committee was chaired by Giblin and included Roland Wilson (secretary of the Department of Labor and National Service and holder of doctorates in economics from Oxford and Chicago), Melville, Copland, and Coombs. Giblin quickly drafted a paper arguing that the key consideration in Article VII was the reference to maintaining employment and production.[8] Melville agreed, judging that unless Australia obtained guarantees from the larger countries, they would not adopt policies aimed at maintaining employment, and no other considerations under Article VII should be accepted; as he put it, "[we] must put ourselves in the position of leaving our hands entirely free to take any action regarding tariffs, exchange rates, exchange control, etc."[9] Coombs went even further, proposing that all signatories to postwar agreements should sign an agreement committing themselves to maintaining full employment.[10] It was a rare moment when technical economic advice, domestic political considerations, and foreign policy were all aligned.

Coombs became the dominant figure in the development of the "positive approach" from early in 1943, as the result of being appointed head of the new, powerful federal Department of Post-War Reconstruction. With Giblin and Melville, Coombs oversaw preparation of the proposed international employment agreement: countries would be asked to submit a plan for approval by an international agency setting out how they intended to maintain full employment and would be required to report at regular intervals whether they were achieving their employment objectives.[11]

Australia signed the Mutual Aid Agreement on September 3, 1942. Australia's response to Article VII assumed that the United States would give priority to removing trade barriers—the second part of "the Consideration" in Article VII. In contrast, Australian authorities argued for giving priority to the first part—expanding "employment" and "production" by "appropriate international and domestic measures." This interpretation formed the basis of Australia's "positive approach" to the postwar talks.[12] Because it gave priority to maintaining employment and production, Australia's delegates to international conferences believed they were pursuing a "Keynesian crusade": high levels of employment and production were to be achieved by domestic policies keeping aggregate demand at full-employment levels. If all countries adopted full-employment policies, demand for exports would remain high and there would be greater scope to reduce barriers to imports.

REACTION TO THE "POSITIVE APPROACH" BEFORE BRETTON WOODS

The first international conference on postwar issues that Australian officials attended was in London in October–November 1942 (see table 8.1). The other countries present were Britain, Canada, New Zealand, South Africa, and India. Roland Wilson represented Australia. Britain presented John Maynard Keynes's plan to address postwar monetary problems through an International Currency (or Clearing) Union. When Wilson cabled back to Australia the details of the Keynes Plan, the Australian government was concerned that it placed insufficient pressure on creditor countries to adjust their economies, and excessive pressure on debtor countries. The government was also critical of an apparent overemphasis on exchange rate stability and an inadequate emphasis on maintaining full employment, augmenting production, and promoting development.[13]

TABLE 8.1. CHRONOLOGY OF AUSTRALIA'S "POSITIVE APPROACH"

1936	Leslie Melville develops aspects of the "positive approach."
September 3,1939	Australia enters World War II with Britain.
September 3, 1942	Australia agrees with the United States to accept the principles of the Anglo-American Mutual Aid agreement signed February 23, 1942; its Article VII is the springboard for the "positive approach."
October–November 1942	British Commonwealth conference on postwar planning, London
May 18–June 3, 1943	United Nations Conference on Food and Agriculture, Hot Springs, Virginia, adopts an Australian resolution on employment.
February–March 1944	British Commonwealth conference on IMF and World Bank, London, endorses a weaker version of Australia's employment proposal.
April 20–May 12, 1944	International Labour Organization meeting, Philadelphia, adopts Australian resolution for international conference on employment.
June 15–30, 1944	Atlantic City, New Jersey, preparatory conference for Bretton Woods
July 1–22, 1944	United Nations Monetary and Financial Conference, Bretton Woods, New Hampshire, mostly disappoints Australian hopes on employment.
April 25–June 26, 1945	United Nations Conference, San Francisco, adopts Australian full-employment provision in UN charter.
September–December 1946	Preparatory meeting on trade and employment, London
April–October 1947	Preparatory meeting on trade and employment, Geneva
August 5, 1947	Australia joins IMF and World Bank.
November 21, 1947–March 24, 1948	United Nations Conference on Trade and Employment, Havana, adopts Australian proposals on employment; agreement not ratified.

Source: Table by Selwyn Cornish and Kurt Schuler.

On his return to Australia by way of the United States, Wilson learned of the rival American plan for a United Nations Stabilization Fund, devised by Harry Dexter White of the US Treasury. The Americans envisioned the Stabilization Fund as a kind of global credit union. The American plan preserved the existing orthodoxy under which national central banks had primacy in influencing national monetary conditions, whereas the Keynes Plan in effect proposed a global central bank. From the outset, Australia preferred the Keynes Plan, believing the White Plan to be too restrictive and inflexible. In Washington, however, Wilson found the "most serious criticism . . . was that the British proposals were too 'unrealistic'—meaning, I gathered, that it was felt that it would be exceedingly difficult to get Congress to accept them. Put in its crudest form, the critics hold that the British plan is simply one which would confer on other countries an unlimited right to purchase United States goods with their own currencies." Wilson's view was that while the White Plan was "generous," it was constructed along "very much more orthodox lines than the British proposals." His advice to the Australian government was to press the case for the Clearing Union but to back the US plan for a world bank.[14]

Australia continued to pursue its "positive approach" even though American and British officials often told it that the US Congress would never agree to a treaty mandating the application of government-sponsored full-employment policies. Writing to a colleague in April 1943, Keynes, for instance, mentioned that the Australians "are taking the line that, before any plan at all is considered, it must be laid down in advance that the primary duty of every country is to raise its own employment and production to the maximum by its own efforts. They will not get far with the Americans on this."[15] On the other hand, Australia's representatives were acutely aware that the Australian government would not give its approval to any international agreement that failed to commit the signatories to full employment.

Australia's concerns were conveyed to Secretary Henry Morgenthau of the US Treasury and to his deputies White and Edward Bernstein by Minister for External Affairs Herbert V. Evatt and by Coombs, at meetings in Washington in 1943. Australia's delegation also raised those concerns at the United Nations Conference on Food and Agriculture at Hot Springs, Virginia, in May–June 1943. The conference was the first gathering of all the nations allied against the Axis powers, and its subject matter was broader than its title implies. Coombs succeeded in having a resolution carried that recognized "the close interdependence between the level of employment in all countries, the character and extent of industrial development, the management of currencies, the direction of national and international investment, and the policy adopted by the nations toward foreign trade." The conference also affirmed that economic development was a prerequisite for securing "freedom from want of food," and recommended that governments "take action individually, and in concert, in order to secure this objective."[16]

After the conference, Coombs highlighted the "positive approach" in talks with US Treasury officials in Washington. For Coombs, the major problem of both the White and Keynes Plans was that they placed inadequate weight on maintaining full employment. In response, White was adamant that the US Congress would never accept Australia's position. At the conclusion of these talks, Coombs discussed Australia's plan for an international agreement on full employment with Keynes at meetings in London. Afterward, Coombs wrote to Keynes proposing that Australia take the initiative in calling for an international conference to discuss employment, the ultimate objective being a formal recognition that maintaining full employment was a necessary prerequisite for achieving other postwar plans, including trade liberalization. Keynes thought a conference on employment in the near future would be premature, but he sought to reassure Coombs that maintaining full employment would be placed "to the forefront" of Article VII negotiations with the United States and that a conference along the lines of what Coombs was proposing might be possible at some time in the future.[17]

At a series of meetings beginning in September 1943, American and British officials, led by White and Keynes, worked toward producing a joint document on international monetary policy after the war. By then it was clear to Keynes that the United States would not accept his plan for an International Clearing Union and that he should concentrate on modifying the White Plan. These discussions led to the publication on April 21, 1944, of the "Joint Statement by Experts on the Establishment of an International Monetary Fund," presented as a compromise between the White and Keynes Plans, though in reality it was the White Plan with amendments requested by Britain.

A draft of the "Joint Statement" formed the basis of the British Commonwealth talks in London in February–March 1944. Melville was appointed leader of the Australian delegation for the London talks. Before he left for the talks, Australia's response to the Anglo-American draft plan for an International Monetary Fund and a Bank for Reconstruction and Development (World Bank) had been worked out in considerable detail. There were four issues of major contention. First, Australia wanted members of the proposed institutions to commit themselves to the "positive approach." Second, it wanted the size of the fund to be enlarged and Australia's quota and drawing rights raised. Third, it wanted greater flexibility of exchange rates. Fourth, countries should not have to commit themselves to membership in the fund and bank until the details of the negotiations that were shortly to commence on trade liberalization were known.[18]

In his opening statement at the talks on February 23, Melville warned that "unless there was assurance that the larger countries would maintain a high level of employment by domestic measures, it was unlikely that smaller countries like Australia could significantly reduce barriers to international trade, many of which had been set up in desperate efforts to deal with the employment problem."[19] Keynes, in his reply to Melville on February 29, admitted that reference to employment policy at the most recent talks in Washington between the United States and British governments on the monetary, commodity, and investment plans "was limited and unambitious, largely because of American antagonism to the creation of an international institution which would advise governments on domestic policy matters."[20] Melville responded by saying that he intended to produce a document proposing that governments commit themselves to maintaining full employment after the war. Lionel Robbins of the British Cabinet Office, in his reply to Melville, said he did not believe that such a document was necessary since the compromises that had been worked out by White and Keynes in Washington late in 1943 would ensure that full employment would be maintained.[21]

The following day, Melville produced a copy of the full-employment agreement. It asserted that "the lack of effective demand [was] the most serious enduring world economic problem." Signatories to the agreement were "to undertake certain specified things, including taking necessary internal measures to maintain full employment."[22] They would be liable to censure if unemployment exceeded a particular rate of unemployment, or "quota," which was to be set by each country according to local conditions and the country's exposure to the international economy and to seasonal and other influences. Should a country exceed its quota, it would be required "to consider" measures including the stimulation of private investment, an increase in public investment, increased consumption expenditure, and expansion, under appropriate circumstances, of overseas investment. Melville thought the "appropriate organization" overseeing all of this would need to be little more than a "small secretariat," which could rely on other organizations, such as the International Labour Organization, for research and the collection of data.

Keynes responded to the Australian plan on March 6 with the announcement that the British government was preparing a white paper on employment policy after the war; it would commit the government to maintaining a "high and stable" level of employment.[23] Canada argued that an international employment agreement was unnecessary, but New Zealand and South Africa supported Australia's plan. As it turned out, the conference endorsed a weaker version of the Australian document. In his report to Prime Minister John Curtin of Australia after the conference, Melville considered the United Kingdom's acceptance of the amended employment agreement to be a "big step forward" and the amendments to be "quite satisfactory." All the same, he believed Australia still had a steep hill to climb. For one thing, the British government's approach to full employment relied overwhelmingly on monetary policy and gave inadequate attention to public works and taxation measures. As for the United States, he agreed with Keynes that maintaining full employment there would require "unconventional measures,"[24] for which American public opinion was not yet ready.

The other issue of great concern to Australia at the London talks was exchange rate flexibility. Melville argued that the US and British proposals were both too limiting for countries, like Australia, that regularly suffered violent swings in their terms of trade. In fact, Australia, he said, would oppose any limits on its ability to adjust the exchange rate. As Keynes was ill on the day that exchange rate policy was discussed, he wrote a long letter to Melville seeking to clarify the latest Anglo-American thinking on the subject. In short, Keynes's advice was that Australia should not "act on the assumption that the Fund is an intrinsically unreasonable body, which always refuses everything. Much better that we should expect them to be kind and complacent and reasonable when any respectable ground of change is produced."[25]

Keynes then questioned Melville's claim that Australia needed the discretion to change its exchange rate in order to deal with swings in its terms of trade. He found "it extraordinarily difficult to see how an alteration in the exchanges could possibly be the right remedy for a catastrophic fall in some export commodity, such as wool." He took the view that, to "maintain incomes of the wool producers by greatly increasing the incomes of all other exporters and diminishing the purchasing power of the public generally, is something like burning down the house for roast pork."[26] Moreover, if the fall in prices was the result of oversupply, he considered an exchange rate depreciation to be an altogether inappropriate remedy; if it were appropriate, a very large depreciation might be required. Rather than manipulating exchange rates, Keynes's preferred solution to a slump in the terms of trade was to establish international buffer stocks to smooth the short-term fluctuations of commodity prices while still adjusting to long-term trends. The buffer-stock plan was part of Keynes's wider vision for international planning for the postwar era. About this, Keynes told Melville that he was disappointed by the lack of enthusiasm for the plan by primary export-producing countries.

On his return to Australia through Ottawa and Washington, Melville met with White, who was adamant that agreement on an International Monetary Fund should be pressed to a conclusion without waiting for progress on other proposals, including an employment agreement. He was also strongly opposed to making provision in the fund for greater exchange rate flexibility. From Washington, Melville advised the Australian government that the "monetary fund as now drafted is quite unsatisfactory for Australia." He thought there would be great difficulty in attempting to secure fundamental changes at the proposed monetary conference. Australia, he insisted, should not accept any commitments until it was known what obligations would be attached to membership in other organizations being proposed for the postwar world and unless it was clear that membership in the monetary fund would not be a condition for membership in other international organizations.[27]

In this period, Australia also took the opportunity of the annual meeting of the International Labour Organization in Philadelphia to try to win support for the international employment agreement. Melville and Coombs, among others, did not consider the Philadelphia meeting an appropriate time or forum to raise the matter. The politicians, led by Evatt, the minister for External Affairs, forced the issue. Australia's delegation was led by J. A. "Jack" Beasley, the left-wing minister for Supply and Shipping. At the conference, fundamental differences between Australia and the United States over the meaning of Article VII rose to the surface. Beasley attacked a US resolution on employment, proposed by Secretary of Labor Frances Perkins, that highlighted the importance of removing "unreasonable restrictions" on trade for the creation of employment in the postwar world. In the end a rather meaningless compromise was agreed on. Still, the Australian delegation managed to come away from Philadelphia with a resolution calling for a further conference to consider "an international agreement on domestic policies of employment and unemployment."[28]

AT BRETTON WOODS

On May 25, 1944, President Franklin Roosevelt issued invitations to governments of the Allied nations inviting them to send delegates to an international monetary and financial conference at Bretton Woods, New Hampshire, starting on July 1. Despite some internal disagreement, the Australian government sent a delegation. It included Melville, as leader; James Brigden, a former professor of economics and departmental secretary, now economic consultant to the Australian legation in Washington; Frederick Wheeler, the head of the Australian Treasury's Financial and Economic Policy Division; and Arthur Tange, senior economist at the Department of External Affairs. The government instructed the delegation to press "strongly" for an increased quota and annual drawing rights (in effect, allowing members limited exchanges of their currencies for US dollars almost automatically); to have included in the Articles of Agreement a firm undertaking that the IMF would not reject a request to change the exchange rate to meet a "serious and persistent deficit in the balance of payments on current account accompanied by a substantially adverse change in the terms of trade"; to seek an alteration of the "purposes and policies of the Fund" to give more emphasis to employment and less to exchange stability; to strengthen the safeguards against the IMF interfering with the domestic policies of a country; to ask that it should be made clear that the right of withdrawal from the fund should not be prejudiced by making membership in the IMF a condition of membership in any other international body; to urge that an employment agreement be concluded before a final decision had to be made by countries to join the IMF; and to report any proposals made concerning the time of commencement of benefits and obligations before Australia decided its attitude to membership. The government gave the delegation no formal instructions about the proposed Bank for Reconstruction and Development. No clear proposal for it existed until the Atlantic City, New Jersey, conference held just before Bretton Woods.[29] The Atlantic City conference, attended by a select group of fifteen countries, including Australia, versus the forty-four countries at Bretton Woods, developed drafts of the main documents elaborated and made final at Bretton Woods.

These instructions formed the basis of Australia's concerns expressed at Atlantic City and at Bretton Woods. With a small delegation, Melville and his team found it difficult to attend all meetings, many occurring simultaneously. Communication between the delegation and Australia was difficult, given that the technology of the time did not permit quick responses between Bretton Woods and Canberra, which were at opposite ends of the earth.[30]

The Bretton Woods Conference was divided into three major groups, called commissions. Commission I dealt with the IMF; Commission II with the Bank for Reconstruction and Development (World Bank); and Commission III with matters not handled by the other commissions. In Commission I, Australia, with New Zealand and India, pressed for language in the IMF Articles of Agreement more explicitly specifying economic development as one of the IMF's purposes. Melville raised concerns that without such language, the IMF would overemphasize exchange rate considerations in cases where they might conflict with considerations of economic growth. Australia's proposed employment agreement was assigned to the catchall Commission III.[31] The Final Act of the conference contained only a weak recommendation that the participating governments "reach agreement as soon as possible on ways and means whereby they may best . . . facilitate by cooperative effort the harmonization of national policies of Member States designed to promote and maintain high levels of employment and progressively rising standards of living."[32]

In a covering note attached to his postmortem to the prime minister on the conference, Melville highlighted the numerous "misunderstandings" that he had encountered at Bretton Woods "about Australia's attitude to international agreements. The delegation was constantly being confronted by the belief that we were unwilling to cooperate with other countries on economic matters."[33] He lamented that there had been little opportunity at the main meetings of the conference to dispel this misunderstanding, although Commission III had provided some scope to clarify Australia's views. The atmosphere became particularly difficult when Australia hesitated to sign the Final Act. (The government ultimately instructed Melville to sign "for purposes of certification"—in other words, not indicating agreement with the result.)

As a result of the difficulties experienced at Bretton Woods, Melville's advice to the government was that Australia "should state her general attitude toward international arrangements as soon as possible, on the highest plane." Not only should Australia explain its attitude, but it should become "a spokesman for a positive and constructive policy of international cooperation, which would make the various international proposals now under discussion subsidiary to the general requirement that all nations should commit themselves to maintain high and stable levels of employment." He thought that "such a policy for international cooperation of this kind based on a commitment to maintain high levels of employment would . . . receive a sympathetic hearing in many countries and even from an important section of the United States public. What has been interpreted as a negative approach by Australia to international questions would then appear in its positive aspect, as a constructive attempt to direct international activities towards objectives which the people of all countries wish to attain."[34]

Melville gave special prominence in his report to the failure to have the employment agreement adopted. In Commission III Melville had moved that governments accepting membership in the fund should agree concurrently to an "international agreement in which signatories will pledge themselves to their own people and to one another to maintain high levels of employment in their respective countries, and to exchange information on measures necessary to prevent the growth of unemployment and its spread to other countries." The United States opposed the resolution on the grounds that more time was needed to consider whether matters of domestic policy could legitimately be included in an international agreement and proposed that the subject would be better left to subsequent Article VII conversations. No reference at the conference, Melville informed the prime minister, was made to "the United States political difficulties, but I believe these to be dominant in their opposition to our resolution at the conference."[35]

He added that, in the debate on the employment issue, and at the final vote in Commission III, Australia had "the full support" of Britain, New Zealand, France, Poland, and "a few of the smaller countries." It seems that they were the countries most sympathetic to Keynesian thinking. Several of the South American countries had lent their support at an early stage but, as the discussion progressed, they "were more interested in the special bargains they were making with the United States and in gaining some acknowledgement of the need to reduce tariffs." This was particularly important, since nineteen of the forty-four countries represented at Bretton Woods were from Latin America.

There was fairly general opposition to the specific proposal that countries represented at the conference should sign the employment agreement concurrently with the monetary agreement. The United States and Canada argued that while they recognized the relationship between employment and monetary policy, any resolution implying that acceptance of the fund should be contingent on signing the employment agreement was outside the terms of reference of the conference. The USSR, China, and India also gave little support to

Australia, since they appeared more interested in promoting the development of their economies than in policies to maintain full employment. Even so, after the educational work that Australian representatives had undertaken at Hot Springs, London, Philadelphia, and Bretton Woods, Melville believed there "were good prospects of securing widespread support for an employment agreement as part of a program of international economic cooperation." Because of political difficulties, he agreed the United States might continue to oppose it. To try to secure the support of the United States and other countries, it was "urgently necessary," he said, for Australia to restate its case, calling on governments to organize an international conference at which they would be asked to accept an employment agreement along the lines proposed by Australia.[36]

The government would now have to consider what IMF membership would mean for the commitment it had given to the Australian people to maintain full employment after the war. Membership in the fund might limit Australia's ability to respond to external instability while attempting to retain full employment—but not inevitably, Melville emphasized. "Provided we built up international reserves outside the fund, for use in the event of the fund denying us the use of our drawing rights," he was confident that "our freedom to follow a policy of maintaining a high level of employment in Australia should, therefore, not be hampered by membership of the Fund."[37]

While Melville and his colleagues were disappointed that they were unable to secure the adoption of the employment agreement, they achieved some success on other fronts. Australia's quota was increased from A£47 million to A£62.5 million. (The Australian pound, the currency at the time, was worth US$3.224.) The 25 percent annual limit on drawing rights was not changed, but a waiver provision was inserted to meet the needs of countries like Australia that were subject "to conditions of a periodic and exceptional nature." The draft IMF agreement had proposed that members must have the IMF's permission to alter exchange rates outside a band of 10 percent above or below the rates they registered when joining the IMF, but the final agreement allowed members to go outside the band without the IMF's consent, though in that case their drawing rights would cease. With regard to the "purposes and policies of the Fund," Melville continued to think that too much weight was assigned to exchange rate stability and not enough to employment. There was also some uncertainty as to whether a country withdrawing from the IMF would forfeit its membership in other international bodies. But as the IMF was now more satisfactory from Australia's viewpoint, Melville thought it "unlikely that we should ever need to withdraw."[38]

Weighing the benefits and costs of IMF membership, Melville concluded that, on balance, it would be to Australia's advantage to accept membership. As to the International Bank for Reconstruction and Development (the "International" had been added to the name at the conference), he foresaw no difficulties arising from membership, especially since Australia was unlikely to be a borrower or large lender. From Australia's point of view, the "successful reconstruction of the devastated countries means the very necessary restoration of our old export markets. The development loans mean the expansion of new markets and the prospects of exports of capital equipment to the Far East and Netherlands East Indies." Since the bank seemed to fit in with Australia's "positive approach" to Article VII, Melville again proposed that the government should accept membership.[39]

AFTER BRETTON WOODS

When the IMF and World Bank held their inaugural meetings at Savannah, Georgia, in March 1946, Australia had not decided whether to join. Even so, Melville attended as an official observer. In his report to the government on his return, he wrote that if "there were reason to expect that the economic collaboration resulting from current discussions were likely to restore world trade and maintain economic stability, it would, I believe, be in Australia's interests to join the Fund and the Bank." But he thought the recently concluded Anglo-American loan agreement and the proposals for an International Trade Organization (ITO), as presently drafted, "do not seem to me to hold out that promise." The loan agreement, which had reduced the transition period for the convertibility of sterling from five years to one year, would "make the restoration of her [Britain's] economy, and consequently our own, much more difficult." The proposed ITO was likely to "impose restraints on other action that the U.K. might have taken to restore her export income and upon measures which Australia has, in the past, found necessary to protect her domestic economy from adverse international conditions and to provide a balanced development of her resources"; here he was referring to the imperial preferences, import tariffs and export subsidies. Furthermore, there was "little guarantee that, in return, the United States will follow domestic policies likely to maintain internal economic stability, or international investment, commercial and tariff policies that will secure satisfactory world conditions."[40]

Melville recommended that Australia wait until the obligations of ITO membership were determined and future US policy was clearer. Australia finally decided to join the fund and bank in 1947, after the deadline for acceptance as an original member of the institutions had passed. There were two predominant reasons for joining. One involved domestic politics. The prime minister, now J. B. "Ben" Chifley, had always supported Australia's membership in principle; when he became prime minister in 1945 on the death of John Curtin, his authority within the governing Labor Party was enhanced. The other reason was the success Australia achieved after Bretton Woods in gaining recognition for its "positive approach." At the United Nations conference at San Francisco in 1945, Roland Wilson succeeded in having the promotion of full employment included in the UN charter. Article 55 of the charter states that the UN "shall promote:

a. higher standards of living, full employment, and conditions of economic and social progress and development;

b. solutions of international economic, social, health, and related problems; and international cultural and educational cooperation . . ."[41]

Article 56 states, "All members pledge themselves to take joint and separate action in co-operation with the Organization for the achievement of the purposes set forth in Article 55." Upon its creation, the UN established an Economic and Employment Commission under the Economic and Social Council (ECOSOC); among the commission's tasks was monitoring employment levels in member countries. Wilson himself was appointed to the commission.[42]

After the Bretton Woods Conference, the Australian, New Zealand, and British governments on several occasions stressed to the US government the need for an international conference to discuss employment. In March 1945, Secretary of State Edward Stettinius of the United States wrote to the three governments advising them that the United States "recognizes the desirability of international collaboration for the attainment of full employment in agreement with the view of the Australian government that the employment policy should be considered at an international conference." It also believed, though, that "there can be no sound basis for stability of productive employment at a high level in the various nations if there is not a general agreement to remove excessive barriers and prevent discriminatory practices in the past." That said, the US government "would be pleased to participate at the earliest practicable date in an international conference on trade and employment."[43]

Preparatory meetings for such a conference were held in London in late 1946 and Geneva in mid-1947, leading up to the Trade and Employment Conference at Havana in late 1947 and early 1948. Coombs led the Australian delegation to the London conference and attended both the Geneva and Havana conferences, which were led by the minister for Post-War Reconstruction (now John Dedman). At Havana, Australia was again successful in having full employment recognized as a key objective of economic and social policy. Chapter 1, Article 1, of the charter of the proposed ITO declared that member countries "pledge themselves to promote national and international action to increase the production, consumption and exchange of goods; to foster the economic development of underdeveloped countries; and to promote the reduction of tariffs and other barriers to trade and the elimination of discriminatory treatment in international commerce. They establish the International Trade Organization through which to achieve these objectives." Chapter 11, Articles 2–7 stated that the "avoidance of unemployment or underemployment is necessary to the achievement of the aims set out in Chapter 1. Internal measures by individual countries to avoid unemployment should be supplemented by concerted action under the sponsorship of the Economic and Social Organization of the United Nations in collaboration with the appropriate intergovernmental organizations." Ultimately, however, the decisions made at Havana came to nothing because the US government never submitted the ITO charter for Senate ratification.[44]

When he announced in Parliament on March 13, 1947, that Australia would join the Bretton Woods institutions, Prime Minister Chifley noted that Australia had "consistently maintained the view that the successful working of international economic organizations, and the expansion of international investment and trade, depends to a very great degree on the achievement and preservation of full employment in the major industrial countries." After "a long series of formal and informal discussions," he declared that the "positive approach" had "finally succeeded," pointing specifically to the UN charter and Britain having "obtained from the Fund a ruling that steps necessary to protect a member country from chronic or persistent unemployment arising from pressure upon its balance of payments are among the measures necessary to correct a fundamental disequilibrium."[45]

He went on to explain that Australia would review its membership when the final outcome of the present trade negotiations was known. But such a review never occurred, in part because the ITO was not established, and in part because the government was defeated at the general election in

December 1949; its successor warmly welcomed Australia's membership. But there was another important reason. Chifley had made it clear to the Parliament that Australia's application for membership was "on the basis of admission on the same conditions as those applying to an original member." Australia could not be admitted as an original member since the deadline had long passed. But he said that "the conditions of the proposal is that we will be admitted on the same basis as original members"; the government, he added, "would not be prepared to accept any new condition as a prerequisite to admittance to the Fund and Bank." Australia became a member on August 5, 1947, on the same basis as original members. When the number of executive directors of the fund was increased from thirteen to fourteen in February 1948, Stuart McFarlane, the secretary to the Australian Treasury, was elected to fill the new position; Roland Wilson became the alternative director.

FULL EMPLOYMENT IN LATER YEARS

The feared postwar stagnation did not come to pass. The years of the Bretton Woods system constituted a new golden age for Australia, resembling in some ways the decades before the 1890s: the economy expanded rapidly and unemployment and inflation remained low. Whether Australia's prosperity would have occurred without the Bretton Woods institutions is impossible to say, but Australia never regretted its membership in them. Leslie Melville was appointed Australia's Executive Director at the IMF and World Bank from 1950 to 1953; "Nugget" Coombs, as governor of the central bank, was responsible in part for managing Australia's economic affairs in accordance with the principles established at Bretton Woods.

This chapter has explained the historical background that led to Australia's "positive approach." What were the potential shortcomings of the "positive approach"? The 1930s had shown the costs of high unemployment. Understandably, in the 1940s there was scant concern that monetary policy aiming for full employment might create uncomfortably high inflation. Labor market reform and the supply-side aspect of taxation were also underemphasized. Australia's employment proposal relied on the pressure of opinion to keep countries in line. The IMF and World Bank could stop lending to countries violating their agreements, but there were no sanctions for violations of the employment agreement. The employment proposal was aimed mainly at rich countries, especially the United States and Britain because of their size and their importance in world trade. It was, and remains, less clear what full employment means in poor, mainly rural economies; whether government policy there can make it happen; and whether policy should emphasize industrialization over employment. To the extent that full employment in rich countries promoted demand for imports, it would have benefited poor countries as well as rich ones like Australia that were commodity exporters, but there was a potential tension between full employment and openness to foreign trade.

Although Australia was unsuccessful at Bretton Woods in making full employment a central concern of the IMF or of a parallel international agreement, the question of whether some type of international coordination regarding employment is desirable remains a live issue. The global financial crisis of 2008–2009 resulted in the most severe economic problems since the 1930s. In response, the newly influential Group of 20 economies focused on the financial system, because that was where the crisis had originated, but they acknowledged its effects on employment and pledged to address them.[46] The crisis and the years since have also seen a revival of the Keynesian ideas that had inspired Melville, Coombs, and other Australian figures in the 1930s and 1940s. Although the international agreement on full employment that Australia wanted in the 1940s has not proved politically feasible, after decades of being subordinate to issues relating to monetary policy and the financial system, full employment now has a high place on the agenda of international policy makers.

Notes

1. See Ian McLean, *Why Australia Prospered: The Shifting Sources of Economic Growth* (Princeton, NJ: Princeton University Press, 2013); and Chay Fisher and Christopher Kent, "Two Depressions, One Banking Collapse," Reserve Bank of Australia, Research Discussion Paper 1999–06 (June 1999).

2. For short biographies of Melville and Coombs, see the entries by Selwyn Cornish in J. E. King, ed., *A Biographical Dictionary of Australian and New Zealand Economists* (Cheltenham, UK: Edward Elgar, 2007). Rodney Maddock and Janet Penny cover the membership and work of the Financial and Economic Committee (hereafter F & E), in "Economists at War: The Financial and Economic Committee 1939–44," *Australian Economic History Review* 23, no. 1 (March 1983).

3. L. G. Melville, "Statement of Evidence," in *Royal Commission to Inquire into the Monetary and Banking Systems at Present in Operation in Australia*, vol. 2 (Canberra: Commonwealth Government Printer, 1937), 1117, 1119–20.

4. L. G. Melville, "The Post-War Economy," in Melville et al., *Australia's Post-War Economy* (Sydney: Australasian Publishing, 1945), 9.

5. J. G. Crawford, *Australian Trade Policy 1942–1966: A Documentary History* (Canberra: ANU Press, 1968), 9–10.

6. William Coleman, Selwyn Cornish, and Alf Hagger, *Giblin's Platoon: The Trials and Triumphs of the Economist in Australian Public Life* (Canberra: ANU Press, 2006), 199.

7. Interdepartmental Committee on External Relations (ICER), "Australia's Position in Relation to Article VII of the Anglo-American Mutual Aid Agreement," August 20, 1942, National Archives of Australia, Commonwealth Persons (hereafter NAA CP) index 43/1/1, Bundle 5/1943/444/pt.1.

8. L. F. Giblin, "Mutual Aid and Article VII," F & E, 36k, NAA CP184/7/1, B1-25. See also Giblin, *The Australian Problem of Maintaining Full Employment* (Melbourne: Melbourne University Press, 1943).

9. L. G. Melville, "Notes on F&E Meeting 21/1/43," NAA CP184/4/1, Bundle 1.

10. H. C. Coombs, "Notes on Article Seven," F & E, 36am, October 5, 1942.

11. H. C. Coombs, "International Aspects of Reconstruction," Address to the Economic Society of Australia and New Zealand, Sydney, October 15, 1943, NAA M448/1/125. See "The Employment Agreement," in the "Historical Documents" section of this book.

12. Australian economists saw the genesis of their so-called "Keynesian crusade" in John Maynard Keynes, *The General Theory of Employment, Interest and Money* (London: Macmillan, 1936), especially 382–83 (chap. 24, sec. iv).

13. Roland Wilson, "Post-war Economic Talks, London, October–November 1942," January 16, 1943, NAA A601/1, 4011/8 (hereafter Wilson, "Post-war Economic Talks").

14. Ibid.

15. Donald Moggridge, ed., *The Collected Writings of John Maynard Keynes*, vol. 25, *Activities 1940–1944; Shaping the Post-War World: The Clearing Union* (London: Macmillan/Cambridge University Press, 1980) (hereafter Keynes, vol. 25), Keynes to Sir Frederick Phillips, April 22, 1943, 251.

16. H. C. Coombs, *Trial Balance* (Melbourne: Macmillan, 1981), 39–40; Tim Rowse, *Nugget Coombs: A Reforming Life* (Cambridge: Cambridge University Press, 2002), 141; J. B. Brigden, "Discussions on the Stabilization Fund," April 23, 1943, NAA A981/1.

17. Keynes to Coombs, September 3, 1943, NAA CP43/1, 43/1324.

18. Evatt to Melville, January 27, 1944, NAA CP43/1/1, Bundle 6/1943/484/pt.1.

19. L. G. Melville, "Report on London Discussions on Article VII, February–March 1944," NAA A5954, box 658.

20. "Mutual Aid Agreement, Article 7: Discussions with Dominions. Employment," February–March 1944, NAA CP43/1/1, Bundle 6/1943/484/pt.2 (hereafter "Mutual Aid Agreement").

21. "Mutual Aid Agreement."

22. "An International Employment Agreement," NAA A989/1, 43/735/27/1, pt. 3.

23. "Mutual Aid Agreement."

24. L. G. Melville, "Report on Discussions at United Nations Monetary and Financial Conference Held at Bretton Woods, USA, from 1st July to 22nd July, 1944" (hereafter Melville, "Report on Discussions"), Reserve Bank of Australia Archives (hereafter RBA) c.3.9.1.78.

25. Keynes to Melville, March 14, 1944, in Keynes, vol. 25, 413–15.

26. Ibid.

27. Melville to Evatt and Chifley, April 27, 1944, NAA A989, 44/735/56/6.

28. Beasley to Perkins, May 3, 1944, NAA A989, 44/1320/13/3; Beasley to Evatt, May 4, 6, and 11, 1944.

29. Melville, "Report on Discussions."

30. Melville to Curtin, August 26, 1944, RBA c.3.9.1.77.

31. The conference discussions on these points are in Kurt Schuler and Andrew Rosenberg, eds., *The Bretton Woods Transcripts* (New York: Center for Financial Stability, 2013), 305–6, 314–17, 328–29, 346, 545–46, 570–84.

32. United Nations Monetary and Financial Conference, *Final Act*, Article VII, para. 4 (Bretton Woods, NH, 1944); also see "Final Act (22 July 1944)" in the "Historical Documents" section of this book.

33. Melville to Curtin, December 14, 1944, NAA c.3.9.1.77.

34. Melville, "Report on Discussions."

35. Ibid.

36. Ibid.

37. Ibid.

38. Ibid.

39. Ibid.

40. L. G. Melville, "Report of the Inaugural Meeting of the Governors of the World Fund and Bank held at Savannah, USA, from 8th to 18th March 1946," RBA c.3.9.1.79.

41. United Nations, *Charter of the United Nations and Statute of the International Court of Justice* (San Francisco, 1945), https://treaties.un.org/doc/publication/ctc/uncharter.pdf.

42. Coleman, Cornish and Hagger, *Giblin's Platoon*, 203–5; L. F. Crisp, "The Australian Full Employment Pledge at San Francisco," *Australian Outlook* 19, no. 1 (1965): 5–19.

43. Sir Frederic Eggleston to Department of External Affairs, "Employment Conference," March 16, 1945, NAA A/1066, ER45/2/3/2 45.

44. Crawford, *Australian Trade Policy*, 43–44. The abortive agreement is also available at United Nations Conference on Trade and Employment (Havana, 1948), *Final Act and Related Documents*, https://www.wto.org/english/docs_e/legal_e/havana_e.pdf.

45. "International Monetary Agreements Bill," Second Reading Speech, March 13, 1947, RBA IT-f-525.

46. G20 London Summit Leaders' Statement, April 2, 2009, para. 26, available at https://www.imf.org/external/np/sec/pr/2009/pdf/g20_040209.pdf; G20 Pittsburgh Summit Leaders' Statement, September 24–25, 2009, paras. 9, 43–45, available at https://www.treasury.gov/resource-center/international/g7-g20/Documents/pittsburgh_summit_leaders_statement_250909.pdf.

Chapter 9

How the Bretton Woods Negotiations Helped to Pioneer International Development

Eric Helleiner

Histories of the Bretton Woods negotiations often devote very little space to international development issues. A common assumption is that the negotiators focused primarily on economic problems facing industrialized countries, particularly those of the leading financial powers. As Gerald Meier put it, "The political power lay with the United States and Britain, and from the outset it was apparent that issues of development were not to be on the Bretton Woods agenda."[1] Richard Gardner—whose writings established much of the conventional wisdom about the origins of Bretton Woods—reinforced this point, arguing that the question of how to assist the development of poorer countries "was not recognized as a major issue in the postwar planning."[2]

Gardner and many others have gone further to argue that even the creation at Bretton Woods of the International Bank for Reconstruction and Development (IBRD; later the World Bank) was not driven primarily by a desire to support the development of poorer countries. In Gardner's words, "There was simply no conception of the vast needs of the less developed countries and of the role the Bank should play in meeting them. Indeed, the Bank was conceived mainly as an institution for reconstruction. Incredible as it seems today, the word 'development' did not even appear in Harry White's first draft circulated within the US Treasury Department."[3] Detailed histories of the World Bank have echoed this view, arguing that development "played a bit role at Bretton Woods" and that "the distinction between developed and less developed and between north and south—the special problems of the 'third world'—had scarcely swum into the ken of postwar planners."[4]

This common story has been reinforced by much scholarship on the history of international development. A frequent argument in this literature is that the birth of international development came *after* the Bretton Woods Conference with President Harry Truman's 1949 inauguration speech. In that address, Truman announced that the United States would "embark on a bold new program for making the benefits of our scientific advances and industrial progress available for the improvement and growth of underdeveloped areas." This speech is said to have "inaugurated the 'development age'" by promoting the idea that rich countries should be actively engaged in supporting and promoting the development of "underdeveloped" countries.[5]

This chapter shows how these lines of argument overlook the fact that there were very extensive discussions of international development issues during the Bretton Woods negotiations.[6] Indeed, it goes further to argue that the Bretton Woods architects should be recognized for their important role in helping to pioneer modern concepts of international development. Their particular contribution was to establish for the first time a new kind of multilateral economic framework that aimed to assist the economic development of poorer countries. This framework involved much more ambitious ideas about international development than Truman's subsequent thinking.

The chapter begins by highlighting how the Bretton Woods discussions on international development built upon some important precursors from the interwar period. It then shows how US support for a development-friendly multilateral economic framework was evident in White's earliest plans and the initial conceptions of the IBRD. Support for such a framework was also apparent among policy makers from many other countries, particularly those from poorer regions such as Latin America and Asia, whose role in the Bretton Woods negotiations is often neglected. At the Bretton Woods Conference itself, this wide support led to the endorsement of key provisions in the Articles of Agreement of the IBRD and IMF that were aimed at supporting development goals. The chapter concludes with a suggestion about why this history is often overlooked and some brief comments about its relevance for the evolution of subsequent international development debates of the 1960s and 1970s.

SOME PRECURSORS

To understand the Bretton Woods discussions about international development, it is necessary first to review some ideas about the topic that emerged in the interwar period. One of the earliest proposals for a formal international development institution was put forward by China's Sun Yat-sen at the time of the creation of the League of Nations. In detailed plans sent to the Paris Peace Conference of 1919, Sun—who had no official position at the time—urged the creation of an "International Development Organization" that could help to mobilize foreign capital, technology, and expertise to promote the development of China and raise the standard of living of its people.[7]

Published as a book in 1920 under the title of *The International Development of China,* Sun's proposal was for this organization to be created by governments of "the Capital-supplying Powers" which would negotiate a formal loan contract with the Chinese government. The loans would support development projects whose property would then be owned by the Chinese state and "managed for the benefit of the whole nation." While foreign private bankers had "entirely disregarded the will of the Chinese people" in their past loans, Sun argued that this new form of international lending would ensure that the livelihood of the Chinese people was better served. Sun argued that this proposal could become "the keystone in the arch of the League of Nations" by promoting peace (by minimizing imperialist rivalries in China) as well as the prosperity of both China and the lending powers.[8]

Although Sun's proposal was ignored by the creators of the League of Nations, it was later invoked by some US advocates of international development lending at the time of the Bretton Woods negotiations.[9] It also served as the key inspiration for the Chinese government itself during those same negotiations. It is often forgotten that the Chinese government was actively involved in the Bretton Woods negotiations and sent the second largest delegation to the 1944 conference. In a formal statement near the start of the conference, China's head delegate, H. H. Kung, invoked Sun's book: "After the first World War, Dr. Sun Yat-sen proposed a plan for what he called 'the international development of China.' . . . Dr. Sun's teaching constituted the basis of China's national policy. America and others of the United Nations, I hope, will take an active part in aiding the post-war development of China."[10]

Not surprisingly, Kung and other Chinese officials strongly supported the creation of the IBRD and its development lending function, seeing this initiative as the final realization of Sun's ideas (despite the considerable differences between Sun's proposal and the IBRD's design).[11]

Although the founders of the League had ignored Sun's ideas, some of the activities of that organization during the interwar period also foreshadowed the international development focus of Bretton Woods. After its creation, the League began in a rather ad hoc fashion to support various technical assistance missions to poorer regions of the world that addressed issues such as agriculture, public health, education, and transportation, particularly during the 1930s.[12] By the late 1930s, top officials in the League also began to advocate international cooperation aimed at boosting living standards and nutrition levels in poorer parts of the world as a strategy for bolstering world prosperity and peace.[13] Although most of these League figures were on the sidelines of the Bretton Woods negotiations themselves, their arguments helped to boost support for international development more generally in international policy circles by the time of the Bretton Woods negotiations in early 1940s.

The Bretton Woods discussions of international development were influenced even more strongly by a set of inter-American initiatives in the late 1930s and early 1940s designed to support Latin American economic development. These initiatives included public international lending to finance not just long-term development projects (as in Sun's early proposal) but also short-term balance-of-payment deficits of the kind that plagued many Latin American commodity-exporting countries. These loans were initially extended bilaterally by US government agencies, but in 1939–1940 US and Latin American officials went further to design a new multilateral intergovernmental Inter-American Bank (IAB) to offer such lending. Although the US Congress refused to ratify the IAB plan, the negotiation of its detailed charter represented the first time that governments had ever attempted to construct a multilateral financial institution with a core mandate of promoting economic development in poorer countries.[14]

The United States pursued some other initiatives in Latin America during this time that were also designed to promote the region's economic development. These included efforts to restructure Latin American debts as well as to stabilize the prices of key Latin American commodity exports, including the creation of an Inter-American Coffee Agreement in 1940. The United States also launched financial advisory missions to the region—beginning with one to Cuba in 1941–1942—that recommended reforms aimed at strengthening the capacity of Latin American governments to pursue state-led development strategies, including through the use of unorthodox capital controls and adjustable exchange rates.[15]

Despite lingering concerns about US imperialism in the region, most Latin American governments backed these various initiatives as a form of useful international support for their increasingly ambitious state-led economic development strategies that had emerged in the wake of the Great Depression. Latin American concerns were also assuaged to some extent by the fact that US president Franklin Roosevelt cast these policies as part of his Good Neighbor policy that had renounced US military intervention in Latin America. Many Latin Americans also appreciated how the new US lending programs were government-to-government instead of coming from profit-seeking private US bankers that had been associated with US imperialism in the past. Even leading anti-imperialist politicians in the region, such as Peru's Víctor Raúl Haya de la Torre, became convinced by the late 1930s of the potential usefulness of new US-led international development policies in the inter-American region.[16]

From the US side, officials in the Roosevelt administration were driven to develop these innovative international development initiatives by a complex mix of motives, including economic and strategic interests in the region (particularly in the context of growing German influence) as well as some more idealistic values associated with the New Deal and the Good Neighbor policy. Not surprisingly, the initiatives also generated some opposition within the United States, particularly from isolationists, conservatives, and financial interests. That opposition was effective in blocking congressional ratification of the IAB and in diluting the ambition of other initiatives in this area.[17]

Despite some setbacks, these inter-American initiatives were critically important in setting the scene for the Bretton Woods negotiations. As noted below, Latin American governments played a major role in supporting the development content of the Bretton Woods Agreements, seeing them as building directly on the inter-American experience. The history also had an important impact on US negotiators. Many of the US officials at the center of the Bretton Woods negotiations, including Harry Dexter White himself, had been deeply involved in pioneering the Good Neighbor international development policies. They brought this experience into the Bretton Woods negotiations, where the inter-American initiatives served as key templates for the Bretton Woods Agreements. This link was very apparent in the content of White's initial drafts of the Bretton Woods Agreements that were developed in early 1942.

THE INTERNATIONAL DEVELOPMENT CONTENT OF WHITE'S FIRST PLANS

These plans highlighted the kinds of international development goals and techniques that had been developed in the inter-American context.[18] For example, the design of both the IMF and IBRD built directly on the US bilateral lending programs to Latin America as well as on the stillborn IAB charter. Despite the claims of Gardner and others, the IBRD's mandate to lend for "development" purposes was clearly outlined from the very start. The plans also gave both institutions a formal role in facilitating international debt restructuring, a role that White justified with reference to his experiences in Latin America. In addition, White assigned the IBRD the task of supporting international commodity price stabilization.

In discussing his proposed international fund, White also included some passages backing the need for infant-industry trade protection in poor country contexts, an issue he had previously written about in the Latin American context. The strength of his wording on this point deserves underlining because, as noted below, the issue became significant to discussions of the fund's purposes at the Bretton Woods meeting two years later. As he put it in his March 1942 draft of the fund, free trade policy rested on assumptions that were "unreal and unsound" and it "grossly underestimates the extent to which a country can virtually lift itself by its bootstraps in one generation from a lower to a higher standard of living, from a backward agricultural to an advanced industrialized country, provided always it is willing to pay the price."[19]

Finally, White's plans also provided for the kinds of adjustable exchange rates and capital controls that he and other US officials were recommending to Latin American governments at the time in their financial advisory work. Scholars have often noted that these provisions were designed to provide policy space for rich countries to pursue activist policies aimed at boosting employment and social security commitments. But the provisions were also intended by White and other US officials to protect policy space in poorer countries to pursue state-led development strategies. White also went out of his way in his early plans to highlight the useful role that capital controls could play in curtailing flight capital from poorer countries, an issue he had encountered in his financial advisory work in Cuba in 1941–1942 and in the negotiations of the IAB.

Taken together, these provisions represented a quite innovative multilateral economic framework for supporting state-led development strategies of poorer countries. No such comprehensive framework had ever been developed by a leading power for this purpose. White went out of his way in these early plans to highlight the significance of promoting the development of poorer countries. As he put it in his very first detailed draft of January 1942, "It is true that rich and powerful countries can for long periods safely and easily ignore the interests of poorer or weaker neighbors or competitors, but by doing so they only imperil the future and reduce the potential of their own level of prosperity." Using language that invoked the Good Neighbor policy, he continued: "The lesson that must be learned is that prosperous neighbors are the best neighbors; that a higher standard of living in one country begets higher standards in others, and that a high level of trade and business is most easily attained when generously and widely shared."[20]

White also added one more provision that was supportive of the interests of poorer countries: he proposed that the construction of the postwar international financial order take place through a multilateral conference that would give formal voice to all members of the United Nations (as well as what were called the "Associated Nations," that is, those countries that were neutral in the war but that had broken diplomatic relations with the Axis powers). White's proposal contrasted with Keynes's preference for an exclusive bilateral Anglo-American negotiation, which the latter argued would avoid "the delays and confused counsels of an international conference."[21] Keynes's view lost out, as White insisted on a more inclusive and democratic multilateral procedure to avoid giving the impression of an Anglo-American "gang-up."[22] Between White's initial plans and the 1944 multilateral conference, White and his US colleagues also went out of their way to consult with many countries beyond Britain, including poorer countries.

White's broad international development goals had the strong backing not just of his direct boss, US Treasury secretary Henry Morgenthau, but also of Roosevelt himself. The US president had already indicated in early 1941 that he hoped to promote "freedom from want . . . everywhere in the world," a goal that was subsequently incorporated into the Atlantic Charter of August of that year.[23] During the war, Roosevelt also went out of his way to signal his strong commitment to the idea of raising living standards in poorer regions of the world through international cooperation. Roosevelt saw "freedom from want" as a kind of internationalization of New Deal values that would lay a key foundation for postwar world peace and prosperity. US policy makers also argued that international development would help bolster US exports, create new opportunities for US investments, and secure strategic alliances during the war with governments in Latin America and other poorer regions where elites had become committed to state-led development. In justifying his plans, White also invoked these various idealistic, economic, and strategic objectives.

As the US plans evolved in internal discussions in 1942–1943, some of White's initial ideas were dropped. The provisions for mandatory international debt restructuring and commodity price stabilization were considered too controversial, while White's language about infant-industry protectionism related more to the international trade negotiations. But the core US commitment to international development remained in subsequent drafts and at the Bretton Woods Conference itself.

SUPPORT FOR INTERNATIONAL DEVELOPMENT BEYOND THE UNITED STATES

Keynes also shared this commitment. His support for international development was evident in his first specific proposals about the postwar international financial order drafted in the fall of 1941 and early 1942. When Keynes discussed how surplus countries within his proposed International Clearing Union (ICU) could restore equilibrium, one of his four suggestions was that they could be encouraged to offer "international loans for the development of backward countries." He also anticipated his ICU working in support of an "International Investment or Development Corporation" that US economist Alvin Hansen (who was involved in official US postwar planning) had been promoting at the time to fund development projects in poorer countries after the war.[24]

In the first published version of Keynes's ICU plan in April 1943, these ideas remained, and Keynes also went out of his way to add in a preface that the postwar world would need "investment aid, both medium and long term, for the countries whose economic development needs assistance from outside."[25] At the Bretton Woods Conference itself, Keynes also reiterated his support for international development lending in his role as chair of the commission that drafted the IBRD's charter. In his opening comments to the group, he noted the bank's duty "to develop the resources and productive capacity of the world, with special attention to the less developed countries" and "to raising the standard of life and the conditions of labour everywhere."[26]

Although Keynes supported the international development focus of Bretton Woods in these ways, his commitment to the issue was less strong than that of White. The latter had become very interested in the economic development of poorer countries through his extensive travel and work in Latin America. By contrast, Keynes had little travel experience in poorer regions of the world and had not shown a significant interest in the economic problems of those regions beyond his early writings about Indian currency and finance. Like many other British officials, Keynes also did not share White's support for arguments backing infant-industry protection to support industrialization in poorer regions, and he was much less critical of imperialism than many US New Dealers. While White was committed to consulting with poorer countries in the Bretton Woods negotiations, Keynes was also very dismissive of their potential contributions. In addition, Keynes's rhetorical support for international development sat very uneasily alongside British resistance to freeing up enormous sterling balances accumulated during the war by its Indian colony as well as by poor countries such as Egypt.[27]

US and British officials were not the only ones backing the inclusion of international development issues in the Bretton Woods negotiations. In discussions about postwar plans in the early 1940s, the prominent Dutch policy maker Johan Willem Beyen called for an international lending institution that could encourage the "development of backward countries." A Canadian official, Robert Bryce, also argued in 1943 that "we must have substantial loans from the richer states to the poorer states of the United Nations" in order to improve the standard of living of the world's poor.[28] Many of the strongest calls for international development, however, came from officials from poorer countries who were involved in postwar planning discussions.

One such country was China, whose enthusiasm at the Bretton Woods Conference for the IBRD's development lending role has already been mentioned. Chinese officials had in fact been pushing for greater development content in postwar planning well before the conference. When Keynes's and White's plans (which did not yet include the detailed public IBRD proposal) were first made public in the spring of 1943, the Chinese Ministry of Finance had complained that "neither plan gives sufficient consideration to the development of industrially weak nations." After the United States finally made public a draft of the IBRD in late 1943, Chinese officials backed the creation of this institution very strongly, telling US officials that it was "of very great importance to China."[29]

Drawing directly on their experience with the Good Neighbor development initiatives, Latin American countries also assumed a prominent role in supporting international development goals. Analyses that focus exclusively on the Anglo-American dimensions of the Bretton Woods negotiations overlook the important participation of countries from this region. It is worth recalling, for example, that White first discussed his postwar international financial plans with a Latin American audience in early 1942 before they were even shared with Britain.[30] Latin American officials continued to comment actively on evolving US plans up until the Bretton Woods meeting and then had a major presence at the conference itself, where they represented nineteen of the forty-four governments represented. Voting often as a bloc at the meeting, they used their numerical advantage to strengthen the development content of the final Bretton Woods Agreements in several ways, as will be noted.[31]

The delegation from India was another prominent backer of international development objectives during the Bretton Woods negotiations. Although still a British colony, the delegation included Indian officials, who took the lead role in speaking for India at the Bretton Woods Conference. Like their Chinese and Latin American counterparts, these figures saw state-led industrialization as the path to higher living standards. Indeed, one of the delegates, Ardeshir Darabshaw Shroff, had coauthored the high profile "Bombay Plan," which outlined such a strategy in detail in January 1944. At Bretton Woods, Shroff and the other Indian officials urged the conference to endorse provisions that would support these aspirations, including the freeing up of British sterling balances. If the latter remained inconvertible, Shroff argued that India would be placed "in a situation which I may compare to the position of a man with a million dollar balance in the bank but not sufficient cash to pay his taxi fare."[32]

There would likely have been even more voices of this kind from poorer regions of the world but for the fact that most parts of colonized Asia and Africa were not represented at the conference. Aside from India and the Philippines (which had been promised independence by the United States after its liberation from Japan), no other colony was represented.[33] The lack of representation did not stop colonial powers such as the Dutch from invoking their colonies' trade to justify demands for larger national quotas (and thus voting shares) in the IMF. Some US delegates privately suggested that it might be better to establish separate quotas for colonies to prevent any perception that the Bretton Woods Conference was endorsing colonial rule. After a quiet debate within the American delegation about this idea, however, they decided not to raise it, in order to prevent a major political row at the meeting.[34]

STRENGTHENING THE DEVELOPMENT MANDATE OF THE BANK

Given the broad support for international development among those present at Bretton Woods, it is not surprising that the conference devoted considerable attention to the issue. Morgenthau set the tone in his welcoming speech to the delegates, in which he referred to the goal of establishing "a satisfactory standard of living for all the people of all the countries on this earth." He also made the following argument: "Prosperity, like peace, is indivisible. We cannot afford to have it scattered here or there among the fortunate or to enjoy it at the expense of others. Poverty, wherever it exists, is menacing to us all and undermines the well-being of each of us."[35] Morgenthau's argument echoed a statement endorsed by an International Labour Organization conference in April that "poverty anywhere constitutes a danger to prosperity everywhere"—a statement that Roosevelt had enthusiastically endorsed at the time as "a guide to all of our international economic deliberations."[36]

The Bretton Woods delegates then proceeded to strengthen the development focus of some of the draft documents that had been prepared in advance of the conference. Particularly important were some changes made to the draft of the IBRD's Articles of Agreement. The first of these changes took place in response to an Indian complaint about the draft purposes of the other proposed institution: the IMF. In a draft document prepared by the United States and Britain, the IMF's purposes had included the following passage: "to facilitate the expansion and balanced growth of international trade, and to contribute in this way to the maintenance of a high level of employment and of real income which must be a primary object of economic policy." The Indian delegation argued that this wording "gives undue emphasis to the high level of income and of employment in already highly industrial countries. . . . The fund should have as its objective also to bring low-income countries up to a high level quite as much as to maintain the high level in other countries."[37] To address this situation, the Indian delegation proposed the addition of the following italicized wording: "To facilitate the expansion and balanced growth of international trade, *to assist in the fuller utilisation of the resources* of *economically underdeveloped countries* and to contribute thereby to the maintenance in the world as a whole of a high level of employment and real income, which must be a primary objective of economic policy."[38]

While some countries, such Ecuador and Australia, immediately supported the proposal, others did not, including Britain and the United States. The Anglo-American stance on this issue is sometimes invoked in contemporary scholarship to support the idea that they were uninterested in development issues. But US and British officials made clear that they were very supportive of India's general desire to see the needs of poorer countries recognized at the Bretton Woods Conference. They were only concerned that India's proposal might confuse the purposes of the fund with the development lending role of the IBRD. Other countries that were deeply committed to the development focus of Bretton Woods, such as Brazil, shared this Anglo-American concern.[39]

To signal their support for the broader Indian goal, those resisting the specific Indian proposal proposed a strengthening of the wording of the formal development purposes of the IBRD as an alternative. As one British official told the conference after a speech from one Indian delegate, "We are all in sympathy with those aspirations [to recognize the special needs of poorer countries]. Some of us have them very much at heart, but I would urge our Indian friends to reflect at this late hour whether those aspirations are not better satisfied in the framework of the preambles of the bank than in the framework of the preambles of the fund."[40] To accommodate the Indian goal, new wording was proposed that made explicit reference to the development needs of poorer countries in the first formal purpose of the bank. In an Anglo-American draft proposal developed before the conference, the IBRD's purposes referred to "development" in more general ways, such as its role in assisting "in the reconstruction and development of member countries" and "encouraging international investment for the development of the productive resources of member countries."[41] New wording was now proposed and quickly approved that spoke directly about "less developed countries" in the first formal purpose of the bank: "To assist in the reconstruction and development of territories of members by facilitating the investment of capital for productive purposes, including the restoration of economies destroyed or disrupted by war, the reconversion of productive facilities to peacetime needs and *the encouragement of the development of productive facilities and resources in less developed countries.*"[42]

In addition to strengthening the bank's explicit purpose of supporting the development of poorer countries, the Bretton Woods delegates also changed the wording of its general loan provisions to reinforce its development focus. In this case, the change was made in response to lobbying from Latin American delegates who were concerned that the bank might devote more attention to loans supporting European reconstruction than to those for development. To minimize this risk, Victor Urquidi of the Mexican delegation proposed the addition of the following sentence to the bank's loan provisions: "The Bank shall give equal consideration to projects for development and to projects for reconstruction, and its resources and facilities shall always be made available to the same extent for either kind of project."[43]

Explaining this proposal, Urquidi clarified that Mexico did not want "to impose on the Bank a rigid fifty-fifty rule," but that the new sentence was important to reassure Latin American governments that their "requests for capital for development purposes" would be given equal consideration as those for reconstruction. More generally, Urquidi highlighted the importance of international development, using language that he hoped would appeal to Keynes, who was chairing the discussion: "in the very short run, perhaps reconstruction will be more urgent for the world as a whole, but in the long run, Mr. Chairman—before we are all too dead, if I may say so—development must prevail if we are to sustain and increase real income everywhere."[44]

The general goal of the Mexican proposal was well received, but a Dutch official noted that the specific Mexican wording would require development lending to decline when reconstruction loans diminished. To avoid this problem, Keynes proposed a slight change to the wording which was then refined as follows: "The resources and the facilities of the Bank shall be used exclusively for the benefit of members with equitable consideration to projects for development and projects for reconstruction alike."[45] When Poland tried to suggest a further refinement that would prioritize reconstruction lending, Latin American delegations and others opposed the proposal and secured the approval of the wording above.

STRENGTHENING THE IMF'S DEVELOPMENT FOCUS

The IMF's draft Articles of Agreement were also altered in some ways that were seen to benefit development goals. One of the changes was to the very clause that Indian delegates had objected to in the IMF's draft purposes. Although India's specific proposal was rejected, the conference agreed to alter the clause—after much debate and several redrafts—to the following wording: "To facilitate the expansion and balanced growth of international trade, and to contribute thereby to the promotion and maintenance of high levels of employment and real income and to the development of the productive resources of all members as primary objectives of economic policy."[46] The addition of the word "promotion" in front of "high levels of employment and real income" and the inclusion of the phrase "the development of the productive resources of all members" were both made in response to the issue India had raised. Although the Indian delegation remained unhappy about the omission of any specific reference to less-developed countries in the IMF's formal purposes, this new phrasing did link the IMF's purposes more closely to development goals.[47]

The relationship of development goals to the IMF's mandate was also brought out in some interesting discussions that took place when the new wording was approved. Before the approval, an Indian delegate had advanced one last proposal to add the following statement at the end of the new clause: "with due regard to the needs of economically backward countries."[48] He argued that the wording would ensure that the commitment to the "balanced growth of international trade" would be interpreted in a manner that recognized the need for poorer countries to industrialize:

> We attach great importance also to the balanced character and composition of international trade. A predominant flow of raw materials and food stuffs in one direction and highly manufactured goods in the other direction is not a really balanced international trade from this latter point of view. It is only by greater attention to the industrial needs of countries like India that you can achieve a real and rational balance. It is for this reason that the India Delegation wants to mention specifically the needs of economically backward countries, in the description of objectives of economic policy, which the fund cannot directly assist but may indirectly facilitate.[49]

Although India's new proposal was rejected, other delegates supported India's development-oriented interpretation of the wording about the "balanced growth of international trade." Just before the final wording of the fund's purposes was approved, Colombia's Carlos Lleras Restrepo made a formal statement endorsing the final wording on the grounds that it had accommodated India's desire "to include among the ultimate purposes of the new facilities for the growth of international trade the development of the means of production of the member countries." As he put it, the wording implied recognition of "the right of new nations whose resources are not suf-ficiently developed to move forward on the road which they have already started to travel toward a more complex economy, toward a growing indus-trialization which may alter, and probably will alter, the volume of interna-tional trade in many commodities." He added that future trade agreements could not "become obstacles to the necessary protection which must be given in the new countries to their infant industries" and Colombia was agreeing to the fund's purposes, assuming that they were not "contrary to the devel-opment of our own domestic production and to the integration of our econ-omy through a steady access to new industrial techniques."[50]

It is important to note that White responded to Restrepo's speech by call-ing it "a splendid statement in support of the recommendation."[51] White's apparent endorsement of this interpretation of the wording of the IMF's pur-poses was likely sincere given his strong wording in favor of infant-industry protection in his first drafts of the fund quoted earlier in this chapter. It is understandable, then, that Indian delegates such as Shroff claimed after the conference that one of the IMF's objectives was "to see that the economically backward countries got suitable opportunities for rapid development, and that a substantial increase in the standard of living and real income of the people is brought about."[52]

Another reason that this interpretation made sense was that some specific provisions of the IMF Articles of Agreement were also seen by delegates to be supportive of the development goals of poorer countries. These included provisions that helped protect their policy space to pursue state-led develop-ment strategies, such as capital controls and adjustable exchange rates. The final Articles were in fact more permissive in these areas than White's initial drafts had been. For example, White's early plans had required IMF approval for governments to use capital controls, but the final Articles of Agreement gave governments the right to control all capital movements, as long as the controls did not restrict payments for current account transactions.[53] In the IMF's final Articles of Agreement, adjustments of exchange pegs of up to 10 percent were also permitted without Fund approval.[54] In financial advi-sory missions to Latin America, US policy makers had already indicated their support for poorer countries to use these policy tools in order to back state-led development strategies. They continued to signal this message through their backing of important domestic financial reforms in the immediate wake of the conference in countries such as Paraguay, Guatemala, the Philippines, and Ethiopia.[55]

Officials from poorer countries also saw the IMF's role of providing balance-of-payments support as particularly helpful to commodity-exporting countries that experienced large balance-of-payments fluctuations. At the Bretton Woods Conference, Latin American countries in fact lobbied successfully to strengthen the IMF's capacity to lend to countries that might experience unexpected fluctuations in their balance of payments. Brazilian delegates took the lead in proposing a clause that would allow the IMF's regular lending limits to be overruled in special circumstances. With Mexican delegates, they then participated in a special conference committee that developed this "waiver" clause in the IMF's Articles of Agreement, a clause whose final wording instructed the fund to "take into consideration periodic or exceptional requirements of the member requesting the waiver."[56] The Brazilian government hailed the approval of this wording by the conference as a victory for the interests of commodity-exporting countries.[57]

CONCLUSION

In these various ways, White's initial core goal of building a more development-friendly multilateral economic order remained intact and was even strengthened in some ways at the Bretton Woods Conference itself with the help of lobbying by delegates from poorer countries. The Bretton Woods delegates did not invent the idea of international development from scratch, since they drew upon and consolidated various ideas that had already emerged, such as Sun Yat-sen's early proposal, initiatives of the League of Nations, and especially the inter-American activities in the late 1930s and early 1940s. But their innovation was to locate these emerging ideas firmly within a new multilateral economic framework for the first time in a more comprehensive way.

After the conference, delegates highlighted this innovation prominently. For example, in a high profile article in *Foreign Affairs* in early 1945, Morgenthau went out of his way to speak to the importance of economic relations between rich and poor countries: "Nothing would be more menacing to world security than to have the less developed countries, comprising more than half the population of the world, ranged in economic battle against the less populous but industrially more advanced nations of the west." He then trumpeted how the international development goals of Bretton Woods would help avoid such a battle: "The Bretton Woods approach is based on the realization that it is to the economic and political advantage of countries such as India and China, and also of countries such as England and the United States, that the industrialization and betterment of living conditions in the former be achieved with the aid and encouragement of the latter."[58]

Given all this history, why has the important role of Bretton Woods in pioneering a multilateral framework for international development been often overlooked? A key reason may be that US policy makers withdrew much of their support for the framework very quickly after Roosevelt's death in 1945. The New Dealers who had been key drivers of this policy, such as White and Morganthau, lost influence in the new Truman administration, while critics of the policy—including Wall Street interests and more conservative thinkers—emerged more powerful. The strategic reasons for US support of state-led development goals in poorer regions such as Latin America also dramatically diminished with the end of the war.[59]

Although the onset of the Cold War then triggered some revival of US interest in international development, Truman's famous 1949 speech outlined only a very limited development vision focused primarily on the provision of technical assistance. In the new ideological environment of the Cold War, the more ambitious ideas of White and other New Dealers were viewed more skeptically. US financial assistance also came to be focused on its key strategic allies in Europe and Japan rather than on poorer parts of the world (with some exceptions of some frontline states such as South Korea).[60]

The United States' turn away from the ambitious Bretton Woods development framework during the early postwar years generated much resentment in Latin America and other poorer regions of the world. That resentment then grew in political influence with the decolonization movement of the 1950s and 1960s and culminated in the demands for a more development-friendly New International Economic Order (NIEO) in the 1970s. The NIEO proposal was portrayed by both its supporters and its opponents at the time as a challenge to the Bretton Woods order. But its broad goal of reforming the multilateral economic order to be more supportive of state-led development strategies of poorer countries in fact echoed the original Bretton Woods vision in some ways.[61]

Indeed, many of the specific issues that were at the top of the NIEO agenda reiterated topics extensively discussed during the Bretton Woods negotiations: long-term international development finance, compensatory short-term balance-of-payments financing for commodity exporters, the need for policy space, the control of capital flows, debt restructuring, commodity price stabilization, and support for infant-industry trade protectionism. In this way, the Bretton Woods negotiations deserve to be recognized for their role in pioneering modern concepts of international development that were at the center of international development debates later in the postwar period. They also remain politically salient today, particularly as emerging economies acquire greater influence in global economic governance.

Notes

For their helpful comments, I thank Ian Shapiro, Naomi Lamoreaux, and the other participants in this project. I am also grateful to the Social Sciences and Humanities Research Council of Canada for helping to fund the research underlying this chapter.

1. Gerald Meier, "The Formative Period," in *Pioneers in Development*, ed. G. Meier and Dudley Seers (Oxford: Oxford University Press, 1984), 9.

2. Richard Gardner, "Sterling Dollar Diplomacy in Current Perspective," *International Affairs* 62, no. 1 (1985): 30.

3. Ibid.

4. Quotes from Devesh Kapur, John Lewis, and Richard Webb, *The World Bank: Its First Half Century* (Washington, DC: Brookings Institution, 1997), 68; and Edward Mason and Robert Asher, *The World Bank Since Bretton Woods* (Washington, DC: Brookings Institution, 1973), 4.

5. Quotes from Gilbert Rist, *The History of Development*, trans. Patrick Camiller (London: Zed Books, 1997), 71.

6. See also Martin Daunton's contribution, "Nutrition, Food, Agriculture, and the World Economy," to this volume (chap. 7).

7. Quote from Sun Yat-sen, *The International Development of China* (New York: G. P. Putnam's Sons, 1922), 219. For an analysis of the origins of Sun's ideas, see Eric Helleiner, "Sun Yat-sen as a Pioneer of International Development," *History of Political Economy* 50, no. S1 (2018): 76–103.

8. Quotes from Sun, *International Development*, 9–11.

9. See, for example, David Ekbladh, *The Great American Mission: Modernization and the Construction of an American World Order* (Princeton, NJ: Princeton University Press, 2010), 74.

10. US State Department, *Proceedings and Documents of the United Nations Monetary and Financial Conference, Bretton Woods, New Hampshire, July 1–22, 1944* (Washington, DC: Government Printing Office, 1948), 1165–66.

11. Eric Helleiner, *Forgotten Foundations of Bretton Woods: International Development and the Making of the Postwar Order* (Ithaca, NY: Cornell University Press, 2014), chap. 7; Helleiner, "Sun Yat-sen."

12. Margherita Zanasi, "Exporting Development: The League of Nations and Republican China," *Comparative Studies in Society and History* 49, no. 1 (2007): 143–69.

13. Patricia Clavin, *Securing the World Economy: The Reinvention of the League of Nations, 1920–46* (Oxford: Oxford University Press, 2013).

14. Helleiner, *Forgotten Foundations*, chaps. 1–2

15. Ibid., chaps. 1, 3.

16. Robert Alexander, ed., *Aprismo: The Ideas and Doctrines of Víctor Raúl Haya de la Torre* (Kent, OH: Kent State University Press, 1973), 247, 289–94, 330. For Haya's anti-imperialist views, see Eric Helleiner and Antulio Rosales, "Towards Global IPE: The Neglected Significance of the Haya-Mariátegui Debate," *International Studies Review* 19, no. 4 (2017): 667–91. For Latin American views, see Helleiner, *Forgotten Foundations*, chaps. 1–3; and Christy Thorton, "Voice and Vote for the Weaker Nations: Mexico's Bretton Woods," in *Global Perspectives on the Bretton Woods Conference and the Post-War World Order*, ed. Giles Scott-Smith and J. Simon Rolfe (New York: Palgrave Macmillan, 2017).

17. Helleiner, *Forgotten Foundations*, chaps. 1–3.

18. The section draws on ibid., chap. 4.

19. J. Keith Horsefield, *The International Monetary Fund 1945–1965: Twenty Years of International Monetary Cooperation*, vol. 3 (Washington, DC: IMF, 1969), 70.

20. Quoted in Helleiner, *Forgotten Foundations*, 103.

21. John Maynard Keynes, *The Collected Writings of John Maynard Keynes*, vol. 25, ed. Donald Moggridge (London: Macmillan, 1980), 54.

22. Quote from E. F. Penrose, *Economic Planning for the Peace* (Princeton, NJ: Princeton University Press, 1953), 48.

23. Quoted in Helleiner, *Forgotten Foundations*, 120.

24. Keynes, *Collected Writings*, 80, 91; see also 47, 59, 91.

25. See Keynes's "Proposals for an International Clearing Union (April 1943)," in the "Historical Documents" section of this book.

26. US State Department, *Proceedings*, 85.

27. Helleiner, *Forgotten Foundations*, chap. 8.

28. Both quotes from ibid., 216–17.

29. Quotes from ibid., 192, 197.

30. Ibid., 107.

31. Ibid., chap. 6.

32. Quoted in US State Department, *Proceedings*, 1173. For India's role in the negotiations, see Eric Helleiner, "India and the Neglected Development Dimensions of Bretton Woods," *Economic and Political Weekly* 50, no. 29 (July 18, 2015): 31–39.

33. The only Asian delegations at Bretton Woods beyond India, China, and the Philippines were Iran and Iraq, while the only African delegations included Egypt, Ethiopia, Liberia, and South Africa.

34. Helleiner, *Forgotten Foundations*, 184–85.

35. US State Department, *Proceedings*, 81–82.

36. Quotes from Helleiner, *Forgotten Foundations*, 122.

37. Kurt Schuler and Andrew Rosenberg, eds., *The Bretton Woods Transcripts* (New York: Center for Financial Stability, 2012), 306.

38. US State Department, *Proceedings*, 23 [emphasis in the original].

39. Helleiner, "India."

40. Schuler and Rosenberg, *Bretton Woods Transcripts*, 130.

41. US State Department, *Proceedings*, 366–67.

42. IBRD's Article I (i) [emphasis added]. See "Articles of Agreement of the International Bank for Reconstruction and Development, July 22, 1944," in the "Historical Documents" section of this book.

43. US State Department, *Proceedings*, 373–74.

44. Ibid., 1176–77.

45. IBRD's Article III, Section 1 (a). See "Articles of Agreement of the International Bank for Reconstruction and Development, July 22, 1944," in the "Historical Documents" section of this book.

46. IMF's Article I (ii). See "Articles of Agreement of the International Monetary Fund, July 22, 1944," in the Historical Documents section of this book.

47. Helleiner, "India."

48. US State Department, *Proceedings*, 184.

49. Ibid., 1180–81.

50. Ibid., 1185–86.

51. Schuler and Rosenberg, *Bretton Woods Transcripts*, 247.

52. Quoted in Helleiner, *Forgotten Foundations*, 254.

53. IMF's Article VI, Section 3. See "Articles of Agreement of the International Monetary Fund, July 22, 1944," in the "Historical Documents" section of this book.

54. IMF's Article IV, Section 5 (c) (i). See "Articles of Agreement of the International Monetary Fund, July 22, 1944," in the "Historical Documents" section of this book.

55. Helleiner, *Forgotten Foundations*, chaps. 5–9.

56. IMF's Article 5, Section 4. See "Articles of Agreement of the International Monetary Fund, July 22, 1944," in the "Historical Documents" section of this book.

57. Helleiner, *Forgotten Foundations*, 166–68. At the Bretton Woods conference, Latin American countries also sought to resurrect White's early proposals for commodity price stabilization. When supporting the waiver clause, the Cuban delegation argued that the fund's resources were unlikely to be fully adequate to compensate for the kinds of balance-of-payments fluctuations that Cuba and other commodity exporters experienced. For that reason, they urged the convening of a future conference to create an international agency that helped stabilize commodity prices. Brazil and many other Latin American countries backed this idea, and their lobbying resulted in the passage of a vague conference resolution that recommended governments seek "to reach agreement as soon as possible on ways and means whereby they may best . . . bring about the orderly marketing of staple commodities at prices fair to the producer and consumer alike." US State Department, *Proceedings*, 1097–98. See also Helleiner, *Forgotten Foundations*, 169–70.

58. Henry Morgenthau, "Bretton Woods and International Cooperation," *Foreign Affairs* 23, no. 1 (1945): 190, also found in the "Historical Documents" section of this book.

59. Helleiner, *Forgotten Foundations*, 258–64.

60. Ibid., 264–68.

61. Ibid., 268–75.

Part IV

DENOUEMENT AND LEGACY

Chapter 10

The Operation and Demise of the Bretton Woods System, 1958–1971

Michael D. Bordo

The Bretton Woods system established in the 1944 agreements was a compromise between the fixed exchange rates of the gold standard, seen as conducive to rebuilding the network of global trade and finance, and the greater flexibility to which countries had resorted in the 1930s in the effort to restore and maintain domestic economic and financial stability. Each member would declare a par value of its currency in terms of dollars, while the United States declared the par value of the dollar as $35 per ounce of gold. The Articles of Agreement formally obliged member countries to ask the IMF for permission in advance before adjusting their parities, as a way of preventing opportunistic, beggar-thy-neighbor exchange rate changes. Adjustment would occur in the face of a fundamental disequilibrium that was never defined but that has later been construed to mean an imbalance requiring a change in the real exchange rate.

The agreements further obliged countries to remove restrictions on the current account while permitting them to maintain controls on transactions on capital accounts (so as to limit destabilizing capital flows). Capital controls and the ability to adjust parities in the face of shocks gave members the flexibility to use domestic monetary and fiscal policy to alleviate business-cycle shocks, but adherence to the pegged parities limited the size of these policy actions. The IMF, based on the principle of a credit union, whereby members could withdraw more than their original gold quotas,[1] was to provide relief to members for temporary current account shortfalls.

The system evolved differently than what the framers of Bretton Woods first imagined. Originally, currencies were treated as equal in the Articles. In theory, each country was required to maintain their par values by intervening in terms of the currency of every other country, but because the United States was the only country that pegged its exchange rate to gold, the others set their parities in terms of dollars and intervened in the dollar market. Thus, the system evolved into a gold-dollar standard that in many ways resembled the interwar gold-exchange standard.

The dollar emerged into prominence in the 1950s because of the sheer size of the role that the United States played in the world economy, its importance in world trade, and its open and deep capital markets. Thus, the dollar emerged in the 1950s as a private international money.[2] By the 1960s it was used as a unit of account in invoicing imports and exports, as a medium of exchange in serving as a vehicle currency for interbank transactions, and as a store of value for private claims for much of the world, although some countries closely linked to British trade and payments primarily used sterling. At the same time, the dollar emerged as an official international money. This stemmed from its use as a unit of account to define the parities of the member countries and because the dollar was used as the primary intervention currency. Finally, because of its role as a unit of account and a medium of exchange and its growing private acceptance, it became the dominant international store of value to be used as reserves. The growing private and official demands for dollars were supported through private and official long-term capital outflows in excess of a current account surplus, which produced a series of official settlement balance-of-payments deficits beginning as early as 1950.[3]

This essay focuses on the Bretton Woods system in the period 1958 to 1971, after the Western European members declared current account convertibility until the closing of the gold window by President Richard Nixon on August 15, 1971, which effectively ended it. I describe the problems in getting the system started, the operation of the system, and the problems faced by the United States, which ran continuous balance-of-payments deficits leading to a buildup in outstanding dollar liabilities in the rest of the world relative to the US gold reserves to back them. This created a threat of a run on the dollar. This structural weakness was magnified after 1965, when the United States began following an inflationary policy leading to the ultimate collapse of the system in 1971. I also discuss the problems faced by other key members (especially the United Kingdom, whose currency was also a reserve currency), and the eventually unsuccessful policies adopted by governments, the IMF, and other international institutions to preserve the system.

GETTING THE SYSTEM STARTED

It took close to fifteen years to get the Bretton Woods system fully operating. A number of overwhelming obstacles stood in the way. The first was bilateralism: for most countries, with the major exception of the United States, there were pervasive exchange controls and controls on international trade. Along with exchange controls, every country negotiated a series of bilateral agreements with each of the trading partners. The rationale for the use of controls and bilateralism was a shortage of international reserves. The devastated economies of Europe and Asia were unable to produce the exports needed to generate foreign exchange.

The second problem facing the system was a dollar shortage. By the end of World War II the United States held two-thirds of the world's monetary gold stock, and gold and dollar reserves were depleted in the rest of the world. Europe ran a massive current account deficit reflecting the demand for essential imports and the reduced capacity of its export industries. The dollar shortage was aggravated by overvalued official parities by the major European industrial countries set at the end of 1946. The IMF pressured its members to declare par values as soon as possible, and if the exchange rate chosen was inappropriate, it could be corrected later. Indeed, most countries adopted their prewar parities on the assumption that wartime and postwar inflation did not seriously disrupt their competitive position relative to the United States.[4]

By the early 1950s both problems had been solved by two developments: the Marshall Plan and the European Payments Union (EPU). The Marshall Plan funneled approximately $13 billion in grants and loans to Western Europe between 1948 and 1952. The Economic Cooperation Act of 1948, which created the Marshall Plan, was designed to help the European countries expand their economies, restore their export capacity, and, by creating economic stability, preserve political stability. These results would follow from providing relief from the burden of financing a massive payments deficit.

The EPU was established in 1952 under the auspices of the OEEC (Organization of European Economic Cooperation) to simplify bilateral clearing and pave the way to multilateralism.[5] The EPU followed the basic principle of a commercial bank clearinghouse. At the end of each month, each member would clear its net debit or credit position against all of its members with the EPU, with the Bank for International Settlement (BIS) acting as its agent. The EPU became the center of a worldwide multilateral settlement area, including the countries of the sterling and franc zones. The process of multilateralism culminated when eight European countries declared their currencies convertible for current account transactions on December 27, 1958.[6]

The third problem getting started concerned the role of the IMF. The IMF, by intention, was not equipped to deal with the postwar reconstruction problem. Most of the structural balance-of-payments assistance in this period was provided by the Marshall Plan and other US aid, including the Anglo-American loan of 1945. In a sense the United States replaced the IMF. As a consequence, new institutions, such as the OEEC, and existing institutions, such as the BIS, emerged as competing sources of international monetary authority. Moreover, the fund did very little to speed up the process of achieving multilateralism.

The fund also was criticized by prominent economists for seeking a declaration of par values too soon. The resultant fixed parities then set in motion forces within each country to resist devaluation, until it was done in the face of a currency crisis. The crisis associated with the 1949 sterling devaluation (following and as a result of the 1947 sterling crisis) in turn created further resistance by monetary authorities to changes in parity,[7] which ultimately changed the nature of the international monetary system from the adjustable peg intended in the Articles to a fixed-exchange-rate regime.

The fund's prestige was dealt a severe blow by three events in the preconvertibility period.[8] The first occurred when France devalued the franc in 1948 and created a multiple-exchange-rate system.[9] This violated Article IV, Section 5 of the Articles, and France was then denied access to the fund's resources until 1952. Since France had access to Marshall Plan aid, the fund's actions had little effect.

Second was the sterling devaluation of September 1949, when the fund was given only twenty-four hours of advance notice, which also violated Article IV, Section 5. This event revealed the fund's inability to deter a major power from following its sovereign interest.

Third was Canada's decision to float its currency in 1950 again in violation of the Articles. The fund was highly critical of the action. The Canadian authorities assured the fund that it was only a temporary expedient reflecting a massive capital inflow from the United States during the Korean War. As it turned out, Canada did not return to the par-value system until 1961, and in contrast to the fund's warnings, while the Canadian dollar freely floated there were only limited swings in it and the Canadian economy performed better than it did when it was part of the par-value system.[10]

The final development that preceded the full operation of the Bretton Woods system was the decline of sterling as a reserve currency. At the outset it was expected that sterling would play an important role in the postwar period. At the end of World War II, Britain ran a massive balance of payments deficit in gold and dollars. It also had an outstanding sterling debt of £3.7 billion amassed by borrowing from the British Empire, most of which was made inconvertible into dollars. The 1946 Anglo-American loan of $3.75 billion from the United States and $1.25 billion from Canada was to allow Britain to ratify the Bretton Woods Articles and restore current account convertibility in dollars. Current account convertibility was restored in July 15, 1947, quickly followed by a run on sterling, which rapidly depleted the United Kingdom's reserves and led to the suspension of convertibility on August 20, 1947. This event as well as the devaluation of sterling in 1949 greatly weakened sterling's credibility as a reserve currency. Sterling's devaluation was quickly followed by twenty-three countries.

The devaluation of 1949 was important for the system because it and Marshall Plan aid (by both boosting trade liberalization and removing political uncertainty) helped move key European countries from a current account deficit to a surplus, which was important to the eventual restoration of convertibility. It was also important because it revealed a basic weakness with the adjustable-peg arrangement—the one-way option of speculating against parity. By allowing changes in parity only in the event of a fundamental disequilibrium, the system encouraged the monetary authorities to delay adjustment until they were sure it was necessary. By then, speculators would also be sure and they would take a position from which they could not lose.[11]

THE OPERATION AND FLAWS OF THE BRETTON WOODS SYSTEM

The Bretton Woods system became functional in December 1958 almost fifteen years after the original conference, when the Western European countries declared current account convertibility. Japan followed in 1961.

Although the Bretton Woods system was short-lived, it lasted in its convertible phase from 1959 to 1971, and as we will discuss, it had many problems, yet economic performance during its existence was remarkable.

The Bretton Woods system (along with trade liberalization under the General Agreement on Tariffs and Trade—GATT) was associated with higher and more stable economic growth than in any other period in the past 150 years, with the exception of the Great Moderation from 1983 to 2006. In addition, inflation performance, both in terms of levels and variation, was also superior to previous and subsequent regimes, with the principal exception of the classical gold standard and the Great Moderation periods.[12] However, as we will discuss, inflation began to rise in 1965, leading to the Great Inflation of the 1970s.

Nevertheless, as the system evolved into a gold-dollar standard, the three big problems of the interwar gold-exchange standard reemerged: the adjustment, confidence, and liquidity problems.

THE ADJUSTMENT PROBLEM

The adjustment problem in Bretton Woods reflected downward rigidity in wages and prices, which prevented the normal price adjustment of the gold standard price-specie flow mechanism to operate. Consequently, payments deficits would be associated with rising unemployment and recessions. The reluctance to follow tight monetary and fiscal policies (in most advanced countries with the principal exceptions of Germany and Switzerland), except in the face of a currency crisis, reflected the strong commitment to full employment and a social safety net. For surplus countries, inflationary pressure would ensue, which they would try to block by sterilization and capital controls.

The United Kingdom between 1959 and 1967 alternated between expansionary monetary and fiscal policies designed to maintain full employment and encourage economic growth and austerity programs—a strategy referred to as "stop-go." The connecting link was the state of the balance of payments. Expansionary policy inevitably led to deterioration in the current account, a decline in international reserves, and speculation against the sterling parity.

On several occasions, standby loans were drawn from the IMF and rescue packages arranged by the G10 through the BIS.[13] These took place in 1957, 1961, and 1964. The final crisis occurred in 1966–1967, ending in sterling's devaluation in November 1967, in which the Federal Reserve and other central banks contributed to a $3 billion rescue package. which was insufficient to stem the speculative attack. After the November 1967 devaluation and the 1968 Basel Agreement (in which the members of the sterling area received a dollar guarantee of their sterling holdings) sterling ceased to be an effective international reserve currency.[14]

The experience of the United Kingdom was important for the adjustment issue because it was a country with a chronic balance-of-payments deficit forced to take corrective action.[15] For the United States, sterling as an alternative reserve currency was viewed as a first line of defense for the dollar.[16]

During this period, every technique and tool recommended by the Organization for Economic Cooperation and Development (OECD) Working Party 3 on adjustment was used. Other facilities to provide the liquidity needed for adjustment were developed (Basel arrangements, short-term swaps (extensions of inter–central bank credit lines), and longer-term facilities. The IMF instituted the General Arrangements to Borrow (GAB) in 1961, in which the G10 countries provided a $6 billion line of credit in hard currencies to the IMF.

West Germany from 1959 to 1967 (also the Netherlands) was a surplus country facing the opposite problem to the United Kingdom's. Rapid economic and export growth and relatively slow inflation led to a series of current account surpluses and reserve inflows in the 1950s and 1960s. Concern over the inflationary consequences of the balance-of-payments surplus led the German monetary authorities in 1955 to both follow tight monetary policy and to institute measures to prevent capital inflows, including the prohibition of interest payments and the imposition of discriminatory reserve requirements on foreign deposits. Finally, in 1961 the deutsche mark was revalued by 5 percent. The package of tight money and capital controls was repeated again in 1964–1966 and 1968. Germany resisted further adjustment during the Bretton Woods era. The German monetary authorities believed that the key problem of the international monetary system was inflation imported from abroad.[17]

ASYMMETRIC ADJUSTMENT BETWEEN THE UNITED STATES AND THE REST OF THE WORLD

In the Bretton Woods pegged exchange rate system the United States as central-reserve country did not have to adjust to its balance-of-payments deficit. It was the n-1th currency in the system of n currencies.[18] Other countries had to intervene in their foreign exchange markets and buy or sell dollars to maintain their pegs. The US Treasury only had to intervene in the gold market to maintain the fixed dollar price of gold at $35 per ounce. Indeed, as

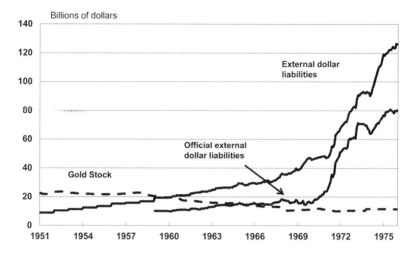

Figure 10.1: U.S. monetary gold stock and external liabilities, 1951–1975. Source: *Banking and Monetary Statistics 1941–1970.* Washington, DC: Board of Governors of the Federal Reserve System, September 1976, tables 14.1, 15.1.

a matter of routine, the Federal Reserve automatically sterilized dollar outflows.

This asymmetry of adjustment was resented by the Europeans. The Germans viewed the United States as exporting inflation to surplus countries through its deficits.[19] The French resented US financial hegemony and the seigniorage[20] that the United States earned on its outstanding liabilities.[21] They preferred jettisoning the gold dollar system and returning to the classical gold standard.

The US monetary authorities began to worry about the balance-of-payments deficit because of its effect on confidence. As official dollar liabilities held abroad mounted with successive deficits, the likelihood increased that these dollars would be converted into gold and that the US monetary gold stock would eventually reach a point low enough to trigger a run. This was actually what happened to the gold-exchange standard in the interwar period. Indeed, by 1959, the US monetary gold stock equaled total external dollar liabilities and the rest of the world's monetary gold stock exceeded that of the United States. By 1964, official dollar liabilities held by foreign monetary authorities exceeded the US monetary gold stock (see fig. 10.1).

A second source of concern, which also echoed the role of sterling in the interwar, was the dollar's role in providing liquidity to the rest of the world. Elimination of the US balance-of-payments deficit (as the Germans and French urged) could create a worldwide liquidity shortage. Much concern through the 1960s was over how to provide this liquidity.

Robert Triffin captured the problems in his famous dilemma.[22] Because the Bretton Woods parities that were declared in the 1940s had undervalued the price of gold, gold production would be insufficient to provide the reserves to finance the growth of global trade. Moreover, the main sources of supply at the time, the USSR and South Africa, were unreliable.[23] Under the gold-dollar standard, the shortfall would be met by US dollars provided by capital outflows from the US manifest in its balance-of-payments deficit. Triffin posited that as outstanding US dollar liabilities mounted they would increase the likelihood of a classic bank run, when the rest of the world's monetary authorities would convert their dollar holdings into gold.[24] According to Triffin, when the tipping point would occur, the US monetary authorities would tighten monetary policy and this would lead to global deflationary pressure and, in the face of nominal rigidities, global depression, as in the 1930s.[25] Triffin's solution was to create a form of global liquidity, like Keynes's bancor,[26] to act as a substitute for US dollars in international reserves. This was achieved in 1969 with the creation of the SDR (Special Drawing Rights, sometimes referred to as paper gold). This was too little and too late to save the system.

Another way to think about the problems of Bretton Woods is in terms of the open economy trilemma posited by Obstfeld and Taylor.[27] According to the trilemma, only two of three conditions could prevail: fixed exchange rates, an open capital account, and independent monetary policy. In the Bretton Woods system, the trilemma would be solved by imposing capital controls. This would allow the domestic monetary authorities to maintain full employment and low inflation while keeping the exchange rate pegged. As events unfolded, member states followed financial policies inconsistent with the pegged rates, and capital controls were increasingly evaded, leading to speculative attacks.

POLICIES TO SHORE UP THE SYSTEM

The problems of the Bretton Woods system were dealt with by the IMF, the G10 plus Switzerland, and by the US monetary authorities. The remedies that followed often worked in the short run but not in the long run. The main threat to the system as a whole was the Triffin problem, which was exacerbated after 1965 by expansionary US monetary and fiscal policy that led to rising inflation. Misalignments between member countries other than the United States also aggravated the basic problem because deficit countries like the United Kingdom would settle their imbalances with surplus countries like Germany in dollars, which in turn increased the threat of eventual conversion into US monetary gold.

The event that galvanized action was a spike in the London price of gold to $40.50 in October 1960. It was based on the fear in the financial markets that if John F. Kennedy were to be elected as president, he would pursue inflationary policies. The US Treasury developed policies to discourage conversion of dollars into gold by the Europeans: moral suasion on Germany with the threat to pull out US troops; the creation of the Gold Pool in 1961 (eight central banks pooled their gold reserves to be used to keep the London price of gold close to the $35-per-ounce parity price); the issue of Roosa bonds (foreign currency denominated bonds to discourage US allies from converting dollars into gold, originated by Robert Roosa, undersecretary of the Treasury for Monetary Affairs); the General Arrangements to Borrow (GAB) in 1961, which created an IMF lending facility large enough to offer substantial credit to the United States; Operation Twist in 1962 (the US Treasury bought long-term debt to lower long-term interest rates and encourage investment while the Federal Reserve simultaneously sold short-term Treasury bills to raise short-term interest rates to attract capital inflows); and the Interest Equalization Tax in 1963 (which imposed a tax on capital outflows).

The US Treasury also engaged in sterilized exchange market intervention, both spot and forward, using the Exchange Stabilization Fund, which had been created in 1934 from the proceeds of Roosevelt's devaluation of the dollar.[28] In 1961, to tap the Fed's greater resources, the Treasury requested it to join in the intervention. The main instrument used by the Fed to protect the gold stock was the swap network. It was designed to protect the US gold stock by temporarily providing an alternative to foreign central-bank conversion of their dollar holdings into gold. In a typical swap transaction, the Federal Reserve and a foreign central bank would undertake simultaneous and offsetting spot and forward exchange transactions typically at the same exchange rates and equal interest rates.

The swaps in turn became valuable to foreign monetary authorities in the face of a currency crisis, that is, in the United Kingdom from 1961 to 1967 and in France from 1968 to 1969. The Federal Reserve swap lines increased from $900 million to $11.2 billion between March 1962 and the closing of the gold window in August 1971[29] (see figs. 10.2 and 10.3). Until 1967 sterling took up the lion's share of the swap lines (see fig. 10.3).

The swaps and the ancillary Treasury policies did protect the US gold reserve until the mid-1960s and were viewed at the time as successful policies. Indeed, during the period of 1959 to 1967 the Bretton Woods system functioned reasonably well with the various cooperative arrangements that had been worked out by the G10, the BIS, and the IMF.[30]

In addition to the many policies designed to solve the US adjustment problem, following Triffin's approach, a number of plans were instituted to provide alternative forms of liquidity for the international monetary system to gold and dollars. Triffin's own solution was to go back to the Keynes Plan and have the IMF serve as the world's central bank and issue bancor (international fiat money). An alternative plan was that of Edward Bernstein (first research director of the IMF) to issue CRUs—composite reserve units. Under Bernstein's plan, each member of the G10 would subscribe an amount of its own currency to a pool and receive in exchange a corresponding amount of

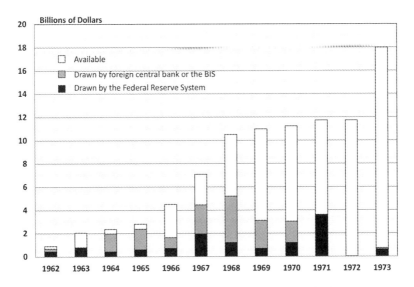

Figure 10.2: Federal Reserve swap lines, 1962–1973. Source: Federal Reserve System.

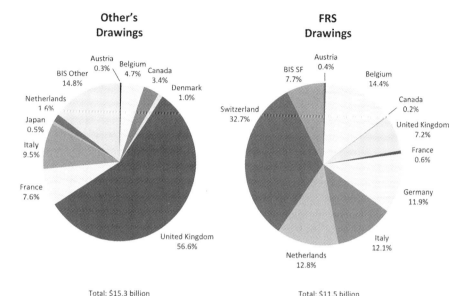

Figure 10.3: Composition of drawings on the Federal Reserve swap line 1962–1971. Source: Federal Reserve System.

CRUs, which could then be used as equivalent to gold. An extension of the CRU system was the Special Drawing Rights (SDR) which were adopted under the First Amendment to the IMF Articles in 1969. In the SDR scheme, a special drawing account was set up at the fund, separate from the general account. In contrast to CRUs, access to SDRs was made available to all members, not just the G10. Members were credited SDRs in proportion to their quotas. Also unlike with the CRUs, SDRs carried a fiat obligation and were not backed by gold, although they were valued in terms of gold at par with the US dollar. Their acceptability derived from the obligation by other members to accept SDRs in exchange for dollars. Members had to accept SDRs when the fund mandated their acceptance, as long as their holdings were less than three times their quotas. The IMF Articles were amended in 1969 creating SDRs. They were activated in 1970.

Several plans were also suggested to alleviate the confidence problem. These included substituting SDRs for gold and dollars as reserve assets, "the substitution account."[31] Many felt that this would just put the pressure onto the new asset, doubling the official price of gold.[32] It would create sufficient liquidity to alleviate both the liquidity and adjustment problems. Also, the rise in the official price of gold would encourage gold production and discourage private demand. Growth in the world monetary gold stock would be sufficient to finance the growth of real output and prevent a threat to US gold reserves for the foreseeable future. Doubling the price of gold was opposed on the grounds that it was time inconsistent, that if the official price of gold were raised once, why would it not happen again? Market agents would expect a change in gold's price in the future and would reduce their holdings of dollars permanently. Second, it would only postpone the problem because eventually, in the face of rapid real growth, scarcity would reappear.[33]

THE BREAKDOWN OF BRETTON WOODS, 1968–1971

A key force that led to the breakdown of the BWS was the rise in inflation in the central country, the United States, beginning in 1965. Until that year Federal Reserve chairman William McChesney Martin had maintained low inflation. The Fed also attached high importance to the balance of payments and the US monetary gold stock in its policy deliberations.[34] Beginning in 1965 Martin's Fed shifted to an inflationary policy, which continued until the early 1980s and in the 1970s became known as the Great Inflation. The Federal Reserve shifted its stance in the mid-1960s away from monetary orthodoxy in response to the growing influence of Keynesian economics in the Kennedy and Johnson administrations, with its primary objective of full employment and the belief that the Fed could manage the Phillips-curve trade-off between inflation and unemployment.[35] The shift in policy reflected the accommodation of growing fiscal deficits—a strategy referred to as "fiscal dominance."[36] Rising deficits reflected the increasing expense of the Vietnam War and Lyndon Baines Johnson's Great Society. One way that fiscal pressure led to accommodative monetary policy was by the use of "Even Keel" policies, under which the Federal Reserve would stabilize interest rates during Treasury funding operations. This operation prevented the Fed from tightening monetary policy to offset inflationary pressure.[37]

In addition, as the inflation rate ratcheted up, fear that the tight monetary policies required to reduce it would lead to rising unemployment, and a political backlash against the Fed made first Chairman Martin and then Arthur Burns, his successor, reluctant to stop it.[38]

Increasing US monetary growth led to rising inflation. Rising US inflation then spread to the rest of the world through growing US balance-of-payments deficits. A well-understood transmission mechanism was via the classical price-specie flow mechanism supplemented by capital flows. This led to growing balance-of-payment surpluses in Germany and other countries. The German monetary authorities (and those in other surplus countries) attempted to sterilize the inflows but were eventually unsuccessful, leading to growing inflationary pressure.[39]

In addition to the rise in US inflation as a source of strain on the international monetary system, world gold production leveled off in the mid-1960s and even declined in 1966. At the same time, private demand for gold increased, leading to a drop in the world monetary gold stock after 1966. Beginning in 1966, the Gold Pool became a net seller of gold.[40]

After the devaluation of sterling in November 1967, pressure mounted against the dollar via the London gold market. From December 1967 to March 1968, the Gold Pool lost $3 billion in gold with the US share at $2.2 billion.[41] In the face of the pressure, the Gold Pool was disbanded on March 17, 1968, and a two-tier arrangement was put in its place. The monetary authorities of the Gold Pool agreed neither to sell nor to buy gold from the market and would transact among themselves at the official $35 price. As a consequence, the link between gold production and other sources of gold and official reserves was cut. In the following three years the United States put considerable pressure on other monetary authorities to refrain from converting their dollar holdings into gold.

The world had switched to a de facto dollar standard. However gold convertibility still played a role. Although the major industrial countries tacitly agreed not to convert their outstanding dollar liabilities into US monetary gold, the threat of doing so was always present. The system also developed into a de facto fixed-exchange-rate system. Exchange rates became more rigid out of fear of the consequences of members allowing them to change. Moreover, because of increased capital mobility, the pressure for altering the parities of countries with persistent deficits and surpluses became harder to stop through the use of domestic policy tools and the aid of international rescue packages.

1968–1969 was characterized by currency crises in France and Germany, leading to a devaluation in France and a temporary float and then revaluation in Germany, taking the pressure temporarily off the United States. In 1970 US interest rates fell in response to rapid monetary expansion, and the US balance of payments mushroomed to $9 billion. The deficit exploded to $30 billion by August 1971. The dollar flood increased the reserves of the surplus countries, auguring inflation. German money growth nearly doubled from 6.8 percent to 12 percent in 1971, and the German inflation rate increased from 1.8 percent in 1969 to 5.3 percent in 1971.[42] In April 1971 the dollar inflow to Germany reached $3 billion. On May 5, 1971, the Bundesbank suspended official operations in the foreign exchange market and allowed the deutsche mark to float. Similar actions by Austria, Belgium, the Netherlands, and Switzerland followed.[43]

In April 1971, the US balance of trade turned to a deficit for the first time. The decision to suspend gold convertibility by President Richard Nixon on August 15, 1971, was triggered by French and British intentions in early August to convert dollars into gold. The US decision to suspend gold convertibility ended a key aspect of the Bretton Woods system. The remaining part of the system, the adjustable peg, disappeared by March 1973.

The Bretton Woods system collapsed for three basic reasons. First inflationary US monetary policy was inappropriate for the key currency country of the system. Although the acceleration of inflation from 1965 to 1971 was low compared to what happened in the 1970s, it was sufficient to trigger a speculative attack on the world's monetary gold stock in 1968, leading to the collapse of the Gold Pool.[44] Once the system had evolved into a de facto dollar standard after the collapse of the Gold Pool, the obligation of the United States was to maintain price stability. Instead it conducted an inflationary monetary policy that ultimately destroyed the system. Indeed, the Bretton Woods system was based on rules. The most important of them was to follow monetary and fiscal policies consistent with the official peg. The United States violated this rule after 1965.[45]

Second, the surplus countries were increasingly unwilling to adjust and absorb dollar balances and revalue their currencies. This reflected basic differences in the underlying inflation rates that they were willing to accept. It also reflected growing productivity differences between Germany and Japan, on the one hand, and the United States, on the other, which changed real exchange rates.[46] The growing gap between the sovereign interests of the United States and the other major powers likely reflected the decline in US power. At the same time as US power declined relative to the continental countries, European countries, and Japan, the G10 lost effectiveness and no other focal points of power emerged. The stage was set for a decentralized system.

Finally, the collapse of the Bretton Woods system was related to two major design flaws. The first was the gold-dollar/ gold-exchange system, which placed the United States under threat of a convertibility crisis. In reaction it pursued policies that in the end made adjustment more difficult. The second flaw was the adjustable peg. Because, in the face of growing capital mobility, the costs of discrete changes in parities were deemed so high, the system evolved into a reluctant fixed-exchange-rate system without any effective adjustment.

CONCLUSION

The collapse of the Bretton Woods system between 1971 and 1973 led to the general adoption by advanced countries of a managed floating exchange rate system, which is still with us. Yet this outcome (at least at the time) was not inevitable.[47] As was argued by Despres, Kindleberger, and Salant,[48] in contra distinction to Triffin, the ongoing US balance-of-payments deficit was not really a problem. The rest of the world voluntarily held dollar balances because of their valuable service flow: the deficit was demand-determined. They viewed the United States as supplying financial intermediation services to the rest of the world. Europeans borrowed long-term capital from the United States because the US capital markets were deeper and more efficient and interest rates were lower. In turn, Europeans maintained short-term balances in American banks because of a higher return. In their view the Bretton Woods system could have continued indefinitely.

This of course was not the case, but although the par-value system ended in 1973, the dollar standard without gold is still with us, as McKinnon had long argued.[49] Both private entities and official agencies hold dollars because of their superior attributes as money. This was the case in the 1960s when under the gold-dollar standard, and it still is the case today with fiat money. The key requirement to maintain the pure dollar standard is for the Federal Reserve to follow credible monetary policy geared to price stability. In the 1970s the Federal Reserve's inflationary policy led to a shift out of dollar holdings in the rest of the world and culminated in a speculative attack on the dollar in 1978. Paul Volcker was appointed chairman of the Federal Reserve to end the inflationary spiral and restore credibility. He succeeded in doing this by following a vigorous disinflationary policy, which by the mid-1980s greatly reduced the inflation rate but at the expense of a serious recession in 1980–1982. Since the mid-1980s the Fed has followed a policy of maintaining credibility for low inflation, and the international stature of the dollar has been more than fully restored.[50]

The dollar standard was resented by the French in the 1960s and referred to as conferring "the exorbitant privilege" on the United States, and the same argument was made in 2010 by the governor of the Central Bank of China. However, the likelihood that the dollar will be replaced as the dominant international reserve currency in the foreseeable future seems remote. The alternative candidates are the euro and the Chinese renminbi. The euro is still in crisis, and the likelihood that the Eurozone will ever be a secure and stable political and economic entity is doubtful. China is not yet financially developed and does not have the open financial system free from capital controls or the presence of the rule of law necessary to backstop a true international reserve currency. The dollar standard and the legacy of the Bretton Woods system will be with us for a long time.

Notes

For helpful comments, I thank Owen Humpage, Allan Meltzer, Eric Monnet, Catherine Schenk, and John Taylor.

1. Each member contributed a gold quota determined by its economic size in 1944. Then each member was allowed to borrow beyond their original quotas; the amounts they could borrow (the multiples of the original gold quota), up to the amount of their original contribution (in both gold and their own currencies), was determined by the IMF based on conditions that the members would fulfill, e.g., reducing their budget deficits by a certain amount.

2. See Ronald I. McKinnon, "An International Gold Standard without Gold," *Cato Journal* 8 (Fall 1988): 351–73.

3. See Michael D. Bordo, "The Bretton Woods International Monetary System: A Historical Overview," in *A Retrospective on the Bretton Woods System, Lessons for International Monetary Reform*, ed. Michael Bordo and Barry Eichengreen (Chicago: University of Chicago Press, 1993), 47.

4. See Robert Triffin, *Europe and the Money Muddle* (New Haven, CT: Yale University Press, 1957).

5. See Jacob Kaplan and Gunther Schleiminger, *The European Payments Union: Financial Diplomacy in the 1950s* (Oxford: Clarendon Press, 1989).

6. See Bordo, "Bretton Woods International Monetary System," 431.

7. See Catherine Schenk, *The Decline of Sterling: Managing the Retreat of an International Currency, 1945 to 1992* (New York: Cambridge University Press, 2010).

8. See Robert A. Mundell, "The International Monetary Fund," *Journal of World Trade Law* 3 (1969): 455–97.

9. A multiple-exchange-rate system means having different exchange rates for different types of activities, e.g., investment goods vs. consumption goods.

10. See Michael D. Bordo, Ali Dib, and Larry Schembri, "Canada's Pioneering Experience with a Flexible Exchange Rate in the 1950s," *International Journal of Central Banking* (October 2010).

11. See Milton Friedman, "The Case for Flexible Exchange Rates," in *Essays in Positive Economics*, 157–203 (Chicago: University of Chicago Press, 1953).

12. See Michael D. Bordo and Anna J. Schwartz, "Monetary Policy Regimes and Economic Performance: The Historical Record," chap. 3 of the *Handbook of Macroeconomics*, vol. 1, ed. John Taylor and Michael Woodford (New York: North Holland Press, 1999); and Luca Benati and Charles Goodhart, "Monetary Policy Regimes and Economic Performance: The Historical Record 1979–2008," chap. 21 of the

Handbook of Monetary Economics, vol. 3, ed. Benjamin Friedman and Michael Woodford (New York: North Holland Press, 2010).

13. Referred to as Basel Operations and Arrangements. See Michael D. Bordo and Catherine Schenk, "Monetary Policy Cooperation and Coordination: An Historical Perspective on the Importance of Rules," in *Rules for International Monetary Stability: Past, Present, and Future*, ed. Michael Bordo and John Taylor (Stanford, CA: Hoover Institution Press, 2017).

14. See Schenk, *Decline of Sterling.*

15. France had been in a similar position in 1950.

16. See Michael D. Bordo, Owen Humpage, and Anna J. Schwartz, *Strained Relations: US Foreign Exchange Operations and Monetary Policy in the Twentieth Century* (Chicago: University of Chicago Press, 2015).

17. See Bordo, "Bretton Woods International Monetary System," 54–55.

18. See Robert A. Mundell, "Problems of the International Monetary System," in *Monetary Problems of the International Economy*, ed. Robert A. Mundell and Alexander Swoboda (Chicago: University of Chicago Press, 1969).

19. See Otmar Emminger, "Practical Aspects of the Problem of Balance of Payments Adjustment," *Journal of Political Economy* 75 (August 1967): 512–22.

20. "Seigniorage" originally meant the fee that was paid to the sovereign for the right to mint coins. In the modern context of fiat money it means the foregone interest that central banks earn by issuing costless paper currency.

21. See Jacques Rueff, "Increase the Price of Gold," in *The International Monetary System: Problems and Proposals*, ed. Lawrence H. Officer and Thomas D. Willett (Englewood Cliffs, NJ: Prentice Hall, 1967), 179–90.

22. See Robert Triffin, *Gold and the Dollar Crisis* (New Haven, CT: Yale University Press, 1960).

23. See Martin Gilbert, *The Gold Dollar System: Conditions of Equilibrium and the Price of Gold*, Essays in International Economics, International Finance Section, Department of Economics, Princeton University, 1968.

24. See Peter M. Garber, "The Collapse of the Bretton Woods Fixed Exchange Rate Regime," in *A Retrospective on the Bretton Woods System: Lessons for International Monetary Reform*, ed. Michael D. Bordo and Barry Eichengreen (Chicago: University of Chicago Press, 1993), 461–85.

25. See Michael D. Bordo, Christopher Erceg, and Charles Evans, "Money, Sticky Wages, and the Great Depression," *American Economic Review* (December 2000). As it turned out Triffin's predictions never came true. As it is argued below, the system did not collapse into deflation but exploded into inflation. See the mimeo of Michael D. Bordo and Robert N. McCauley, "Triffin: Dilemma or Myth?" (Basel: Bank for International Settlement [BIS], 2017).

26. See John Maynard Keynes, "Proposals for an International Clearing Union" (1943), in *The International Monetary Fund 1945–1965: Twenty Years of International Monetary Cooperation*, vol. 1: *Chronicle*, ed. Keith Horsefield et al. (Washington, DC: International Monetary Fund, 1969).

27. See Maurice Obstfeld and Alan Taylor, *Global Capital Markets: Integration, Crises, and Growth* (New York: Cambridge University Press, 2004).

28. See Bordo, Humpage, and Schwartz, *Strained Relations*, chap. 3.

29. Ibid.

30. See Bordo and Schenk, "Monetary Policy Cooperation and Coordination."

31. See Robert McCauley and Catherine Schenk, "Reforming the International Monetary System in the 1970s and 2000s: Would an SDR Substitution Account Have Worked?," *International Finance* 18, no. 2 (2015): 187–206.

32. See Jacques Rueff, "Increase the Price of Gold," 179–90; and Martin Gilbert, *Gold Dollar System*. Doubling the official price of gold from $35 per ounce to $70 per ounce would double the value of US gold reserves, which would greatly reduce the likelihood of a run on the dollar.

33. See Bordo, "Bretton Woods International Monetary System," 72.

34. See Michael D. Bordo and Barry Eichengreen, "Bretton Woods and the Great Inflation," chap. 9 in *The Great Inflation*, ed. Michael Bordo and Athanasios Orphanides (Chicago: University of Chicago Press, 2013).

35. See Allan H. Meltzer, *A History of the Federal Reserve*, vol. 2, bk. 1 (Chicago: University of Chicago Press, 2010).

36. See Eric Leeper and Todd Walker, "Perceptions and Misperceptions of Fiscal Inflation" (BIS Working Paper 364, December 2011).

37. See Meltzer, *History of the Federal Reserve*; and Owen Humpage, "Even Keel and the Great Inflation" (Federal Reserve Bank of Cleveland Working Paper, 2015), 15–32.

38. See "Introduction," in Bordo and Orphanides, *Great Inflation*.

39. Sterilization, whereby the effects of an inflow of dollar reserves on the money supply is offset by an open market sale of domestic securities, is limited by the supply of such securities. See Michael Darby, James Lothian, et al., *The International Transmission of Inflation* (Chicago: University of Chicago Press, 1983).

40. The Gold Pool was designed to keep the price of gold at $35 per ounce. It would buy gold to raise the price and reduce downward pressure on the price, and sell gold to reduce upward pressure on the price. Selling gold also reduces the size of the Gold Pool, and since the United States was the largest member, it would also reduce US gold reserves.

41. See Robert Solomon, *The International Monetary System, 1945–1976: An Insider's View* (New York: Harper & Row, 1976); and Michael Bordo, Eric Monnet, and Alain Naef, "The Gold Pool (1961–1968) and the Fall of Bretton Woods: Lessons for Central Bank Cooperation" (NBER Working Paper, November 2017).

42. See Allan H. Meltzer, "U.S. Policy in the Bretton Woods Era," *Federal Reserve Bank of St. Louis Review* 73 (May/June 1991): 54–83 (73).

43. See Solomon, *International Monetary System*, 179.

44. See Garber, "Collapse of the Bretton Woods Fixed Exchange Rate Regime," 461–85.

45. See Bordo, "Bretton Woods International Monetary System," 84.

46. See Richard Marston, "Real Exchange Rates and Productivity Growth in the United States and Japan," in *Real Financial Linkages among Open Economies*, ed. Sven Arndt (Cambridge, MA: MIT Press, 1987).

47. See Michael D. Bordo and Barry Eichengreen, "Implications of the Great Depression for the Development of the International Monetary System," in *The Defining Moment: The Great Depression and the American Economy in the Twentieth Century*, ed. Michael D. Bordo, Claudia Goldin, and Eugene N. White (Chicago: University of Chicago Press, 1998) for an analysis, based on a model of the global gold standard, of how the life of Bretton Woods could have been prolonged.

48. See Emil Despres, Charles Kindleberger, and William Salant, "The Dollar and World Liquidity: A Minority View," *Economist* 5 (February 1966): 526–29.

49. See Ronald I. McKinnon, *Private and Official International Money: The Case for the Dollar*, Princeton Essays in International Economics, International Finance Section, Department of Economics, Princeton University, 1969; McKinnon, "International Gold Standard Without Gold," 351–73; and Ronald I. McKinnon, *The Unloved Dollar Standard: From Bretton Woods to the Rise of China* (New York: Oxford University Press, 2014).

50. See Barry Eichengreen, *Exorbitant Privilege: The Rise and Fall of the Dollar and the Future of the International Monetary System* (New York: Oxford University Press, 2010).

Chapter 11

Japan and the Collapse of Bretton Woods

Frances McCall Rosenbluth and James Sundquist

Japan's postwar exchange rate, set by the US occupation in 1949 at 360 yen to the dollar, was not only a "nice round number."[1] US officials deliberately lowered the exchange rate from its prewar rate to buoy Japanese exports and to lift the economy from utter devastation. The notion that Japanese exports would threaten American corporations' market share would have seemed laughable had anyone voiced it. US businesses were far more worried about the tax implications of US aid to Japan and were eager for Japan to recover. The Truman administration, dismayed by the collapse of Nationalist China in its civil war with the Communists, wanted Japan to recover for another reason: it sought to build a powerful Asian ally in the intensifying Cold War.[2]

Within twenty years, Japan had achieved the unthinkable: not only had the economy achieved a complete recovery, but many Japanese firms were also accelerating their gains in foreign markets. In a pattern that would be repeated in Taiwan and South Korea, strategic American generosity sparked rapid economic growth. Yet the Bretton Woods system never managed to adapt to Japan's spectacular success, because exchange rate adjustments could not take place except through mutual agreement. When the United States responded to the surge in Japanese exports by calling for revaluation of the yen, Japanese firms dug in their heels in defense of a low yen.

Trade tensions, having been intentionally set aside at the original Bretton Woods Conference, thus returned in force during the 1960s.[3] Congress, which had approved an expansion of the president's authority to negotiate free-trade agreements with an overwhelming majority in 1962, increasingly became a mouthpiece for US industrial anxiety as the decade brought growing evidence of Japanese and German economic resurgence. Economic nationalism pushed aside Congress's postwar concern for the reconstruction of Europe and Japan, as well as the Atlantic and Pacific partnerships at the heart of American national security alliances. Exporters and import-competitors, and textile manufacturers in particular, dominated the microphones in both the United States and Japan, sinking multiple proposed deals that might have alleviated economic tensions.

Nixon's decision to break the dollar's link to gold, which forced Japan to revalue the yen, demonstrated that America's ability to prioritize global monetary stability had its limits. Bretton Woods contributed to the recovery of postwar trade and economic prosperity by providing exchange rate stability, but when confronted with a choice between saving Bretton Woods and addressing the pressing concerns of their own producers, the Japanese and American governments alike chose the latter.[4]

The respective positions of Japanese and American businesses are easy enough to fathom. More interesting but harder to read is whether the Japanese government realized that its dogged defense of the 360-yen exchange rate was fatal to the very advantages it sought to retain for domestic industry. Japanese efforts to freeze economic relations the way they had been in 1949 frustrated American presidents and ultimately figured centrally in Richard Nixon's decision to abandon the Bretton Woods system. The paper that follows documents the reasons behind the Japanese government's vigorous support of the weak yen and its unintended consequences.

BRETTON WOODS UNDER STRESS

In 1948 when the exchange rate was set at 360 yen to the dollar, Japan's economy was still only at 70 percent of the output level of 1930–1934.[5] Japan imported substantially more than it exported, and its firms had no market power outside of the country. In order to pay for raw materials that no longer came from occupied China or its colonies in Taiwan and Korea, Japan had to use scarce US dollars. Although the exchange rate was significantly lower than it had been before the war, Japan still ran a persistent current account deficit (see fig. 11.1) and ran low on foreign currency in 1953, 1957,

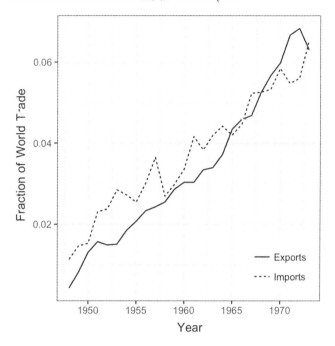

Figure 11.1: Japanese exports and imports as a share of world trade. More important than the emergence of a net trade surplus by 1970 was the steadily increasing volume of Japanese exports, which competed with domestic producers in the United States and elsewhere. Source: World Bank. Image courtesy of James Sundquist.

and 1961, each time requiring assistance from the United States and the IMF.[6] These repeated crises, combined with the fact that Japan had very little gold, contributed to a sense of vulnerability to global finance among Japanese policy makers.

Yet during this time, the Japanese economy strengthened rapidly, changing its relationship with the United States. Exports to the United States increased, stirring protectionist sentiment in that country. Japan recorded a surplus in trade with the United States for the first time in 1959, and large, systemic surpluses appeared in the second half of the 1960s. These trade imbalances were fueled in part by a shifting monetary landscape: as Japan followed a relatively austere monetary policy, at first dictated by the American occupiers and then designed to ease the foreign exchange crunch, while

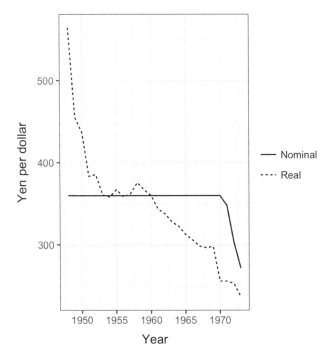

Figure 11.2: Yen per dollar real and nominal exchange rates. Real exchange rate calculated from GDP deflator data, using 1960 as a base year. Though unreliable in the short run, this approach gives an accurate picture of the monetary pressures on the yen-dollar exchange rate: the 360 rate became undervalued over the course of the 1960s. Sources: Federal Reserve Economic Data, World Bank, Bank of Japan. Graph modeled on that in David Flath, "A Perspective on Japanese Trade Policy and Japan-U.S. Trade Friction" (NCSU Department of Economics Working Paper, 1998), 2005, 149. Image courtesy of James Sundquist.

the United States expanded its money supply to provide liquidity to the Bretton Woods system, the nominal exchange rate of 360 yen to the dollar became undervalued relative to the yen's purchasing power (see fig. 11.2).

West Germany, also tending toward trade surpluses, agreed to higher values of the deutsche mark three times, in 1961, 1969, and 1971, while Japan steadfastly refused over the same period. The main difference between Germany and Japan was the Bundesbank's stronger influence on German policy than its Japanese counterpart in its vigilant fight against inflation. The Bundesbank had sold large quantities of deutsche marks to keep the currency at par, but this increase in supply of marks threatened price stability, eventually leading to the decision to revalue.[7] The Bank of Japan, which was under the close supervision of the Ministry of Finance, instead dutifully carried out the government's commitment to the 360 rate. This satisfied domestic constituencies (discussed in the following section), but increased the strain on the United States' commitment to back its currency with gold and to do so in the face of trade deficits.

In the Bretton Woods system, the dollar was the principal intervention currency, the store of value, and the currency of trade. Each member of the Bretton Woods system bought or sold dollars to maintain parity within small margins of their fixed rates, and the United States, in turn, pegged the dollar at $35 per ounce of gold as a commitment device to maintain price stability.[8] On one hand, this granted the United States an "exorbitant privilege": since every nation in the world wanted to hold its currency, it could effectively print money and run trade deficits with impunity.[9] The French government particularly resented the advantages that American banks enjoyed on account of the dollar's indispensable role in international transactions and reserve currency status. Japan and West Germany were angered by American inflationary policies, particularly after 1967, which buoyed the American domestic economy at the unintended but nevertheless real cost of increasing inflationary pressures abroad.[10]

Yet even though the United States enjoyed major advantages at the international level, the Bretton Woods system still became a domestic political burden. US corporations had begun to lose market share to Japanese and German firms, both at home and abroad. American consumers, buoyed by relatively loose monetary policy, snapped up Japanese and German imports, while consumers in Japan and Germany, restrained by tighter credit, bought fewer imports from the United States. To American producers, the monetary system seemed to tilt the playing field in their competitors' favor. They viewed the growth of Japanese and German sales in the United States with alarm and insisted on revaluation of the yen and the mark.

Pressure was building on Japan to revalue the yen, but it clung tightly to the 360 rate. As we will see, domestic politics precluded any other action.

THE CONTAGION OF PROTECTIONISM

As economic tensions grew between them during the 1960s, the United States and Japan could agree on neither the problem nor the solution. Where Japan felt vulnerable to global finance, the United States felt that Japan was exploiting the fact that the United States could not devalue its currency without breaking Bretton Woods. Where American manufacturers demanded protection, their Japanese competitors demanded that their own government stand firm.

In Japan, the government offered a wide array of trade protections to its industries. Heavy industries such as ship building, steel, and machinery, which had grown during the war, protected their large sunk costs by purchasing political influence in the Liberal Democratic Party (LDP). This influence was amplified by electoral rules that put a premium on campaign contributions. Each district elected multiple representatives, but individuals could only vote for a single candidate, requiring any party seeking an electoral majority to divide the vote among multiple candidates in most districts. The result was a party of internally divided politicians who vied with one another for votes. Electoral politics were famously corrupt and expensive because LDP politicians traded government policy favors—protection, subsidies, tax breaks—for campaign contributions with which they cultivated personal support among the electorate.

Given its members' dependence on corporate contributions, the LDP was a reluctant trade liberalizer. Not only did the government seek to keep the 360-yen rate on behalf of exporters and import-competitors, but it was also reluctant to lower tariffs and quotas.[11] In this, Japan was far from alone; European countries had also emerged from the Great Depression and World War II with electoral mandates to rebuild their economies with protectionist legislation.

The United States, however, favored freer trade and took the lead in negotiating several rounds of tariff-cutting agreements under the auspices of the 1947 General Agreement on Tariffs and Trade (GATT). Immediately after the war, US firms were the most efficient producers in many industries and thus stood to benefit from trade liberalization. Yet the United States also proved particularly generous in opening its own economy, using market access as a tool to secure alliances in the Cold War. Behind the scenes, the State Department repeatedly clashed with Commerce, arguing that trade concessions were indispensable in the fight against Communism.[12] The State Department won most of these battles, assisted by the powerful chair of the House Ways and Means Committee, Wilbur Mills. Mills pushed the Trade Expansion Act through Congress, which authorized the administration to lead a new round of tariff-cutting negotiations.[13] The Kennedy Round, as the negotiations came to be known, were ambitious but encountered growing opposition from the

US steel, chemical, textile, and oil industries, which feared competition from low-cost imports.[14] By the end of the 1960s, American concern about the loss of market share in manufacturing industries led the principal constituencies of both major political parties—capital and labor—to swing against unconditional free trade, profoundly affecting exchange rate negotiations.

US-Japanese textile trade already had a history of friction before Kennedy's time. The manufacturing of textiles had been the engine of Japan's industrialization prior to World War II. With technical and financial assistance from the United States, the Japanese textile industry had recovered to peak prewar levels by 1950, and within five years, Japanese exports of cotton blouses to the United States had risen to one-quarter of US production.[15] Favoring free trade in principle but succumbing to relentless domestic pressure, the Eisenhower administration convinced Japan to accept "voluntary" textile export limits in 1955 and again in 1957 to avoid an open trade war.[16] The US textile industry employed 2.4 million workers, one-eighth of American manufacturing labor. Textile plants were located across the country but most concentrated in the Carolinas; and 80 percent of the industry was represented by a single organization, the American Textile Manufacturers Institute (ATMI), giving it a strong collective voice. In Japan, 1.8 million textile workers comprised an even bigger portion of the Japanese workforce.[17]

Despite an overarching US interest in expanding world trade, making peace with the textile industry remained a priority for American presiden tial aspirants. As part of his hard-fought campaign against Richard Nixon in 1960, John F. Kennedy himself promised to limit textile imports to protect the US industry, a pledge that may have helped him carry the three leading textile states of North Carolina, South Carolina, and Georgia.[18] Lyndon Johnson reached an agreement with the Japanese in 1964 to retain limits on textile imports against the advice of the free-traders on his staff.[19]

Meanwhile, trade tensions began to emerge in other sectors. The American Iron and Steel Institute started to lobby for protection in 1966, which bore fruit the next year when William Harsha, Republican of Ohio, introduced the Iron and Steel Orderly Trade Act of 1967. In testimony before the Ways and Means Committee, the chair of Republic Steel Corporation and the president of the United Steelworkers presented a united front of capital and labor in opposition to soaring steel imports.[20] Automobiles also appeared as a trade issue for the first time in 1967, when Japan unexpectedly failed to include them in its first round of capital liberalization.[21]

Confronted by demands for protection at home and weakening confidence in the dollar abroad, the Johnson administration announced that it was considering a levy on all imports of between 2 and 10 percent. Although fears of reprisals and a successful conclusion to the Kennedy Round meant that the tariff never came to pass, it sufficiently alarmed the Japanese government that the LDP and business lobbying group Keidanren sent delegations to protest the idea; both returned to Japan worried by the depth of protectionist sentiment in Washington.[22]

The 1968 presidential election offered US manufacturers another chance to demand help from the White House. Even after the Deep South abandoned the Democratic Party following the civil rights movement, Republicans had to fight for southern support, and Richard Nixon, once again a presidential aspirant in 1968, promised to defend the textile industry in exchange for southern backing (over George Wallace) at the Republican National Convention.[23] Although Nixon opposed outright trade quotas and tariffs, the effort to make good on this promise became one of the most significant economic issues of his first term.

TIED UP OVER TEXTILES

One piece of leverage available to Nixon in his negotiations with Japan was control over the Okinawa Islands, still held by the United States since the end of the war. Aware that Prime Minister Eisaku Sato was under pressure to secure their return, Nixon made export quotas on textiles a condition of any US agreement to restore Okinawa to Japanese sovereignty. The exchange reflected the new state of détente in the Cold War: the United States had less strategic need of Japan and its islands and thus took a less tolerant view of its imports. In secret negotiations during November 1969, Sato agreed to meet American terms on export restrictions in exchange for the return of Okinawa and the removal of nuclear weapons stationed on the island.[24]

Sato, however, had promised more than he could deliver. Members of Sato's own Liberal Democratic Party, struggling against a decline in vote share, regarded the Sato-Nixon agreement as a betrayal of Japanese corporate interests. The fact that Sato could not bring along the other factions of the LDP reflected the party's structural dependence on campaign support from protected industries.[25] The Japanese textile industry had agreed to continue the export restraints of the past years, but Sato could not secure their acquiescence to the Multifiber Arrangement that Nixon sought to curb Japan's booming exports of new synthetic fabrics. In response, the Nixon administration continued to dangle the prospect of Okinawa's reversion as a quid pro quo for American satisfaction on textiles, as well as a new item on America's list: steel.[26]

In April 1970, the US global balance of trade turned to a deficit for the first time. Also that month, Wilbur Mills submitted a bill (H.R. 16920) calling for textile and footwear quotas. Mills, himself a free-trader, wanted both to buy time with protectionists in Congress (who favored still harsher measures) and to signal seriousness to the Japanese. The "Mills bill" limited textile imports for 1970 to the 1967–1968 average, with increases thereafter in proportion to American consumption growth. The legislation allocated quotas by country, including now Hong Kong, Korea, and Taiwan, which were gaining on Japan.[27]

Rather than bowing to the American threat, however, a Japanese textile industry spokesman immediately declared "absolute opposition to any comprehensive control in violation of the GATT rules, however temporary it might be."[28] Much of educated Japanese public opinion was on their side. As an editorial in the center-left *Asahi Shimbun* wrote on June 20, 1970, "It should be a matter of first priority for Japan to make her best efforts in articulating the essence of the problem . . . so that the . . . American people may realize how selfish and anachronistic the U.S. demand really is."[29] *The New York Times* editorialized along similar lines on June 28 and July 5. New York senator Jacob Javits, who represented American multinationals that would be hurt in a trade war, called the bill a "backward-looking, protectionist quota bill."[30]

Sato and Nixon met personally on October 24, 1970, to hammer out an overall bilateral deal that would encompass both the textile problem and America's reversion of Okinawa to Japan. But when word leaked that Japan would agree to unilateral export restraints, leaders of the Japanese textile industry were outraged. On November 16, Toyosaburo Taniguchi, head of the textile industry association of Japan, spoke at a rally of eight hundred textile industry executives: "We will not agree to an inappropriate concession and we will fight it to the end."[31] Sato had managed to win a fourth term as LDP president on October 29, 1970, but he still hoped to hold off American action until the Upper House elections of summer 1971 were behind him.[32] According to Prime Minister Sato's diary, minister of Foreign Affairs Kiichi Aichi advised Sato on November 23 that Japan might have to bite the bullet on textiles. Three weeks later, on December 16, Wakaizumi Kei, who was negotiating the terms of the Okinawan reversion, urged Sato to "concede on textiles for the sake of the world economy." But minister of International

Trade and Industry Kiichi Miyazawa counseled Sato to take the industry's side in the face of America's unprincipled demands, and the prime minister did not budge.[33]

Congress moved ahead on its own schedule. Frustrated with the administrations of both countries, Wilbur Mills told a *Wall Street Journal* reporter on December 30, 1970, "I've told both sides they have until March to come up with something. We need a trade bill, but we don't need quotas if they can come to an agreement." Mills met directly with Japanese textile leaders in January 1971 to agree on export limits in order to forestall the stricter measures now developing in Congress.[34] As he warned in a speech later that month, "Time is running out, and if concrete results are not forthcoming soon, the Congress will necessarily have to respond to the special needs of the textile industry at the time it considers overall trade legislation."[35] Senator Javits also favored compromise, recommending that a special presidential task force be charged with documenting injury to the American textile industry, information that "would be useful in providing the Japanese government with ammunition to use against their own potent textile lobby."[36]

The US textile industry and its backers, however, were equally implacable. They preferred the strict quotas in the congressional bill and wanted to see their own defender, Mills, fail at mediation. American Textile Manufacturing Institute (ATMI) president Donald F. McCulloch called Mills's intervention "a calculated effort to block realistic controls."[37]

American industry remained unmoved when on March 8 the Japanese government, despite stiff domestic opposition, issued a blueprint for Japanese export restraints.[38] Mills urged the US textile industry to give the Japanese offer "a most deliberate review in light of its own long-run interest"; but Frederick Dent, chairman of the ATMI's international trade committee, said, "The Japanese plan for self-regulation of textile exports is worse than no agreement at all." South Carolina Senator Hollings and Georgia Senator Talmadge piled on, calling the plan a "sorry spectacle."[39]

The question now was whether Nixon would get behind a compromise deal to avert a trade war or back the American textile industry's intransigence. He chose the latter. However squeamish Nixon may have been about outright quotas, his reelection plans trumped other considerations. Nixon lost no time denouncing the agreement as insufficient protection for American industry, and he pledged to "strongly support" legislation to impose quotas on Japanese textile imports.[40] Not only did Nixon seek to advance his "Southern strategy" for reelection, but he aimed specifically to undermine Mills, who was contemplating a presidential run of his own. By no means was Nixon willing to let a Democrat come away with the credit for solving the textile problem. ATMI representatives praised Nixon's "forceful rejection" of the "unworkable" Japanese plan, and expressed their regret that Mills had "become identified" with it.[41]

With this latest collapse of negotiations, the US-Japanese relationship reached its lowest point since the end of the Pacific War.[42] Prime Minister Sato had tried and failed to bring along Japanese textile manufacturers; President Nixon, if he couldn't secure relief for American textiles, faced the prospect of yet more stringent protectionist legislation coming out of Congress. In July 1971, he received a report that noted "a developing crisis of confidence in the system" of international trade. The primary reason for declining faith in free trade "without doubt, is the increased pressure of imports in the U.S. market."[43] Manufacturers in both countries had succeeded in pressuring their governments to stand strong, as the crisis barreled toward a unilateral resolution.

SHOCKED

Late though they were, some voices in Japan expressed the inevitability and perhaps even the desirability of revaluing the yen in order to dampen American protectionism. In May 1970, Yoshitomi Ishimaru of the trading firm Toyomenka warned that yen revaluation of at least 10 percent was probably inevitable, bringing losses to export-dependent sectors of the economy, particularly small firms without deep financial reserves.[44] A year later, in April 1971, Kazutaka Kikawada, the chair of Tokyo Power and Electric and chair of the national business organization Keizai Doyukai, publicly raised the question of revaluation, eliciting howls from the Japanese shipbuilding industry that revaluation would be too costly.[45] After Germany revalued the mark again in May 1971, Matsuyuki Wakasugi, head of Japan's Association of General Trading Companies, also hinted that revaluation could be coming Japan's way. In June, University of Tokyo economics professor Ryutaro Komiya advised the government unilaterally to raise the yen's value along a crawling peg.[46] The director of the Economic Research Institute of the government's Economic Planning Agency, Miyohei Shinohara, went further: Japan should float the yen and let it appreciate to around 280 or even 260 to the dollar.[47]

The LDP's Upper House victory of June 27, 1971, bought Sato domestic room for maneuvering. Reshuffling his cabinet, Sato appointed Takeo Fukuda as foreign minister and Kakuei Tanaka to head MITI, rivals for succession as party leader, who both favored textile concessions.[48] No one, however, signaled dramatic moves. It was no secret that Fukuda and Tanaka were vying to be Sato's successor, and neither wanted to run on the ticket of "sellout to America."[49] MITI minister Tanaka judged the textile industry to be implacably opposed to export restraints.[50]

That summer, Nixon settled things decisively. On July 15, 1971, he took the first of the two momentous actions that summer that would go down in history as the "Nixon Shocks." His first announcement was his intention to send Henry Kissinger to China to begin serious rapprochement, a shift in the tectonic plates of global politics. A month later, on August 15, Nixon dropped the second bomb. He suspended dollar convertibility to gold, while slapping on a 10 percent surcharge on all imports. From his taped conversations, we know that the 10 percent surcharge was a bargaining device to force the Japanese to a sizable revaluation, after which the United States would remove the surcharge.[51]

As Nixon hammered out the details of what he called his New Economic Policy, textiles featured prominently in the discussion. Nixon favored the import tax to placate manufacturing interests without resorting to explicit quotas. As he noted, demanding quotas for textiles would be "opening Pandora's box, and I'll have to do it for steel, and it's stretching one hell of a lot."[52] In his memoirs of the discussions, future Fed chairman and then undersecretary of the Treasury for international monetary affairs Paul Volcker bemoaned the amount of time spent on the "side issue" of textiles, which he observed Nixon "felt more strongly about than gold."[53] Given his position, Volcker understood better than anyone the need for a US devaluation, but he opposed the import surcharge, which he could see was politically motivated. Yet as President, Nixon understood that the protectionist demands would only intensify if he did nothing about them.

Many Japanese, and most of all Prime Minister Sato, took Nixon's "shocks" personally.[54] The press and opposition parties ridiculed Sato and his cabinet for not anticipating Nixon's moves. Still, the government seemed paralyzed. To the astonishment of the Nixon administration, Japan continued to defend the yen in the markets at the 360 rate, losing billions of dollars in bets against the market in a few days. With every option exhausted, Japan finally abandoned the 360 rate. The US view, as Secretary of State William Rogers put it, was that ". . . any country in chronic surplus as Japan is, has an obligation to take the necessary measures—increasing imports, eliminating export incentives, stimulating capital outflow and revaluating its exchange rate—to bring its global balance of payments into equilibrium."[55] The view in Japan was that the United States was throwing its weight around.

The United States did in fact continue to throw its weight around. In September Nixon issued an ultimatum: Japan would agree to textile export restrictions on American terms or the United States would impose quotas under the stinging title of the "Trading with the Enemy Act" of 1917. MITI minister Tanaka began negotiations on behalf of Japan that produced an agreement on January 3, 1972, whereby the American industry got its comprehensive quota agreement and at levels double those proposed early in the negotiations.[56] With less leverage than before, it was a deal Japan had to accept. Tanaka won the cooperation of the Japanese textile industry at the cost of 200 billion yen in aid.[57]

In a narrow sense, the United States got what it wanted: export restraints on textiles and a currency revaluation from Japan. But the end of Bretton Woods did not change the tenor of economic relations between the two countries, which continued to be tense for another two decades. The true change had already occurred when the Japanese economy regained its former competitiveness, ending US concern for rebuilding Japan and triggering a protectionist backlash. Japanese politicians had preserved the benefits of this system for as long as they could, but they could do nothing once the United States decided to abandon Bretton Woods. Meanwhile, trade tensions and accusations of currency undervaluation would persist into the new era of floating exchange rates.

The United States continued to demand that the Japanese—and Europeans—voluntarily limit their exports to the United States in a range of industries. The 1974 US Trade Act included Section 301, which authorized the president to retaliate against a foreign country that maintains "unjustifiable or unreasonable" tariff or other import restrictions that reduce the sales of the competitive American product. To textiles and steel were added automobiles beginning in 1981 and machine tools in 1987.[58]

Although Japan did not welcome these demands for voluntary export restraints, it accepted them as preferable to retaliatory tariffs. Not only were export restraints more easily circumvented by building factories in foreign markets (as Japanese car manufacturers did in the southern United States), but even when effective, they were more producer-friendly. Whereas a tariff increases prices by adding a tax that generates revenue for the government, an export restraint increases prices by restricting the quantity of goods sold. Rather than going to a government treasury, the higher prices translated to a rise in profit margins for those producers still able to export. Japanese auto companies, in particular, were able to use export restraints as a means of reducing competition between themselves, effectively operating as a cartel.[59]

The textile industry was not so fortunate. Indeed, part of the reason that textile manufacturers in both countries had fought so hard for protection was that the industry was in decline in both Japan and the United States. Less than a decade after they had influenced negotiations over the return of Okinawa and the future of Bretton Woods, textile manufacturers in both countries shrank rapidly in size and influence. Yet even though the actors changed, new industries were ready to play the role of aggrieved victim of foreign competition.

CONCLUSIONS

In retrospect, it is clear that the Bretton Woods system was freighted with problems that its structure could not carry, including insufficient liquidity except through much-resented American inflation. Japan did not break Bretton Woods on its own; nevertheless, it is interesting to consider whether the Japanese brought on themselves a worse outcome than if they had agreed to successive revaluations earlier, as the Germans had done. A timely revaluation by Japan might at least have altered the way Bretton Woods ended. After all, the system did not collapse when other nations reached a tipping point in their tolerance for US inflation; it collapsed when pressure from domestic producers and an international impasse over how to keep the system alive compelled Nixon to place the interests of US manufacturers before a global public good. However, Japan's export industries could not bring themselves to accept the inevitability of revaluation or export restraints before it was too late, and Japanese politicians were too hamstrung by factional rivalry and too dependent on campaign contributions to make the decision on the industries' behalf.

Japanese politicians also failed to realize that their country occupied a completely different role in Richard Nixon's mind than it had in Harry Truman's. Détente with the Soviet Union and a diplomatic coup in opening relations with China meant that Japan was not as strategically vital, while its renewed competitiveness meant that the United States could less afford Japan economic privileges. Japan and the Bretton Woods system in general failed to adapt to these changes until the events of summer 1971 forced adjustment.

After an experiment in allowing currencies to move within a wider band than under the Bretton Woods system, between December 1971 and

February 1973, the major industrial countries abandoned the fixed rate system altogether and allowed their currencies to float. Floating exchange rates did not end the trade wars; Japan's continuing export drive, in automobiles and electronics, was in precisely the industries in which US unions were strongest and America's comparative advantage was slipping. As Kissinger's economic adviser Fred Bergsten warned with some prescience in 1971, "Japan's competitiveness will probably continue to grow and thus keep Japan in the forefront of protectionist attacks in the United States whatever the policies which it pursues."[60]

Driven by concerns about its growing trade deficit, the United States engineered another devaluation with respect to the yen (and several other currencies) in the 1985 Plaza Accords. To cushion the effects of the yen's appreciation, the Bank of Japan made credit freely available, contributing to the growth of an asset bubble, which burst in 1991. Not until that falling from grace did the United States turn its attention away from the feared but never realized Japanese takeover of the world economy. By then, it was China's turn to earn the ire of the United States for an undervalued currency.

Notes

We are grateful to William Liang and Michiyo Seto for exceptional research assistance, and to the Yale University Council on East Asian Studies for generous funding.

1. US Government interim directive to General MacArthur, December 6, 1948. The 360 yen to the dollar required an enormous depreciation of the yen compared to its 1941 value. Before fixing the exchange rate at 360 yen to the dollar, the occupation had in fact allowed multiple exchange rates: undervalued for exports and overvalued for imports. Orville J. McDiarmid, "The Japanese Exchange Rate," *Far Eastern Survey* 18, no. 12 (1949): 133–35.

2. As recently declassified documents reveal, the CIA knew by the fall of 1948 that the Nationalists were sure to lose the civil war. CIA Office of Reports and Estimates (ORE) 27–48, "Possible Developments in China," 1948. Available at the Central Intelligence Agency Freedom of Information Act Electronic Reading Room.

3. Harold James, "The Multiple Contexts of Bretton Woods," *Oxford Review of Economic Policy* 28, no. 3 (2012): 416.

4. Michael Bordo, "The Bretton Woods International Monetary System: A Historical Overview," in *A Retrospective of the Bretton Woods System: Lessons for International Monetary Reform*, ed. Michael Bordo and Barry Eichengreen (Chicago: University of Chicago Press, 1993), 27. As John Williamson put it, "Bretton Woods worked for a while because its rules were consistent with the needs of the time and, until emergence of the dollar overvaluation, acceptable to the dominant power." John Williamson, "On the System in Bretton Woods," *American Economic Review* 75, no. 2 (1985): 74–79.

5. McDiarmid, "Japanese Exchange Rate," 134.

6. Yoshio Asai, "The IMF and Japan: Liberalization of Foreign Exchange and Pursuit of High Growth," in *History of the IMF: Organization, Policy, and Market*, ed. Kazuhiko Yago, Yoshio Asai, and Masanao Itoh (Tokyo: Springer, 2015), 249–74 (250–63).

7. Paul Volcker and Toyoo Gyohten, *Changing Fortunes: The World's Money and the Threat to American Leadership* (New York: Times Books, 1992), 51–58.

8. Bordo, "Bretton Woods International Monetary System," 49.

9. Valery Giscard d'Estaing coined the term "exorbitant privilege" when describing American latitude as the key currency issuer.

10. Bordo, "Bretton Woods International Monetary System," 74–78.

11. Nobuhito Kishi, *Keizai hakusho monogatari* [The saga of the economic white papers] (Tokyo: Bungei Shunju Press, 1999); Economic Planning Agency, *Economic White Paper*, 1970, 1971; *Shukan Asahi*, September 18, 1970, 17; Kent E. Calder, *Crisis and Compensation: Public Policy and Political Stability in Japan, 1949–1986* (Princeton, NJ: Princeton University Press, 1988).

12. Alfred Eckes, *Opening America's Market: U.S. Foreign Trade Policy since 1776* (Chapel Hill: University of North Carolina Press, 1995), 170–74.

13. This was a period in American legislative history in which Wilbur Mills controlled Ways and Means assignments to maintain nonpartisan consensus around free trade and fiscal conservatism. John Manley, *The Politics of Finance: The House Committee on Ways and Means* (New York: Little, Brown, 1970), 52. Zelizer calls Mills "the most important player in the House of Representatives." Julian E. Zelizer, *The Fierce Urgency of Now: Lyndon Johnson, Congress, and the Battle for the Great Society* (New York: Penguin Press, 2015), 280.

14. "Protectionists Balk at Kennedy Round Tariff Cuts," *Congressional Quarterly Almanac 1967*, 23rd ed., (Washington, DC: Congressional Quarterly, 1968), available online at http://library.cqpress.com/cqalmanac /document.php?id=cqal67-1312913.

15. I. M. Destler, Haruhiro Fukui, and Hideo Sato, *The Textile Wrangle: Conflict in Japanese-American Relations, 1969–1971* (Ithaca, NY: Cornell University Press, 1979), 28.

16. Dean Spinanger, "Textiles Beyond the MFA Phase-Out," *World Economy* 22, no. 4 (1999): 456–57; Pietra Rivoli, *The Travels of a T-shirt in the Global Economy* (Hoboken, NJ: John Wiley, 2005).

17. Destler, Fukui, and Sato, *Textile Wrangle*, 29–30. As Lawrence Krause pointed out, US organized labor overrepresented manufacturing interests since service-sector firms are less likely to be unionized. Lawrence Krause, "Trade Policy for the Seventies," *Columbia Journal of World Business* 6, no. 1 (1971): 5–14.

18. For accounts of how hard Kennedy worked for the Deep South, see Guy Paul Land, "John F. Kennedy's Southern Strategy, 1956–1960," *North Carolina Historical Review* 56, no. 1 (1979): 41–63; and Patrick Novotny, "John F. Kennedy, the 1960 Election, and Georgia's Unpledged Electors in the Electoral College," *Georgia Historical Quarterly* 88, no. 3 (2004): 375–97. Kennedy's first "Long Term Agreement" on textiles, from 1962 to 1967, rested on the "voluntary export constraints" established by the Eisenhower administration.

19. James Cochrane and Gary Griepentrog, "Cotton Textile Prices, 1965–66: The Microeconomics of Moral Suasion," *Southern Economic Journal* 44, no. 1 (1977): 78.

20. William Hogan, *The 1970s: Critical Years for Steel* (Lexington, KY: Lexington Books, 1972), 52–54.

21. William Duncan, *U.S.-Japan Automobile Diplomacy: A Study in Economic Confrontation* (Cambridge: Ballinger Publishing, 1973), 1.

22. Ibid., 15–18.

23. Destler, Fukui, and Sato, *Textile Wrangle*, 58.

24. See Wakaizumi Kei, *The Best Course Available: A Personal Account of the Secret U.S.-Japan Okinawa Reversion Negotiations* (Honolulu: University of Hawai'i Press, 2002) for details on the terms of Okinawa's reversion, including a secret agreement that the United States would be able to return nuclear weapons to Okinawa in times of emergency, and arrangements on textiles.

25. According to Prime Minister Sato's diary in January 1970, Sato lost confidence in minister of International Trade and Industry (and rival faction leader) Masayoshi Ohira over the failed textile negotiations. Sato replaced Ohira with Ohira's lieutenant Kiichi Miyazawa as MITI minister, but it was soon clear that Miyazawa was no better able to construct a deal with the textile industry. Recounted in Sakuji Horikoshi, *Sengo seiji rimenshi* [The inside history of postwar politics]: *"Satō Eisaku nikki" ga kataru mono* [What Sato's diary tells us] (Tokyo: Iwanami Shoten, 1998), 228–29.

26. Haruhiro Fukui, "Review of Wakaizumi Kei, *The Best Course Available*," *Journal of Japanese Studies* 29, no. 2 (2003): 451.

27. Destler, Fukui, and Sato, *Textile Wrangle*, 181.

28. Quoted in ibid., 193.

29. Quoted in ibid., 197.

30. On June 28, 1970, *The New York Times* wrote, "The Administration might well be reluctant to adopt mandatory quotas. For one thing, they put the United States in violation of the General Agreement on Tariffs and Trade. For another, they will almost certainly provoke retaliation against the United States by Japan and other countries hurt by American quotas. And they are sure to intensify problems of domestic inflation." On July 5, *The NYT* was more insistent: "It would be difficult to conceive of legislation worse suited to the interests of the nation . . . it would contract world trade whose growth had contributed so much to international economic development since World War II."

31. Horikoshi, *Sengo seiji rimenshi*, 231–32.

32. Ibid., 232.

33. Kiichi Miyazawa, *Kikigaki Miyazawa Kiichi Kaikoroku*, ed. Mikuriya Takashi and Nakamura Takafusa (Tokyo: Iwanami Shoten, 2005), 328; Horikoshi, *Sengo seiji rimenshi*, 233.

34. Destler, Fukui, and Sato, *Textile Wrangle*, 251.

35. Quoted in ibid., 163.

36. Quoted in ibid., 165. Meanwhile, Donald Kendall, president of Pepsi Cola and chairman of the Emergency Committee for American Trade, an anti-protectionism group of some fifty American multinationals, traveled to Tokyo in March 1971 in search of an arrangement along Javits's lines. The so-called "Kendall plan" met with the relief and approval of major business leaders in both countries, but not by the textile industries of either country.

37. Ibid., 264.

38. Ministry of Foreign Affairs of Japan, *Diplomatic Bluebook*, March 12, 1971, 1–2.

39. "Mills Welcomes Offer by Japan to Restrict Textile Exports to U.S.," *Wall Street Journal*, March 9, 1971.

40. "Nixon Turns Down Japanese Textile Plan, Will Back Legislation for Import Quotas," *Wall Street Journal*, March 12, 1971.

41. Ibid.

42. Destler, Fukui, and Sato, *Textile Wrangle*, 252.

43. *United States International Economic Policy in an Interdependent World*, Report to the President submitted by the Commission on International Trade and Investment Policy, 1971. Viewable online at https://catalog.hathitrust.org/Record/007395326.

44. *Shukan Posuto*, May 15, 1970, 40. See also comments by Hara of Asahi's Washington bureau, warning Japanese readers that Americans viewed Japanese trading practices as highly protectionist and unfair. *Shukan Asahi*, September 18, 1970, 17.

45. Robert Angel, *Explaining Economic Policy Failure* (New York: Columbia University Press, 1991), 78.

46. Ibid., 105.

47. Alice Amsden and Kotaro Suzumura, "An Interview with Miyohei Shinohara: Nonconformism in Japanese Economic Thought," *Journal of the Japanese and International Economies* 15 (2001): 341–60 (346); Miyohei Shinohara, "360 en reeto e no kasetsu" [Hypothesis about the 360 yen rate], *Riron Keizai Gaku* [Theoretical economics] (April 1974).

48. Yo Mizuki, *Tanaka Kakuei: Sono kyozen to kyoaku* [Kakuei Tanaka: His gigantic strengths and gigantic faults] (Tokyo: Nihon Keizai Shimbunsha, 1998), 179.

49. Akira Asaga, *Tanaka Kakuei: Jo to chie no seijika* [Kakuei Tanaka: A sensitive and wise politician] (Tokyo: Daiichi Hoki, 2016), 90.

50. According to Tanaka's top aide for five decades, Akira Asaga, Tanaka could be tough with big firms, but with the small firms of the kind that made up a large part of the textile industry, Tanaka showed

his softer side. When he finally did cut a deal with them after the fall of Bretton Woods, it was only after Nixon had made compromise unavoidable; and even then it was after much consultation, patient explanation, a liberal flow of government subsidies, and tearful apologies by Tanaka himself. Interview with Asaga, June 24, 2016, Tokyo, Japan.

51. Douglas Brinkley and Luke Nichter, eds., *The Nixon Tapes: 1971–1972* (New York: Houghton Mifflin Harcourt, 2014).

52. Ibid.

53. Volcker and Gyohten, *Changing Fortunes*, 79.

54. Eisaku Sato, *Sato Eisaku Daiarii*, vol. 4 (Tokyo: Asahi Shimbunsha, 1997), 399.

55. Quoted in Destler, Fukui, and Sato, *Textile Wrangle*, 296.

56. Ibid., 311.

57. Mizuki, *Tanaka Kakuei*, 186.

58. David Flath, "A Perspective on Japanese Trade Policy and Japan-U.S. Trade Friction" (North Carolina State University Department of Economics Working Paper, 1998), 11.

59. Ibid., 11–12.

60. Fred Bergsten, "Crisis in U.S. Trade Policy," *Foreign Affairs* 49, no. 4 (1971): 619–35 (629).

Chapter 12

The Multiple Contexts of Bretton Woods

Harold James

Bretton Woods has become a powerful myth. It is the only instantly recognizable location of the series of conferences of the wartime coalition (the United Nations) held shortly before and after the end of the Second World War. Hot Springs (the conference in May and June 1943 that discussed food and agriculture) and Dumbarton Oaks (the meetings from August to October 1944 that sketched out a future international organization) are easily forgotten; even the San Francisco conference (April–June 1945) that established the postwar United Nations system is scarcely identifiable to any but the expert in United Nations history. By contrast, the United Nations Monetary and Financial Conference, held in July 1944 at Bretton Woods, New Hampshire, is still instantly recognizable as a view of the world.

This essay suggests that this view stems from a unique confluence of contemporary contexts—in terms of trade policy, stabilization policy (especially in response to currency instability), and policies to control capital movements. But the iconic conference also was shaped by a powerful interpretation, a retrospective context, that lent a golden halo to the whole exercise. In that sense, our interpretation of a very specific historical event is inseparably intertwined with views of what happened *after* as well as *before* that event. In retrospect, the Bretton Woods order looks like a solution, not just to the question of postwar reconstruction but to the problem of recasting capitalism in such a way that it would not permanently destabilize both itself and the international political and legal order. As Robert Skidelsky has recently reminded us, it thus has a continuing actuality.[1]

Any contemplation of the Bretton Woods Conference has to begin with the godlike (the phrase is Lionel Robbins's, not mine) figure who presided over it.[2] Bretton Woods was about reconstruction, but not simply about reconstruction after a war or about trying to return to the prewar order. The conference continued a debate about the appropriate form of an international economic order that had intensified in the course of the Second World War, as the competition of contrasting systems became increasingly obvious. When in 1940 the German minister of economics, Walther Funk, presented a plan after the fall of France and at the height of German euphoria about a Nazi "New Order," the British government asked John Maynard Keynes to prepare a counterscheme. Funk had presented his plan as an alternative to the outdated and discredited gold standard; Keynes, when preparing a counter-project, insisted that any response could not offer reconstruction as it had been done after the First World War. He wrote that it would not be enough to restore "good old 1920–1921 [the postwar slump] or 1930–1933 [the Great Depression], i.e. gold standard or international exchange laissez-faire aggravated by heavy tariffs, unemployment etc. etc."[3] He did not want the solution that the United States preferred, extensive trade liberalization, as that would simply open up other, less competitive economies to a renewed onslaught of the forces of depression. Bretton Woods was about reconstructing a system that had not been adequately reconstructed in 1919. But how could a world order, one that had evolved rather than been created spontaneously, be negotiated by different powers that wanted to protect their national interest?

Keynes had a powerful reputation as a critic of counterproductive or destructive attempts at international cooperation—of the Paris Peace Conference of 1919, but also of the attempts to deal with the Great Depression of the early 1930s. In 1933, Keynes had commented on the abortive London World Economic Conference that "a pow-wow of sixty-six nations" could never be expected to agree. A workable plan could only be realized at the insistence of "a single power or like-minded group of powers."[4] In 1919, in *The Economic Consequences of the Peace*, John Maynard Keynes wrote plaintively, "But if America recalls for a moment what Europe has meant to her, what Europe, the mother of art and knowledge, in spite of everything, still is and still will be, will she not reject these counsels of indifference and isolation, and interest herself in what may be decisive issues for the progress and civilization of all mankind?"[5] The turn in 1944 to a different postwar policy from that of 1919 was a consequence of new power politics, as well as of a new intellectual direction that would overcome American isolationism.

Bretton Woods was obviously a unique occasion, whose magic was produced in part by felicitous timing: the conference convened just after the Normandy landings, when the prospect of a very speedy end to the European conflict appeared much greater than in reality it subsequently proved to be. Treasury secretary Henry Morgenthau told a strategy meeting preparing for Bretton Woods quite candidly that "we felt that it was good for the world, good for the nation, and good for the Democratic Party, for us to move." Why was what was good for the Democratic Party really what was good for America or the world?

Was this naked power masked as idealism? At the inaugural session of the conference, Morgenthau had propounded a vision:

> I hope that this Conference will focus its attention upon two elementary economic axioms. The first of these is this: that prosperity has no fixed limits. It is not a finite substance to be diminished by division. On the contrary, the more of it that other nations enjoy, the more each nation will have for itself. [. . .] The second axiom is a corollary of the first. Prosperity, like peace, is indivisible. We cannot afford to have it scattered here or there among the fortunate or to enjoy it at the expense of others. Poverty, wherever it exists, is menacing to us all and undermines the well-being of each of us. It can no more be localized than war, but spreads and saps the economic strength of all the more-favored areas of the earth.[6]

Along with the idealism, there were three specific lessons, in all of which idealism was tempered by a precise calculation of the balance of national interest: (1) in trade relations, where the United States wanted to pry open other economies, especially those of the great European colonial empires; (2) in internationalizing the New Deal, so that the United States would be competing against industrial economies organized in a similar way; and (3) in solving the question of capital mobility by curtailing hot money flows. The American negotiators themselves were quite aware of their negotiating advantage and knew that they should use it. As Morgenthau told Assistant Secretary Harry Dexter White, the principal negotiator of the Bretton Woods settlement, "Now the advantage is ours here, and I personally think we should take it." White replied, "If the advantage were theirs, they would take it."[7]

These lessons were substantively lost in a retrospective context, as a new dynamism developed in the course of postwar recovery, but they were lost in different ways. The trade lessons proved the most resilient and provided the bedrock of the postwar order, at least until export growth faltered in the aftermath of the 2008 global financial crisis. But the New Deal and its thinking were only rather partially internationalized, and the major industrial countries all developed quite individual prescriptions for the best philosophy underlying economic policy, from ordoliberalism in Germany, a revival of classical economic liberalism in Italy, state-orchestrated *planisme* in France, and a state developmental strategy in Japan. By the 1970s all of these ran into trouble, and a new debate about economic philosophy developed. Finally, the vision of a world in which capital movements were controlled was gradually undermined in the 1960s, as offshore financial markets (notably the so-called "Eurodollar market") developed, and then radically subverted by the development of large-scale international banking in the 1970s.

THE TRADE LESSON

The Bretton Woods Conference represented both an attempt to learn the lessons of the Great Depression (in the mind of the Democratic Party, that is, of the New Deal), and a part of the preparation for peace and the postwar order. The conference was preceded by negotiations involving initially the United States and the United Kingdom, and then the other members of the United Nations (the wartime coalition against the Axis powers). The fundamental insight that made it possible to agree on an outcome was that destructive disputes over trade could be overcome by an agreement on monetary matters.

In this respect, Bretton Woods broke through the paralysis that had afflicted interwar attempts at international cooperation. The World Monetary and Economic Conference held in London in 1933 was generally seen as the last, and lost, opportunity to arrive at a settlement.[8] It had treated the trade and monetary issues separately. Even at the preparatory stage, work on the agenda of the London conference had been divided between two subcommittees. The Monetary Subcommittee dealt with financial issues and with currency stabilization, and the Economic Subcommittee with trade. The result of this division of labor was predictable and would have been comic if the results had not been so tragic. The monetary discussion arrived at the conclusion that a prerequisite for stabilization was the dismantling of barriers to trade. "Freer trade was a prerequisite of a return to normal economic conditions and a return to the gold standard." On the other hand, the trade debates produced agreement that nothing could be done without an overhaul of the international financial system, since "for ten years the world has been attempting to adjust the balance of payments by lending and borrowing instead of buying and selling."[9] This was patently a perfect recipe for a deadlock, in which trade and currency experts thought that the other side should be the one to make the first move.

The fundamental cause of the intellectual shift between 1932 and 1933 and the wartime discussions lay in the unflinching commitment of the world's most powerful state and economy to the principle of multilateral negotiations to reduce tariff levels and eliminate, as far as possible, trade quotas. This was a specifically Democratic (especially southern Democratic) vision: its major champion was Secretary of State Cordell Hull. Hull had been a congressman and then senator for Tennessee and was deeply influenced by the traditional interpretation of southern interests, which saw free trade as beneficial to southern cotton exporters and other farmers, and protection as the imposition of the interests of the manufacturing states of the Northeast and the Midwest. In the 1930s, as secretary of state, he had used bilateral negotiations as a way of creating reciprocal commitments to trade liberalization. His wartime diplomacy simply followed this pattern.

In the 1940s, however, the new policy consensus held that the overall goal of trade liberalization was to be generalized rather than advanced as it had been in the 1930s through bilateral deals. In particular, the wartime negotiations had offered the opportunity of undercutting British imperial preference and the protectionism that the United Kingdom had adopted in 1932. The principle of the obligation to introduce currency convertibility, limits on discriminatory trading practices, and increased access to each other's markets had been inserted into Anglo-American relations as Article VII of the Lend-Lease Agreement, which was generally known as "the Consideration" and was regarded by Keynes with much bitterness. The original draft of the State Department specified that the two countries would commit themselves to "promote mutually advantageous economic relations between them and the betterment of world-wide economic relations; they shall provide against discrimination in either the United States of America or the United Kingdom against the importation of any product originating in the other country."[10] The measure appeared in Washington as a sledgehammer to break the carapace of British imperial preference. The same language was used in Clause Four of the Atlantic Charter, drawn up in shipboard meetings on the ocean at the first visit of Winston Churchill to Roosevelt. The governments committed themselves "to further the enjoyment by all States, great or small, victor or vanquished, of access, on equal terms, to the trade and to the raw materials of the world."[11]

Hull's strategy for limiting protectionist impulses rested on two pillars. First, following what had become a standard political science interpretation of the origins of the Smoot-Hawley Tariff and the disasters of depression-era trade policy, there was a need to limit congressional or parliamentary politics. The political scientist Elmer Schattschneider had shown how the tariff had changed its nature in the course of congressional debate, as individual parliamentarians added on measures to protect particular interests associated with their locality. The logic of this argument is analogous to the collective-action mechanism suggested by Mancur Olson: an accumulation of small interests will lead to a suboptimal outcome, as each small interest will see major gains in a protectionist measure, and the collectivity is happy to accept this, as the overall cost of each measure is relatively trivial. Olson's suggestion is that only an overarching articulation of a general interest can solve the collective-action problem: in terms of concrete politics, this meant the strengthening of the executive and the presidency at the expense of the legislature. This was exactly the course Hull took with legislation (the Reciprocal Trade Agreements Act of 1934), which allowed the president to conclude bilateral trade treaties.[12]

The logic behind Hull's strategy lay in the perception that it is safer to anchor liberal arrangements in a legal or constitutional form, and in this way also remove them from party and parliamentary politics. But a further logic posited that international treaties were an even more secure barrier to alteration than domestic legal and constitutional arrangements. Anchoring the open economy in international agreements would be a way of tying political hands, or—in today's political science terminology—embedding the liberal international order.[13] In this way, an international order might create permanent constitutional guarantees for preferences of the United States as a collectivity (but not necessarily of individual Americans or individual parliamentarians).

The uncompromising attitude of the United States brought the inescapable conclusion even to opponents and skeptics (such as Keynes) that trade liberalization could not be the subject of discussion or bargaining. The British may have suspected that the US intention was to impose free trade on other countries so that there would be ready markets for the powerful manufacturing machine but that Congress would still maintain some domestic protection. So Keynes was eager to move ahead at the time of Bretton Woods with some kind of mechanism in the form of an International Trade Organization to ensure that the United States too was constrained. How fortunate for the world that there were no trade negotiations! When after the conclusion of the war, countries started haggling about the exemptions they desired from a proposed International Trade Organization, the US Congress indeed revolted, and the proposed institution collapsed. Bretton Woods in this sense had already succeeded before the delegates even met because of the already established wartime consensus that trade should not be debated and, thus, that an initial conference should deal with currency stabilization. The order was already embedded in preexisting diplomacy.

THE NEW DEAL CONTEXT

The second component was born out of the character of the conflict, when Allied policy makers thought of how to create a common vision reflecting the vision of the New Deal, which might be set against the Nazi continental European economy and *Grossraumwirtschaft*. Very different types of economies needed to be integrated into the common vision: ones that relied (as would the United Kingdom and the United States) on Keynesian macroeconomic demand management, as well as economies with central planning, including of external trade, on the Soviet model. The Soviet delegation was a part of Bretton Woods, and some of the obscurer wording of the IMF agreement is the result of the need to take into account Soviet peculiarities.

How could the domestic priorities that were the mainstay of the New Deal be reconciled with peace and broad international objectives? There were three alternative possibilities:

1. States might come to see their self-interest as lying in international harmony. The experience of the 1930s, however, did not seem encouraging.
2. An international juridical framework might be established for economic issues to arbitrate in cases where national and international objectives clashed.
3. An entirely automatic mechanism might point states in the direction of peace and prosperity without a complex and lengthy bureaucratic or juridical process.

Discussions of the postwar order swung between acceptance of the second and third of these choices and ended by taking elements of both. It was important to stop a mechanism such as the gold standard (which a new fixed-exchange-rate regime might resemble) from dragging the world into deflation. The legacy of the New Deal depended on resisting deflation. In the 1930s, this could only be done in a domestically sheltered setting, and trade protection appeared as a second-best answer to monetary induced deflation.[14] But a better way was to keep the international system from deflation by instituting better policy coordination. Automatism was attractive because it was apolitical, but it might not always fit in with widely perceived needs. An element of discretion was needed, which might best be provided through the creation of an institution with legal powers established by treaty. The resulting compromise is the foundation of the Bretton Woods achievement.

Keynes's scheme proposed an international bank, which he called the Clearing Union, with a new unit of account that would be the basis for the issue of a new international currency.[15] The proposed currency's name, "bancor," indicates the way in which the new money was conceived as an artificially created replacement for gold, which should gradually be expelled from the civilized conduct of international economics. Gold might be sold by central banks to the new international bank for bancor, but it would not be bought.

The object of the union's activities would be to avoid balance-of-payments imbalances through the creation of a body of rules and practices relating to the overdrafts on the bank accumulated by debtors and the positive balances acquired by creditors. The quotas for each country in the union were to be fixed as half of the average of imports and exports over the past five years. These quotas determined the limits up to which debtors could borrow (at interest rates that rose with the quantity of their debts). Creditors had to transfer to the union surpluses above their quota and pay charges to the union if their balances rose above a quarter of their quota. The Keynes scheme created a nearly perfect symmetry: it was to be as unpleasant and as costly to hold credit balances as to be a debtor. The result would be the impossibility of policies such as those followed by the United States and France in the later 1920s: the rules of the Clearing Union would drive such creditor states to expand.[16]

In subsequent drafts of his proposal, Keynes wrestled with "the most difficult question": "to determine [. . .] how much to decide by rule and how much to leave to discretion."[17] An abstract and impersonal operation would give the most scope for the operation of markets, and also for the preservation of national sovereignty. The most extreme version of a rule-bound system, however, the gold standard, had led to deflation and depression. Successive British drafts, tossed forward and backward between Keynes and the British Treasury and the Bank of England, gradually increased the discretionary element in what had originally been a neat and simple automatic principle of operation. Monetary authorities preferred (often they still do) "to operate by vague requests backed by vague sanctions, rather than by publishing definite rules."[18] By the fourth draft, the balance had shifted toward discretion. The Governing Board of the international bank might set conditions under which countries would be allowed to increase their debit balances, including the surrender of their gold reserve, the control of capital transactions, and a devaluation of the currency. But even with the introduction of consultations about policy in the place of rules of conduct, there still existed a symmetry between the constraints on debtors and creditors. If a credit balance exceeded half the quota, the country would be required to "discuss with the Governing Board (but still retain the ultimate decision in its own hands)" an expansion of domestic credit and demand, an exchange rate revaluation, an increase in wages, tariff reductions, or international loans for the development of backward countries.[19]

By April 1945, this symmetry had disappeared. What was left in the "Joint Statement by Experts on the Establishment of an International Monetary Fund (April 1944)" was a rather vaguer responsibility of the institution (now called the International Monetary Fund) to guide policy adjustment in surplus countries whose currencies had been deemed "scarce" by the fund and against whom deficit countries might take restrictive measures: "When a currency is thus declared scarce, the Fund shall issue a report embodying the causes of the scarcity and containing recommendations designed to bring it to an end."[20]

The final Bretton Woods settlement reflected a successful intervention by the American negotiators to undermine Keynes's original proposal.[21] The United States gradually, persistently, and effectively intervened in the negotiations to avoid being forced into expansionary policies simply by virtue of its debtor position. This was possible, because international capital movements would largely be controlled.

Article VI, Section 1 (a) of the IMF's Articles of Agreement specifically required countries to impose controls to meet large capital outflows: "A member may not make net use of the Fund's resources to meet a large or sustained outflow of capital, and the Fund may request a member to exercise controls to prevent such use of the resources of the Fund. If, after receiving such a request, a member fails to exercise appropriate controls, the Fund may declare the member ineligible to use the resources of the Fund."[22]

Article VII, Section 1, followed the April 1945 "Joint Statement" and contained the "scarcity of currency" clause that looked as if it might be targeted against the only country for the foreseeable future likely to have a currency that could not easily be obtained, the United States. But this measure would in practice require a majority of votes on the executive board, which would not be realizable in the case of attempting to punish the United States. From the beginning, in consequence, the capacity of the fund to exercise what would now be called surveillance "with teeth" was limited. The teeth were really not more than an optical illusion in the Articles. In practice, countries went on to develop idiosyncratic approaches that were not necessarily compatible with international equilibrium. In particular, by the 1960s, Japan and Germany began to run large current account surpluses, as part of an industrial development strategy in which export industry was promoted.

THE INTELLECTUAL CONTEXT

The final vital context for Bretton Woods was the prior crystallization of an intellectual consensus about the way the world economy functioned, and in particular about the costs and benefits of capital flows (where the economists now reached a negative verdict). Keynes did not believe in what might be called the "globalization paradigm"—the theory, elaborated already by Montesquieu and celebrated by Richard Cobden and John Bright as well as by Norman Angell, that commerce and commercial interconnectedness would by themselves bring international peace and order. In the *Economic Consequences of the Peace* Keynes had written,

> Bankers are used to this system, and believe it to be a necessary part of the permanent order of society. They are disposed to believe, therefore, by analogy with it, that a comparable system between Governments, on a far vaster and definitely oppressive scale, represented by no real assets, and less closely associated with the property system, is natural and reasonable and in conformity with human nature. I doubt this view of the world. Even capitalism at home, which engages many local sympathies, which plays a real part in the daily process of production, and upon the security of which the present organisation of society largely depends, is not very safe.[23]

The Bretton Woods scheme depended on a worldwide agreement on the control of capital movements, which was presented as a "permanent feature" of the postwar system.[24] That was the core intellectual bedrock on which the new institutions would be built. The Clearing Union would work closely not only with an agency dedicated to stabilizing prices (in order "to control the Trade Cycle"), but also with a supernational peacekeeping agency ("charged with the duty of preserving the peace and maintaining international order"). The British draft concluded that the proposal was "capable of arousing enthusiasm because it makes a beginning at the future economic ordering of the world between nations and the 'winning of the peace,' and might help to create the conditions and the atmosphere in which much else would be made easier."[25]

A new consensus on the causes of the Great Depression had shifted the emphasis away from the favorite villains of the 1930s literature—the uneven distribution of gold and the sterilizing policies of the Banque de France and the Federal Reserve System, or the allegedly excessive monetary inflation of the 1920s, or structural weaknesses in major industrial centers. Rather, the new view looked at the transmission process of depression and came to the conclusion that the large short-term capital flows of the 1920s and 1930s had led to disaster. These movements had made it impossible for states to pursue stable monetary policies; they threatened exchange rate stability, and they made fiscal stabilization highly hazardous.

This approach to the interwar economy oriented toward the diagnosis of capital movements as the fundamental ill had been developed by League of Nations economists in the 1930s. The most influential academic statement was Ragnar Nurkse's *International Currency Experience* (1944). "In the absence of international reserves large enough to meet such speculative and often self-perpetuating capital movements, many countries had to resort to exchange control and to other less insidious means of correcting the balance of payments." From this historical experience, Nurkse drew the conclusion that greater international cooperation was needed: "But if, owing to anticipated exchange adjustments, political unrest or similar causes, closer control of hot money movements is inevitable, then some of its difficulties and dangers might be overcome by international understanding." As a consequence, when he wrote about plans for an international bank or monetary fund, Nurkse added: "If, in addition to trade and other normal transactions, such a fund had to cover all kinds of capital flight, it might have to be endowed with enormous resources. In fact, no fund of any practicable size might be sufficient to offset mass movements of nervous flight capital."[26] It was obviously hard to distinguish what exactly constituted "flight capital."

The restoration of a multilateral financial system depended in the view of almost every analyst on control of capital movements for an unlimited time. This approach appealed to Keynes, who had repeatedly asserted his skepticism about the benefits of both capital exports and capital imports. Keynes fully shared the belief that capital flight had been the major international interwar problem: "There is no country which can, in future, safely allow the flight of funds for political reasons or to evade domestic taxation or in anticipation of the owner turning refugee. Equally, there is no country that can safely receive fugitive funds, which constitute an unwanted import of capital, yet cannot safely be used for fixed investment."[27] It is true that Keynes added that the new controls, which might become a "permanent feature of the post-war system," should not bring an end to the "era of international investment"; but it would need states and international agreements to define (in accordance with national priorities) what was desirable investment and what was unwanted capital movement. The British economist Sir Hubert Henderson noted, "It has been generally agreed in the United Kingdom that we must retain the right to regulate capital movements, effectively and indefinitely."[28] Many Americans also shared this view.

In the United States, the feeling that the capital exports of the 1920s had largely been a result of banks' misspelling of foreign securities (especially government and municipal bonds) to naive investors was a commonplace for the New Deal. Harry Dexter White, assistant to the US Treasury secretary, and the other major architect of what would be the Bretton Woods Agreements, fully concurred with Keynes that

> The theoretical bases for the belief still so widely held, that interference with trade and with capital and gold movements etc., are harmful, are hangovers from a Nineteenth Century economic creed, which held that international economic adjustments, if left alone, would work themselves out toward an "equilibrium" with a minimum of harm to world trade and prosperity. . . . The task before us is not to prohibit instruments of control but to develop those measures of control, those policies of administering such control, as will be the most effective in obtaining the objectives of world-wide sustained prosperity.[29]

White's immediate superior, Treasury secretary Henry Morgenthau, made the target of these controls much more explicit. The new institutions of the international order would be "instrumentalities of sovereign governments and not of private financial interests." The task that the statesmen should set themselves was to "drive the usurious moneylenders from the temple of international finance."[30] But this was primarily a political task.

Producing an agreement was possible because of the wide extent of agreement in the initial bargaining positions.[31] Keynes wrote of his proposals that they "lay no claim to originality. They are an attempt to reduce to practical shape certain general ideas belonging to the contemporary climate of economic opinion, which have been given publicity in recent months by writers of several different nationalities. It is difficult to see how any plan can be successful which does not use these general ideas, which are born of the spirit of the age."[32]

THE RETROSPECTIVE CONTEXT

It is striking that in retrospect Bretton Woods appears as the only really successful example of a multilateral redesign of the world's international monetary order: Napoleon III had tried to establish a world money at the World Monetary Conference of 1867; the Genoa conference in 1922 was ineffective in proposing a blueprint for monetary stability after the First World War; in 1971 Richard Nixon termed the Smithsonian meeting the most important monetary conference since the birth of Jesus Christ, but the new exchange rates held for less than two years; and ever since the disintegration of the Bretton Woods regime in the early 1970s economists and policy makers have been calling in vain for a new Bretton Woods. Such reforms never materialized after 1945 because of monetary multilateralism: there is no single power or like-minded group of powers that can impose their plan on a complicated and perhaps uncontrollable market of ideas and interests.

The negotiations at the Bretton Woods Conference involved representatives of forty-five countries. But the preceding negotiation had been largely bilateral, between the United Kingdom and the United States. The French Plan and an analogous Canadian proposal had been aimed at mediating between the two contrasting positions.[33] It took a long time for anything like the Bretton Woods system to come into operation. The right in the United States was hostile, and American bankers lobbied against the Bretton Woods Agreements, which they saw as costly concessions to foreigners and to socialist and redistributive principles. For them, there was too much of the New Deal in the scheme.[34] In the United Kingdom, the agreements were attacked by economic nationalists both on the left of the Labour Party and on the right of the Conservative Party. For these politicians, the scheme was simply too American.

The opposition to Bretton Woods in the immediate aftermath of the Second World War was driven in both countries by what would now be seen as an incoherent anti-globalization consensus—analogous to the passions that drove Brexit in 2016 both from anti–free trade leftists and from rightists who also emphasized national sovereignty, or to the debates in the US primaries of 2016, where both Donald Trump and Bernard "Bernie" Sanders fanned anxieties about the effects of free trade and of immigration. The ratification of the Bretton Woods settlement held off that backlash, for the moment— and it was a moment that lasted seventy years.

The United States in practice then made the Bretton Woods order (and globalization) work by keeping open markets and pressuring other countries to liberalize their trading regimes. It provided dollar liquidity, perhaps by the late 1960s too much; and as a financial center it took short-term deposits while engaging in long-term lending and in foreign direct investment. But most of all the perpetuation of the New Deal mind-set as an international ideal created an emotional or cultural model of openness. The world looked to American culture as much as American economics; and that aspect was preserved when the narrow financial framework of the Bretton Woods order fell apart.

A large part of the institutional mechanism of Bretton Woods, the fixed but adjustable exchange rate system, eventually collapsed in the early 1970s. Exchange rates had become inflexible, and countries with large trade surpluses (Japan and West Germany) were reluctant to conduct revaluations that might correct the imbalance. In part they justified their hesitance by an argument that also struck a chord with deficit countries that disliked the political humiliation of devaluing: frequent parity changes might lead speculators to bet on an impending change, selling in the anticipation of devaluation or buying in the expectation of revaluation. The adjustable-peg system created the potential for one-way bets that could force countries into crisis measure adjustment. Unwillingness to adjust on the part of countries pegged to the dollar (the one country that could not change its exchange rate) increased the sense that the dollar's role was problematical, and more and more US policy makers felt trapped.

The heart of the story of the so-called "breakdown" of Bretton Woods in the early 1970s lies in the political economy of the reaction in the United States to the surge of exports from the "emergers" of the time, in particular from Japan, but also Germany. US Treasury secretary John Connally took up this theme again and again, notably in his May 1971 Munich speech at the International Banking Conference. The idea that the international monetary order benefited foreigners became a part of congressional politics with the August 6, 1971, report of the Joint Economic Committee's Subcommittee on International Exchange and Payments, which presented the "inescapable conclusion" that the "dollar is overvalued."[35] But the only way that the United States could change its exchange rate was by temporarily escaping from the system altogether. Connally wanted to use exchange rates as a weapon to secure market opening in Japan and Europe, especially since the question of Japanese textile exports to the United States was producing major congressional pressure for immediate action and was likely to become a central issue in the 1972 election. The dollar crisis, and the associated temporary import surcharge, was used to deal with a pressing issue in domestic politics by an administration that was not particularly engaged in multilateral international financial diplomacy.

The dollar remained the world's leading currency after 1971, contrary to most expectations after August 15, 1971. Almost the sole exception to the doom-laden commentary was Robert Mundell, who predicted the continuation of a dollar-dominated world in a short and quite remarkable essay of 1970, which also (incidentally) accurately forecast European monetary integration and the collapse of Communism.[36] The centrality of the American dollar, which remained after 1971 and persists until today, was the real legacy of Bretton Woods.

The principal achievement of 1971 was a negative one: by shifting political discontent directed at the trade regime (the undisputed source of the world's massive post-1945 wealth creation, and indeed the heart of Cordell Hull's vision) onto the prominent and emotional issues around the international role of the dollar, the world escaped (though only just) a major trade war. In the earlier age of worries about globalization at the beginning of the twentieth century, a backlash began, which in the end produced restrictions on migration and high levels of trade protection. When national protection became the major priority of most countries, in the 1920s and 1930s, the world became both poorer and less safe. There was a vicious cycle, in which external forces were blamed for loss and disaster, and high levels of trade protection destroyed national prosperity.

By contrast, though there was a great deal of pressure for protection in the US Congress (and in other countries also) in the 1970s, the world did not go back to protectionism, and trade continued to expand faster than world production. Trade thus acted as the locomotive of economic growth, and the higher rate of growth relative to output only reversed in 2013.

Most countries avoided a protectionist backlash in the second half of the twentieth century, although their citizens often relived the trade anxieties of the nineteenth and early twentieth centuries. There are obvious parallels between British concerns about German competition with cheap labor and the power of the new German industries in the 1880s and 1890s and debates in the United States and Western Europe about the Japanese "threat" in the 1960s and 1980s, and indeed about today's China challenge. Changing employment patterns are a constant accompaniment of growth. In the early 1970s and again in the 1980s, US workers and producers were upset about the loss of jobs to Japan. Some of the most skilled jobs, in automobiles, were lost; household appliances like TVs were no longer made in the United States. In the later twentieth century, the US administration tried to respond to the job-loss worries not by trade restrictions but by exchange rate alterations that would make the US products more competitive: first the end of the gold convertibility of the dollar in 1971, and then in 1985 the Plaza Accord to depreciate the dollar. Monetary and exchange rate policy initiatives offered a way of absorbing adjustment pain. The focus of trade discontent was shifted to the monetary arena in a way that helped to undermine the legitimacy of institutional means of regulating the international financial system.

Trade problems were in fact routinely dealt with by shifting the emphasis to the monetary arena. The world has developed its institutional arrangements in the setting of globalization away from the Bretton Woods settlement by making them harder in the trade arena and softer in the monetary one. The trade settlement, which was not explicitly tackled at the 1944 conference but was left to the postwar era, was thus the longest and most powerful legacy of the Bretton Woods order.

The use of monetary policy and exchange rate adjustment to de-escalate trade conflict is harder today, since many of the countries whose products are entering the United States peg their own currencies in more or less formal ways to the dollar (in a manner that is reminiscent of the old Bretton Woods order of fixed exchange rates). Governments in industrial countries still feel that they need some response in an attempt to "feel the pain," and to show that they are doing something.

In the wake of the 2008 financial crisis, the threat of trade protection and a reversal of the globalization impetus have increased. Trade collapsed in the immediate aftermath of the financial crisis, but from 2009 recovered. From 2013, however, trade growth was substantially slower than world output growth: a dramatic reversal of the relationship prevailing in the classic years of the Bretton Woods order. Some of the impetus for twenty-first-century trade slowing may be technical in origin. New technologies allow cost-saving automated production, so that the wage-costs benefits of distant production appear less, while demands to respond to instant demands of fashion or of production schedules produce a "just in time" focus that has led to a reversal of production off-shoring (or "on-shoring").

Major central banks—in particular the Fed—engaged in a large-scale exercise of "unconventional" monetary policy, or quantitative easing. While this looked like an appropriate policy to deal with problems in the Unites States or the United Kingdom, the spillover effects created substantial problems in emerging markets. Cheap borrowing in particular fueled large-scale capital inflows, with inflationary effects.

The actions of the major industrial countries seemed to be eroding monetary and financial stability in the periphery. The standard reply of US officials was that the spillovers could be dealt with easily through the use of domestic policy levers such as interest rates, but also through the imposition of capital controls. But that argument ignored the real practical difficulties of maintaining watertight controls. Some emerging market policy makers claimed that the extraordinarily low interest rates were part of a strategy of currency depreciation by the United States ("currency wars" in the oft-quoted phrase of Brazilian finance minister Guido Mantega).[37] Japan and Europe subsequently seemed to adopt similar strategies, in which it looked as if a depreciated exchange rate was a major part of the plan for economic recovery. The repeated accusations that exchange rates are being manipulated in order to achieve trade advantages recall the bitter polemics of the 1930s.

Economic outcomes are often attributed to a specific part of the institutional architecture. There are both negative and positive versions. The Versailles Treaty produced a negative mythology, in which all the bad and unstable elements of interwar politics were attributed to the peace treaty rather than to the destruction that had been wrought by the First World War. By contrast, Bretton Woods formed part of a positive mythology. The conference was a backlash against the interwar backlash against globalization. It was driven by the perception that poverty, autarky, and war were causally interlinked. According to the new vision, an act of enlightened creative internationalism removed obstacles to aligning the interests of multiple nation-states and of economic agents, providing a new synthesis of state and market. Bretton Woods was the intellectual sugar covering and masking the bitter taste of the pill of Realpolitik dollar hegemony. But it also provided a sugar coating for the unpleasant taste of internationalism in the domestic context of American politics. Gradually—probably inevitably—the sugar coating gave way, and in each large country a dynamic of national politics reasserted itself.

Notes

1. Robert Skidelsky, *Keynes: The Return of the Master* (New York: Public Affairs, 2009).

2. For Lionel Robbins's description of the "godlike" Keynes, see Roy F. Harrod, *The Life of John Maynard Keynes* (Harmondsworth, UK: Penguin, 1972), 740; also Donald Moggridge, *Maynard Keynes: An Economist's Biography* (London: Routledge, 1992).

3. Walther Funk, *The Economic Future of Europe* (Berlin: Terramare Office, 1940); Armand van Dormael, *Bretton Woods: Birth of a Monetary System* (New York: Holmes and Meier, 1978), 6–7; Joseph Gold, *Legal and Institutional Aspects of the International Monetary System: Selected Essays*, vol. 2 (Washington, DC: IMF, 1984), 19; Moggridge, *Maynard Keynes*, 654.

4. Cited in Robert Skidelsky, *John Maynard Keynes: The Economist as Saviour* (London: Macmillan, 1992), 482.

5. John Maynard Keynes, *The Economic Consequences of the Peace* (London: Macmillan, 1919), 268.

6. John Morton Blum, *From the Morgenthau Diaries*, vol. 3: *Years of War 1941–1945* (Boston: Houghton Mifflin, 1967), 248.

7. Armand van Dormael, *Bretton Woods: Birth of a Monetary System* (New York: Holmes and Meier, 1978), 211.

8. See Patricia Clavin, "The World Economic Conference 1933: The Failure of British Internationalism," *Journal of European Economic History* 20 (1991): 489–527.

9. League of Nations Archive (Geneva: United Nations), R2672, 1 xi 1932, Second Meeting of Monetary Sub-Committee; R2671, 7 xi 1932, Third Meeting of Preparatory Committee.

10. US Department of State, Foreign Relations of the United States Diplomatic Papers, 1941, The British Commonwealth; The Near East and Africa, vol. 3, *Draft Proposal for a Temporary Lend-Lease Agreement Handed by Mr. Acheson to Mr. Keynes on July 28, 1941*, https://history.state.gov/historicaldocuments/frus1941v03/d9 (p. 13).

11. "Inter-Allied Council Statement on the Principles of the Atlantic Charter: September 24, 1941," http://avalon.law.yale.edu/wwii/interall.asp.

12. E. E. Schattschneider, *Politics, Pressures and the Tariff: A Study of Free Private Enterprise in Pressure Politics, as Shown in the 1929–1930 Revision of the Tariff* (New York: Prentice-Hall, 1935); Mancur Olson, *The Logic of Collective Action: Public Goods and the Theory of Groups* (Cambridge, MA: Harvard University Press, 1971).

13. John Gerard Ruggie, *Winning the Peace: America and World Order in the New Era* (New York: Columbia University Press, 1996); G. John Ikenberry, *After Victory: Institutions, Strategic Restraint, and the Rebuilding of Order after Major Wars* (Princeton, NJ: Princeton University Press, 2001).

14. See W. Arthur Lewis, *Economic Survey 1919–1939* (London: Allen & Unwin, 1949).

15. See Keynes's, "Proposals for an International Clearing Union (April 1943)," in the "Historical Documents" section of this book.

16. There is a possibility that Keynes envisaged a world in which there would be more exchange rate alterations as the major adjustment mechanism for the international monetary system, with deficit countries depreciating and surplus countries appreciating (see David Vines, review of Robert Skidelsky, *John Maynard Keynes*, vol. 3: *Fighting for Freedom, 1937–1946*, in *Economic Journal* 113 (June 2003): 338–61. The practice of the Bretton Woods system was remarkably different, however, with only two (contentious)

appreciations of surplus currencies in 1961 and 1969, and it would have been difficult in 1944–1945 to envisage the circumstances in which the United States, where the surpluses were likely to be for the foreseeable future, would agree to an appreciation of the dollar.

17. J. Keith Horsefield, *The International Monetary Fund 1945–1965: Twenty Years of International Monetary Cooperation*, vol. 3 (Washington, DC: International Monetary Fund, 1969), 6.

18. Samuel Brittan, *A Restatement of Economic Liberalism* (London: Macmillan, 1988), 87.

19. Harold James, *International Monetary Cooperation Since Bretton Woods* (New York: Oxford University Press, 1995), 37.

20. See "Joint Statement by Experts on the Establishment of an International Monetary Fund (April 1944)," in the "Historical Documents" section of this book.

21. See "Final Act (22 July 1944)," in the "Historical Documents" section of this book.

22. See Article VI, Section 1 (a) of the "Articles of Agreement" in the "Historical Documents" section of this book.

23. Keynes, *Economic Consequences*, 263–64.

24. Horsefield, *International Monetary Fund*, 3:13.

25. See Keynes, *Proposals for an International Currency (or Clearing) Union* [February 11, 1942], at http://www.elibrary.imf.org/staticfiles/IMF_History/IMF_45-65_vol3.pdf.

26. Ragnar Nurkse, *International Currency Experience: Lessons from the Inter-War Period* (Geneva: League of Nations, 1944), 188, 220, 222.

27. Horsefield, *International Monetary Fund*, 3:31; see also Moggridge, *Maynard Keynes*, 673.

28. Bank of England Archive, London, OV38/49, Sir Hubert Henderson note of 1 August 1944.

29. Horsefield, *International Monetary Fund*, 3:64.

30. Richard N. Gardner, *Sterling-Dollar Diplomacy: The Origins and the Prospects of Our International Economic Order* (New York: McGraw-Hill, 1969), 76.

31. A modern commentator speaks of the existence of a "primitive epistemic community" of expert economic opinion-makers: G. John Ikenberry, "A World Economy Restored: Expert Consensus and the Anglo-American Postwar Settlement," *International Organization* 46 (1992): 293.

32. Horsefield, *International Monetary Fund*, 3:21.

33. See "Suggestions Regarding International Monetary Relations (May 1943)," in the "Historical Documents" section of this book.

34. See Eric Rauchway, *The Money Makers: How Roosevelt and Keynes Ended the Depression, Defeated Fascism, and Secured a Prosperous Peace* (New York: Basic Books, 2015).

35. *Action Now to Strengthen the U.S. Dollar: Report of the Subcommittee on International Exchange and Payments of the Joint Economic Committee*, 92nd Congress of the United States, Together with Minority Views (Washington, DC: Government Printing Office, 1971).

36. Robert Mundell, in *L'Union monétaire en Europe*, ed. Alexandre Swoboda (Geneva: Institut de Hautes Études Internationales, 1971).

37. "Brazil in 'Currency War' Alert," *Financial Times*, September 27, 2010.

HISTORICAL DOCUMENTS

ARTICLES OF AGREEMENT

ARTICLES OF AGREEMENT OF THE

INTERNATIONAL MONETARY FUND,

July 22, 1944

The Governments on whose behalf the present Agreement is signed agree as follows:

INTRODUCTORY ARTICLE

The International Monetary Fund is established and shall operate in accordance with the following provisions:

ARTICLE I. PURPOSES

The purposes of the International Monetary Fund are:

(i) To promote international monetary cooperation through a permanent institution which provides the machinery for consultation and collaboration on international monetary problems.

(ii) To facilitate the expansion and balanced growth of international trade, and to contribute thereby to the promotion and maintenance of high levels of employment and real income and to the development of the productive resources of all members as primary objectives of economic policy.

(iii) To promote exchange stability, to maintain orderly exchange arrangements among members, and to avoid competitive exchange depreciation.

(iv) To assist in the establishment of a multilateral system of payments in respect of current transactions between members and in the elimination of foreign exchange restrictions which hamper the growth of world trade.

(v) To give confidence to members by making the Fund's resources available to them under adequate safeguards, thus providing them with opportunity to correct maladjustments in their balance of payments without resorting to measures destructive of national or international prosperity.

(vi) In accordance with the above, to shorten the duration and lessen the degree of disequilibrium in the international balances of payments of members.

The Fund shall be guided in all its decisions by the purposes set forth in this Article.

ARTICLE II. MEMBERSHIP
Section 1. Original Members

The original members of the Fund shall be those of the countries represented at the United Nations Monetary and Financial Conference whose governments accept membership before the date specified in Article XX, Section 2 (e).

Section 2. Other Members

Membership shall be open to the governments of other countries at such times and in accordance with such terms as may be prescribed by the Fund.

ARTICLE III. QUOTAS AND SUBSCRIPTIONS
Section 1. Quotas

Each member shall be assigned a quota. The quotas of the members represented at the United Nations Monetary and Financial conference which accept membership before the date specified in article XX, Section 2 (e), shall be those set forth in Schedule A. The quotas of other members shall be determined by the Fund.

Section 2. Adjustment of Quotas

The Fund shall at intervals of five years review, and if it deems it appropriate propose an adjustment of, the quotas of the members. It may also, if it thinks fit, consider at any other time the adjustment of any particular quota at the request of the member concerned. A four-fifths majority of the total voting power shall be required for any change in quotas and no quota shall be changed without the consent of the member concerned.

Section 3. Subscriptions: Time, Place, and Form of Payment

(a) The subscription of each member shall be equal to its quota and shall be paid in full to the Fund at the appropriate depository on or before the date when the member becomes eligible under Article XX, Section 4 (c) or (d), to buy currencies from the Fund.

(b) Each member shall pay in gold, as a minimum, the smaller of

(i) twenty-five percent of its quota; or

(ii) ten percent of its net official holdings of gold and United States dollars as at the date when the Fund notifies members under Article XX, Section 4 (a) that it will shortly be in a position to begin exchange transactions.

Each member shall furnish to the Fund the data necessary to determine its net official holdings of gold and United States dollars.

(c) Each member shall pay the balance of its quota in its own currency.

(d) If the net official holdings of gold and United States dollars of any member as at the date referred to in (b) (ii) above are not ascertainable because its territories have been occupied by the enemy, the Fund shall fix an appropriate alternative date for determining such holdings. If such date is later than that on which the country becomes eligible under Article XX, Section 4 (c) or (d), to buy currencies from the Fund, the Fund and the member shall agree on a provisional gold payment to be made under (b) above, and the balance of the member's subscription shall be paid in the member's currency, subject to appropriate adjustment between the member and the Fund when the net official holdings have been ascertained.

Section 4. Payments when Quotas are Changed

(a) Each member which consents to an increase in its quota shall, within thirty days after the date of its consent, pay to the Fund twenty-five percent of the increase in gold and the balance in its own currency. If, however, on the date when the member consents to an increase, its monetary reserves are less than its new quota, the Fund may reduce the proportion of the increase to be paid in gold.

(b) If a member consents to a reduction in its quota, the Fund shall, within thirty days after the date of the consent, pay to the member an amount equal to the reduction. The payment shall be made in the member's currency and in such amount of gold as may be necessary to prevent reducing the Fund's holdings of the currency below seventy-five percent of the new quota.

Section 5. Substitution of Securities for Currency

The Fund shall accept from any member in place of any part of the member's currency which in the judgment of the Fund is not needed for its operations, notes or similar obligations issued by the member or the depository designated by the member under Article XIII, Section 2, which shall be non-negotiable, non-interest bearing and payable at their par value on demand by crediting the account of the Fund in the designated depository. This Section shall apply not only to currency subscribed by members but also to any currency otherwise due to, or acquired by, the Fund.

ARTICLE IV. PAR VALUES OF CURRENCIES
Section 1. Expression of Par Values

(a) The par value of the currency of each member shall be expressed in terms of gold as a common denominator or in terms of the United States dollar of the weight and fineness in effect on July 1, 1944.

(b) All computations relating to currencies of members for the purpose of applying the provisions of this Agreement shall be on the basis of their par values.

Section 2. Gold Purchases based on Par Values

The Fund shall prescribe a margin above and below par value for transactions in gold by members, and no member shall buy gold at a price above par value plus the prescribed margin, or sell gold at a price below par value minus the prescribed margin.

Section 3. Foreign Exchange Dealings based on Parity

The maximum and the minimum rates for exchange transactions between the currencies of members taking place within their territories shall not differ from parity

(i) in the case of spot exchange transactions, by more than one percent; and

(ii) in the case of other exchange transactions, by a margin which exceeds the margin for spot exchange transactions by more than the Fund considers reasonable.

Section 4. Obligations Regarding Exchange Stability

(a) Each member undertakes to collaborate with the Fund to promote exchange stability, to maintain orderly exchange arrangements with other members, and to avoid competitive exchange alterations.

(b) Each member undertakes, through appropriate measures consistent with this Agreement, to permit within its territories exchange transactions between its currency and the currencies of other members only within the limits prescribed under Section 3 of this Article. A member whose monetary authorities, for the settlement of international transactions, in fact freely buy and sell gold within the limits prescribed by the Fund under Section 2 of this Article shall be deemed to be fulfilling this undertaking.

Section 5. Changes in Par Values

(a) A member shall not propose a change in the par value of its currency except to correct a fundamental disequilibrium.

(b) A change in the par value of a member's currency may be made only on the proposal of the member and only after consultation with the Fund.

(c) When a change is proposed, the Fund shall first take into account the changes, if any, which have already taken place in the initial par value of the member's currency as determined under Article XX, Section 4. If the proposed change, together with all previous changes, whether increases or decreases,

(i) does not exceed ten percent of the initial par value, the Fund shall raise no objection,

(ii) does not exceed a further ten percent of the initial par value, the Fund may either concur or object, but shall declare its attitude within seventy-two hours if the member so requests,

(iii) is not within (i) or (ii) above, the Fund may either concur or object, but shall be entitled to a longer period in which to declare its attitude.

(d) Uniform changes in par values made under Section 7 of this Article shall not be taken into account in determining whether a proposed change falls within (i), (ii), or (iii) of (c) above.

(e) A member may change the par value of its currency without the concurrence of the Fund if the change does not affect the international transactions of members of the Fund.

(f) The Fund shall concur in a proposed change which is within the terms of (c) (ii) or (c) (iii) above if it is satisfied that the change is necessary to correct a fundamental disequilibrium. In particular, provided it is so satisfied, it shall not object to a proposed change because of the domestic social or political policies of the member proposing the change.

Section 6. Effect of Unauthorized Changes

If a member changes the par value of its currency despite the objection of the Fund, in cases where the Fund is entitled to object, the member shall be ineligible to use the resources of the Fund unless the Fund otherwise determines; and if, after the expiration of a reasonable period, the difference between the member and the Fund continues, the matter shall be subject to the provisions of Article XV, Section 2 (b).

Section 7. Uniform Changes in Par Values

Notwithstanding the provisions of Section 5 (b) of this Article, the Fund by a majority of the total voting power may make uniform proportionate changes in the par values of the currencies of all members provided each such change is approved by every member which has ten percent or more of the total of the quotas. The par value of a member's currency shall, however, not be changed under this provision if, within seventy-two hours of the Fund's action, the member informs the Fund that it does not wish the par value of its currency to be changed by such action.

Section 8. Maintenance of Gold Value of the Fund's Assets

(a) The gold value of the Fund's assets shall be maintained notwithstanding changes in the par or foreign exchange value of the currency of any member.

(b) Whenever (i) the par value of a member's currency is reduced, or (ii) the foreign exchange value of a member's currency has, in the opinion of the Fund, depreciated to a significant extent within that member's territories, the member shall pay to the Fund within a reasonable time an amount of its own currency equal to the reduction in the gold value of its currency held by the Fund.

(c) Whenever the par value of a member's currency is increased, the Fund shall return to such member within a reasonable time an amount in its currency equal to the increase in the gold value of its currency held by the Fund.

(d) The provisions of this Section shall apply to a uniform proportionate change in the par values of the currencies of all members, unless at the time when such a change is proposed the Fund decides otherwise.

Section 9. Separate Currencies within a Member's Territories

A member proposing a change in the par value of its currency shall be deemed, unless it declares otherwise, to be proposing a corresponding change in the par value of the separate currencies of all territories in respect of which it has accepted this Agreement under Article XX, Section 2 (g). It shall, however, be open to a member to declare that its proposal relates either to the metropolitan currency alone, or only to one or more specified separate currencies, or to the metropolitan currency and one or more specified separate currencies.

ARTICLE V. TRANSACTIONS WITH THE FUND
Section 1. Agencies Dealing with the Fund

Each member shall deal with the Fund only through its Treasury, central bank, stabilization fund or other similar fiscal agency and the Fund shall deal only with or through the same agencies.

Section 2. Limitation on the Fund's Operations

Except as otherwise provided in this Agreement, operations on the account of the Fund shall be limited to transactions for the purpose of supplying a member, on the initiative of such member, with the currency of another member in exchange for gold or for the currency of the member desiring to make the purchase.

Section 3. Conditions Governing use of the Fund's Resources

(a) A member shall be entitled to buy the currency of another member from the Fund in exchange for its own currency subject to the following conditions:

(i) The member desiring to purchase the currency represents that it is presently needed for making in that currency payments which are consistent with the provisions of this Agreement;

(ii) The Fund has not given notice under Article VII, Section 3, that its holdings of the currency desired have become scarce;

(iii) The proposed purchase would not cause the Fund's holdings of the purchasing member's currency to increase by more than twenty-five percent of its quota during the period of twelve months ending on the date of the purchase nor to exceed two hundred percent of its quota, but the twenty-five percent limitation shall apply only to the extent that the Fund's holdings of the member's currency have been brought above seventy-five percent of its quota if they had been below that amount;

(iv) The Fund has not previously declared under Section 5 of this Article, Article IV, Section 6, Article VI, Section 1, or Article XV, Section 2 (a), that the member desiring to purchase is ineligible to use the resources of the Fund.

(b) A member shall not be entitled without the permission of the Fund to use the Fund's resources to acquire currency to hold against forward exchange transactions.

Section 4. Waiver of Conditions

The Fund may in its discretion, and on terms which safeguard its interests, waive any of the conditions prescribed in Section 3 (a) of this Article, especially in the case of members with a record of avoiding large or continuous use of the Fund's resources. In making a waiver it shall take into consideration periodic or exceptional requirements of the member requesting the waiver. The Fund shall also take into consideration a member's willingness to pledge as collateral security gold, silver, securities, or other acceptable assets having a value sufficient in the opinion of the Fund to protect its interests and may require as a condition of waiver the pledge of such collateral security.

Section 5. Ineligibility to use the Fund's Resources

Whenever the Fund is of the opinion that any member is using the resources of the Fund in a manner contrary to the purposes of the Fund, it shall present to the member a report setting forth the views of the Fund and prescribing a suitable time for reply. After presenting such a report to a member, the Fund may limit the use of its resources by the member. If no reply to the report is received from the member within the prescribed time, or if the reply received is unsatisfactory, the Fund may continue to limit the member's use of the Fund's resources or may, after giving reasonable notice to the member, declare it ineligible to use the resources of the Fund.

Section 6. Purchases of Currencies from the Fund for Gold

(a) Any member desiring to obtain, directly or indirectly, the currency of another member for gold shall, provided that it can do so with equal advantage, acquire it by the sale of gold to the Fund.

(b) Nothing in this Section shall be deemed to preclude any member from selling in any market gold newly produced from mines located within its territories.

Section 7. Repurchase by a Member of its Currency held by the Fund

(a) A member may repurchase from the Fund and the Fund shall sell for gold any part of the Fund's holdings of its currency in excess of its quota.

(b) At the end of each financial year of the Fund, a member shall repurchase from the Fund with gold or convertible currencies, as determined in accordance with Schedule B, part of the Fund's holdings of its currency under the following conditions:

(i) Each member shall use in repurchases of its own currency from the Fund an amount of its monetary reserves equal in value to one-half of any increase that has occurred during the year in the Fund's holdings of its currency plus one-half of any increase, or minus one-half of any decrease, that has occurred during the year in the member's monetary reserves. This rule shall not apply when a member's monetary reserves have decreased during the year by more than the Fund's holdings of its currency have increased.

(ii) If after the repurchase described in (i) above (if required) has been made, a member's holdings of another member's currency (or of gold acquired from that member) are found to have increased by reason of transactions in terms of that currency with other members or persons in their territories, the member whose holdings of such currency (or gold) have thus increased shall use the increase to repurchase its own currency from the Fund.

(c) None of the adjustments described in (b) above shall be carried to a point at which

(i) the member's monetary reserves are below its quota, or

(ii) the Fund's holdings of its currency are below seventy-five percent of its quota, or

(iii) the Fund's holdings of any currency required to be used are above seventy-five percent of the quota of the member concerned.

Section 8. Charges

(a) Any member buying the currency of another member from the Fund in exchange for its own currency shall pay a service charge uniform for all members of three-fourths percent in addition to the parity price. The Fund in its discretion may increase this service charge to not more than one percent or reduce it to not less than one-half percent.

(b) The Fund may levy a reasonable handling charge on any member buying gold from the Fund or selling gold to the Fund.

(c) The Fund shall levy charges uniform for all members which shall be payable by any member on the average daily balances of its currency held by the Fund in excess of its quota. These charges shall be at the following rates:

(i) *On amounts not more than twenty-five percent in excess of the quota:* no charge, for the first three months; one-half percent per annum for the next nine months; and thereafter an increase in the charge of one-half percent for each subsequent year.

(ii) *On amounts more than twenty-five percent and not more than fifty percent in excess of the quota:* an additional one-half percent for the first year; and an additional one-half percent for each subsequent year.

(iii) *On each additional bracket of twenty-five percent in excess of the quota:* an additional one-half percent for the first year; and an additional one-half percent for each subsequent year.

(d) Whenever the Fund's holdings of a member's currency are such that the charge applicable to any bracket for any period has reached the rate of four percent per annum, the Fund and the member shall consider means by which the Fund's holdings of the currency can be reduced. Thereafter, the charges shall rise in accordance with the provisions of (c) above until they reach five percent and failing agreement, the Fund may then impose such charges as it deems appropriate.

(e) The rates referred to in (c) and (d) above may be changed by a three-fourths majority of the total voting power.

(f) All charges shall be paid in gold. If, however, the member's monetary reserves are less than one-half of its quota, it shall pay in gold only that proportion of the charges due which such reserves bear to one-half of its quota, and shall pay the balance in its own currency.

ARTICLE VI. CAPITAL TRANSFERS
Section 1. Use of the Fund's Resources for Capital Transfers

(a) A member may not make net use of the Fund's resources to meet a large or sustained outflow of capital, and the Fund may request a member to exercise controls to prevent such use of the resources of the Fund. If, after receiving such a request, a member fails to exercise appropriate controls, the Fund may declare the member ineligible to use the resources of the Fund.

(b) Nothing in this Section shall be deemed

(i) to prevent the use of the resources of the Fund for capital transactions of reasonable amount required for the expansion of exports or in the ordinary course of trade, banking or other business, or

(ii) to affect capital movements which are met out of a member's own resources of gold and foreign exchange, but members undertake that such capital movements will be in accordance with the purposes of the Fund.

Section 2. Special Provisions for Capital Transfers

If the Fund's holdings of the currency of a member have remained below seventy-five percent of its quota for an immediately preceding period of not less than six months, such member, if it has not been declared ineligible to use the resources of the Fund under Section 1 of this Article, Article IV, Section 6, Article V, Section 5, or Article XV, Section 2 (a), shall be entitled, notwithstanding the provisions of Section 1 (a) of this Article, to buy the currency of another member from the Fund with its own currency for any purpose, including capital transfers. Purchases for capital transfers under this Section shall not, however, be permitted if they have the effect of raising the Fund's holdings of the currency of the member desiring to purchase above seventy-five percent of its quota, or of reducing the Fund's holdings of the currency desired below seventy-five percent of the quota of the member whose currency is desired.

Section 3. Controls of Capital Transfers

Members may exercise such controls as are necessary to regulate international capital movements, but no member may exercise these controls in a manner which will restrict payments for current transactions or which will unduly delay transfers of funds in settlement of commitments, except as provided in Article VII, Section 3 (b), and in Article XIV, Section 2.

ARTICLE VII. SCARCE CURRENCIES
Section 1. General Scarcity of Currency

If the Fund finds that a general scarcity of a particular currency is developing, the Fund may so inform members and may issue a report setting forth the causes of the scarcity and containing recommendations designed to bring it to an end. A representative of the member whose currency is involved shall participate in the preparation of the report.

Section 2. Measures to Replenish the Fund's Holdings of Scarce Currencies

The Fund may, if it deems such action appropriate to replenish its holdings of any member's currency, take either or both of the following steps:

(i) Propose to the member that, on terms and conditions agreed between the Fund and the member, the latter lend its currency to the

Fund or that, with the approval of the member, the Fund borrow such currency from some other source either within or outside the territories of the member, but no member shall be under any obligation to make such loans to the Fund or to approve the borrowing of its currency by the Fund from any other source.

(ii) Require the member to sell its currency to the Fund for gold.

Section 3. Scarcity of the Fund's Holdings

(a) If it becomes evident to the Fund that the demand for a member's currency seriously threatens the Fund's ability to supply that currency, the Fund, whether or not it has issued a report under Section 1 of this Article, shall formally declare such currency scarce and shall thenceforth apportion its existing and accruing supply of the scarce currency with due regard to the relative needs of members, the general international economic situation and any other pertinent considerations. The Fund shall also issue a report concerning its action.

(b) A formal declaration under (a) above shall operate as an authorization to any member, after consultation with the Fund, temporarily to impose limitations on the freedom of exchange operations in the scarce currency. Subject to the provisions of Article IV, Sections 3 and 4, the member shall have complete jurisdiction in determining the nature of such limitations, but they shall be no more restrictive than is necessary to limit the demand for the scarce currency to the supply held by, or accruing to, the member in question; and they shall be relaxed and removed as rapidly as conditions permit.

(c) The authorization under (b) above shall expire whenever the Fund formally declares the currency in question to be no longer scarce.

Section 4. Administration of Restrictions

Any member imposing restrictions in respect of the currency of any other member pursuant to the provisions of Section 3 (b) of this Article shall give sympathetic consideration to any representations by the other member regarding the administration of such restrictions.

Section 5. Effect of Other International Agreements on Restrictions

Members agree not to invoke the obligations of any engagements entered into with other members prior to this Agreement in such a manner as will prevent the operation of the provisions of this Article.

ARTICLE VIII. GENERAL OBLIGATIONS OF MEMBERS
Section 1. Introduction

In addition to the obligations assumed under other articles of this Agreement, each member undertakes the obligations set out in this Article.

Section 2. Avoidance of Restrictions on Current Payments

(a) Subject to the provisions of Article VII, Section 3 (b), and Article XIV, Section 2, no member shall, without the approval of the Fund, impose restrictions on the making of payments and transfers for current international transactions.

(b) Exchange contracts which involve the currency of any member and which are contrary to the exchange control regulations of that member maintained or imposed consistently with this Agreement shall be unenforceable in the territories of any member. In addition, members may, by mutual accord, co-operate in measures for the purpose of making the exchange control regulations of either member more effective, provided that such measures and regulations are consistent with this Agreement.

Section 3. Avoidance of Discriminatory Currency Practices

No member shall engage in, or permit any of its fiscal agencies referred to in Article V, Section 1, to engage in, any discriminatory currency arrangements or multiple currency practices except as authorized under this Agreement or approved by the Fund. If such arrangements and practices are engaged in at the date when this Agreement enters into force the member concerned shall consult with the Fund as to their progressive removal unless they are maintained or imposed under Article XIV, Section 2, in which case the provisions of Section 4 of that Article shall apply.

Section 4. Convertibility of Foreign held Balances

(a) Each member shall buy balances of its currency held by another member if the latter, in requesting the purchase, represents

(i) that the balances to be bought have been recently acquired as a result of current transactions; or

(ii) that their conversion is needed for making payments for current transactions.

The buying member shall have the option to pay either in the currency of the member making the request or in gold.

(b) The obligation in (a) above shall not apply

(i) when the convertibility of the balances has been restricted consistently with Section 2 of this Article, or Article VI, Section 3; or

(ii) when the balances have accumulated as a result of transactions effected before the removal by a member of restrictions maintained or imposed under Article XIV, Section 2; or

(iii) when the balances have been acquired contrary to the exchange regulations of the member which is asked to buy them; or

(iv) when the currency of the member requesting the purchase has been declared scarce under Article VII, Section 3 (a); or

(v) when the member requested to make the purchase is for any reason not entitled to buy currencies of other members from the Fund for its own currency.

Section 5. Furnishing of Information

(a) The Fund may require members to furnish it with such information as it deems necessary for its operations, including, as the minimum necessary for the effective discharge of the Fund's duties, national data on the following matters:

(i) Official holdings at home and abroad, of (1) gold, (2) foreign exchange.

(ii) Holdings at home and abroad by banking and financial agencies, other than official agencies, of (1) gold, (2) foreign exchange.

(iii) Production of gold.

(iv) Gold exports and imports according to countries of destination and origin.

(v) Total exports and imports of merchandise, in terms of local currency values, according to countries of destination and origin.

(vi) International balance of payments, including (1) trade in goods and services, (2) gold transactions, (3) known capital transactions, and (4) other items.

(vii) International investment position, i.e., investments within the territories of the member owned abroad and investments abroad owned by persons in its territories so far as it is possible to furnish this information.

(viii) National income.

(ix) Price indices, i.e., indices of commodity prices in wholesale and retail markets and of export and import prices.

(x) Buying and selling rates for foreign currencies.

(xi) Exchange controls, i.e., a comprehensive statement of exchange controls in effect at the time of assuming membership in the Fund and details of subsequent changes as they occur.

(xii) Where official clearing arrangements exist, details of amounts awaiting clearance in respect of commercial and financial transactions, and of the length of time during which such arrears have been outstanding.

(b) In requesting information the Fund shall take into consideration the varying ability of members to furnish the data requested. Members shall be under no obligation to furnish information in such detail that the affairs of individuals or corporations are disclosed. Members undertake, however, to furnish the desired information in as detailed and accurate a manner as is practicable, and, so far as possible, to avoid mere estimates.

(c) The Fund may arrange to obtain further information by agreement with members. It shall act as a centre for the collection and exchange of information on monetary and financial problems, thus facilitating the preparation of studies designed to assist members in developing policies which further the purposes of the Fund.

Section 6. Consultation between Members Regarding Existing International Agreements

Where under this Agreement a member is authorized in the special or temporary circumstances specified in the Agreement to maintain or establish restrictions on exchange transactions, and there are other engagements between members entered into prior to this Agreement which conflict with the application of such restrictions, the parties to such engagements will consult with one another with a view to making such mutually acceptable adjustments as may be necessary. The provisions of this Article shall be without prejudice to the operation of Article VII, Section 5.

ARTICLE IX. STATUS, IMMUNITIES AND PRIVILEGES
Section 1. Purposes of Article

To enable the Fund to fulfill the functions with which it is entrusted, the status, immunities and privileges set forth in this Article shall be accorded to the Fund in the territories of each member.

Section 2. Status of the Fund

The Fund shall possess full juridical personality, and, in particular, the capacity:

(i) to contract;

(ii) to acquire and dispose of immovable and movable property;

(iii) to institute legal proceedings.

Section 3. Immunity from Judicial Process

The Fund, its property and its assets, wherever located and by whomsoever held, shall enjoy immunity from every form of judicial process except to the extent that it expressly waives its immunity for the purpose of any proceedings or by the terms of any contract.

Section 4. Immunity from other Action

Property and assets of the Fund, wherever located and by whomsoever held, shall be immune from search, requisition, confiscation, expropriation or any other form of seizure by executive or legislative action.

Section 5. Immunity of Archives

The archives of the Fund shall be inviolable.

Section 6. Freedom of Assets from Restrictions

To the extent necessary to carry out the operations provided for in this Agreement, all property and assets of the Fund shall be free from restrictions, regulations, controls and moratoria of any nature.

Section 7. Privilege for Communications

The official communications of the Fund shall be accorded by members the same treatment as the official communications of other members.

Section 8. Immunities and Privileges of Officers and Employees

All governors, executive directors, alternates, officers and employees of the Fund

(i) shall be immune from legal process with respect to acts performed by them in their official capacity except when the Fund waives this immunity;

(ii) not being local nationals, shall be granted the same immunities from immigration restrictions, alien registration requirements and national service obligations and the same facilities as regards exchange restrictions as are accorded by members to the representatives, officials, and employees of comparable rank of other members;

(iii) shall be granted the same treatment in respect of travelling facilities as is accorded by members to representatives, officials and employees of comparable rank of other members.

Section 9. Immunities from Taxation

(a) The Fund, its assets, property, income and its operations and transactions authorized by this Agreement, shall be immune from all taxation and from all customs duties. The Fund shall also be immune from liability for the collection or payment of any tax or duty.

(b) No tax shall be levied on or in respect of salaries and emoluments paid by the Fund to executive directors, alternates, officers or employees of the Fund who are not local citizens, local subjects, or other local nationals.

(c) No taxation of any kind shall be levied on any obligation or security issued by the Fund, including any dividend or interest thereon, by whomsoever held

(i) which discriminates against such obligation or security solely because of its origin; or

(ii) if the sole jurisdictional basis for such taxation is the place or currency in which it is issued, made payable or paid, or the location of any office or place of business maintained by the Fund.

Section 10. Application of Article

Each member shall take such action as is necessary in its own territories for the purpose of making effective in terms of its own law the principles set forth in this Article and shall inform the Fund of the detailed action which it has taken.

ARTICLE X. RELATIONS WITH OTHER INTERNATIONAL ORGANIZATIONS

The Fund shall cooperate within the terms of this Agreement with any general international organization and with public international organizations having specialized responsibilities in related fields. Any arrangements for such cooperation which would involve a modification of any provision of this Agreement may be effected only after amendment to this Agreement under Article XVII.

ARTICLE XI. RELATIONS WITH NON-MEMBER COUNTRIES
Section 1. Undertakings Regarding Relations with Non-Member Countries

Each member undertakes:

(i) Not to engage in, nor to permit any of its fiscal agencies referred to in Article V, Section 1, to engage in, any transactions with a non-member or with persons in a non-member's territories which would be contrary to the provisions of this Agreement or the purposes of the Fund;

(ii) Not to cooperate with a non-member or with persons in a non-member's territories in practices which would be contrary to the provisions of this Agreement or the purposes of the Fund; and

(iii) To cooperate with the Fund with a view to the application in its territories of appropriate measures to prevent transactions with non-members or with persons in their territories which would be contrary to the provisions of this Agreement or the purposes of the Fund.

Section 2. Restrictions on Transactions with Non-Member Countries

Nothing in this Agreement shall affect the right of any member to impose restrictions on exchange transactions with non-members or with persons in their territories unless the Fund finds that such restrictions prejudice the interests of members and are contrary to the purposes of the Fund.

ARTICLE XII. ORGANIZATION AND MANAGEMENT
Section 1. Structure of the Fund

The Fund shall have a Board of Governors, Executive Directors, a Managing Director and a staff.

Section 2. Board of Governors

(a) All powers of the Fund shall be vested in the Board of Governors, consisting of one governor and one alternate appointed by each member in such manner as it may determine. Each governor and each alternate shall serve for five years, subject to the pleasure of the member appointing him, and may be reappointed. No alternate may vote except in the absence of his principal. The Board shall select one of the governors as chairman.

(b) The Board of Governors may delegate to the Executive Directors authority to exercise any powers of the Board, except the power to:

(i) Admit new members and determine the conditions of their admission.

(ii) Approve a revision of quotas.

(iii) Approve a uniform change in the par value of the currencies of all members.

(iv) Make arrangements to cooperate with other international organizations (other than informal arrangements of a temporary or administrative character).

(v) Determine the distribution of the net income of the Fund.

(vi) Require a member to withdraw.

(vii) Decide to liquidate the Fund.

(viii) Decide appeals from interpretations of this Agreement given by the Executive Directors.

(c) The Board of Governors shall hold an annual meeting and such other meetings as may be provided for by the Board or called by the Executive Directors. Meetings of the Board shall be called by the Directors whenever requested by five members or by members having one quarter of the total voting power.

(d) A quorum for any meeting of the Board of Governors shall be a majority of the governors exercising not less than two-thirds of the total voting power.

(e) Each governor shall be entitled to cast the number of votes allotted under Section 5 of this Article to the member appointing him.

(f) The Board of Governors may by regulation establish a procedure whereby the Executive Directors, when they deem such action to be in the best interests of the Fund, may obtain a vote of the governors on a specific question without calling a meeting of the Board.

(g) The Board of Governors, and the Executive Directors to the extent authorized, may adopt such rules and regulations as may be necessary or appropriate to conduct the business of the Fund.

(h) Governors and alternates shall serve as such without compensation from the Fund, but the Fund shall pay them reasonable expenses incurred in attending meetings.

(i) The Board of Governors shall determine the remuneration to be paid to the Executive Directors and the salary and terms of the contract of service of the Managing Director.

Section 3. Executive Directors

(a) The Executive Directors shall be responsible for the conduct of the general operations of the Fund, and for this purpose shall exercise all the powers delegated to them by the Board of Governors.

(b) There shall be not less than twelve directors who need not be governors, and of whom

(i) five shall be appointed by the five members having the largest quotas;

(ii) not more than two shall be appointed when the provisions of (c) below apply;

(iii) five shall be elected by the members not entitled to appoint directors, other than the American Republics; and

(iv) two shall be elected by the American Republics not entitled to appoint directors.

For the purposes of this paragraph, members means governments of countries whose names are set forth in Schedule A, whether they become members in accordance with Article XX or in accordance with Article II, Section 2. When governments of other countries become members, the Board of Governors may, by a four-fifths majority of the total voting power, increase the number of directors to be elected.

(c) If, at the second regular election of directors and thereafter, the members entitled to appoint directors under (b) (i) above do not include the two members, the holdings of whose currencies by the Fund have been, on the average over the preceding two years, reduced below their quotas by the largest absolute amounts in terms of gold as a common denominator, either one or both of such members, as the case may be, shall be entitled to appoint a director.

(d) Subject to Article XX, Section 3 (b) elections of elective directors shall be conducted at intervals of two years in accordance with the provisions of Schedule C, supplemented by such regulations as the Fund deems appropriate. Whenever the Board of Governors increases the number of directors to be elected under (b) above, it shall issue regulations making appropriate changes in the proportion of votes required to elect directors under the provisions of Schedule C.

(e) Each director shall appoint an alternate with full power to act for him when he is not present. When the directors appointing them are present, alternates may participate in meetings but may not vote.

(f) Directors shall continue in office until their successors are appointed or elected. If the office of an elected director becomes vacant more than ninety days before the end of his term, another director shall be elected for the remainder of the term by the members who elected the former director. A majority of the votes cast shall be required for election. While the office remains vacant, the alternate of the former director shall exercise his powers, except that of appointing an alternate.

(g) The Executive Directors shall function in continuous session at the principal office of the Fund and shall meet as often as the business of the Fund may require.

(h) A quorum for any meeting of the Executive Directors shall be a majority of the directors representing not less than one-half of the voting power.

(i) Each appointed director shall be entitled to cast the number of votes allotted under Section 5 of this Article to the member appointing him. Each elected director shall be entitled to cast the number of votes which counted towards his election. When the provisions of Section 5 (b) of this Article are applicable, the votes which a director would otherwise be entitled to cast shall be increased or decreased correspondingly. All the votes which a director is entitled to cast shall be cast as a unit.

(j) The Board of Governors shall adopt regulations under which a member not entitled to appoint a director under (b) above may send a representative to attend any meeting of the Executive Directors when a request made by, or a matter particularly affecting, that member is under consideration.

(k) The Executive Directors may appoint such committees as they deem advisable. Membership of committees need not be limited to governors or directors or their alternates.

Section 4. Managing Director and Staff

(a) The Executive Directors shall select a Managing Director who shall not be a governor or an executive director. The Managing Director shall be chairman of the Executive Directors, but shall have no vote except a deciding vote in case of an equal division. He may participate in meetings of the Board of Governors, but shall not vote at such meetings. The Managing Director shall cease to hold office when the Executive Directors so decide.

(b) The Managing Director shall be chief of the operating staff of the Fund and shall conduct, under the direction of the Executive Directors, the ordinary business of the Fund. Subject to the general control of the Executive Directors, he shall be responsible for the organization, appointment and dismissal of the staff of the Fund.

(c) The Managing Director and the staff of the Fund, in the discharge of their functions, shall owe their duty entirely to the Fund and to no other authority. Each member of the Fund shall respect the international character of this duty and shall refrain from all attempts to influence any of the staff in the discharge of his functions.

(d) In appointing the staff the Managing Director shall, subject to the paramount importance of securing the highest standards of efficiency and of technical competence, pay due regard to the importance of recruiting personnel on as wide a geographical basis as possible.

Section 5. Voting

(a) Each member shall have two hundred fifty votes plus one additional vote for each part of its quota equivalent to one hundred thousand United States dollars.

(b) Whenever voting is required under Article V, Section 4 or 5, each member shall have the number of votes to which it is entitled under (a) above, adjusted:

(i) by the addition of one vote for the equivalent of each four hundred thousand United States dollars of net sales of its currency up to the date when the vote is taken, or

(ii) by the subtraction of one vote for the equivalent of each four hundred thousand United States dollars of its net purchases of the currencies of other members up to the date when the vote is taken; provided, that neither net purchases nor net sales shall be deemed at any time to exceed an amount equal to the quota of the member involved.

(c) For the purpose of all computations under this Section, United States dollars shall be deemed to be of the weight and fineness in effect on July 1, 1944, adjusted for any uniform change under Article IV, Section 7, if a waiver is made under Section 8 (d) of that Article.

(d) Except as otherwise specifically provided, all decisions of the Fund shall be made by a majority of the votes cast.

Section 6. Distribution of Net Income

(a) The Board of Governors shall determine annually what part of the Fund's net income shall be placed to reserve and what part, if any, shall be distributed.

(b) If any distribution is made, there shall first be distributed a two percent non-cumulative payment to each member on the amount by which seventy-five percent of its quota exceeded the Fund's average holdings of its currency during that year. The balance shall be paid to all members in proportion to their quotas. Payments to each member shall be made in its own currency.

Section 7. Publication of Reports

(a) The Fund shall publish an annual report containing an audited statement of its accounts, and shall issue, at intervals of three months or less, a summary statement of its transactions and its holdings of gold and currencies of members.

(b) The Fund may publish such other reports as it deems desirable for carrying out its purposes.

Section 8. Communication of Views to Members

The Fund shall at all times have the right to communicate its views informally to any member on any matter arising under this Agreement. The Fund may, by a two-thirds majority of the total voting power, decide to publish a report made to a member regarding its monetary or economic conditions and developments which directly tend to produce a serious disequilibrium in the international balance of payments of members. If the member is not entitled to appoint an executive director, it shall be entitled to representation in accordance with Section 3 (j) of this Article. The Fund shall not publish a report involving changes in the fundamental structure of the economic organization of members.

ARTICLE XIII. OFFICES AND DEPOSITORIES
Section 1. Location of Offices

The principal office of the Fund shall be located in the territory of the member having the largest quota, and agencies or branch offices may be established in the territories of other members.

Section 2. Depositories

(a) Each member country shall designate its central bank as a depository for all the Fund's holdings of its currency, or if it has no central bank it shall designate such other institution as may be acceptable to the Fund.

(b) The Fund may hold other assets, including gold, in the depositories designated by the five members having the largest quotas and in such other designated depositories as the Fund may select. Initially at least one-half of the holdings of the Fund shall be held in the depository designated by the member in whose territories the Fund has its principal office and at least forty percent shall be held in the depositories designated by the remaining four members referred to above. However, all transfers of gold by the Fund shall be made with due regard to the costs of transport and anticipated requirements of the Fund. In an emergency the Executive Directors may transfer all or any part of the Fund's gold holdings to any place where they can be adequately protected.

Section 3. Guarantee of the Fund's Assets

Each member guarantees all assets of the Fund against loss resulting from failure or default on the part of the depository designated by it.

ARTICLE XIV. TRANSITIONAL PERIOD
Section 1. Introduction

The Fund is not intended to provide facilities for relief or reconstruction or to deal with international indebtedness arising out of the war.

Section 2. Exchange Restrictions

In the post-war transitional period members may, notwithstanding the provisions of any other articles of this Agreement, maintain and adapt to changing circumstances (and, in the case of members whose territories have been occupied by the enemy, introduce where necessary) restrictions on payments and transfers for current international transactions. Members shall, however, have continuous regard in their foreign exchange policies to the purposes of the Fund; and, as soon as conditions permit, they shall take all possible measures to develop such commercial and financial arrangements with other members as will facilitate international payments and the maintenance of exchange stability. In particular, members shall withdraw restrictions maintained or imposed under this Section as soon as they are satisfied that they will be able, in the absence of such restrictions, to settle their balance of payments in a manner which will not unduly encumber their access to the resources of the Fund.

Section 3. Notification to the Fund

Each member shall notify the Fund before it becomes eligible under Article XX, Section 4 (c) or (d), to buy currency from the Fund, whether it intends to avail itself of the transitional arrangements in Section 2 of this Article, or whether it is prepared to accept the obligations of Article VIII, Sections 2, 3, and 4. A member availing itself of the transitional arrangements shall notify the Fund as soon thereafter as it is prepared to accept the above-mentioned obligations.

Section 4. Action of the Fund Relating to Restrictions

Not later than three years after the date on which the Fund begins operations and in each year thereafter, the Fund shall report on the restrictions still in force under Section 2 of this Article. Five years after the date on which the Fund begins operations, and in each year thereafter, any member still retaining any restrictions inconsistent with Article VIII, Sections 2, 3, or 4, shall consult the Fund as to their further retention. The Fund may, if it deems such action necessary in exceptional circumstances, make representations to any member that conditions are favorable for the withdrawal of any particular restriction, or for the general abandonment of restrictions, inconsistent with the provisions of any other articles of this

Agreement. The member shall be given a suitable time to reply to such representations. If the Fund finds that the member persists in maintaining restrictions which are inconsistent with the purposes of the Fund, the member shall be subject to Article XV, Section 2 (a).

Section 5. Nature of Transitional Period

In its relations with members, the Fund shall recognize that the post-war transitional period will be one of change and adjustment and in making decisions on requests occasioned thereby which are presented by any member it shall give the member the benefit of any reasonable doubt.

ARTICLE XV. WITHDRAWAL FROM MEMBERSHIP
Section 1. Right of Members to Withdraw

Any member may withdraw from the Fund at any time by transmitting a notice in writing to the Fund at its principal office. Withdrawal shall become effective on the date such notice is received.

Section 2. Compulsory Withdrawal

(a) If a member fails to fulfill any of its obligations under this Agreement, the Fund may declare the member ineligible to use the resources of the Fund. Nothing in this Section shall be deemed to limit the provisions of Article IV, Section 6, Article V, Section 5, or Article VI, Section 1.

(b) If, after the expiration of a reasonable period the member persists in its failure to fulfill any of its obligations under this Agreement, or a difference between a member and the Fund under Article IV, Section 6, continues, that member may be required to withdraw from membership in the Fund by a decision of the Board of Governors carried by a majority of the governors representing a majority of the total voting power.

(c) Regulations shall be adopted to ensure that before action is taken against any member under (a) or (b) above, the member shall be informed in reasonable time of the complaint against it and given an adequate opportunity for stating its case, both orally and in writing.

Section 3. Settlement of Accounts with Members Withdrawing

When a member withdraws from the Fund, normal transactions of the Fund in its currency shall cease and settlement of all accounts between it and the Fund shall be made with reasonable despatch by agreement between it and the Fund. If agreement is not reached promptly, the provisions of Schedule D shall apply to the settlement of accounts.

ARTICLE XVI. EMERGENCY PROVISIONS
Section 1. Temporary Suspension

(a) In the event of an emergency or the development of unforeseen circumstances threatening the operations of the Fund, the Executive Directors by unanimous vote may suspend for a period of not more than one hundred twenty days the operation of any of the following provisions:

    (i) Article IV, Sections 3 and 4 (b).

    (ii) Article V, Sections 2, 3, 7, 8 (a) and (f).

    (iii) Article VI, Section 2.

    (iv) Article XI, Section 1.

(b) Simultaneously with any decision to suspend the operation of any of the foregoing provisions, the Executive Directors shall call a meeting of the Board of Governors for the earliest practicable date.

(c) The Executive Directors may not extend any suspension beyond one hundred twenty days. Such suspension may be extended, however, for an additional period of not more than two hundred forty days, if the Board of Governors by a four-fifths majority of the total voting power so decides, but it may not be further extended except by amendment of this Agreement pursuant to Article XVII.

(d) The Executive Directors may, by a majority of the total voting power, terminate such suspension at any time.

Section 2. Liquidation of the Fund

(a) The Fund may not be liquidated except by decision of the Board of Governors. In an emergency, if the Executive Directors decide that liquidation of the Fund may be necessary, they may temporarily suspend all transactions, pending decision by the Board.

(b) If the Board of Governors decides to liquidate the Fund, the Fund shall forthwith cease to engage in any activities except those incidental to the orderly collection and liquidation of its assets and the settlement of its liabilities, and all obligations of members under this Agreement shall cease except those set out in this Article, in Article XVIII, paragraph (c), in Schedule D, paragraph 7, and in Schedule E.

(c) Liquidation shall be administered in accordance with the provisions of Schedule E.

ARTICLE XVII. AMENDMENTS

(a) Any proposal to introduce modifications in this Agreement, whether emanating from a member, a governor or the Executive Directors, shall be communicated to the chairman of the Board of Governors who shall bring the proposal before the Board. If the proposed amendment is approved by the Board the Fund shall, by circular letter or telegram, ask all members whether they accept the proposed amendment. When three-fifths of the members, having four-fifths of the total voting power, have accepted the proposed amendment, the Fund shall certify the fact by a formal communication addressed to all members.

(b) Notwithstanding (a) above, acceptance by all members is required in the case of any amendment modifying

(i) the right to withdraw from the Fund (Article XV, Section 1);

(ii) the provision that no change in a member's quota shall be made without its consent (Article III, Section 2);

(iii) the provision that no change may be made in the par value of a member's currency except on the proposal of that member (Article IV, Section 5 (b)).

(c) Amendments shall enter into force for all members three months after the date of the formal communication unless a shorter period is specified in the circular letter or telegram.

ARTICLE XVIII. INTERPRETATION

(a) Any question of interpretation of the provisions of this Agreement arising between any member and the Fund or between any members of the Fund shall be submitted to the Executive Directors for their decision. If the question particularly affects any member not entitled to appoint an executive director it shall be entitled to representation in accordance with Article XII, Section 3 (j).

(b) In any case where the Executive Directors have given a decision under (a) above, any member may require that the question be referred to the Board of Governors, whose decision shall be final. Pending the result of the reference to the Board the Fund may, so far as it deems necessary, act on the basis of the decision of the Executive Directors.

(c) Whenever a disagreement arises between the Fund and a member which has withdrawn, or between the Fund and any member during liquidation of the Fund, such disagreement shall be submitted to arbitration by a tribunal of three arbitrators, one appointed by the Fund, another by the member or withdrawing member and as umpire who, unless the parties otherwise agree, shall be appointed by the President of the Permanent Court of International Justice or such other authority as may have been prescribed by regulation adopted by the Fund. The umpire shall have full power to settle all questions of procedure in any case where the parties are in disagreement with respect thereto.

ARTICLE XIX. EXPLANATION OF TERMS

In interpreting the provisions of this Agreement the Fund and its members shall be guided by the following:

(a) A member's monetary reserves means its net official holdings of gold, of convertible currencies of other members, and of the currencies of such non-members as the Fund may specify.

(b) The official holdings of a member means central holdings (that is, the holdings of its Treasury, central bank, stabilization fund, or similar fiscal agency).

(c) The holdings of other official institutions or other banks within its territories may, in any particular case, be deemed by the Fund, after consultation with the member, to be official holdings to the extent that they are substantially in excess of working balances; provided that for the purpose of determining whether, in a particular case, holdings are in excess of working balances, there shall be deducted from such holdings amounts of currency due to official institutions and banks in the territories of members or non-members specified under (d) below.

(d) A member's holdings of convertible currencies means its holdings of the currencies of other members which are not availing themselves of the transitional arrangements under Article XIV, Section 2, together with its holdings of the currencies of such non-members as the Fund may from time to time specify. The term currency for this purpose includes without limitation coins, paper money, bank balances, bank acceptances, and government obligations issued with a maturity not exceeding twelve months.

(e) A member's monetary reserves shall be calculated by deducting from its central holdings the currency liabilities to the Treasuries, central banks, stabilization funds, or similar fiscal agencies of other members or non-members specified under (d) above, together with similar liabilities to other official institutions and other banks in the territories of members, or non-members specified under (d) above. To these net holdings shall be added the sums deemed to be official holdings of other official institutions and other banks under (c) above.

(f) The Fund's holdings of the currency of a member shall include any securities accepted by the Fund under Article III, Section 5.

(g) The Fund, after consultation with a member which is availing itself of the transitional arrangements under Article XIV, Section 2, may deem holdings of the currency of that member which carry specified rights of conversion into another currency or into gold to be holdings of convertible currency for the purpose of the calculation of monetary reserves.

(h) For the purpose of calculating gold subscriptions under Article III, Section 3, a member's net official holdings of gold and United States dollars shall consist of its official holdings of gold and United States currency after deducting central holdings of its currency by other countries and holdings of its currency by other official institutions and other banks if these holdings carry specified rights of conversion into gold or United States currency.

(i) Payments for current transactions means payments which are not for the purpose of transferring capital, and includes, without limitation:

(1) All payments due in connection with foreign trade, other current business, including services, and normal short-term banking and credit facilities;

(2) Payments due as interest on loans and as net income from other investments;

(3) Payments of moderate amount for amortization of loans or for depreciation of direct investments;

(4) Moderate remittances for family living expenses.

The Fund may, after consultation with the members concerned, determine whether certain specific transactions are to be considered current transactions or capital transactions.

ARTICLE XX. FINAL PROVISIONS
Section 1. Entry into Force

This Agreement shall enter into force when it has been signed on behalf of governments having sixty-five percent of the total of the quotas set forth in Schedule A and when the instruments referred to in Section 2 (a) of this Article have been deposited on their behalf, but in no event shall this Agreement enter into force before May 1, 1945.

Section 2. Signature

(a) Each government on whose behalf this Agreement is signed shall deposit with the Government of the United States of America an instrument setting forth that it has accepted this Agreement in accordance with its law and has taken all steps necessary to enable it to carry out all of its obligations under this Agreement.

(b) Each government shall become a member of the Fund as from the date of the deposit on its behalf of the instrument referred to in (a) above, except that no government shall become a member before this Agreement enters into force under Section 1 of this Article.

(c) The Government of the United States of America shall inform the governments of all countries whose names are set forth in Schedule A, and all governments whose membership is approved in accordance with Article II, Section 2, of all signatures of this Agreement and of the deposit of all instruments referred to in (a) above.

(d) At the time this Agreement is signed on its behalf, each government shall transmit to the Government of the United States of America one one-hundredth of one percent of its total subscription in gold or United States dollars for the purpose of meeting administrative expenses of the Fund. The Government of the United States of America shall hold such funds in a special deposit account and shall transmit them to the Board of Governors of the Fund when the initial meeting has been called under Section 3 of this Article. If this Agreement has not come into force by December 31, 1945, the Government of the United States of America shall return such funds to the governments that transmitted them.

(e) This Agreement shall remain open for signature at Washington on behalf of the governments of the countries whose names are set forth in Schedule A until December 31, 1945.

(f) After December 31, 1945, this Agreement shall be open for signature on behalf of the government of any country whose membership has been approved in accordance with Article II, Section 2.

(g) By their signature of this Agreement, all governments accept it both on their own behalf and in respect of all their colonies, overseas territories, all territories under their protection, suzerainty, or authority and all territories in respect of which they exercise a mandate.

(h) In the case of governments whose metropolitan territories have been under enemy occupation, the deposit of the instrument referred to in (a) above may be delayed until one hundred eighty days after the date on which these territories have been liberated. If, however, it is not deposited by any such government before the expiration of this period the signature affixed on behalf of that government shall become void and the portion of its subscription paid under (d) above shall be returned to it.

(i) Paragraphs (d) and (h) shall come into force with regard to each signatory government as from the date of its signature.

Section 3. Inauguration of the Fund

(a) As soon as this Agreement enters into force under Section 1 of this Article, each member shall appoint a governor and the member having the largest quota shall call the first meeting of the Board of Governors.

(b) At the first meeting of the Board of Governors, arrangements shall be made for the selection of provisional executive directors. The governments of the five countries for which the largest quotas are set forth in Schedule A shall appoint provisional executive directors. If one or more of such governments have not become members, the executive directorships they would be entitled to fill shall remain vacant until they become members, or until January 1, 1946, whichever is the earlier. Seven provisional executive directors shall be elected in accordance with the provisions of Schedule C and shall remain in office until the date of the first regular election of executive directors which shall be held as soon as practicable after January 1, 1946.

(c) The Board of Governors may delegate to the provisional executive directors any powers except those which may not be delegated to the Executive Directors.

Section 4. Initial Determination of Par Values

(a) When the Fund is of the opinion that it will shortly be in a position to begin exchange transactions, it shall so notify the members and shall request each member to communicate within thirty days the par value of its currency based on the rates of exchange prevailing on the sixtieth day before the entry into force of this Agreement. No member whose metropolitan territory has been occupied by the enemy shall be required to make such a communication while that territory is a theater of major hostilities or for such period thereafter as the Fund may determine. When such a member communicates the par value of its currency the provisions of (d) below shall apply.

(b) The par value communicated by a member whose metropolitan territory has not been occupied by the enemy shall be the par value of that member's currency for the purposes of this Agreement unless, within ninety days after the request referred to in (a) above has been received, (i) the member notifies the Fund that it regards the par value as unsatisfactory, or (ii) the Fund notifies the member that in its opinion the par value cannot be maintained without causing recourse to the Fund on the part of that member or others on a scale prejudicial to the Fund and to members. When notification is given under (i) or (ii) above, the Fund and the member shall, within a period determined by the Fund in the light of all relevant circumstances, agree upon a suitable par value for that currency. If the Fund and the member do not agree within the period so determined, the member shall be deemed to have withdrawn from the Fund on the date when the period expires.

(c) When the par value of a member's currency has been established under (b) above, either by the expiration of ninety days without notification, or by agreement after notification, the member shall be eligible to buy from the Fund the currencies of other members to the full extent permitted in this Agreement, provided that the Fund has begun exchange transactions.

(d) In the case of a member whose metropolitan territory has been occupied by the enemy, the provisions of (b) above shall apply, subject to the following modifications:

(i) The period of ninety days shall be extended so as to end on a date to be fixed by agreement between the Fund and the member.

(ii) Within the extended period the member may, if the Fund has begun exchange transactions, buy from the Fund with its currency the currencies of other members, but only under such conditions and in such amounts as may be prescribed by the Fund.

(iii) At any time before the date fixed under (i) above, changes may be made by agreement with the Fund in the par value communicated under (a) above.

(e) If a member whose metropolitan territory has been occupied by the enemy adopts a new monetary unit before the date to be fixed under (d) (i) above, the par value fixed by that member for the new unit shall be communicated to the Fund and the provisions of (d) above shall apply.

(f) Changes in par values agreed with the Fund under this Section shall not be taken into account in determining whether a proposed change falls within (i), (ii), or (iii) of Article IV, Section 5 (c).

(g) A member communicating to the Fund a par value for the currency of its metropolitan territory shall simultaneously communicate a value, in terms of that currency, for each separate currency, where such exists, in the territories in respect of which it has accepted this Agreement under Section 2 (g) of this Article, but no member shall be required to make a communication for the separate currency of a territory which has been occupied by the enemy while that territory is a theater of major hostilities or for such period thereafter as the Fund may determine. On the basis of the par value so communicated, the Fund shall compute the par value of each separate currency. A communication or notification to the Fund under (a), (b) or (d) above regarding the par value of a currency, shall also be deemed, unless the contrary is stated, to be a communication or notification regarding the par value of all the separate currencies referred to above. Any member may, however, make a communication or notification relating to the metropolitan or any of the separate currencies alone. If the member does so, the provisions of the preceding paragraphs (including (d) above, if a territory where a separate currency exists has been occupied by the enemy) shall apply to each of these currencies separately.

(h) The Fund shall begin exchange transactions at such date as it may determine after members having sixty-five percent of the total of the quotas set forth in Schedule A have become eligible, in accordance with the preceding paragraphs of this Section, to purchase the currencies of other members, but in no event until after major hostilities in Europe have ceased.

(i) The Fund may postpone exchange transactions with any member if its circumstances are such that, in the opinion of the Fund, they would lead to use of the resources of the Fund in a manner contrary to the purposes of this Agreement or prejudicial to the Fund or the members.

(j) The par values of the currencies of governments which indicate their desire to become members after December 31, 1945, shall be determined in accordance with the provisions of Article II, Section 2.

DONE at Washington, in a single copy which shall remain deposited in the archives of the Government of the United States of America, which shall transmit certified copies to all governments whose names are set forth in Schedule A and to all governments whose membership is approved in accordance with Article II, Section 2.

ARTICLES OF AGREEMENT OF THE INTERNATIONAL BANK FOR RECONSTRUCTION AND DEVELOPMENT,

July 22, 1944

The Governments on whose behalf the present Agreement is signed agree as follows:

INTRODUCTORY ARTICLE

The International Bank for Reconstruction and Development is established and shall operate in accordance with the following provisions:

ARTICLE I. PURPOSES

The purposes of the Bank are:

(i) To assist in the reconstruction and development of territories of members by facilitating the investment of capital for productive purposes, including the restoration of economies destroyed or disrupted by war, the reconversion of productive facilities to peacetime needs and the encouragement of the development of productive facilities and resources in less developed countries.

(ii) To promote private foreign investment by means of guarantees or participations in loans and other investments made by private investors; and when private capital is not available on reasonable terms, to supplement private investment by providing, on suitable conditions, finance for productive purposes out of its own capital, funds raised by it and its other resources.

(iii) To promote the long-range balanced growth of international trade and the maintenance of equilibrium in balances of payments by encouraging international investment for the development of the productive resources of members, thereby assisting in raising productivity, the standard of living and conditions of labor in their territories.

(iv) To arrange the loans made or guaranteed by it in relation to international loans through other channels so that the more useful and urgent projects, large and small alike, will be dealt with first.

(v) To conduct its operations with due regard to the effect of international investment on business conditions in the territories of members and, in the immediate post-war years, to assist in bringing about a smooth transition from a wartime to a peacetime economy.

The Bank shall be guided in all its decisions by the purposes set forth above.

ARTICLE II. MEMBERSHIP IN AND CAPITAL OF THE BANK
Section 1. Membership

(a) The original members of the Bank shall be those members of the International Monetary Fund which accept membership in the Bank before the date specified in Article XI, Section 2 (e).

(b) Membership shall be open to other members of the Fund, at such times and in accordance with such terms as may be prescribed by the Bank.

Section 2. Authorized Capital

(a) The authorized capital stock of the Bank shall be $10,000,000,000, in terms of United States dollars of the weight and fineness in effect on July 1, 1944. The capital stock shall be divided into 100,000 shares having a par value of $100,000 each, which shall be available for subscription only by members.

(b) The capital stock may be increased when the Bank deems it advisable by a three-fourths majority of the total voting power.

Section 3. Subscription of Shares

(a) Each member shall subscribe shares of the capital stock of the Bank. The minimum number of shares to be subscribed by the original members shall be those set forth in Schedule A. The minimum number of shares to be subscribed by other members shall be determined by the Bank, which shall reserve a sufficient portion of its capital stock for subscription by such members.

(b) The Bank shall prescribe rules laying down the conditions under which members may subscribe shares of the authorized capital stock of the Bank in addition to their minimum subscriptions.

(c) If the authorized capital stock of the Bank is increased, each member shall have a reasonable opportunity to subscribe, under such conditions as the Bank shall decide, a proportion of the increase of stock equivalent to the proportion which its stock theretofore subscribed bears to the total capital stock of the Bank, but no member shall be obligated to subscribe any part of the increased capital.

Section 4. Issue Price of Shares

Shares included in the minimum subscriptions of original members shall be issued at par. Other shares shall be issued at par unless the Bank by a majority of the total voting power decides in special circumstances to issue them on other terms.

Section 5. Division and Calls of Subscribed Capital

The subscription of each member shall be divided into two parts as follows:

(i) twenty percent shall be paid or subject to call under Section 7 (i) of this Article as needed by the Bank for its operations;

(ii) the remaining eighty percent shall be subject to call by the Bank only when required to meet obligations of the Bank created under Article IV, Sections I (a) (ii) and (iii).

Calls on unpaid subscriptions shall be uniform on all shares.

Section 6. Limitation on Liability

Liability on shares shall be limited to the unpaid portion of the issue price of the shares.

Section 7. Method of Payment of Subscriptions for Shares

Payment of subscriptions for shares shall be made in gold or United States dollars and in the currencies of the members as follows:

(i) under Section 5 (i) of this Article, two percent of the price of each share shall be payable in gold or United States dollars, and, when calls are made, the remaining eighteen percent shall be paid in the currency of the member;

(ii) when a call is made under Section 5 (ii) of this Article, payment may be made at the option of the member either in gold, in United States dollars or in the currency required to discharge the obligations of the Bank for the purpose for which the call is made;

(iii) when a member makes payments in any currency under (i) and (ii) above, such payments shall be made in amounts equal in value to the member's liability under the call. This liability shall be a proportionate part of the subscribed capital stock of the Bank as authorized and defined in Section 2 of this Article.

Section 8. Time of Payment of Subscriptions

(a) The two percent payable on each share in gold or United States dollars under Section 7 (i) of this Article, shall be paid within sixty days of the date on which the Bank begins operations, provided that

(i) any original member of the Bank whose metropolitan territory has suffered from enemy occupation or hostilities during the present war shall be granted the right to postpone payment of one-half percent until five years after that date;

(ii) an original member who cannot make such a payment because it has not recovered possession of its gold reserves which are still seized or immobilized as a result of the war may postpone all payment until such date as the Bank shall decide.

(b) The remainder of the price of each share payable under Section 7 (i) of this Article shall be paid as and when called by the Bank, provided that

(i) the Bank shall, within one year of its beginning operations, call not less than eight percent of the price of the share in addition to the payment of two percent referred to in (a) above;

(ii) not more than five percent of the price of the share shall be called in any period of three months.

Section 9. Maintenance of Value of Certain Currency Holdings of the Bank

(a) Whenever (i) the par value of a member's currency is reduced, or (ii) the foreign exchange value of a member's currency has, in the opinion of the Bank, depreciated to a significant extent within that member's territories, the member shall pay to the Bank within a reasonable time an additional amount of its own currency sufficient to maintain the value, as of the time of initial subscription, of the amount of the currency of such member which is held by the Bank and derived from currency originally paid in to the Bank by the member under Article II, Section 7 (i), from currency referred to in Article IV, Section 2 (b), or from any additional currency furnished under the provisions of the present paragraph, and which has not been repurchased by the member for gold or for the currency of any member which is acceptable to the Bank.

(b) Whenever the par value of a member's currency is increased, the Bank shall return to such member within a reasonable time an amount of that member's currency equal to the increase in the value of the amount of such currency described in (a) above.

(c) The provisions of the preceding paragraphs may be waived by the Bank when a uniform proportionate change in the par values of the currencies of all its members is made by the International Monetary Fund.

Section 10. Restriction on Disposal of Shares

Shares shall not be pledged or encumbered in any manner whatever and they shall be transferable only to the Bank.

ARTICLE III. GENERAL PROVISIONS RELATING TO LOANS AND GUARANTEES
Section 1. Use of Resources

(a) The resources and the facilities of the Bank shall be used exclusively for the benefit of members with equitable consideration to projects for development and projects for reconstruction alike.

(b) For the purpose of facilitating the restoration and reconstruction of the economy of members whose metropolitan territories have suffered great devastation from enemy occupation or hostilities, the Bank, in determining the conditions and terms of loans made to such members, shall pay special regard to lightening the financial burden and expediting the completion of such restoration and reconstruction.

Section 2. Dealings between Members and the Bank

Each member shall deal with the Bank only through its Treasury, central bank, stabilization fund or other similar fiscal agency, and the Bank shall deal with members only by or through the same agencies.

Section 3. Limitations on Guarantees and Borrowings of the Bank

The total amount outstanding of guarantees, participations in loans and direct loans made by the Bank shall not be increased at any time, if by such increase the total would exceed one hundred percent of the unimpaired subscribed capital, reserves and surplus of the Bank.

Section 4. Conditions on which the Bank may Guarantee or make Loans

The Bank may guarantee, participate in, or make loans to any member or any political sub-division thereof and any business, industrial, and agricultural enterprise in the territories of a member, subject to the following conditions:

(i) When the member in whose territories the project is located is not itself the borrower, the member or the central bank or some comparable agency of the member which is acceptable to the Bank, fully guarantees the repayment of the principal and the payment of interest and other charges on the loan.

(ii) The Bank is satisfied that in the prevailing market conditions the borrower would be unable otherwise to obtain the loan under conditions which in the opinion of the Bank are reasonable for the borrower.

(iii) A competent committee, as provided for in Article V, Section 7, has submitted a written report recommending the project after a careful study of the merits of the proposal.

(iv) In the opinion of the Bank the rate of interest and other charges are reasonable and such rate, charges and the schedule for repayment of principal are appropriate to the project.

(v) In making or guaranteeing a loan, the Bank shall pay due regard to the prospects that the borrower, and, if the borrower is not a member, that the guarantor, will be in position to meet its obligations under the loan; and the Bank shall act prudently in the interests both of the particular member in whose territories the project is located and of the members as a whole.

(vi) In guaranteeing a loan made by other investors, the Bank receives suitable compensation for its risk.

(vii) Loans made or guaranteed by the Bank shall, except in special circumstances, be for the purpose of specific projects of reconstruction or development.

Section 5. Use of Loans Guaranteed, Participated in or made by The Bank

(a) The Bank shall impose no conditions that the proceeds of a loan shall be spent in the territories of any particular member or members.

(b) The Bank shall make arrangements to ensure that the proceeds of any loan are used only for the purposes for which the loan was granted, with due attention to considerations of economy and efficiency and without regard to political or other non-economic influences or considerations.

(c) In the case of loans made by the Bank, it shall open an account in the name of the borrower and the amount of the loan shall be credited to this account in the currency or currencies in which the loan is made. The borrower shall be permitted by the Bank to draw on this account only to meet expenses in connection with the project as they are actually incurred.

ARTICLE IV. OPERATIONS
Section 1. Methods of Making or Facilitating Loans

(a) The Bank may make or facilitate loans which satisfy the general conditions of Article III in any of the following ways:

(i) By making or participating in direct loans out of its own funds corresponding to its unimpaired paid-up capital and surplus and, subject to Section 6 of this Article, to its reserves.

(ii) By making or participating in direct loans out of funds raised in the market of a member, or otherwise borrowed by the Bank.

(iii) By guaranteeing in whole or in part loans made by private investors through the usual investment channels.

(b) The Bank may borrow funds under (a) (ii) above or guarantee loans under (a) (iii) above only with the approval of the member in whose markets the funds are raised and the member in whose currency the loan is denominated, and only if those members agree that the proceeds may be exchanged for the currency of any other member without restriction.

Section 2. Availability and Transferability of Currencies

(a) Currencies paid into the Bank under Article II, Section 7 (i), shall be loaned only with the approval in each case of the member whose currency is involved; provided, however, that if necessary, after the Bank's subscribed capital has been entirely called, such currencies shall, without restriction by the members whose currencies are offered, be used or exchanged for the currencies required to meet contractual payments of interest, other charges or amortization on the Bank's own borrowings, or to meet the Bank's liabilities with respect to such contractual payments on loans guaranteed by the Bank.

(b) Currencies received by the Bank from borrowers or guarantors in payment on account of principal of direct loans made with currencies referred to in (a) above shall be exchanged for the currencies of other members or reloaned only with the approval in each case of the members whose currencies are involved; provided, however, that if necessary, after the Bank's subscribed capital has been entirely called, such currencies shall, without restriction by the members whose currencies are offered, be used or exchanged for the currencies required to meet contractual payments of interest, other charges or amortization on the Bank's own borrowings, or to meet the Bank's liabilities with respect to such contractual payments on loans guaranteed by the Bank.

(c) Currencies received by the Bank from borrowers or guarantors in payment on account of principal of direct loans made by the Bank under Section 1 (a) (ii) of this Article, shall be held and used, without restriction by the members, to make amortization payments, or to anticipate payment of or repurchase part or all of the Bank's own obligations.

(d) All other currencies available to the Bank, including those raised in the market or otherwise borrowed under Section 1 (a) (ii) of this Article, those obtained by the sale of gold, those received as payments of interest and other charges for direct loans made under Sections 1 (a) (i) and (ii), and those received as payments of commissions and other charges under Section 1 (a) (iii), shall be used or exchanged for other currencies or gold required in the operations of the Bank without restriction by the members whose currencies are offered.

(e) Currencies raised in the markets of members by borrowers on loans guaranteed by the Bank under Section 1 (a) (iii) of this Article, shall also be used or exchanged for other currencies without restriction by such members.

Section 3. Provision of Currencies for Direct Loans

The following provisions shall apply to direct loans under Sections 1 (a) (i) and (ii) of this Article:

(a) The Bank shall furnish the borrower with such currencies of members, other than the member in whose territories the project is located, as are needed by the borrower for expenditures to be made in the territories of such other members to carry out the purposes of the loan.

(b) The Bank may, in exceptional circumstances when local currency required for the purposes of the loan cannot be raised by the borrower on reasonable terms, provide the borrower as part of the loan with an appropriate amount of that currency.

(c) The Bank, if the project gives rise indirectly to an increased need for foreign exchange by the member in whose territories the project is located, may in exceptional circumstances provide the borrower as part of the loan with an appropriate amount of gold or foreign exchange not in excess of the borrower's local expenditure in connection with the purposes of the loan.

(d) The Bank may, in exceptional circumstances, at the request of a member in whose territories a portion of the loan is spent, repurchase with gold or foreign exchange a part of that member's currency thus spent but in no case shall the part so repurchased exceed the amount by which the expenditure of the loan in those territories gives rise to an increased need for foreign exchange.

Section 4. Payment Provisions for Direct Loans

Loan contracts under Section 1 (a) (i) or (ii) of this Article shall be made in accordance with the following payment provisions:

(a) The terms and conditions of interest and amortization payments, maturity and dates of payment of each loan shall be determined by the Bank. The Bank shall also determine the rate and any other terms and conditions of commission to be charged in connection with such loan.

In the case of loans made under Section 1 (a) (ii) of this Article during the first ten years of the Bank's operations, this rate of commission shall be not less than one percent per annum and not greater than one and one-half percent per annum, and shall be charged on the outstanding portion of any such loan. At the end of this period of ten years, the rate of commission may be reduced by the Bank with respect both to the outstanding portions of loans already made and to future loans, if the reserves accumulated by the Bank under Section 6 of this Article and out of other earnings are considered by it sufficient to justify a reduction. In the case of future loans the Bank shall also have discretion to increase the rate of commission beyond the above limit, if experience indicates that an increase is advisable.

(b) All loan contracts shall stipulate the currency or currencies in which payments under the contract shall be made to the Bank. At the option of the borrower, however, such payments may be made, in gold, or subject to the agreement of the Bank, in the currency of a member other than that prescribed in the contract.

(i) In the case of loans made under Section 1 (a) (i) of this Article, the loan contracts shall provide that payments to the Bank of interest, other charges and amortization shall be made in the currency loaned, unless the member whose currency is loaned agrees that such payments shall be made in some other specified currency or currencies. These payments, subject to the provisions of Article II, Section 9 (c), shall be equivalent to the value of such contractual payments at the time the loans were made, in terms of a currency specified for the purpose by the Bank by a three-fourths majority of the total voting power.

(ii) In the case of loans made under Section 1 (a) (ii) of this Article, the total amount outstanding and payable to the Bank in any one currency shall at no time exceed the total amount of the out-standing borrowings made by the Bank under Section 1 (a) (ii) and payable in the same currency.

(c) If a member suffers from an acute exchange stringency, so that the service of any loan contracted by that member or guaranteed by it or by one of its agencies cannot be provided in the stipulated manner, the member concerned may apply to the Bank for a relaxation of the conditions of payment. If the Bank is satisfied that some relaxation is in the interests of the particular member and of the operations of the Bank and of its members as a whole, it may take action under either, or both, of the following paragraphs with respect to the whole, or part, of the annual service:

(i) The Bank may, in its discretion, make arrangements with the member concerned to accept service payments on the loan in the member's currency for periods not to exceed three years upon appropriate terms regarding the use of such currency and the maintenance of its foreign exchange value; and for the repurchase of such currency on appropriate terms.

(ii) The Bank may modify the terms of amortization or extend the life of the loan, or both.

Section 5. Guarantees

(a) In guaranteeing a loan placed through the usual investment channels, the Bank shall charge a guarantee commission payable periodically on the amount of the loan outstanding at a rate determined by the Bank. During the first ten years of the Bank's operations, this rate shall be not less than one percent per annum and not greater than one and one-half percent per annum. At the end of this period of ten years, the rate of commission may be reduced by the Bank with respect both to the outstanding portions of loans already guaranteed and to future loans if the reserves accumulated by the Bank under Section 6 of this Article and out of other earnings are considered by it sufficient to justify a reduction. In the case of future loans the Bank shall also have discretion to increase the rate of commission beyond the above limit, if experience indicates that an increase is advisable.

(b) Guarantee commissions shall be paid directly to the Bank by the borrower.

(c) Guarantees by the Bank shall provide that the Bank may terminate its liability with respect to interest if, upon default by the borrower and by the guarantor, if any, the Bank offers to purchase, at par and interest accrued to a date designated in the offer, the bonds or other obligations guaranteed.

(d) The Bank shall have power to determine any other terms and conditions of the guarantee.

Section 6. Special Reserve

The amount of commissions received by the Bank under Sections 4 and 5 of this Article shall be set aside as a special reserve, which shall be kept available for meeting liabilities of the Bank in accordance with Section 7 of this Article. The special reserve shall he held in such liquid form, permitted under this Agreement, as the Executive Directors may decide.

Section 7. Methods of Meeting Liabilities of the Bank in Case of Defaults

In cases of default on loans made, participated in, or guaranteed by the Bank:

(a) The Bank shall make such arrangements as may be feasible to adjust the obligations under the loans, including arrangements under or analogous to those provided in Section 4 (c) of this Article.

(b) The payments in discharge of the Bank's liabilities on borrowings or guarantees under Sections 1 (a) (ii) and (iii) of this Article shall be charged:

(i) first, against the special reserve provided in Section 6 of this Article;

(ii) then, to the extent necessary and at the discretion of the Bank, against the other reserves, surplus and capital available to the Bank.

(c) Whenever necessary to meet contractual payments of interest, other charges or amortization on the Bank's own borrowings, or to meet the Bank's liabilities with respect to similar payments on loans guaranteed by it, the Bank may call an appropriate amount of the unpaid subscriptions of members in accordance with Article II, Sections 5 and 7. Moreover, if it believes that a default may be of long duration, the Bank may call an additional amount of such unpaid subscriptions not to exceed in any one year one percent of the total subscriptions of the members for the following purposes:

(i) To redeem prior to maturity, or otherwise discharge its liability on, all or part of the outstanding principal of any loan guaranteed by it in respect of which the debtor is in default.

(ii) To repurchase, or otherwise discharge its liability on, all or part of its own outstanding borrowings.

Section 8. Miscellaneous Operations

In addition to the operations specified elsewhere in this Agreement, the Bank shall have the power:

(i) To buy and sell securities it has issued and to buy and sell securities which it has guaranteed or in which it has invested, provided that the Bank shall obtain the approval of the member in whose territories the securities are to be bought or sold.

(ii) To guarantee securities in which it has invested for the purpose of facilitating their sale.

(iii) To borrow the currency of any member with the approval of that member.

(iv) To buy and sell such other securities as the Directors by a three-fourths majority of the total voting power may deem proper for the investment of all or part of the special reserve under Section 6 of this Article.

In exercising the powers conferred by this Section, the Bank may deal with any person, partnership, association, corporation or other legal entity in the territories of any member.

Section 9. Warning to be Placed on Securities

Every security guaranteed or issued by the Bank shall bear on its face a conspicuous statement to the effect that it is not an obligation of any government unless expressly stated on the security.

Section 10. Political Activity Prohibited

The Bank and its officers shall not interfere in the political affairs of any member; nor shall they be influenced in their decisions by the political character of the member or members concerned. Only economic considerations shall be relevant to their decisions, and these considerations shall be weighed impartially in order to achieve the purposes stated in Article I.

ARTICLE V. ORGANIZATION AND MANAGEMENT
Section 1. Structure of the Bank

The Bank shall have a Board of Governors, Executive Directors, a President and such other officers and staff to perform such duties as the Bank may determine.

Section 2. Board of Governors

(a) All the powers of the Bank shall be vested in the Board of Governors consisting of one governor and one alternate appointed by each member in such manner as it may determine. Each governor and each alternate shall serve for five years, subject to the pleasure of the member appointing him, and may be reappointed. No alternate may vote except in the absence of his principal. The Board shall select one of the governors as Chairman.

(b) The Board of Governors may delegate to the Executive Directors authority to exercise any powers of the Board, except the power to:

(i) Admit new members and determine the conditions of their admission;

(ii) Increase or decrease the capital stock;

(iii) Suspend a member;

(iv) Decide appeals from interpretations of this Agreement given by the Executive Directors;

(v) Make arrangements to cooperate with other international organizations (other than informal arrangements of a temporary and administrative character);

(vi) Decide to suspend permanently the operations of the Bank and to distribute its assets;

(vii) Determine the distribution of the net income of the Bank.

(c) The Board of Governors shall hold an annual meeting and such other meetings as may be provided for by the Board or called by the Executive Directors. Meetings of the Board shall be called by the Directors whenever requested by five members or by members having one-quarter of the total voting power.

(d) A quorum for any meeting of the Board of Governors shall be a majority of the Governors, exercising not less than two-thirds of the total voting power.

(e) The Board of Governors may by regulation establish a procedure whereby the Executive Directors, when they deem such action to be in the best interests of the Bank, may obtain a vote of the Governors on a specific question without calling a meeting of the Board.

(f) The Board of Governors, and the Executive Directors to the extent authorized, may adopt such rules and regulations as may be necessary or appropriate to conduct the business of the Bank.

(g) Governors and alternates shall serve as such without compensation from the Bank, but the Bank shall pay them reasonable expenses incurred in attending meetings.

(h) The Board of Governors shall determine the remuneration to be paid to the Executive Directors and the salary and terms of the contract of service of the President.

Section 3. Voting

(a) Each member shall have two hundred fifty votes plus one additional vote for each share of stock held.

(b) Except as otherwise specifically provided, all matters before the Bank shall be decided by a majority of the votes cast.

Section 4. Executive Directors

(a) The Executive Directors shall be responsible for the conduct of the general operations of the Bank, and for this purpose, shall exercise all the powers delegated to them by the Board of Governors.

(b) There shall be twelve Executive Directors, who need not be governors, and of whom:

(i) five shall be appointed, one by each of the five members having the largest number of shares;

(ii) seven shall be elected according to Schedule B by all the Governors other than those appointed by the five members referred to in (i) above.

For the purpose of this paragraph, "members" means governments of countries whose names are set forth in Schedule A, whether they are original members or become members in accordance with Article II, Section I (b). When governments of other countries become members, the Board of Governors may, by a four-fifths majority of the total voting power, increase the total number of directors by increasing the number of directors to be elected.

Executive directors shall be appointed or elected every two years.

(c) Each executive director shall appoint an alternate with full power to act for him when he is not present. When the executive directors appointing them are present, alternates may participate in meetings but shall not vote.

(d) Directors shall continue in office until their successors are appointed or elected. If the office of an elected director becomes vacant more than ninety days before the end of his term, another director shall be elected for the remainder of the term by the governors who elected the former director. A majority of the votes cast shall be required for election. While the office remains vacant, the alternate of the former director shall exercise his powers, except that of appointing an alternate.

(e) The Executive Directors shall function in continuous session at the principal office of the Bank and shall meet as often as the business of the Bank may require.

(f) A quorum for any meeting of the Executive Directors shall be a majority of the Directors, exercising not less than one-half of the total voting power.

(g) Each appointed director shall be entitled to cast the number of votes allotted under Section 3 of this Article to the member appointing him. Each elected director shall be entitled to cast the number of votes which counted toward his election. All the votes which a director is entitled to cast shall be cast as a unit.

(h) The Board of Governors shall adopt regulations under which a member not entitled to appoint a director under (b) above may send a representative to attend any meeting of the Executive Directors when a request made by, or a matter particularly affecting, that member is under consideration.

(i) The Executive Directors may appoint such committees as they deem advisable. Membership of such committees need not be limited to governors or directors or their alternates.

Section 5. President and Staff

(a) The Executive Directors shall select a President who shall not be a governor or an executive director or an alternate for either. The President shall be Chairman of the Executive Directors, but shall have no vote except a deciding vote in case of an equal division. He may participate in meetings of the Board of Governors, but shall not vote at such meetings. The President shall cease to hold office when the Executive Directors so decide.

(b) The President shall be chief of the operating staff of the Bank and shall conduct, under the direction of the Executive Directors, the ordinary business of the Bank. Subject to the general control of the Executive Directors, he shall be responsible for the organization, appointment and dismissal of the officers and staff.

(c) The President, officers and staff of the Bank, in the discharge of their offices, owe their duty entirely to the Bank and to no other authority. Each member of the Bank shall respect the international character of this duty and shall refrain from all attempts to influence any of them in the discharge of their duties.

(d) In appointing the officers and staff the President shall, subject to the paramount importance of securing the highest standards of efficiency and of technical competence, pay due regard to the importance of recruiting personnel on as wide a geographical basis as possible.

Section 6. Advisory Council

(a) There shall be an Advisory Council of not less than seven persons selected by the Board of Governors including representatives of banking, commercial, industrial, labor, and agricultural interests, and with as wide a national representation as possible. In those fields where specialized international organizations exist, the members of the Council representative of those fields shall be selected in agreement with such organizations. The Council shall advise the Bank on matters of general policy. The Council shall meet annually and on such other occasions as the Bank may request.

(b) Councillors shall serve for two years and may be reappointed. They shall be paid their reasonable expenses incurred on behalf of the Bank.

Section 7. Loan Committees

The committees required to report on loans under Article III, Section 4, shall be appointed by the Bank. Each such committee shall include an expert selected by the governor representing the member in whose territories the project is located and one or more members of the technical staff of the Bank.

Section 8. Relationship to other International Organizations

(a) The Bank, within the terms of this Agreement, shall cooperate with any general international organization and with public international organizations having specialized responsibilities in related fields. Any arrangements for such cooperation which would involve a modification of any provision of this Agreement may be effected only after amendment to this Agreement under Article VIII.

(b) In making decisions on applications for loans or guarantees relating to matters directly within the competence of any international organization of the types specified in the preceding paragraph and participated in primarily by members of the Bank, the Bank shall give consideration to the views and recommendations of such organization.

Section 9. Location of Offices

(a) The principal office of the Bank shall be located in the territory of the member holding the greatest number of shares.

(b) The Bank may establish agencies or branch offices in the territories of any member of the Bank.

Section 10. Regional Offices and Councils

(a) The Bank may establish regional offices and determine the location of, and the areas to be covered by, each regional office.

(b) Each regional office shall be advised by a regional council representative of the entire area and selected in such manner as the Bank may decide.

Section 11. Depositories

(a) Each member shall designate its central bank as a depository for all the Bank's holdings of its currency or, if it has no central bank, it shall designate such other institution as may be acceptable to the Bank.

(b) The Bank may hold other assets, including gold, in depositories designated by the five members having the largest number of shares and in such other designated depositories as the Bank may select. Initially, at least one-half of the gold holdings of the Bank shall be held in the depository designated by the member in whose territory the Bank has its principal office, and at least forty percent shall be held in the depositories designated by the remaining four members referred to above, each of such depositories to hold, initially, not less than the amount of gold paid on the shares of the member designating it. However, all transfers of gold by the Bank shall be made with due regard to the costs of transport and anticipated requirements of the Bank. In an emergency the Executive Directors may transfer all or any part of the Bank's gold holdings to any place where they can be adequately protected.

Section 12. Form of Holdings of Currency

The Bank shall accept from any member, in place of any part of the member's currency, paid in to the Bank under Article II, Section 7 (i), or to meet amortization payments on loans made with such currency and not needed by the Bank in its operations, notes or similar obligations issued by the Government of the member or the depository designated by such member, which shall be non-negotiable, non-interest-bearing and payable at their par value on demand by credit to the account of the Bank in the designated depository.

Section 13. Publication of Reports and Provision of Information

(a) The Bank shall publish an annual report containing an audited statement of its accounts and shall circulate to members at intervals of three months or less a summary statement of its financial position and a profit and loss statement showing the results of its operations.

(b) The Bank may publish such other reports as it deems desirable to carry out its purposes.

(c) Copies of all reports, statements and publications made under this section shall be distributed to members.

Section 14. Allocation of Net Income

(a) The Board of Governors shall determine annually what part of the Bank's net income, after making provision for reserves, shall be allocated to surplus and what part, if any, shall be distributed.

(b) If any part is distributed, up to two percent non-cumulative shall be paid, as a first charge against the distribution for any year, to each member on the basis of the average amount of the loans outstanding during the year made under Article IV, Section 1 (a) (i), out of currency corresponding to its subscription. If two percent is paid as a first charge, any balance remaining to be distributed shall be paid to all members in proportion to their shares. Payments to each member shall be made in its own currency, or if that currency is not available in other currency acceptable to the member. If such payments are made in currencies other than the member's own currency, the transfer of the currency and its use by the receiving member after payment shall be without restriction by the members.

ARTICLE VI. WITHDRAWAL AND SUSPENSION OF MEMBERSHIP: SUSPENSION OF OPERATIONS
Section 1. Right of Members to Withdraw

Any member may withdraw from the Bank at any time by transmitting a notice in writing to the Bank at its principal office. Withdrawal shall become effective on the date such notice is received.

Section 2. Suspension of Membership

If a member fails to fulfill any of its obligations to the Bank, the Bank may suspend its membership by decision of a majority of the Governors, exercising a majority of the total voting power. The member so suspended shall automatically cease to be a member one year from the date of its suspension unless a decision is taken by the same majority to restore the member to good standing.

While under suspension, a member shall not be entitled to exercise any rights under this Agreement, except the right of withdrawal, but shall remain subject to all obligations.

Section 3. Cessation of Membership in International Monetary Fund

Any member which ceases to be a member of the International Monetary Fund shall automatically cease after three months to be a member of the Bank unless the Bank by three-fourths of the total voting power has agreed to allow it to remain a member.

Section 4. Settlement of Accounts with Governments Ceasing to be Members

(a) When a government ceases to be a member, it shall remain liable for its direct obligations to the Bank and for its contingent liabilities to the Bank so long as any part of the loans or guarantees contracted before it ceased to be a member are outstanding; but it shall cease to incur liabilities with respect to loans and guarantees entered into thereafter by the Bank and to share either in the income or the expenses of the Bank.

(b) At the time a government ceases to be a member, the Bank shall arrange for the repurchase of its shares as a part of the settlement of accounts with such government in accordance with the provisions of (c) and (d) below. For this purpose the repurchase price of the shares shall be the value shown by the books of the Bank on the day the government ceases to be a member.

(c) The payment for shares repurchased by the Bank under this section shall be governed by the following conditions:

(i) Any amount due to the government for its shares shall be withheld so long as the government, its central bank or any of its agencies remains liable, as borrower or guarantor, to the Bank and such amount may, at the option of the Bank, be applied on any such liability as it matures. No amount shall be withheld on account of the liability of the government resulting from its subscription for share under Article II, Section 5 (ii). In any event, no amount due to a member for its shares shall be paid until six months after the date upon which the government ceases to be a member.

(ii) Payments for shares may be made from time to time, upon their surrender by the government, to the extent by which the amount due as the repurchase price in (b) above exceeds the aggregate of liabilities on loans and guarantees in (c) (i) above until the former member has received the full repurchase price.

(iii) Payments shall be made in the currency of the country receiving payment or at the option of the Bank in gold.

(iv) If losses are sustained by the Bank on any guarantees, participations in loans, or loans which were outstanding on the date when the government ceased to be a member, and the amount of such losses exceeds the amount of the reserve provided against losses on the date when the government ceased to be a member, such government shall be obligated to repay upon demand the amount by which the repurchase price of its shares would have been reduced, if the losses had been taken into account when the repurchase price was determined. In addition, the former member government shall remain liable on any call for unpaid subscriptions under Article II, Section 5 (ii), to the extent that it would have been required to respond if the impairment of capital had occurred and the call had been made at the time the repurchase price of its shares was determined.

(d) If the Bank suspends permanently its operations under Section 5 (b) of this Article, within six months of the date upon which any government ceases to be a member, all rights of such government shall be determined by the provisions of Section 5 of this Article.

Section 5. Suspension of Operations and Settlement of Obligations

(a) In an emergency the Executive Directors may suspend temporarily operations in respect of new loans and guarantees pending an opportunity for further consideration and action by the Board of Governors.

(b) The Bank may suspend permanently its operations in respect of new loans and guarantees by vote of a majority of the Governors, exercising a majority of the total voting power. After such suspension of operations the

Bank shall forthwith cease all activities, except those incident to the orderly realization, conservation, and preservation of its assets and settlement of its obligations.

(c) The liability of all members for uncalled subscriptions to the capital stock of the Bank and in respect of the depreciation of their own currencies shall continue until all claims of creditors, including all contingent claims, shall have been discharged.

(d) All creditors holding direct claims shall be paid out of the assets of the Bank, and then out of payments to the Bank on calls on unpaid subscriptions. Before making any payments to creditors holding direct claims, the Executive Directors shall make such arrangements as are necessary, in their judgment, to insure a distribution to holders of contingent claims ratably with creditors holding direct claims.

(e) No distribution shall be made to members on account of their subscriptions to the capital stock of the Bank until

(i) all liabilities to creditors have been discharged or provided for, and

(ii) a majority of the Governors, exercising a majority of the total voting power, have decided to make a distribution.

(f) After a decision to make a distribution has been taken under (e) above, the Executive Directors may by a two-thirds majority vote make successive distributions of the assets of the Bank to members until all of the assets have been distributed. This distribution shall be subject to the prior settlement of all outstanding claims of the Bank against each member.

(g) Before any distribution of assets is made, the Executive Directors shall fix the proportionate share of each member according to the ratio of its shareholding to the total outstanding shares of the Bank.

(h) The Executive Directors shall value the assets to be distributed as at the date of distribution and then proceed to distribute in the following manner:

(i) There shall be paid to each member in its own obligations or those of its official agencies or legal entities within its territories, insofar as they are available for distribution, an amount equivalent in value to its proportionate share of the total amount to be distributed.

(ii) Any balance due to a member after payment has been made under (i) above shall be paid, in its own currency, insofar as it is held by the Bank, up to an amount equivalent in value to such balance.

(iii) Any balance due to a member after payment has been made under (i) and (ii) above shall be paid in gold or currency acceptable to the member, insofar as they are held by the Bank, up to an amount equivalent in value to such balance.

(iv) Any remaining assets held by the Bank after payments have been made to members under (i), (ii), and (iii) above shall be distributed *pro rata* among the members.

(i) Any member receiving assets distributed by the Bank in accordance with (h) above, shall enjoy the same rights with respect to such assets as the Bank enjoyed prior to their distribution.

ARTICLE VII. STATUS, IMMUNITIES AND PRIVILEGES
Section 1. Purposes of Article

To enable the Bank to fulfill the functions with which it is entrusted, the status, immunities and privileges set forth in this Article shall be accorded to the Bank in the territories of each member.

Section 2. Status of the Bank

The Bank shall possess full juridical personality, and, in particular, the capacity:

(i) to contract;
(ii) to acquire and dispose of immovable and movable property;
(iii) to institute legal proceedings.

Section 3. Position of the Bank with Regard to Judicial Process

Actions may be brought against the Bank only in a court of competent jurisdiction in the territories of a member in which the Bank has an office, has appointed an agent for the purpose of accepting service or notice of process, or has issued or guaranteed securities. No actions shall, however, be brought by members or persons acting for or deriving claims from members. The property and assets of the Bank shall, wheresoever located and by whomsoever held, be immune from all forms of seizure, attachment or execution before the delivery of final judgment against the Bank.

Section 4. Immunity of Assets from Seizure

Property and assets of the Bank, wherever located and by whomsoever held, shall be immune from search, requisition, confiscation, expropriation or any other form of seizure by executive or legislative action.

Section 5. Immunity of Archives

The archives of the Bank shall be inviolable.

Section 6. Freedom of Assets from Restrictions

To the extent necessary to carry out the operations provided for in this Agreement and subject to the provisions of this Agreement, all property and assets of the Bank shall be free from restrictions, regulations, controls and moratoria of any nature.

Section 7. Privilege for Communications

The official communications of the Bank shall be accorded by each member the same treatment that it accords to the official communications of other members.

Section 8. Immunities and Privileges of Officers and Employees

All governors, executive directors, alternates, officers and employees of the Bank

(i) shall be immune from legal process with respect to acts performed by them in their official capacity except when the Bank waives this immunity;

(ii) not being local nationals, shall be accorded the same immunities from immigration restrictions, alien registration requirements and national service obligations and the same facilities as regards exchange restrictions as are accorded by members to the representatives, officials, and employees of comparable rank of other members;

(iii) shall be granted the same treatment in respect of travelling facilities as is accorded by members to representatives, officials and employees of comparable rank of other members.

Section 9. Immunities from Taxation

(a) The Bank, its assets, property, income and its operations and transactions authorized by this Agreement, shall be immune from all taxation and from all customs duties. The Bank shall also be immune from liability for the collection or payment of any tax or duty.

(b) No tax shall be levied on or in respect of salaries and emoluments paid by the Bank to executive directors, alternates, officials or employees of the Bank who are not local citizens, local subjects, or other local nationals.

(c) No taxation of any kind shall be levied on any obligation or security issued by the Bank (including any dividend or interest thereon) by whomsoever held-

(i) which discriminates against such obligation or security solely because it is issued by the Bank; or

(ii) if the sole jurisdictional basis for such taxation is the place or currency in which it is issued, made payable or paid, or the location of any office or place of business maintained by the Bank.

(d) No taxation of any kind shall be levied on any obligation or security guaranteed by the Bank (including any dividend or interest thereon) by whomsoever held-

(i) which discriminates against such obligation or security solely because it is guaranteed by the Bank; or

(ii) if the sole jurisdictional basis for such taxation is the location of any office or place of business maintained by the Bank.

Section 10. Application of Article

Each member shall take such action as is necessary in its own territories for the purpose of making effective in terms of its own law the principles set forth in this Article and shall inform the Bank of the detailed action which it has taken.

ARTICLE VIII. AMENDMENTS

(a) Any proposal to introduce modifications in this Agreement, whether emanating from a member, a governor or the Executive Directors, shall be communicated to the Chairman of the Board of Governors who shall bring the proposal before the Board. If the proposed amendment is approved by the Board the Bank shall, by circular letter or telegram, ask all members whether they accept the proposed amendment. When three-fifths of the members, having four-fifths of the total voting power, have accepted the proposed amendment, the Bank shall certify the fact by a formal communication addressed to all members.

(b) Notwithstanding (a) above, acceptance by all members is required in the case of any amendment modifying

(i) the right to withdraw from the Bank provided in Article VI, Section 1;

(ii) the right secured by Article II, Section 3 (c);

(iii) the limitation on liability provided in Article II, Section 6.

(c) Amendments shall enter into force for all members three months after the date of the formal communication unless a shorter period is specified in the circular letter or telegram.

ARTICLE IX. INTERPRETATION

(a) Any question of interpretation of the provisions of this Agreement arising between any member and the Bank or between any members of the Bank shall be submitted to the Executive Directors for their decision. If the question particularly affects any member not entitled to appoint an executive director, it shall be entitled to representation in accordance with Article V, Section 4 (h).

(b) In any case where the Executive Directors have given a decision under (a) above, any member may require that the question be referred to the Board of Governors, whose decision shall be final. Pending the result of the reference to the Board, the Bank may, so far as it deems necessary, act on the basis of the decision of the Executive Directors.

(c) Whenever a disagreement arises between the Bank and a country which has ceased to be a member, or between the Bank and any member during the permanent suspension of the Bank, such disagreement shall be submitted to arbitration by a tribunal of three arbitrators, one appointed by the Bank, another by the country involved and an umpire who, unless the parties otherwise agree, shall be appointed by the President of the Permanent Court of International Justice or such other authority as may have been prescribed by regulation adopted by the Bank. The umpire shall have full power to settle all questions of procedure in any case where the parties are in disagreement with respect thereto.

ARTICLE X. APPROVAL DEEMED GIVEN

Whenever the approval of any member is required before any act may be done by the Bank, except in Article VIII, approval shall be deemed to have been given unless the member presents an objection within such reasonable period as the Bank may fix in notifying the member of the proposed act.

ARTICLE XI. FINAL PROVISIONS
Section 1. Entry into Force

This Agreement shall enter into force when it has been signed on behalf of governments whose minimum subscriptions comprise not less than sixty-five percent of the total subscriptions set forth in Schedule A and when the instruments referred to in Section 2 (a) of this Article have been deposited on their behalf, but in no event shall this Agreement enter into force before May 1, 1945.

Section 2. Signature

(a) Each government on whose behalf this Agreement is signed shall deposit with the Government of the United States of America an instrument setting forth that it has accepted this Agreement in accordance with its law and has taken all steps necessary to enable it to carry out all of its obligations under this Agreement.

(b) Each government shall become a member of the Bank as from the date of the deposit on its behalf of the instrument referred to in (a) above, except that no government shall become a member before this Agreement enters into force under Section 1 of this Article.

(c) The Government of the United States of America shall inform the governments of all countries whose names are set forth in Schedule A, and all governments whose membership is approved in accordance with Article II, Section 1 (b), of all signatures of this Agreement and of the deposit of all instruments referred to in (a) above.

(d) At the time this Agreement is signed on its behalf, each government shall transmit to the Government of the United States of America one one-hundredth of one percent of the price of each share in gold or United States dollars for the purpose of meeting administrative expenses of the

Bank. This payment shall be credited on account of the payment to be made in accordance with Article II, Section 8 (a). The Government of the United States of America shall hold such funds in a special deposit account and shall transmit them to the Board of Governors of the Bank when the initial meeting has been called under Section 3 of this Article. If this Agreement has not come into force by December 31, 1945, the Government of the United States of America shall return such funds to the governments that transmitted them.

(e) This Agreement shall remain open for signature at Washington on behalf of the governments of the countries whose names are set forth in Schedule A until December 31, 1945.

(f) After December 31, 1945, this Agreement shall be open for signature on behalf of the government of any country whose membership has been approved in accordance with Article II, Section 1 (b).

(g) By their signature of this Agreement, all governments accept it both on their own behalf and in respect of all their colonies, overseas territories, all territories under their protection, suzerainty, or authority and all territories in respect of which they exercise a mandate.

(h) In the case of governments whose metropolitan territories have been under enemy occupation, the deposit of the instrument referred to in (a) above may be delayed until one hundred and eighty days after the date on which these territories have been liberated. If, however, it is not deposited by any such government before the expiration of this period, the signature affixed on behalf of that government shall become void and the portion of its subscription paid under (d) above shall be returned to it.

(i) Paragraphs (d) and (h) shall come into force with regard to each signatory government as from the date of its signature.

Section 3. Inauguration of the Bank

(a) As soon as this Agreement enters into force under Section 1 of this Article, each member shall appoint a governor and the member to whom the largest number of shares is allocated in Schedule A shall call the first meeting of the Board of Governors.

(b) At the first meeting of the Board of Governors, arrangements shall be made for the selection of provisional executive directors. The governments of the five countries, to which the largest number of shares are allocated in Schedule A, shall appoint provisional executive directors. If one or more of such governments have not become members, the executive directorships which they would be entitled to fill shall remain vacant until they become members, or until January 1, 1946, whichever is the earlier. Seven provisional executive directors shall be elected in accordance with the provisions of Schedule B and shall remain in office until the date of the first regular election of executive directors which shall be held as soon as practicable after January 1, 1946.

(c) The Board of Governors may delegate to the provisional executive directors any powers except those which may not be delegated to the Executive Directors.

(d) The Bank shall notify members when it is ready to commence operations.

Done at Washington, in a single copy which shall remain deposited in the archives of the Government of the United States of America, which shall transmit certified copies to all Governments whose names are set forth in Schedule A and to all governments whose membership is approved in accordance with Article II, Section 1 (b).

SCHEDULE B
Election of Executive Directors

1. The election of the elective executive directors shall be by ballot of the Governors eligible to vote under Article V, Section 4 (b).

2. In balloting for the elective executive directors, each governor eligible to vote shall cast for one person all of the votes to which the member appointing him is entitled under Section 3 of Article V. The seven persons receiving the greatest number of votes shall be executive directors, except that no person who receives less than fourteen percent of the total of the votes which can be cast (eligible votes) shall be considered elected.

3. When seven persons are not elected on the first ballot, a second ballot shall be held in which the person who received the lowest number of votes shall be ineligible for election and in which there shall vote only (a) those governors who voted in the first ballot for a person not elected and (b) those governors whose votes for a person elected are deemed under 4 below to have raised the votes cast for that person above fifteen percent of the eligible votes.

4. In determining whether the votes cast by a governor are to be deemed to have raised the total of any person above fifteen percent of the eligible votes, the fifteen percent shall be deemed to include, first, the votes of the governor casting the largest number of votes for such person, then

SCHEDULE A

Subscriptions

	(millions of dollars)		(millions of dollars)
Australia	200	Iran	24
Belgium	225	Iraq	6
Bolivia	7	Liberia	.5
Brazil	105	Luxembourg	10
Canada	325	Mexico	65
Chile	35	Netherlands	275
China	600	New Zealand	50
Colombia	35	Nicaragua	.8
Costa Rica	2	Norway	50
Cuba	35	Panama	.2
Czechoslovakia	125	Paraguay	.8
*Denmark		Peru	17.5
Dominican Republic	2	Philippine Commonwealth	15
Ecuador	3.2	Poland	125
Egypt	40	Union of South Africa	100
El Salvador	1	Union of Soviet Socialist	
Ethiopia	3	Republics	1200
France	450	United Kingdom	1300
Greece	25	United States	3175
Guatemala	2	Uruguay	10.5
Haiti	2	Venezuela	10.5
Honduras	1	Yugoslavia	40
Iceland	1		
India	400	Total	9100

*The quota of Denmark shall be determined by the Bank after Denmark accepts membership in accordance with these Articles of Agreement.

the votes of the governor casting the next largest number, and so on until fifteen percent is reached.

5. Any governor, part of whose votes must be counted in order to raise the total of any person above fourteen percent, shall be considered as casting all of his votes for such person even if the total votes for such person thereby exceed fifteen percent.

6. If, after the second ballot, seven persons have not been elected, further ballots shall be held on the same principles until seven persons have been elected, provided that after six persons are elected, the seventh may be elected by a simple majority of the remaining votes and shall be deemed to have been elected by all such votes.

THE WHITE PLAN

PRELIMINARY DRAFT OUTLINE OF A PROPOSAL FOR
AN INTERNATIONAL STABILIZATION FUND OF
THE UNITED AND ASSOCIATED NATIONS
(Revised July 10, 1943)

The plan for post-war international currency stability set forth in this pamphlet is a revision of the preliminary draft outline of a proposal for an International Stabilization Fund of the United and Associated Nations made public by the Secretary of the Treasury on April 7, 1943.

The preliminary draft was sent by the Secretary of the Treasury to the finance ministers of the United Nations and the countries associated with them with a request that it be studied by their technical experts. The finance ministers were also invited to send representatives to Washington for informal discussions with the experts of this Government.

Such informal discussions have been held with nearly 30 countries. On the basis of these discussions, the experts of the Treasury with the cooperation of experts of other Departments of this Government have revised the preliminary draft proposal for an international stabilization fund. While suggestions of the representatives of other countries have been included in the revised draft, it does not necessarily reflect the views of the experts of any other country.

This revised draft is in every sense still a preliminary document representing the views of the technical experts of the Treasury and of other Departments of this Government. It has not received the official approval either of the Treasury or this Government.

FOREWORD
BY HENRY MORGENTHAU, JR., *SECRETARY OF THE TREASURY*

When the United Nations have brought this war to a successful conclusion, they will be faced with many urgent international economic and financial problems. Some of these are new problems arising directly from this war; others are continuing consequences of failure to solve the problems that have been with us since the last war. The solution of these problems is essential to the development of a sound economic foundation for world peace and prosperity.

All of the important international economic and financial problems are closely interrelated. Monetary stabilization, commercial policy, the provision of long-term international credit, promotion of stability in the prices of primary products, and arrangements for relief and rehabilitation are problems that join at innumerable points. Nevertheless, because of their complexity, they must be taken up separately, although each in turn must be integrated with the rest.

It is generally recognized that monetary stability and protection against discriminatory currency practices are essential bases for the revival of international commerce and finance. For this reason, an appropriate starting point might well be the consideration of post-war international monetary problems. Success in dealing with international monetary problems in the post-war period will contribute toward final solution of the other international financial and economic problems. Despite the technical difficulties involved, the common interest which all countries have in the solution of post-war monetary problems provides a basis for agreement.

It is still too soon to know the precise form and magnitude of post-war monetary problems. But it is certain that we shall be confronted with three inseparable monetary tasks: to prevent the disruption of foreign exchanges, to avoid the collapse of monetary systems, and to facilitate the restoration and balanced growth of international trade. Clearly, such formidable problems can be successfully handled only through international action.

The creation of instrumentalities adequate to deal with the inevitable post-war monetary problems should not be postponed until the end of hostilities. It would be ill-advised, if not dangerous, to leave ourselves unprepared at the end of the war for the difficult tasks of international monetary cooperation. Specific and practical proposals must be formulated by the experts and must be carefully considered by the policy-shaping officials of the various countries. In each country acceptance of a definitive plan can follow only upon legislative or executive action. And even when a plan is finally adopted, much time will be consumed in preparation before an international institution for monetary cooperation can begin effective work.

There is another important reason for initiating now concrete discussions of specific proposals. A plan for international monetary cooperation can be a factor in winning the war. It has been suggested, and with much cogency, that the task of assuring the defeat of the Axis powers would be made easier if the victims of aggression could have greater assurance that a victory of the United Nations will not mean in the economic sphere a repetition of the exchange instability and monetary collapse that followed the last war. The people in all of the United Nations must be given some assurance that there will not again be two decades of post-war economic disruption. The people must know that we at last recognize the fundamental truth that the prosperity of each country is closely linked to the prosperity of other countries.

One of the appropriate agencies to deal with international economic and monetary problems would be an international stabilization fund with resources and powers adequate to the task of helping to achieve monetary stability and of facilitating the restoration and balanced growth of international trade. A proposal along these lines was drafted by American technical experts and made public on April 7, 1943. There have been informal discussions on this draft in which nearly thirty countries have participated. These discussions have shown that all countries think joint action in this field is necessary for the reconstruction of the world economy.

It is recognized that an international stabilization fund is only one of the instrumentalities which may be needed in the field of international economic cooperation. Other agencies may be needed to provide long-term international credit for post-war reconstruction and development, to provide funds for rehabilitation and relief, and to promote stability in the prices of primary international commodities. There is a strong inclination on the part of some to entrust to a single agency the responsibility for dealing with these and other international economic problems. We believe, however, that an international economic institution can operate most effectively if it is not burdened with diverse duties of a specialized character.

Although an international stabilization fund can provide the facilities for cooperation on monetary questions, the establishment of such an institution would not of itself assure the solution of these difficult problems. The operations of such a fund can be successful only if the powers and resources of the fund are used wisely, and if member countries cooperate with the fund's endeavors to maintain international equilibrium at a high level of international trade. Such cooperation must include commercial policies designed to reduce trade barriers and to terminate discriminatory practices that have in the past hampered the balanced growth of international trade. The nations of this world can be prosperous only if they are good neighbors in their economic as well as their political relations.

The draft proposals that have been put forward on a tentative basis have received wide publicity in the United States, the United Kingdom, Canada, and in other countries. It is in the best democratic tradition that the people should have the fullest opportunity to express their views and to shape the policies of their Governments on the important problems affecting national well-being. And it is an extension of this tradition that all the United Nations should have an opportunity to participate in the formulation of a program for international monetary cooperation.

This revised draft is published with the hope that it will call forth further comments and constructive suggestions. It aims to present only the essential elements of a workable international stabilization fund, and its provisions are in every sense tentative. Obviously, there are many details that have been omitted and that can be better formulated after there is agreement on the more important points. We believe that a workable and acceptable plan can emerge only from the joint efforts of the United Nations support by enlightened public opinion.

PRELIMINARY DRAFT OUTLINE OF A PROPOSAL FOR AN INTERNATIONAL STABILIZATION FUND OF THE UNITED AND ASSOCIATED NATIONS
Preamble

1. There is a growing recognition that progress toward establishment of a functioning democratic world in the post-war period will depend on the ability of free peoples to work together in solving their economic problems. Not the least of these is the problem of how to prevent a widespread breakdown of currencies with resultant international economic disorder. We must assure a troubled world that the free countries will solve these perplexing problems, and that they will not resort to competitive exchange

depreciation, multiple currency practices, discriminatory bilateral clearing, or other destructive foreign exchange devices.

2. These are not transitory problems of the immediate postwar period affecting only a few countries. The history of the past two decades shows that they are continuing problems of vital interest to all countries. There must be a general realization that world prosperity, like world peace, is indivisible. Nations must act together to restore multilateral international trade, and to provide orderly procedure for the maintenance of balanced economic growth. Only through international cooperation will it be possible for countries successfully to apply measures directed toward attaining and maintaining a high level of employment and income which must be the primary objective of economic policy.

3. The International Stabilization Fund of the United and Associated Nations is proposed as a permanent institution for international monetary cooperation. The resources of this Fund would be available under adequate safeguards to maintain currency stability, while giving member countries time to correct maladjustments in their balance of payments without resorting to extreme measures destructive of international prosperity. The resources of the Fund would not be used to prolong a basically unbalanced international position. On the contrary, the Fund would be influential in inducing countries to pursue policies making for an orderly return to equilibrium.

4. The Fund would deal only with member governments and their fiscal agents, and would not intrude in the customary channels for conducting international commerce and finance. The Fund is intended to provide supplemental facilities for the successful functioning of the established foreign exchange institutions and to free international commerce from harmful restrictions.

5. The success of the Fund must ultimately depend upon the willingness of nations to act together on their common problems. International monetary cooperation should not be regarded as a matter of generosity. All countries have a vital interest in the maintenance of international monetary stability, and in the balanced growth of multilateral international trade.

I. Purposes of the Fund

The United Nations and the countries associated with them recognize, as declared in the Atlantic Charter, the need for the fullest cooperation among nations with the object of securing economic advancement and rising standards of living for all. They believe that attainment of these objectives will be facilitated by international monetary cooperation. Therefore, it is proposed that there be established an International Stabilization Fund with the following purposes:

1. To help stabilize the foreign exchange rates of the currencies of the United Nations and the countries associated with them.

2. To shorten the periods and lessen the degree of disequilibrium in the international balance of payments of member countries.

3. To help create conditions under which the smooth flow of foreign trade and of productive capital among the member countries will be fostered.

4. To facilitate the effective utilization of the blocked foreign balances accumulating in some countries as a consequence of the war situation.

5. To reduce the use of such foreign exchange restrictions, bilateral clearing arrangements, multiple currency devices, and discriminatory foreign exchange practices as hamper world trade and the international flow of productive capital.

II. Composition of the Fund

1. The Fund shall consist of gold and the currencies and securities of member governments.

2. Each of the member countries shall subscribe a specified amount, to be called its *quota*. The aggregate of quotas of the member countries shall be the equivalent of at least $5 billion.

3. Each member country shall meet its quota contribution in full on or before the date set by the Board of Directors for the Fund's operations to begin.

(a) A country shall pay in gold not less than an amount determined as follows. If its gold and free foreign exchange holdings are:

(i) In excess of three times its quota, it shall pay in gold 50 percent of its quota.

(ii) More than two but less than three times its quota, it shall pay in gold 40 percent of its quota plus 10 percent of its holdings in excess of twice its quota.

(iii) More than its quota but less than twice its quota, it shall pay in gold 30 percent of its quota plus 10 percent of its holdings in excess of its quota.

(iv) Less than its quota, it shall pay in gold 30 percent of its holdings.

The gold payment required of a member country substantial parts of whose home areas have been wholly or partly occupied by the enemy, shall be only three-fourths of the above. (For other gold provisions, Cf. V-2-a and V-6, 7.)

A member country may include in the legal reserve account and in the published statement of the reserves of gold and foreign exchange in its Treasury or Central Bank, an amount not to exceed its gold contribution to the Fund, minus its net purchases of foreign exchange from the Fund paid for with local currency.

(b) It shall pay the remainder of its quota in local currency, except that a member country may substitute government securities (redeemable at par) for local currency up to 50 percent of its quota.

4. A quota for each member country shall be computed by an agreed upon formula which gives due weight to the important relevant factors, e.g., a country's holdings of gold and free foreign exchange, the magnitude and the fluctuations of its balance of international payments, its national income, etc.

Before computing individual quotas on the basis of the agreed upon formula, there shall be reserved an amount equal to 10 percent of aggregate quotas to be used as a special allotment for the equitable adjustment of quotas. Where the initial quota of a member country as computed by the formula is clearly inequitable, the quota may be increased from this special allotment.

5. Quotas shall be adjusted on the basis of the most recent data 3 years after the establishment of the Fund, and at intervals of 5 years thereafter, in accordance with the agreed upon formula. In the period between adjustment of quotas, the Fund may increase the quota of a country, where it is clearly inequitable, out of the special allotment reserved for the equitable adjustment of quotas.

6. Any changes in the formula by which the quotas of member countries are determined shall be made only with the approval of a four-fifths vote of the Board.

7. No increase shall be made in the quota of a member country under II-4, 5 or 6 without the consent of the representative of the country concerned.

8. The resources of the Fund shall be used exclusively for the benefit of the member countries.

III. Monetary Unit of the Fund

1. The monetary unit of the Fund shall be the *unitas* equal in value to 137-1/7 grains of fine gold (equivalent to $10). No change in the gold value of the unitas shall be made except with the approval of 85 percent of the member votes. When such change is made, the gain or loss sustained by the Fund on its holdings of gold shall be distributed equitably among the members of the Fund.

The Accounts of the Fund shall be kept and published in terms of unitas.

2. The value of the currency of each member country shall be established in terms of unitas and may not be altered except as provided in IV-5, below. (Cf. IV-1, 2, below.)

No member country shall purchase or acquire gold, directly or indirectly, at a price in terms of its national currency in excess of the parity which corresponds to the value of its currency in terms of unitas and to the value of unitas in terms of gold; nor shall any member country sell or dispose of gold, directly or indirectly, at a price in terms of its national currency below the parity which corresponds to the value of its currency in terms of unitas and to the value of unitas in terms of gold. (Cf. VII-1.)

3. No change in the value of the currencies of member countries shall be permitted to alter the value in unitas of the assets of the Fund. Whenever the currency of a member country has depreciated to a significant extent, that country must deliver to the Fund when requested an amount of its local currency or securities equal to the decrease in the unitas value of the Fund's holdings of the local currency and securities of the country. Likewise, if the currency of a member country should appreciate to a significant extent, the Fund must return to that country an amount (in the currency or securities of that country) equal to the resulting increase in the unitas value of the Fund's holdings.

IV. Exchange Rates

1. The rates at which the Fund will buy and sell one member currency for another and at which the Fund will buy and sell gold for local currency shall be established in accordance with the provisions below. (Cf. also III-2 and V-2.)

2. The initial rates of exchange for member countries' currencies shall be determined as follows:

(a) For any country which becomes a member prior to the date on which the Fund's operations begin, the rates initially used by the Fund shall be based upon the value of the currency in terms of United States dollars which prevailed on July 1, 1943.

If, in the judgment of either the member country or the Fund, the above rate is clearly inappropriate, the initial rate shall be determined by consultation between the member country and the Fund. No operations in such currency shall be undertaken by the Fund until a rate has been established which has the approval of the Fund and of the member country in question.

(b) For any member country which has been occupied by the enemy, the Fund shall use the exchange rate fixed by the government of the liberated country in consultation with the Fund and acceptable to the Fund. Prior to the fixing of a definitive rate, operations in such currency may be undertaken by the Fund with the approval of the Board at a tentative rate of exchange fixed by the member country in consultation with the Board. No operations shall be continued under this provision for more than 3 months after the liberation of the country or when the local currency holdings of the Fund exceed the quota of the country, except that under special circumstances the period and the amount of such operations may be extended by the Fund.

3. The Fund shall not come into operation until agreement has been reached on the exchange rates for currencies of countries representing a majority of the aggregate quotas.

4. The Fund shall determine the range within which the rates of exchange of member currencies shall be permitted to fluctuate. (Cf. VII-1.)

5. Changes in the exchange value of the currency of a member country shall be considered only when essential to the correction of fundamental disequilibrium in its balance of payments, and shall be made only with the

approval of three-fourths of the member votes including the representative of the country concerned.

Because of the extreme uncertainties of the immediate post-war period, the following exceptional provisions may be used during the first 3 years of the Fund's operations:

(a) When the existing rate of exchange of a member country is clearly inconsistent with the maintenance of a balanced international payments position for that country, changes from the established rate may be made at the special request of that country and with the approval of a majority of the member votes.

(b) A member country may change the established rate for its currency by not more than 10 percent provided that the member country shall notify the Fund of its intention and shall consult with the Fund on the advisability of its action.

V. Powers and Operations

The Fund shall have the following powers:

1. To buy, sell and hold gold, currencies, and government securities of member countries; to earmark and transfer gold; to issue its own obligations, and to offer them for discount or sale in member countries.

The Fund shall purchase for local currency or needed foreign exchange any member currency in good standing acquired by another member country in settlement of a balance of payments on current account, where such currency cannot be disposed of in the foreign exchange markets within the range established by the Fund.

2. To sell to the Treasury of any member country (or Stabilization Fund or Central Bank acting as its agent) at the accepted rate of exchange, currency of any member country which the Fund holds, provided that:

(a) The foreign exchange demanded from the Fund is required to meet an adverse balance of payments predominantly on current account with any member country. (Cf. V-3, for capital transfers.)

When the gold and free foreign exchange holdings of a member country exceed 50 percent of its quota, the Fund in selling foreign exchange to such member country shall require that one-half of such exchange shall be paid for with gold or foreign exchange acceptable to the Fund. (Cf. V-6, 7; on gold collateral, see V-2-c.)

(b) The Fund's total holdings of the currency and securities of any member country shall not exceed the quota of such country by more than 50 percent during the first year of operation of the Fund, and thereafter shall not exceed such quota by more than 100 percent (except as otherwise provided below). The total holdings thus permitted are termed the permissible quota of a country. When the Fund's holdings of local currency and securities are equal to the permissible quota of a country, the Fund may sell foreign exchange for such additional local currency only with the specific approval of the Board of Directors (cf. VI-3-a, below), and provided that at least one of the following two conditions is met:

(i) In the judgment of the Fund satisfactory measures are being or will be taken by the country whose currency is acquired by the Fund, to correct the disequilibrium in the country's balance of payments; or

(ii) It is believed that the balance of payments of the country whose currency is acquired by the Fund will be such as to warrant the expectation that the excess currency holdings of the Fund can be disposed of within a reasonable time;

Provided further, that when the Fund's holdings of the currency of any member country or countries fall below 20 percent of their respective quotas, the sale shall also require the approval of the representatives of these countries.

(c) When the Fund's holdings of local currency and securities exceed the permissible quota of a country, the Board may require the member country to deposit collateral in accordance with regulations prescribed by the Board. Such collateral shall take the form of gold, foreign or domestic currency or Government bonds, or other suitable collateral within the capacity of the member country.

(d) When, in the judgment of the Fund, a member country, whose currency and securities held by the Fund exceed its quota, is exhausting its permissible quota more rapidly than is warranted, or is using its permissible quota in a manner that clearly has the effect of preventing or unduly delaying the establishment of a sound balance in its international accounts, the Fund may place such conditions upon additional sales of foreign exchange to that country as it deems to be in the general interest of the Fund.

3. The Fund may sell foreign exchange to a member country, under conditions prescribed by the Fund, to facilitate a transfer of capital, or repayment or adjustment of foreign debts, when in the judgment of the Board such a transfer is desirable from the point of view of the general international economic situation, provided the Fund's holdings of the currency and securities of the member country do not exceed ISO percent of the quota of that country. When the Fund's holdings of the local currency and securities of a member country exceed 150 percent of the quota of that country, the Fund may, in exceptional circumstances, sell foreign exchange to the member country for the above purposes with the approval of three-fourths of the member votes. (Cf. V-2-a, above; on voting, VI-3-a, below.)

4. When the Fund's holdings of the currency and securities of a member country become excessively small in relation to prospective acquisitions and needs for that currency, the Fund shall render a report to that country. The report shall embody an analysis of the causes of the depletion of the Fund's holdings of that currency, a forecast of the prospective balance of payments in the absence of special measures, and finally, recommendations designed to increase the Fund's holdings of that currency. The representative of the country in question shall be a member of the Fund committee appointed to draft the report. This report shall be sent to all member countries and, if deemed desirable, be made public. Member countries agree that they will give immediate and careful attention to recommendations made by the Fund.

5. Whenever it becomes evident to the Board of Directors that the anticipated demand for any particular currency may soon exhaust the Fund's holdings of that currency, the Fund shall inform the member countries of the probable supply of the currency and of a proposed method for its equitable distribution, together with suggestions for helping to equate the anticipated demand for and supply of that currency.

The Fund shall make every effort to increase the supply of the scarce currency by acquiring that currency from the foreign balances of member countries. The Fund may make special arrangements with any member country for the purpose of providing an emergency supply under appropriate conditions which are acceptable to both the Fund and the member country.

To facilitate appropriate adjustment in the balance of payments position of member countries, and to help correct the distortions in the pattern of trade balances, the Fund shall apportion its sales of such scarce currency. In such apportionment, it shall be guided by the principle of satisfying the most urgent needs from the point of view of the general international economic situation. It shall also consider the special needs and resources of the particular countries making the request for the scarce currency.

The right of any member country to acquire an amount of other currencies equal to its permissible quota shall be limited by the necessity of assuring an appropriate distribution among the various members of any currency the supply of which is scarce.

6. In order to promote the most effective use of the available and accumulating supply of foreign exchange resources of member countries, each member country agrees that it will offer to sell to the Fund, for its local currency or for foreign currencies which the member country needs, one-half of the foreign exchange resources and gold it acquires in excess of its official holdings at the time it became a member of the Fund, but no country need sell gold or foreign exchange under this provision unless its official holdings (i.e., Treasury, Central Bank, Stabilization Fund, etc.) are in excess of 25 percent of its quota. For the purpose of this provision, only free and liquid foreign exchange resources and gold shall be considered. The Fund may accept or reject the offer. (Cf. II-3-a, V-2-a, and V-7.)

To help achieve this objective each member country agrees to discourage the excessive accumulation of foreign exchange resources and gold by its nationals. The Fund shall inform any member country when, in its opinion, any further growth of privately held foreign exchange resources and gold appears unwarranted.

7. When the Fund's holdings of the local currency and securities of a member country exceed the quota of that country, the Fund shall, upon request of the member country, resell to the member country the Fund's excess holdings of the currency of that country for gold or acceptable foreign exchange. (Cf. V-14, for charges on holdings in excess of quota.)

8. To buy from the governments of member countries, blocked foreign balances held in other member countries, provided all the following conditions are met:

(a) The blocked balances are held in member countries and are reported as such (for the purpose of this provision) by the member governments and are verified by the Fund.

(b) The member country selling the blocked balances to the Fund agrees to transfer these balances to the Fund and to repurchase from the Fund 40 percent of them (at the same price) with gold or such free currencies as the Fund may wish to accept, at the rate of 2 percent of the transferred balances each year for 20 years beginning not later than 3 years after the date of transfer.

(c) The country in which the blocked balances are held agrees to transfer to the Fund the balances described in (b) above, and to repurchase from the Fund 40 percent of them (at the same price) with gold or such free currencies as the Fund may wish to accept, at the rate of 2 percent of the transferred balances each year for 20 years beginning not later than 3 years after the date of transfer.

(d) A charge of 1 percent on the amount of blocked balances sold to the Fund, payable in gold, shall be levied against the country selling its blocked balances and against the country in which the balances are held. In addition a charge of not less than one percent, payable in gold, shall be levied annually against each country on the amount of such balances remaining to be purchased by it.

(e) If the country selling blocked balances to the Fund asks for foreign exchange rather than local currency, the request will not be granted unless the country needs the foreign exchange for the purpose of meeting an adverse balance of payments not arising from the acquisition of gold, the accumulation of foreign balances, or other capital transactions.

(f) Either country may, at its option, increase the amount it repurchases annually. But, in the case of the country selling blocked balances to the Fund, not more than 2 percent per annum of the original sum taken over by the Fund shall become free, and only after 3 years shall have elapsed since the sale of the balances to the Fund.

(g) The Fund has the privilege of disposing of any of its holdings of blocked balances as free funds after the 23-year period is passed, or sooner under the following conditions:

(i) Its holdings of the free funds of the country in which the balances are held fall below 20 percent of its quota; or

(ii) The approval is obtained of the country in which the balances are held.

(h) The country in which the blocked balances are held agrees not to impose any restrictions on the use of the installments of the 40 percent portion gradually repurchased by the country which sold the balances to the Fund.

(i) The Fund agrees not to sell the blocked balances acquired under the above authority, except with the permission or at the request of the country in which the balances are being held. The Fund may invest these balances in the ordinary or special government securities of that country. The Fund shall be free to sell such securities in any country under the provisions of V-11, below.

(j) The Fund shall determine from time to time the maximum proportion of the blocked balances it will purchase under this provision.

Provided, however, that during the first 2 years of its operation, blocked balances purchased by the Fund shall not exceed in the aggregate 10 percent of the quotas of all member countries. At the end of 2 years of operation, the Fund shall propose a plan for the gradual further liquidation of blocked balances still outstanding indicating the proportion of the blocked balances which the Board considers the Fund can appropriately purchase.

Blocked balances acquired under this provision shall not be included either in computing the amount of foreign exchange available to member countries under their quotas (cf. V-2, 3), or in computing charges on balances of local currency in excess of the quotas (cf. V-14).

9. To buy and sell currencies of non-member countries but shall not acquire more than $10 million of the currency of any one non-member country nor hold such currencies beyond 60 days after date of purchase except with the approval of the Board.

10. To borrow the currency of any member country provided the additional amount is needed by the Fund and provided the representative of that country approves.

11. To sell member-country obligations owned by the Fund provided that the representatives of the country issuing the securities and of the country in which the securities are to be sold approve, except that the approval of the representative of the issuing country shall not be necessary if the obligations are to be sold in its own market.

To use its holdings to obtain rediscounts or advances from the Central Bank of any country whose currency the Fund needs.

12. To invest any of its currency holdings in government securities of the country of that currency provided that the representative of the country approves.

13. To lend to any member country its local currency from the Fund for 1 year or less up to 75 percent of the currency of that country held by the Fund, provided the local currency holdings of the Fund are not reduced below 20 percent of the quota.

14. To make a service charge on all gold and exchange transactions.

To levy a charge uniform to all countries, at a rate not less than 1 percent per annum, payable in gold, against any country on the amount of its currency held by the Fund in excess of the quota of that country. An additional charge, payable in gold, shall be levied by the Fund against any member country on the Fund's holdings of its currency in excess of the permissible quota of that country.

In case the Fund finds it necessary to borrow currency to meet the demands of its members, an additional charge, payable in gold, shall be made by the Fund sufficient to cover the cost of the borrowing.

15. To levy upon member countries a *pro rata* share of the expenses of operating the Fund, payable in local currency, not to exceed one-tenth percent per annum of the quota of each country. The levy may be made only to the extent that the earnings of the Fund are inadequate to meet its current expenses.

16. The Fund shall deal only with or through:

(a) The Treasuries, Stabilization Funds, or Central Banks acting as fiscal agents of member governments.

(b) Any international banks owned predominantly by member governments.

The Fund may, nevertheless, with the approval of the representatives of the governments of the countries concerned, sell its own securities, or securities it holds, directly to the public or to institutions of member countries.

VI. Management

1. The administration of the Fund shall be vested in a Board of Directors. Each government shall appoint a director and an alternate, in a manner determined by it, who shall serve for a period of 5 years, subject to the pleasure of their government. Directors and alternates may be reappointed.

2. In all voting by the Board, the director or alternate of each member country shall be entitled to cast an agreed upon number of votes.

The distribution of *basic votes* shall be closely related to the quotas of member countries, although not in precise proportion to the quotas. An appropriate distribution of basic voting power would seem to be the following: Each country shall have 100 votes, plus 1 vote for the equivalent of each 100,000 unitas ($1 million) of its quota.

No country shall be entitled to cast more than one-fifth of the aggregate basic votes, regardless of its quota.

3. All voting shall be according to basic votes except as follows:

(a) In voting on proposals to authorize the sale of foreign exchange, each country shall cast a number of votes modified from its basic vote:

(i) By the addition of one vote for each $2 million of net sales of its currency by the Fund (adjusted for its net transactions in gold), and

(ii) By the subtraction of one vote for each $2 million of its net purchases of foreign exchange from the Fund (adjusted for its net transactions in gold).

(b) In voting on proposals to suspend or restore membership, each member country shall cast one vote, as provided in VI-11, below.

4. All decisions, except where specifically provided otherwise, shall be made by a majority of the member votes.

5. The Board of Directors shall select a Managing Director of the Fund and one or more assistants. The Managing Director shall become an ex officio member of the Board and shall be chief of the operating staff of the Fund. The operating staff shall be selected in accordance with regulations established by the Board of Directors.

6. The Board of Directors shall appoint from among its members an Executive Committee of not less than 11 members. The Chairman of the Board shall be Chairman of the Executive Committee, and the Managing Director of the Fund shall be an *ex officio* member of the Executive Committee.

The Executive Committee shall be continuously available at the head office of the Fund and shall exercise the authority delegated to it by the Board. In the absence of any member of the Executive Committee, his alternate shall act in his place. Members of the Executive Committee shall receive appropriate remuneration.

7. The Board of Directors may appoint such other committees as it finds necessary for the work of the Fund. It may also appoint advisory committees chosen wholly or partially from persons not employed by the Fund.

8. The Board of Directors may at any meeting authorize any officers or committees of the Fund to exercise any specified powers of the Board not requiring more than a majority vote.

The Board may delegate any authority to the Executive Committee, provided that the delegation of powers requiring more than a majority of the member votes can be authorized only by a majority (of the Board) of the same size as specified, and can be exercised by the Executive Committee only by like majority.

Delegated powers shall be exercised only until the next meeting of the Board, and in a manner consistent with the general policies and practices of the Board.

9. The Board of Directors may establish procedural regulations governing the operations of the Fund. The officers and committees of the Fund shall be bound by such regulations.

10. The Board of Directors shall hold an annual meeting and such other meetings as it may be desirable to convene. The annual meeting shall be held in places designated by the Executive Committee, but not more than one annual meeting in any 5-year period shall be held within the same member country.

On request of member countries casting one-fourth of the votes, the Chairman shall call a meeting of the Board for the purpose of considering any matters placed before it.

11. A country failing to meet its obligations to the Fund may be suspended provided a majority of the member countries so decides. While under suspension, the country shall be denied the privileges of membership but shall be subject to the same obligations as any other member of the Fund. At the end of 1 year the country shall be automatically dropped from membership unless it has been restored to good standing by a majority of the member countries.

Any country may withdraw from the Fund by giving notice, and its withdrawal will take effect 1 year from the date of such notice. During the interval between notice of withdrawal and the taking effect of the notice, such country shall be subject to the same obligations as any other member of the Fund.

A country which is dropped or which withdraws from the Fund shall have returned to it an amount in its own currency equal to its contributed quota, plus other obligations of the Fund to the country, and minus any sum owed by that country to the Fund. Any losses of the Fund may be deducted *pro rata* from the contributed quota to be returned to the country that has been dropped or has withdrawn from membership. Local currency holdings of the Fund in excess of the above shall be repurchased by that country with gold or foreign exchange acceptable to the Fund.

When any country is dropped or withdraws from membership, the rights of the Fund shall be fully safeguarded. The obligations of a country to the Fund shall become due at the time it is dropped or withdraws from membership; but the Fund shall have 5 years within which to liquidate its obligations to such country.

12. Net profits earned by the Fund shall be distributed in the following manner:

(a) Fifty percent to reserves until the reserves are equal to 10 percent of the aggregate quotas of the Fund.

(b) Fifty percent to be divided each year among the members in proportion to their quotas. Dividends distributed to each country shall be paid in its own currency or in gold at the discretion of the Fund.

VII. Policies of Member Countries

Each member country of the Fund undertakes the following:

1. To maintain by appropriate action exchange rates established by the Fund on the currencies of other countries, and not to alter exchange rates except as provided in IV-5, above.

Exchange rates of member countries may be permitted to fluctuate within the specified range fixed by the Fund.

2. Not to engage in exchange dealings with member or non-member countries that will undermine stability of exchange rates established by the Fund.

3. To abandon, as soon as the member country decides that conditions permit, all restrictions (other than those involving capital transfers) over foreign exchange transactions with other member countries, and not to impose any additional restrictions (except upon capital transfers) without the approval of the Fund.

The Fund may make representations to member countries that conditions are favorable for the abandonment of restrictions over foreign exchange transactions, and each member country shall give consideration to such representations.

All member countries agree that all of the local currency holdings of the Fund shall be free from any restrictions as to their use. This provision does not apply to blocked foreign balances acquired by the Fund in accordance with the provisions of V-8, above.

4. To cooperate effectively with other member countries when such countries, with the approval of the Fund, adopt or continue controls for the purpose of regulating international movements of capital. Cooperation shall include, upon recommendation by the Fund, measures that can appropriately be taken, such as:

(a) Not to accept or permit acquisition of deposits, securities, or investments by nationals of any member country imposing restrictions on the export of capital except with the permission of the government of that country and the Fund;

(b) To make available to the Fund or to the government of any member country such information as the Fund considers necessary

on property in the form of deposits, securities and investments of the nationals of the member country imposing the restrictions.

5. Not to enter upon any new bilateral clearing arrangements, nor engage in multiple currency practices, which in the judgment of the Fund would retard the growth of world trade or the international flow of productive capital.

6. To give consideration to the views of the Fund on any existing or proposed monetary or economic policy, the effect of which would be to bring about sooner or later a serious disequilibrium in the balance of payments of other countries.

7. To furnish the Fund with all information it needs for its operations and to furnish such reports as the Fund may require in the form and at the times requested by the Fund.

8. To adopt appropriate legislation or decrees to carry out its undertakings to the Fund.

THE KEYNES PLAN

PROPOSALS FOR AN INTERNATIONAL CLEARING UNION

(April 1943)

PREFACE

Immediately after the war all countries who have been engaged will be concerned with the pressure of relief and urgent reconstruction. The transition out of this into the normal world of the future cannot be wisely effected unless we know into what we are moving. It is therefore not too soon to consider what is to come after. In the field of national activity occupied by production, trade and finance, both the nature of the problem and the experience of the period between the wars suggest four main lines of approach:

1. The mechanism of currency and exchange;

2. The framework of a commercial policy regulating the conditions for the exchange of goods, tariffs, preferences, subsidies, import regulations and the like;

3. The orderly conduct of production, distribution and price of primary products so as to protect both producers and consumers from the loss and risk for which the extravagant fluctuations of market conditions have been responsible in recent times;

4. Investment aid, both medium and long term, for the countries whose economic development needs assistance from outside.

If the principles of these measures and the form of the institutions to give effect to them can be settled in advance, in order that they may be in operation when the need arises, it is possible that taken together they may help the world to control the ebb and flow of the tides of economic activity which have, in the past, destroyed security of livelihood and endangered international peace.

All these matters will need to be handled in due course. The proposal that follows relates only to the mechanism of currency and exchange in international trading. It appears on the whole convenient to give it priority, because some general conclusions have to be reached under this head before much progress can be made with the other topics.

In preparing these proposals care has been taken to regard certain conditions, which the groundwork of an international economic system to be set up after the war should satisfy, if it is to prove durable:

(i) There should be the least possible interference with internal national policies, and the plan should not wander from the international *terrain*. Since such policies may have important repercussions on international relations, they cannot be left out of account. Nevertheless in the realm of internal policy the authority of the Governing Board of the proposed Institution should be limited to recommendations, or at the most to imposing conditions for the more extended enjoyment of the facilities which the Institution offers.

(ii) The technique of the plan must be capable of application, irrespective of the type and principle of government and economic policy existing in the prospective member States.

(iii) The management of the Institution must be genuinely international without preponderant power of veto or enforcement to any country or group; and the rights and privileges of the smaller countries must be safeguarded.

(iv) Some qualification of the right to act at pleasure is required by any agreement or treaty between nations. But in order that such arrangements may be fully voluntary so long as they last and terminable when they have become irksome, provision must be made for voiding the obligation at due notice. If many member States were to take advantage of this, the plan would have broken down. But if they are free to escape from its provisions if necessary they may be the more willing to go on accepting them.

(v) The plan must operate not only to the general advantage but also to the individual advantage of each of the participants, and must not require a special economic or financial sacrifice from certain countries. No participant must be asked to do or offer anything which is not to his own true long-term interest.

It must be emphasised that it is not for the Clearing Union to assume the burden of long term lending which is the proper task of some other institution. It is also necessary for it to have means of restraining improvident borrowers. But the Clearing Union must also seek to discourage creditor countries from leaving unused large liquid balances which ought to be devoted to some positive purpose. For excessive credit balances necessarily create excessive debit balances for some other party. In recognising that the creditor as well as the debtor may be responsible for a want of balance, the proposed institution would be breaking new ground.

I.—THE OBJECTS OF THE PLAN

About the primary objects of an improved system of International Currency there is, to-day, a wide measure of agreement:—

(a) We need an instrument of international currency having general acceptability between nations, so that blocked balances and bilateral clearings are unnecessary; that is to say, an instrument of currency used by each nation in its transactions with other nations, operating through whatever national organ, such as a Treasury or a Central Bank, is most appropriate, private individuals, businesses and banks other than Central Banks, each continuing to use their own national currency as heretofore.

(b) We need an orderly and agreed method of determining the relative exchange values of national currency units, so that unilateral action and competitive exchange depreciations are prevented.

(c) We need a *quantum* of international currency, which is neither determined in an unpredictable and irrelevant manner as, for example, by the technical progress of the gold industry, nor subject to large variations depending on the gold reserve policies of individual countries; but is governed by the actual current requirements of world commerce, and is also capable of deliberate expansion and contraction to offset deflationary and inflationary tendencies in effective world demand.

(d) We need a system possessed of an internal stabilising mechanism, by which pressure is exercised on any country whose balance of payments with the rest of the world is departing from equilibrium in *either direction*, so as to prevent movements which must create for its neighbours an equal but opposite want of balance.

(e) We need an agreed plan for starting off every country after the war with a stock of reserves appropriate to its importance in world commerce, so that without due anxiety it can set its house in order during the transitional period to full peace-time conditions.

(f) We need a central institution, of a purely technical and non-political character, to aid and support other international institutions concerned with the planning and regulation of the world's economic life.

(g) More generally, we need a means of reassurance to a troubled world, by which any country whose own affairs are conducted with due prudence is relieved of anxiety for causes which are not of its own making, concerning its ability to meet its international liabilities; and which will, therefore, make unnecessary those methods of restriction and discrimination which countries have adopted hitherto, not on their merits, but as measures of self-protection from disruptive outside forces.

2. There is also a growing measure of agreement about the general character of any solution of the problem likely to be successful. The particular proposals set forth below lay no claim to originality. They are an attempt to reduce to practical shape certain general ideas belonging to the contemporary climate of economic opinion, which have been given publicity in recent months by writers of several different nationalities. It is difficult to see how any plan can be successful which does not use these general ideas, which are born of the spirit of the age. The actual details put forward below are offered, with no dogmatic intention, as the basis of discussion for criticism and improvement. For we cannot make progress without embodying the general underlying idea in a frame of actual working, which will bring out the practical and political difficulties to be faced and met if the breath of life is to inform it.

3. In one respect this particular plan will be found to be more ambitious and yet, at the same time, perhaps more workable than some of the variant versions of the same basic idea, in that it is fully

international, being based on one general agreement and not on a multiplicity of bilateral arrangements. Doubtless proposals might be made by which bilateral arrangements could be fitted together so as to obtain some of the advantages of a multilateral scheme. But there will be many difficulties attendant on such adjustments. It may be doubted whether a comprehensive scheme will ever in fact be worked out, unless it can come into existence through a single act of creation made possible by the unity of purpose and energy of hope for better things to come, springing from the victory of the United Nations, when they have attained it, over immediate evil. That these proposals are ambitious is claimed, therefore to be not a drawback but an advantage.

4. The proposal is to establish a Currency Union, here designated an *International Clearing Union,* based on international bank-money, called (let us say) *bancor,* fixed (but not unalterably) in terms of gold and accepted as the equivalent of gold by the British Commonwealth and the United States and all the other members of the Union for the purpose of settling international balances. The Central Banks of all member States (and also of non-members) would keep accounts with the International Clearing Union through which they would be entitled to settle their exchange balances with one another at their par value as defined in terms of bancor. Countries having a favourable balance of payments with the rest of the world as a whole would find themselves in possession of a credit account with the Clearing Union, and those having an unfavourable balance would have a debit account. Measures would be necessary (see below) to prevent the piling up of credit and debit balances without limit, and the system would have failed in the long run if it did not possess sufficient capacity for self-equilibrium to secure this.

5. The idea underlying such a Union is simple, namely, to generalise the essential principle of banking as it is exhibited within any closed system. This principle is the necessary equality of credits and debits. If no credits can be removed outside the clearing system, but only transferred within it, the Union can never be in any difficulty as regards the honouring of cheques drawn upon it. It can make what advances it wishes to any of its members with the assurance that the proceeds can only be transferred to the clearing account of another member. Its sole task is to see to it that its

members keep the rules and that the advances made to each of them are prudent and advisable for the Union as a whole.

<h2 style="text-align:center">II.—THE PROVISIONS OF THE PLAN</h2>

6. The provisions proposed (the particular proportions and other details suggested being tentative as a basis of discussion) are the following:—

(1) All the United Nations will be invited to become original members of the International Clearing Union. Other States may be invited to join subsequently. If ex-enemy States are invited to join, special conditions may be applied to them.

(2) The Governing Board of the Clearing Union shall be appointed by the Governments of the several member States (as provided in (12) below); the daily business with the Union and the technical arrangements being carried out through their Central Banks or other appropriate authorities.

(3) The member States will agree between themselves the initial values of their own currencies in terms of bancor. A member State may not subsequently alter the value of its currency in terms of bancor without the permission of the Governing Board except under the conditions stated below; but during the first five years after the inception of the system the Governing Board shall give special consideration to appeals for an adjustment in the exchange value of a national currency unit on the ground of unforeseen circumstances.

(4) The value of bancor in terms of gold shall be fixed by the Governing Board. Member States shall not purchase or acquire gold, directly or indirectly, at a price in terms of their national currencies in excess of the parity which corresponds to the value of their currency in terms of bancor and to the value of bancor in terms of gold. Their sales and purchases of gold shall not be otherwise restricted.

(5) Each member State shall have assigned to it a *quota*, which shall determine the measure of its responsibility in the management of the Union and of its right to enjoy the credit facilities provided by the Union. The initial quotas might be fixed by reference to the sum of each country's exports and imports on the average of (say) the three pre-war years, and might be (say) 75 per cent. of this amount, a special assessment being substituted in cases (of which there might be several) where this formula would be, for any reason, inappropriate. Subsequently, after the elapse of the transitional period, the quotas should be revised annually in accor-

dance with the running average of each country's actual volume of trade in the three preceding years, rising to a five-year average when figures for five post-war years are available. The determination of a country's quota primarily by reference to the value of its foreign trade seems to offer the criterion most relevant to a plan which is chiefly concerned with the regulation of the foreign exchanges and of a country's international trade balance. It is, however, a matter for discussion whether the formula for fixing quotas should also take account of other factors.

(6) Member States shall agree to accept payment of currency balances, due to them from other members, by a transfer of bancor to their credit in the books of the Clearing Union. They shall be entitled, subject to the conditions set forth below, to make transfers of bancor to other members which have the effect of overdrawing their own accounts with the Union, provided that the maximum debit balances thus created do not exceed their quota. The Clearing Union may, at its discretion, charge a small commission or transfer fee in respect of transactions in its books for the purpose of meeting its current expenses or any other outgoings approved by the Governing Board.

(7) A member State shall pay to the Reserve Fund of the Clearing Union a charge of 1 per cent. per annum on the amount of its average balance in bancor, whether it is a credit or a debit balance, in excess of a quarter of its quota; and a further charge of 1 per cent. on its average balance, whether credit or debit, in excess of a half of its quota. Thus, only a country which keeps as nearly as possible in a state of international balance on the average of the year will escape this contribution. These charges are not absolutely essential to the scheme. But if they are found acceptable, they would be valuable and important inducements towards keeping a level balance, and a significant indication that the system looks on excessive credit balances with as critical an eye as on excessive debit balances, each being, indeed, the inevitable concomitant of the other. Any member State in debit may, after consultation with the Governing Board, borrow bancor from the balances of any member State in credit on such terms as may be mutually agreed, by which means each would avoid these contributions. The Governing Board may, at its discretion, remit the charges on credit balances, and increase correspondingly those on debit balances, if in its opinion unduly expansionist conditions are impending in the world economy.

(8) —(a) A member State may not increase its debit balance by more than a quarter of its quota within a year without the permission of the

Governing Board. If its debit balance has exceeded a quarter of its quota on the average of at least two years, it shall be entitled to reduce the value of its currency in terms of bancor provided that the reduction shall not exceed 5 per cent. without the consent of the Governing Board; but it shall not be entitled to repeat this procedure unless the Board is satisfied that this procedure is appropriate.

(b) The Governing Board may require from a member State having a debit balance reaching a *half* of its quota the deposit of suitable collateral against its debit balance. Such collateral shall, at the discretion of the Governing Board, take the form of gold, foreign or domestic currency or Government bonds, within the capacity of the member State. As a condition of allowing a member State to increase its debit balance to a figure in excess of a half of its quota, the Governing Board may require all or any of the following measures:—

(i) a stated reduction in the value of the member's currency, if it deems that to be the suitable remedy;
(ii) the control of outward capital transactions if not already in force; and
(iii) the outright surrender of a suitable proportion of any separate gold or other liquid reserve in reduction of its debit balance.

Furthermore, the Governing Board may recommend to the Government of the member State any internal measures affecting its domestic economy which may appear to be appropriate to restore the equilibrium of its international balance.

(c) If a member State's debit balance has exceeded *three-quarters* of its quota on the average of at least a year and is excessive in the opinion of the Governing Board in relation to the total debit balances outstanding on the books of the Clearing Union, or is increasing at an excessive rate, it may, in addition, be asked by the Governing Board to take measures to improve its position, and, in the event of its failing to reduce its debit balance accordingly within two years, the Governing Board may declare that it is in default and no longer entitled to draw against its account except with the permission of the Governing Board.

(d) Each member State, on joining the system, shall agree to pay to the Clearing Union any payments due from it to a country in default towards the discharge of the latter's debit balance and to accept this arrangement in the event of falling into default itself. A member State which resigns from the Clearing Union without making approved arrangements for the discharge of any debit balance shall also be treated as in default.

(9) A member State whose credit balance has exceeded a *half* of its quota on the average of at least a year shall discuss with the Governing Board (but shall retain the ultimate decision in its own hands) what measures would be appropriate to restore the equilibrium of its international balances, including—

(a) Measures for the expansion of domestic credit and domestic demand.

(b) The appreciation of its local currency in terms of bancor, or, alternatively, the encouragement of an increase in money rates of earnings;

(c) The reduction of tariffs and other discouragements against imports.

(d) International development loans.

(10) A member State shall be entitled to obtain a credit balance in terms of bancor by paying in gold to the Clearing Union for the credit of its clearing account. But no one is entitled to demand gold from the Union against a balance of bancor, since such balance is available only for transfer to another clearing account. The Governing Board of the Union shall, however, have the discretion to distribute any gold in the possession of the Union between the members possessing credit balances in excess of a specified proportion of their quotas, proportionately to such balances, in reduction of their amount in excess of that proportion.

(11) The monetary reserves of a member State, viz., the Central Bank or other bank or Treasury deposits in excess of a working balance, shall not be held in another country except with the approval of the monetary authorities of that country.

(12) The Governing Board shall be appointed by the Governments of the member States, those with the larger quotas being entitled to appoint a member individually, and those with smaller quotas appointing in convenient political or geographical groups, so that the members would not exceed (say) 12 or 15 in number. Each representative on the Governing Board shall have a vote in proportion to the quotas of the State (or States) appointing him, except that on a proposal to increase a particular quota, a representative's voting power shall be measured by the quotas of the member States appointing him, increased by their credit balance or

decreased by their debit balance, averaged in each case over the past two years. Each member State, which is not individually represented on the Governing Board, shall be entitled to appoint a permanent delegate to the Union to maintain contact with the Board and to act as *liaison* for daily business and for the exchange of information with the Executive of the Union. Such delegate shall be entitled to be present at the Governing Board when any matter is under consideration which specially concerns the State he represents, and to take part in the discussion.

(13) The Governing Board shall be entitled to reduce the quotas of members, all in the same specified proportion, if it seems necessary to correct in this manner an excess of world purchasing power. In that event, the provisions of 6 (8) shall be held to apply to the quotas as so reduced, provided that no member shall be required to reduce his actual overdraft at the date of the change, or be entitled by reason of this reduction to alter the value of his currency under 6 (8) (a), except after the expiry of two years. If the Governing Board subsequently desires to correct a potential deficiency of world purchasing power, it shall be entitled to restore the general level of quotas towards the original level.

(14) The Governing Board shall be entitled to ask and receive from each member State any relevant statistical or other information, including a full disclosure of gold, external credit and debit balances and other external assets and liabilities, both public and private. So far as circumstances permit, it will be desirable that the member States shall consult with the Governing Board on important matters of policy likely to affect substantially their bancor balances or their financial relations with other members.

(15) Executive offices of the Union shall be situated in London and New York, with the Governing Board meeting alternately in London and Washington.

(16) Members shall be entitled to withdraw from the Union on a year's notice, subject to their making satisfactory arrangements to discharge any debit balance. They would not, of course, be able to employ any credit balance except by making transfers from it, either before or after their withdrawal, to the Clearing Accounts of other Central Banks. Similarly, it should be within the power of the Governing Board to require the withdrawal of a member, subject to the same notice, if the latter is in breach of agreements relating to the Clearing Union.

(17) The Central Banks of non-member States would be allowed to keep credit clearing accounts with the Union; and, indeed, it would be advisable

for them to do so for the conduct of their trade with member States. But they would have no right to overdrafts and no say in the management.

(18) The Governing Board shall make an annual Report and shall convene an annual Assembly at which every member State shall be entitled to be represented individually and to move proposals. The principles and governing rules of the Union shall be the subject of reconsideration after five years' experience, if a majority of the Assembly desire it.

III.—WHAT LIABILITIES OUGHT THE PLAN TO PLACE ON CREDITOR COUNTRIES?

7. It is not contemplated that either the debit or the credit balance of an individual country ought to exceed a certain maximum—let us say, its quota. In the case of debit balances this maximum has been made a rigid one, and, indeed, counter-measures are called for long before the maximum is reached. In the case of credit balances no rigid maximum has been proposed. For the appropriate provision might be to require the eventual cancellation or compulsory investment of persistent bancor credit balances accumulating in excess of a member's quota; and, however desirable this may be in principle, it might be felt to impose on creditor countries a heavier burden than they can be asked to accept before having had experience of the benefit to them of the working of the plan as a whole. If, on the other hand, the limitation were to take the form of the creditor country not being required to accept bancor in excess of a prescribed figure, this might impair the general acceptability of bancor, whilst at the same time conferring no real benefit on the creditor country itself. For, if it chose to avail itself of the limitation, it must either restrict its exports or be driven back on some form of bilateral payments agreements outside the Clearing Union, thus substituting a less acceptable asset for bancor balances which are based on the collective credit of all the member States and are available for payments to any of them, or attempt the probably temporary expedient of refusing to trade except on a gold basis.

8. The absence of a rigid maximum to credit balances does not impose on any member State, as might be supposed at first sight, an unlimited liability outside its own control. The liability of an individual member is determined, not by the quotas of the other members, but by its own policy in controlling its favourable balance of payments. The existence of the Clearing Union does not deprive a member State of any of the facilities which it now possesses for receiving payment for its exports. In the absence

of the Clearing Union a creditor country can employ the proceeds of its exports to buy goods or to buy investments, or to make temporary advances and to hold temporary overseas balances, or to buy gold in the market. All these facilities will remain at its disposal. The difference is that in the absence of the Clearing Union, more or less automatic factors come into play to restrict the volume of its exports after the above means of receiving payment for them have been exhausted. Certain countries become unable to buy and, in addition to this, there is an automatic tendency towards a general slump in international trade and, as a result, a reduction in the exports of the creditor country. Thus, the effect of the Clearing Union is to give the creditor country a choice between voluntarily curtailing its exports to the same extent that they would have been involuntarily curtailed in the absence of the Clearing Union, or, alternatively, of allowing its exports to continue and accumulating the excess receipts in the form of bancor balances for the time being. Unless the removal of a factor causing the involuntary reduction of exports is reckoned a disadvantage, a creditor country incurs no burden but is, on the contrary, relieved, by being offered the additional option of receiving payment for its exports through the accumulation of a bancor balance.

9. If, therefore, a member State asks what governs the maximum liability which it incurs by entering the system, the answer is that this lies entirely within its own control. No more is asked of it than that it should hold in bancor such surplus of its favourable balance of payments as it does not itself choose to employ in any other way, and only for so long as it does not so choose.

IV.—SOME ADVANTAGES OF THE PLAN

10. The plan aims at the substitution of an expansionist, in place of a contractionist, pressure on world trade.

11. It effects this by allowing to each member State overdraft facilities of a defined amount. Thus each country is allowed a certain margin of resources and a certain interval of time within which to effect a balance in its economic relations with the rest of the world. These facilities are made possible by the constitution of the system itself and do not involve particular indebtedness between one member State and another. A country is in credit or debit with the Clearing Union as a whole. This means that the overdraft facilities, whilst a relief to some, are not a real burden to others. For the accumulation of a credit balance with the Clearing Union would

resemble the importation of gold in signifying that the country holding it is abstaining voluntarily from the immediate use of purchasing power. But it would not involve, as would the importation of gold, the withdrawal of this purchasing power from circulation or the exercise of a deflationary and contractionist pressure on the whole world, including in the end the creditor country itself. Under the proposed plan, therefore, no country suffers injury (but on the contrary) by the fact that the command over resources, which it does not itself choose to employ for the time being, is not withdrawn from use. The accumulation of bancor credit does not curtail in the least its capacity or inducement either to produce or to consume.

12. In short, the analogy with a national banking system is complete. No depositor in a local bank suffers because the balances, which he leaves idle, are employed to finance the business of someone else. Just as the development of national banking systems served to offset a deflationary pressure which would have prevented otherwise the development of modern industry, so by extending the same principle into the international field we may hope to offset the contractionist pressure which might otherwise overwhelm in social disorder and disappointment the good hopes of our modern world. The substitution of a credit mechanism in place of hoarding would have repeated in the international field the same miracle, already performed in the domestic field, of turning a stone into bread.

13. There might be other ways of effecting the same objects temporarily or in part. For example, the United States might redistribute her gold. Or there might be a number of bilateral arrangements having the effect of providing international overdrafts, as, for example, an agreement by the Federal Reserve Board to accumulate, if necessary, a large sterling balance at the Bank of England, accompanied by a great number of similar bilateral arrangements, amounting to some hundreds altogether, between these and all the other banks in the world. The objection to particular arrangements of this kind, in addition to their greater complexity, is that they are likely to be influenced by extraneous, political reasons; that they put individual countries in a position of particular obligation towards others; and that the distribution of the assistance between different countries may not correspond to need and to the real requirements, which are extremely difficult to foresee.

14. It should be much easier, and surely more satisfactory for all of us, to enter into a general and collective responsibility, applying to all countries

alike, that a country finding itself in a creditor position *against the rest of the world as a whole* should enter into an arrangement not to allow this credit balance to exercise a contractionist pressure against the world economy and, by repercussion, against the economy of the creditor country itself. This would give everyone the great assistance of multilateral clearing, whereby (for example) Great Britain could offset favourable balances arising out of her exports to Europe against unfavourable balances due to the United States or South America or elsewhere. How, indeed, can any country hope to start up trade with Europe during the relief and reconstruction period on any other terms?

15. The facilities offered will be of particular importance in the transitional period after the war, as soon as the initial shortages of supply have been overcome. Many countries will find a difficulty in paying for their imports, and will need time and resources before they can establish a readjustment. The efforts of each of these debtor countries to preserve its own equilibrium, by forcing its exports and by cutting off all imports which are not strictly necessary, will aggravate the problems of all the others. On the other hand, if each feels free from undue pressure, the volume of international exchange will be increased and everyone will find it easier to re-establish equilibrium without injury to the standard of life anywhere. The creditor countries will benefit, hardly less than the debtors, by being given an interval of *time* in which to adjust their economies, during which they can safely move at their own pace without the result of exercising deflationary pressure on the rest of the world, and, by repercussion, on themselves.

16. It must, however, be emphasised that the provision by which the members of the Clearing Union start with substantial overdraft facilities in hand will be mainly useful, just as the possession of any kind of reserve is useful, to allow time and method for necessary adjustments and a comfortable safeguard behind which the unforeseen and the unexpected can be faced with equanimity. Obviously, it does not by itself provide any long-term solution against a continuing disequilibrium, for in due course the more improvident and the more impecunious, left to themselves, would have run through their resources. But, if the purpose of the overdraft facilities is mainly to give time for adjustments, we have to make sure, so far as possible, that they *will* be made. We must have, therefore, some rules and some machinery to secure that equilibrium is restored. A tentative attempt to provide for this has been made above. Perhaps it might be strengthened and improved.

17. The provisions suggested differ in one important respect from the pre-war system because they aim at putting some part of the responsibility for adjustment on the creditor country as well as on the debtor. This is an attempt to recover one of the advantages which were enjoyed in the nineteenth century, when a flow of gold due to a favourable balance in favour of London and Paris, which were then the main creditor centres, immediately produced an expansionist pressure and increased foreign lending in those markets, but which has been lost since New York succeeded to the position of main creditor, as a result of gold movements failing in their effect, of the breakdown of international borrowing and of the frequent flight of loose funds from one depository to another. The object is that the creditor should not be allowed to remain entirely passive. For if he is, an intolerably heavy task may be laid on the debtor country, which is already for that very reason in the weaker position.

18. If, indeed, a country lacks the productive capacity to maintain its standard of life, then a reduction in this standard is not avoidable. If its wage and price levels in terms of money are out of line with those elsewhere, a change in the rate of its foreign exchange is inevitable. But if, possessing the productive capacity, it lacks markets because of restrictive policies throughout the world, then the remedy lies in expanding its opportunities for export by removal of the restrictive pressure. We are too ready to-day to assume the inevitability of unbalanced trade positions, thus making the opposite error to those who assumed the tendency of exports and imports to equality. It used to be supposed, without sufficient reason, that effective demand is always properly adjusted throughout the world; we now tend to assume, equally without sufficient reason, that it never can be. On the contrary, there is great force in the contention that, if active employment and ample purchasing power can be sustained in the main centres of the world trade, the problem of surpluses and unwanted exports will largely disappear, even though, under the most prosperous conditions, there may remain some disturbances of trade and unforeseen situations requiring special remedies.

V.—THE DAILY MANAGEMENT OF THE EXCHANGES UNDER THE PLAN

19. The Clearing Union restores unfettered multilateral clearing between its members. Compare this with the difficulties and complications of a large number of bilateral agreements. Compare, above all, the provisions by which a country, taking improper advantage of a payments

agreement (for the system is, in fact, a *generalised* payments agreement), as Germany did before the war, is dealt with not by a single country (which may not be strong enough to act effectively in isolation or cannot afford to incur the diplomatic odium of isolated action), but by the system as a whole. If the argument is used that the Clearing Union may have difficulty in disciplining a misbehaving country and in avoiding consequential loss, with what much greater force can we urge this objection against a multiplicity of separate bilateral payments agreements.

20. Thus we should not only obtain the advantages, without the disadvantages, of an international gold currency, but we might enjoy these advantages more widely than was ever possible in practice with the old system under which at any given time only a minority of countries were actually working with free exchanges. In conditions of multilateral clearing, exchange dealings would be carried on as freely as in the best days of the gold standard, without its being necessary to ask anyone to accept special or onerous conditions.

21. The principles governing transactions are: first, that the Clearing Union is set up, not for the transaction of daily business between individual traders or banks, but for the clearing and settlement of the ultimate outstanding balances between Central Banks (and certain other supernational Institutions), such as would have been settled under the old gold standard by the shipment or the earmarking of gold, and should not trespass unnecessarily beyond this field; and, second, that its purpose is to increase *freedom* in international commerce and not to multiply interferences or compulsions.

22. Many Central Banks have found great advantage in centralising with themselves or with an Exchange Control the supply and demand of all foreign exchange, thus dispensing with an outside exchange market, though continuing to accommodate individuals through the existing banks and not directly. The further extension of such arrangements would be consonant with the general purposes of the Clearing Union, inasmuch as they would promote order and discipline in international exchange transactions in detail as well as in general. The same is true of the control of Capital Movements, further described below, which many States are likely to wish to impose on their own nationals. But the structure of the proposed Clearing Union does not *require* such measures of centralisation or of control on the part of a member State. It is, for example, consistent alike with the type of Exchange Control now established in the United Kingdom

or with the system now operating in the United States. The Union does not prevent private holdings of foreign currency or private dealings in exchange or international capital movements, if these have been approved or allowed by the member States concerned. Central Banks can deal direct with one another as heretofore. No transaction in bancor will take place except when a member State or its Central Bank is exercising the right to pay in it. In no case is there any direct control of capital movements by the Union, even in the case of 6 (8) (*b*) (ii) above, but only by the member States themselves through their own institutions. Thus the fabric of international banking organisation, built up by long experience to satisfy practical needs, would be left as undisturbed as possible.

23. It is not necessary to interfere with the discretion of countries which desire to maintain a special intimacy within a particular group of countries associated by geographical or political ties, such as the existing sterling area, or groups, like the Latin Union of former days, which may come into existence covering, for example, the countries of North America or those of South America, or the groups now under active discussion, including Poland and Czechoslovakia or certain of the Balkan States. There is no reason why such countries should not be allowed a double position, both as members of the Clearing Union in their own right with their proper quota, and also as making use of another financial centre along traditional lines, as, for example, Australia and India with London, or certain American countries with New York. In this case, their accounts with the Clearing Union would be in exactly the same position as the independent gold reserves which they now maintain, and they would have no occasion to modify in any way their present practices in the conduct of daily business.

24. There might be other cases, however, in which a dependency or a member of a federal union would merge its currency identity in that of a mother country, with a quota appropriately adjusted to the merged currency area as a whole, and not enjoy a separate individual membership of the Clearing Union, as, for example, the States of a Federal Union, the French colonies or the British Crown Colonies.

25. At the same time countries, which do not belong to a special geographical or political group, would be expected to keep their reserve balances with the Clearing Union and not with one another. It has, therefore, been laid down that balances may not be held in another country except with the approval of the monetary authorities of that country; and, in order that sterling and dollars might not appear to

compete with bancor for the purpose of reserve balances, the United Kingdom and the United States might agree together that they would not accept the reserve balances of other countries in excess of normal working balances except in the case of banks definitely belonging to a Sterling Area or Dollar Area group.

VI.—THE POSITION OF GOLD UNDER THE PLAN

26. Gold still possesses great psychological value which is not being diminished by current events; and the desire to possess a gold reserve against unforeseen contingencies is likely to remain. Gold also has the merit of providing in point of form (whatever the underlying realities may be) an uncontroversial standard of value for international purposes, for which it would not yet be easy to find a serviceable substitute. Moreover, by supplying an automatic means for settling some part of the favourable balances of the creditor countries, the current gold production of the world and the remnant of gold reserves held outside the United States may still have a useful part to play. Nor is it reasonable to ask the United States to de-monetise the stock of gold which is the basis of its impregnable liquidity. What, in the long run, the world may decide to do with gold is another matter. The purpose of the Clearing Union is to supplant gold as a governing factor, but not to dispense with it.

27. The international bank-money which we have designated *bancor* is defined in terms of a weight of gold. Since the national currencies of the member States are given a defined exchange value in terms of bancor, it follows that they would each have a defined gold content which would be their official buying price for gold, above which they must not pay. The fact that a member State is entitled to obtain a credit in terms of bancor by paying actual gold to the credit of its clearing account, secures a steady and ascertained purchaser for the output of the gold-producing countries, and for countries holding a large reserve of gold. Thus the position of producers and holders of gold is not affected adversely, and is, indeed, improved.

28. Central Banks would be entitled to retain their separate gold reserves and ship gold to one another, provided they did not pay a price above parity; they could coin gold and put it into circulation, and, generally speaking, do what they liked with it.

29. One limitation only would be, for obvious reasons, essential. No member State would be entitled to demand gold from the Clearing Union

against its balance of bancor; for bancor is available only for transfer to another clearing account. Thus between gold and bancor itself there would be a one-way convertibility, such as ruled frequently before the war with national currencies which were on what was called a "gold exchange standard." This need not mean that the Clearing Union would only receive gold and never pay it out. It has been provided above that, if the Clearing Union finds itself in possession of a stock of gold, the Governing Board shall have discretion to distribute the surplus between those possessing credit balances in bancor, proportionately to such balances in reduction of their amount.

30. The question has been raised whether these arrangements are compatible with the retention by individual member States of a full gold standard with two-way convertibility, so that, for example, any foreign central bank acquiring dollars could use them to obtain gold for export. It is not evident that a good purpose would be served by this. But it need not be prohibited, and if any member State should prefer to maintain full convertibility for internal purposes it could protect itself from any abuse of the system or inconvenient consequences by providing that gold could only be exported under licence.

31. The value of bancor in terms of gold is fixed but not unalterably. The power to vary its value might have to be exercised if the stocks of gold tendered to the Union were to be excessive. No object would be served by attempting further to peer into the future or to prophesy the ultimate outcome.

VII.—THE CONTROL OF CAPITAL MOVEMENTS

32. There is no country which can, in future, safely allow the flight of funds for political reasons or to evade domestic taxation or in anticipation of the owner turning refugee. Equally, there is no country that can safely receive fugitive funds, which constitute an unwanted import of capital, yet cannot safely be used for fixed investment.

33. For these reasons it is widely held that control of capital movements, both inward and outward, should be a permanent feature of the post-war system. It is an objection to this that control, if it is to be effective, probably requires the machinery of exchange control for all transactions, even though a general permission is given to all remittances in respect of current trade. Thus those countries which have for the time

being no reason to fear, and may indeed welcome, outward capital movements, may be reluctant to impose this machinery, even though a general permission for capital, as well as current, transactions reduces it to being no more than a machinery of record. On the other hand, such control will be more difficult to work by unilateral action on the part of those countries which cannot afford to dispense with it, especially in the absence of a postal censorship, if movements of capital cannot be controlled *at both ends*. It would, therefore, be of great advantage if the United States, as well as other members of the Clearing Union, would adopt machinery similar to that which the British Exchange Control has now gone a long way towards perfecting. Nevertheless, the universal establishment of a control of capital movements cannot be regarded as essential to the operation of the Clearing Union; and the method and degree of such control should therefore be left to the decision of each member State. Some less drastic way might be found by which countries, not themselves controlling outward capital movements, can deter inward movements not approved by the countries from which they originate.

34. The position of abnormal balances in overseas ownership held in various countries at the end of the war presents a problem of considerable importance and special difficulty. A country in which a large volume of such balances is held could not, unless it is in a creditor position, afford the risk of having to redeem them in bancor on a substantial scale, if this would have the effect of depleting its bancor resources at the outset. At the same time, it is very desirable that the countries owning these balances should be able to regard them as liquid, at any rate over and above the amounts which they can afford to lock up under an agreed programme of funding or long-term expenditure. Perhaps there should be some special over-riding provision for dealing with the transitional period only by which, through the aid of the Clearing Union, such balances would remain liquid and convertible into bancor by the creditor country whilst there would be no corresponding strain on the bancor resources of the debtor country, or, at any rate, the resulting strain would be spread over a period.

35. The advocacy of a control of capital movements must not be taken to mean that the era of international investment should be brought to an end. On the contrary, the system contemplated should greatly facilitate the restoration of international loans and credits for legitimate purposes. The object, and it is a vital object, is to have a means—

(a) of distinguishing long-term loans by creditor countries, which help to maintain equilibrium and develop the world's resources, from movements of funds out of debtor countries which lack the means to finance them; and

(b) of controlling short-term speculative movements or flights of currency whether out of debtor countries or from one creditor country to another.

36. It should be emphasised that the purpose of the overdrafts of bancor permitted by the Clearing Union is, not to facilitate long-term, or even medium-term, credits to be made by debtor countries which cannot afford them, but to allow time and a breathing space for adjustments and for averaging one period with another to all member States alike, whether in the long run they are well-placed to develop a forward international loan policy or whether their prospects of profitable new development in excess of their own resources justifies them in long-term borrowing. The machinery and organisation of international medium-term and long-term lending is another aspect of post-war economic policy, not less important than the purposes which the Clearing Union seeks to serve, but requiring another, complementary institution.

VIII.—RELATION OF THE CLEARING UNION TO COMMERCIAL POLICY

37. The special protective expedients which were developed between the two wars were sometimes due to political, social or industrial reasons. But frequently they were nothing more than forced and undesired dodges to protect an unbalanced position of a country's overseas payments. The new system, by helping to provide a register of the size and whereabouts of the aggregate debtor and creditor positions respectively, and an indication whether it is reasonable for a particular country to adopt special expedients as a temporary measure to assist in regaining equilibrium in its balance of payments, would make it possible to establish a general rule not to adopt them, subject to the indicated exceptions.

38. The existence of the Clearing Union would make it possible for member States contracting commercial agreements to use their respective debit and credit positions with the Clearing Union as a test, though this test by itself would not be complete. Thus, the contracting parties, whilst agreeing to clauses in a commercial agreement forbidding, in general, the use of certain measures or expedients in their mutual trade relations, might

make this agreement subject to special relaxations if the state of their respective clearing accounts satisfied an agreed criterion. For example, an agreement might provide that, in the event of one of the contracting States having a debit balance with the Clearing Union exceeding a specified proportion of its quota on the average of a period it should be free to resort to import regulation or to barter trade agreements or to higher import duties of a type which was restricted under the agreement in normal circumstances. Protected by the possibility of such temporary indulgences, the members of the Clearing Union should feel much more confidence in moving towards the withdrawal of other and more dislocating forms of protection and discrimination and in accepting the prohibition of the worst of them from the outset. In any case, it should be laid down that members of the Union would not allow or suffer among themselves any restrictions on the disposal of receipts arising out of current trade or "invisible" income.

IX.—THE USE OF THE CLEARING UNION FOR OTHER INTERNATIONAL PURPOSES

39. The Clearing Union might become the instrument and the support of international policies in addition to those which it is its primary purpose to promote. This deserves the greatest possible emphasis. The Union might become the pivot of the future economic government of the world. Without it, other more desirable developments will find themselves impeded and unsupported. With it, they will fall into their place as parts of an ordered scheme. No one of the following suggestions is a necessary part of the plan. But they are illustrations of the additional purposes of high importance and value which the Union, once established, might be able to serve:—

(1) The Union might set up a clearing account in favour of international bodies charged with post-war relief, rehabilitation and reconstruction. But it could go much further than this. For it might supplement contributions received from other sources by granting preliminary overdraft facilities in favour of these bodies, the overdraft being discharged over a period of years out of the Reserve Fund of the Union, or, if necessary, out of a levy on surplus credit balances. So far as this method is adopted it would be possible to avoid asking any country to assume a burdensome commitment for relief and reconstruction, since the resources would be provided in the first instance by those

countries having credit clearing accounts for which they have no immediate use and are voluntarily leaving idle, and in the long run by those countries which have a chronic international surplus for which they have no beneficial employment.

(2) The Union might set up an account in favour of any supernational policing body which may be charged with the duty of preserving the peace and maintaining international order. If any country were to infringe its properly authorised orders, the policing body might be entitled to request the Governors of the Clearing Union to hold the clearing account of the delinquent country to its order and permit no further transactions on the account except by its authority. This would provide an excellent machinery for enforcing a financial blockade.

(3) The Union might set up an account in favour of international bodies charged with the management of a Commodity Control, and might finance stocks of commodities held by such bodies, allowing them overdraft facilities on their accounts up to an agreed maximum. By this means the financial problem of buffer stocks and "ever-normal granaries" could be effectively attacked.

(4) The Union might be linked up with a Board for International Investment. It might act on behalf of such a Board and collect for them the annual service of their loans by automatically debiting the clearing account of the country concerned. The statistics of the clearing accounts of the member-States would give a reliable indication as to which countries were in a position to finance the Investment Board, with the advantage of shifting the whole system of clearing credits and debits nearer to equilibrium.

(5) There are various methods by which the Clearing Union could use its influence and its powers to maintain stability of prices and to control the Trade Cycle. If an International Economic Board is established, this Board and the Clearing Union might be expected to work in close collaboration to their mutual advantage. If an International Investment or Development Corporation is also set up together with a scheme of Commodity Controls for the control of stocks of the staple primary products, we might come to possess in these three Institutions a powerful means of combating the evils of the Trade Cycle, by exercising contractionist or expansionist influence on the system as a whole or on particular sections. This is a large and important question which cannot be discussed adequately in this paper; and need not be examined

at length in this place because it does not raise any important issues affecting the fundamental constitution of the proposed Union. It is mentioned here to complete the picture of the wider purposes which the foundation of the Clearing Union might be made to serve.

40. The facility of applying the Clearing Union plan to these several purposes arises out of a fundamental characteristic which is worth pointing out, since it distinguishes the plan from those proposals which try to develop the same basic principle along bilateral lines and is one of the grounds on which the Plan can claim superior merit. This might be described as its "anonymous" or "impersonal" quality. No particular member States have to engage their own resources as such to the support of other particular States or of any of the international projects or policies adopted. They have only to agree in general that, if they find themselves with surplus resources which for the time being they do not themselves wish to employ, these resources may go into the general pool and be put to work on approved purposes. This costs the surplus country nothing because it is not asked to part permanently, or even for any specified period, with such resources, which it remains free to expend and employ for its own purposes whenever it chooses; in which case the burden of finance is passed on to the next recipient, again for only so long as the recipient has no use for the money. As pointed out above, this merely amounts to extending to the international sphere the methods of any domestic banking system, which are in the same sense "impersonal" inasmuch as there is no call on the particular depositor either to support as such the purposes for which his banker makes advances or to forgo permanently the use of his deposit. There is no countervailing objection except that which applies equally to the technique of domestic banking, namely that it is capable of the abuse of creating excessive purchasing power and hence an inflation of prices. In our efforts to avoid the opposite evil, we must not lose sight of this risk, to which there is an allusion in 39 (5) above. But it is no more reason for refusing the advantages of international banking than the similar risk in the domestic field is a reason to return to the practices of the seventeenth century goldsmiths (which are what we are still following in the international field) and to forgo the vast expansion of production which banking principles have made possible. Where financial contributions are required for some purpose of general advantage, it is a great facility not to have to ask for specific contributions from any named country, but to depend

rather on the anonymous and impersonal aid of the system as a whole. We have here a genuine organ of truly international government.

X.—THE TRANSITIONAL ARRANGEMENTS

41. It would be of great advantage to agree the general principles of the Clearing Union before the end of the war, with a view to bringing it into operation at an early date after the termination of hostilities. Major plans will be more easily brought to birth in the first energy of victory and whilst the active spirit of united action still persists, than in the days of exhaustion and reaction from so much effort which may well follow a little later. Such a proposal presents, however, something of a dilemma. On the one hand, many countries will be in particular need of reserves of overseas resources in the period immediately after the war. On the other hand, goods will be in short supply and the prevention of inflationary international conditions of much more importance for the time being than the opposite. The expansionist tendency of the plan, which is a leading recommendation of it as soon as peace-time output is restored and the productive capacity of the world is in running order, might be a danger in the early days of a sellers' market and an excess of demand over supply.

42. A reconciliation of these divergent purposes is not easily found until we know more than is known at present about the means to be adopted to finance post-war relief and reconstruction. If the intention is to provide resources on liberal and comprehensive lines outside the resources made available by the Clearing Union and additional to them, it might be better for such specific aid to take the place of the proposed overdrafts during the "relief" period of (say) two years. In this case credit clearing balances would be limited to the amount of gold delivered to the Union, and the overdraft facilities created by the Union in favour of the Relief Council, the International Investment Board or the Commodity Controls. Nevertheless, the immediate establishment of the Clearing Union would not be incompatible with provisional arrangements, which could take alternative forms according to the character of the other "relief" arrangements, qualifying and limiting the overdraft quotas. Overdraft quotas might be allowed on a reduced scale during the transitional period. Or it might be proper to provide that countries in receipt of relief or Lend-Lease assistance should not have access at the same time to overdraft facilities, and that the latter should only become available when the former had come to an end. If, on the other hand, relief from outside sources looks like

being inadequate from the outset, the overdraft quotas may be even more necessary at the outset than later on.

43. We must not be over-cautious. A rapid economic restoration may lighten the tasks of the diplomatists and the politicians in the resettlement of the world and the restoration of social order. For Great Britain and other countries outside the "relief" areas the possibility of exports sufficient to sustain their standard of life is bound up with good and expanding markets. We cannot afford to wait too long for this, and we must not allow excessive caution to condemn us to perdition. Unless the Union is a going concern, the problem of proper "timing" will be nearly insoluble. It is sufficient at this stage to point out that the problem of timing must not be overlooked, but that the Union is capable of being used so as to aid rather than impede its solution.

XI.—CONCLUSION

44. It has been suggested that so ambitious a proposal is open to criticism on the ground that it requires from the members of the Union a greater surrender of their sovereign rights than they will readily concede. But no greater surrender is required than in a commercial treaty. The obligations will be entered into voluntarily and can be terminated on certain conditions by giving notice.

45. A greater readiness to accept super-national arrangements must be required in the post-war world. If the arrangements proposed can be described as a measure of financial disarmament, there is nothing here which we need be reluctant to accept ourselves or to ask of others. It is an advantage, and not a disadvantage, of the scheme that it invites the member States to abandon that licence to promote indiscipline, disorder and bad-neighbourliness which, to the general disadvantage, they have been free to exercise hitherto.

46. The plan makes a beginning at the future economic ordering of the world between nations and "the winning of the peace." It might help to create the conditions and the atmosphere in which much else would be made easier.

THE FRENCH PLAN
SUGGESTIONS REGARDING INTERNATIONAL
MONETARY RELATIONS
(May 1943)

1. PRELIMINARY REMARKS.

There is little doubt that a return to a generalized system of multilateral international trade, excluding foreign-trade control and foreign-exchange control, cannot be expected for some time after the end of hostilities. For numerous countries, a premature suppression of these controls would have ominous effects.

The states of Continental Europe, in particular, devastated by war and by the consequences of German occupation, will have first to feed their population, to import essential supplies, and then to reconstruct their capacity of production for national consumption and for foreign export. It is out of the question to let private importers, each acting independently, import foreign products without restrictions. By reason of the huge size of the requirements and the extreme urgency of some of them, the Government will have to control for a while both the volume and the nature of imports.

Foreign-exchange control will also probably have to be maintained for a while, not so much because of the considerable amount of internal capital requirements, but because it is difficult to visualize how rigid foreign-trade control can be enforced without exchange control.

Anyhow Russia will maintain, for an unpredictable period of time, both foreign-trade and foreign-exchange control.

Also ex-enemy countries will have, for a period of time, to be subjected, under United Nations supervision, to strict foreign-trade and foreign-exchange control.

It is thus necessary to conceive and achieve a practical system of exchange stability and of trade financing with the following characteristics:

a) It must be applicable as soon as hostilities are over and even earlier wherever possible.

b) It must be applicable simultaneously to those countries which will practice foreign-trade control and foreign-exchange control, and to others which will enjoy freedom of foreign trade and foreign exchange.

c) It must be adaptable to the evolution of internal systems of exchange control and of foreign-trade control.

d) Far from paralyzing evolution toward a better system of international economic relations, it should constitute in itself a step toward such a system.

2. FUNDAMENTAL CONDITIONS OF SATISFACTORY MONETARY RELATIONS.

No international monetary system can work satisfactorily unless certain fundamental political and economic conditions are fulfilled. Military security and social order are of course paramount. But among the general conditions, it appears useful to lay particular stress on the following:

a) Commercial treaties should be concluded permitting a rational distribution of productive activities among nations. Such a distribution ought to take into account the natural resources, the geographic and demographic conditions, the level of education as well as various other elements of the cost of production; it ought furthermore, to take into account the creditor or debtor situation of the balance of payments.

b) Certain regulatory measures of an international character should be adopted, designed to stabilize business conditions and to reduce as far as possible the swing of economic cycles.

These measures ought to have a double character: they should operate on the one hand, on the volume of instruments of payment or of credit, in order to adapt them to needs; they ought to operate, on the other hand, directly on the volume of goods in order to adapt them to outlets.

This latter action should, itself, be of a double character: on raw materials, by some kind of regulatory action on stocks and output; on finished goods, by methods devised to accelerate or slow down the rhythm of production.

c) International long term credits should be favored, and might consist, not only in traditional loans, but in direct participation of industry, agriculture, real estate, etc. through the establishment of national or international public or private Investment Trusts, or other forms of financing.

d) Methods should be devised to remedy persistent disequilibria of balances of payments, through fundamental economic adjustments.

During the period immediately after the war it will be necessary to take care of permanent deficits in the balance of payments arising from reconstruction of devastated countries and development of backward countries. This is a problem of long term financing outside of the scope of the present memorandum.

3. *ANALYSIS OF PRECEDENTS SUPPLIED BY PREVIOUS MONETARY AGREEMENTS.*

Various monetary agreements entered in recent years supply interesting precedents and give useful indications concerning the requisites for satisfactory international monetary relations.

Among the most useful precedents, it appears worthwhile to mention the Franco-British agreement of December 1939 which was designed to stabilize the two currencies and to finance trade between the two countries during the war. Its distinctive feature was that the two governments agreed to acquire and keep, through their exchange equalization funds, at the official rates, the other country's exchange offered through authorized channels. Thus was initiated, instead of the traditional method of financial assistance based on credits opened in terms of the money of the creditor country, a new method based on the acquisition by the creditor country of bank balances expressed in terms of the money of the debtor country.

The advantage of this new method arises in part from its flexibility; it arises also from the additional guarantee which it provides to the creditor country. Indeed, when a country opens to another a credit expressed in the currency of the creditor country, the creditor country holds exclusively a promissory note expressed in a currency which the debtor country might be unable to obtain for redeeming its debt. If, however, the creditor country holds the currency of the debtor country, it holds an internal purchasing power inside the country. True, it is conceivable that the debtor country might "freeze" its own currency owned by another country; but between friendly countries, violation of a promise not to "freeze" its own currency is a much more serious offense than failure to refund a foreign currency which the debtor country might be unable to obtain.

Several features of monetary agreements entered during the war were well suited to the special situation involved, but are not satisfactory for purposes of international financial collaboration in the future. Thus, the Franco-British agreement specified an unlimited mutual assistance, which implies risks unsuitable to a peace-time system; it specified also a prohibition of utilizing in third markets the other partner's exchange, which constitutes a bilateral regulation incompatible with the multilateral character of international trade and credit.

4. EXPLANATION OF THE PROPOSED MONETARY SYSTEM.

Let us assume that the principal nations, as in the case of the tripartite agreement of 1936, might conclude a monetary accord among themselves, to which the other United Nations might be invited to adhere, under certain conditions.

a) This agreement would, in the first place, fix the official parities of the currencies of the participating countries; these official rates would not be changed without preliminary consultation (or preferably agreement) of the interested countries. A suitable mechanism of consultation (or preferably agreement) should be set up.

b) The stability of exchange rates thus determined would be assured by the undertaking, on the part of the monetary authorities (either Exchange Equalization Fund or Central Bank) to acquire at the specified rate and to conserve, at their own risks, but with the limitations and guarantees hereafter specified, the exchange of other participating countries offered through authorized channels. (The word "authorized" applies to countries with foreign-exchange control.)

In order to facilitate to participating countries the relaxation of foreign exchange control, treatment, both as regards limitations and guarantees, should be made more favorable as control is relaxed.

c) The foreign exchange thus acquired by the monetary authorities of the participating countries could be utilized for payments to be made in such currencies (purchase of goods, payments for services, payments of interests or dividends, purchase of securities, of real estate, etc.); it might also, under certain conditions, be sold to the monetary authorities of other participating countries.

d) A limit would be fixed, for each participating country, of the amount of exchange of each participating country which its monetary authorities would agree to acquire, if offered, at the specified rate, and conserve if required.

While the limits should correspond to a reasonable amount of international trade, the authors of this memorandum have not attempted, at the present stage, to establish the basis of the determination of these limits.

e) As a guarantee against loss arising from depreciation of its own exchange, each participating country would not only undertake to protect each other participating country against such loss, but would also agree to deposit, on demand, collateral (gold, foreign bills, raw materials, approved securities, etc.) up to a specified percentage (10 to 30% for instance) of the amount of its own currency held by the monetary authorities of another participating country. This collateral should be deposited with the monetary authorities (or warehouses, in the case of raw materials) of the country holding the currency, or a third approved country. Should the currency of the debtor country depreciate, additional collateral might be demanded, like in the case of commercial loans.

f) The proposed monetary system, which amounts to the opening of mutual credits, undoubtedly entails inflationary risks. A method must therefore be devised to counteract, whenever considered advisable, the inflationary effects of the mutual purchases of exchange. The method suggested is a method of sterilization, which would work as follows:

In a normal period, the monetary authorities of a country holding the currency of another country would use this currency so as to favor flow of credit; for instance in the form of current accounts in commercial banks, of Treasury obligations, of discounted bills, etc. In periods of inflation, this currency would be kept in the form of an account with the Central Bank of the debtor country which would refrain from basing credits on them. Thus the debtor country would be enabled to maintain the foreign exchange value of its currency without losing the control of its internal circulation.

5. *OPTIONAL CONSTITUTION OF A MONETARY STABILIZATION OFFICE.*

To assure the smooth working of the system, it would be necessary that the monetary authorities of the participating countries should be constantly in close contact, either by means of periodical meetings or by setting up a permanent committee. It would probably be still preferable to establish a central board which might be called the Monetary Stabilization Office.

This Stabilization Office would keep account of all exchange transactions effected by the monetary authorities of the participating countries. It would not only facilitate clearings, but could also receive and scrutinize collateral. Furthermore, it would be in a position to know the balance of payments of each of the participating countries and thus to furnish valuable information concerning disequilibria of an accidental or permanent character, which should be corrected by financial or economic measures. Thus the Monetary Stabilization Office could serve both as a barometer of economic conditions and as a counsellor on economic affairs.

It should be noted, nevertheless, that the establishment of a Monetary Stabilization Office is not an essential condition for the operation of the proposed system.

6. *THE PLACE OF GOLD IN THE FUTURE MONETARY SYSTEM.*

Under the proposed system, monetary parities are fixed by mutual reference, and mutual credits are opened without movements of gold (except when used as collateral). However, the suggested system may be considered as a first step toward a general return to an international gold standard. Indeed, the establishment of fixed monetary parities,—even if tentative and even if affected by exchange control is tantamount to the adoption of a common monetary unit. Thus the link to gold of the U.S. dollar becomes a link for all other currencies also.

The role of gold could be enhanced by stipulating that any nation which so desired would be authorized to redeem in gold the credits received. Gradually, the various monetary units, as experience would show that parities are well established, could be defined anew in gold ounces.

Nevertheless, the place of gold has undergone deep modifications since 1914 and will remain considerably altered. Gold has ceased, for three decades, to be an instrument of internal circulation. Unlike platinum and silver, which have found new outlets in the chemical industry, gold has found none. So that its industrial use has been greatly reduced and has now become an infinitesimal proportion of an annual production which, in 1940, was three times as high, in dollars, as in 1920. The conception of gold as a "pledge" of internal monetary circulation has been pointedly criticized. Gold, however, has not ceased to be of valuable service for settlement of balances of payment between countries. It has also remained in use for the purpose of hoarding, notwithstanding administrative restrictions in most countries; such restrictions increase the risk of gold hoarding, but increase also its psychological attraction.

To sum up, use of gold is considerably restricted, while its world stock is now, in dollars, about four times as high as in 1914.

The facts themselves, in their evolution, seem to designate the new place of gold. Inasmuch as its stock, considerably increased, is in the hands of the monetary authorities of certain countries, predominantly in the United States, and inasmuch as its other uses have become insignificant, therefore its value depends mainly on the action of monetary authorities, particularly in the United States. The value of gold has thus become similar to the value of a fiduciary currency. Considering the difficulties which nations would encounter if they attempted to agree upon the adoption of a new international currency, is it not providential that they have at hand such a currency, consecrated by a mystic thousands of years old, in the form of yellow metal? Gold is the international currency of the future.

While gold should thus resume its role as an instrument of settlement of international balances and as a common monetary unit, its function as chief economic regulator should not be revived. The latter function should be exercised mainly through the concerted action of the competent authorities on the volume of credits and of goods. (It should be pointed out that the action of competent authorities on credits was already an inherent part of the traditional gold standard which, widely held opinion to the contrary, did not work automatically, but was managed through discount rates.)

7. CONCLUSION.

It may be pointed out that the proposed system is intermediate between two systems which were widely in use in the period 1920–1940. Before Great Britain devalued in 1931, central banks customarily held currencies of certain other countries, without limit nor protection. Under this system, usually designated as the "gold exchange standard," the Bank of France and the Netherlands Central Bank had accumulated large sterling balances. After the heavy losses thus incurred, monetary authorities adhered to the practice of requesting conversion into gold of the foreign exchange balances which they acquired. This system, usually called the "gold bullion standard," was utilized in the tripartite monetary agreement, where each adhering country promised to redeem in gold, within 24 hours the amounts of its own currency acquired by the exchange equalization fund of another adhering country.

Both these systems are unsatisfactory. It is unreasonable, under the "gold exchange standard," to expect one country to hold, without some limit and guarantee, another country's currency. It is also unreasonable, under the "gold bullion standard," to consider the currency of a friendly country as worthless. The proposed system does not, like the gold exchange standard, imply one hundred percent confidence in another country's currency, nor, like the gold bullion standard, imply one hundred percent lack of confidence.

There seems to be no reason why the proposed system, or a similar one, could not be started immediately between the United Nations without waiting for the end of hostilities. The only real problem is to find a proper basis for fixing the limits of the amounts of exchange to be purchased. But should important difficulties arise in this connection, the system could be started nevertheless in an experimental way by fixing at the outset very low limits which could be gradually increased later.

THE AUSTRALIAN EMPLOYMENT AGREEMENT

THE EMPLOYMENT AGREEMENT

(This is the amended version of the Employment Agreement endorsed at the British Commonwealth conference held in London in February–March 1944 and later sent by the British government to the U.S. government together with other proposed amendments to the Joint Statement by Experts.)

(i) Each of the signatory Governments, being determined to do its part to ensure that the victory of the United Nations shall be followed by freedom from want, recognizes that this objective cannot be achieved unless its people are given the fullest opportunities to work and enjoy the rewards of their labour;

(ii) Moreover, each signatory Government recognizes that a high level of employment among its people is not only fundamental to their material well-being, but will also contribute through the channels of trade to the creation of employment for the peoples of other countries and to an increase in their well-being.

(iii) Therefore each signatory Government recognizes and hereby undertakes a national obligation to its own people and an international obligation to the other signatory Governments henceforth to take such measures as may be necessary and practicable to fulfill this purpose.

(iv) Each signatory Government declares to its own people and to other signatory Governments that it will take all measures within its powers to carry out this obligation and, in particular—

(a) To secure the provision of opportunities for work of a kind which will maintain and improve the standard of living of the community.

(b) To mitigate the unemployment due to fluctuations in activity to which certain trades, industries and services are liable.

(v) In addition, each signatory Government undertakes:—

(a) To consult with other Governments and with appropriate international authorities as to methods of collecting on an agreed plan detailed statistics of national employment and unemployment.

(b) To take such internal measures as may be practicable and within its powers to collect the statistics relating to its own country required by the agreed plan.

(c) To submit such statistics to other Governments, through an appropriate international organization at intervals not exceeding three months.

(d) To make a report, for the purpose of an annual conference of the member countries, on the state of employment of its people and on the economic policies which have been used or are contemplated to combat unemployment.

(e) To send representatives concerned with the economic and social policy of the Government to meet with representatives of other Governments and international authorities at a special conference called by the appropriate organization, if, in the opinion of that organization, a serious decline in employment is developing in any of the signatory countries (for causes whether avoidable or unavoidable by the Governments of the countries concerned), for the purpose of examining and reporting upon possible national and international measures to restore the level of employment and to prevent the spread of unemployment to other countries.

(vi) In the event of a serious decline in the level of its employment, a member Government undertakes to consider measures to restore the level of employment such as:

(a) Stimulation of private investment.

(b) Increase in public investment.

(c) Increased consumption expenditure.

(d) Expansion of oversea investment where possible.

THE JOINT STATEMENT
JOINT STATEMENT BY EXPERTS ON THE ESTABLISHMENT
OF AN INTERNATIONAL MONETARY FUND
(April 1944)

Sufficient discussion of the problems of international monetary co-operation has taken place at the technical level to justify a statement of principles. It is the consensus of opinion of the experts of the United and Associated Nations who have participated in these discussions that the most practical method of assuring international monetary co-operation is through the establishment of an International Monetary Fund. The principles set forth below are designed to constitute the basis of this Fund. Governments are not asked to give final approval to these principles until they have been embodied in the form of definite proposals by the delegates of the United and Associated Nations meeting in a formal conference.

I. PURPOSES AND POLICIES OF THE INTERNATIONAL MONETARY FUND.

The Fund will be guided in all its decisions by the purposes and policies set forth below:

1. To promote international monetary co-operation through a permanent institution which provides the machinery for consultation on international monetary problems.

2. To facilitate the expansion and balanced growth of international trade and to contribute in this way to the maintenance of a high level of

employment and real income, which must be a primary objective of economic policy.

3. To give confidence to member countries by making the Fund's resources available to them under adequate safeguards, thus giving members time to correct maladjustments in their balance of payments without resorting to measures destructive of national or international prosperity.

4. To promote exchange stability, to maintain orderly exchange arrangements among member countries, and to avoid competitive exchange depreciation.

5. To assist the establishment of multilateral payments facilities on current transactions among member countries and the elimination of foreign exchange restrictions which hamper the growth of world trade.

6. To shorten the periods and lessen the degree of disequilibrium in the international balance of payments of member countries.

II. SUBSCRIPTION TO THE FUND.

1. Member countries shall subscribe in gold and in their local Funds amounts (quotas) to be agreed, which will amount altogether to about $8 billion if all the United and Associated Nations subscribe to the Fund (corresponding to about $10 billion for the world as a whole).

2. The quotas may be revised from time to time, but changes shall require a four-fifths vote, and no member's quota shall be changed without its assent.

3. The obligatory gold subscription of a member country shall be fixed at 25 per cent, of its subscription (quota) or 10 per cent, of its holdings of gold and gold-convertible exchange, whichever is smaller.

III. TRANSACTIONS WITH THE FUND.

1. Member countries shall deal with the Fund only through their Treasury, Central Bank, Stabilization Fund or other fiscal agencies. The Fund's account in a member's currency shall be kept at the Central Bank of the member country.

2. A member shall be entitled to buy another member's currency from the Fund in exchange for its own currency on the following conditions:

(a) The member represents that the currency demanded is presently needed for making payments in that currency which are consistent with the purposes of the Fund.

(b) The Fund has not given notice that its holdings of the currency demanded have become scarce in which case the provisions of VI, below, come into force.

(c) The Fund's total holdings of the currency offered (after having been restored, if below that figure, to 75 per cent, of the member's quota) have not increased by more than 25 per cent, of the member's quota during the previous twelve months, and do not exceed 200 percent of the quota.

(d) The Fund has not previously given appropriate notice that the member is suspended from making further use of the Fund's resources on the ground that it is using them in a manner contrary to the purposes and policies of the Fund; but the Fund shall not give such notice until it has presented to the member concerned a report setting forth its views and has allowed a suitable time for reply.

The Fund may in its discretion and on terms which safeguard its interests, waive any of the conditions above.

3. The operations on the Fund's account will be limited to transactions for the purpose of supplying a member country on the member's initiative with another member's currency in exchange for its own currency or for gold. Transactions provided for under 4 and 7, below, are not subject to this limitation.

4. The Fund will be entitled at its option with a view to preventing a particular member's currency from becoming scarce:

(a) To borrow its currency from a member country;

(b) To offer gold to a member country in exchange for its currency.

5. So long as a member country is entitled to buy another member's currency from the Fund in exchange for its own currency, it shall be prepared to buy its own currency from that member with that member's currency or with gold. This requirement does not apply to currency subject to restrictions in conformity with IX (3) below or to holdings of currency which have accumulated as a result of transactions of a current account nature effected before the removal by the member country of restrictions on multilateral clearing maintained or imposed under X (2) below.

6. A member country desiring to obtain directly or indirectly the currency of another member country for gold is expected, provided that it can do so with equal advantage, to acquire the currency by the sale of gold

to the Fund. This shall not preclude the sale of newly-mined gold by a gold-producing country on any market.

7. The Fund may also acquire gold from member countries in accordance with the following provisions:

(a) A member country may repurchase from the Fund for gold any part of the latter's holdings of its currency.

(b) So long as a member's holdings of gold and gold-convertible exchange exceed its quota, the Fund in selling foreign exchange to that country shall require that one-half of the net sales of such exchange during the Fund's financial year be paid for with gold.

(c) If at the end of the Fund's financial year a member's holdings of gold and gold-convertible exchange have increased, the Fund may require up to one-half of the increase to be used to repurchase part of the Fund's holdings of its currency so long as this does not reduce the Fund's holdings of a country's currency below 75 per cent of its quota or the member's holdings of gold and gold-convertible exchange below its quota.

IV. PAR VALUES OF MEMBER CURRENCIES.

1. The par value of a member's currency shall be agreed with the Fund when it is admitted to membership and shall be expressed in terms of gold. All transactions between the Fund and members shall be at par subject to a fixed charge payable by the member making application to the Fund; and all transactions in member currencies shall be at rates within an agreed percentage of parity.

2. Subject to 5, below, no change in the par value of a member's currency shall be made by the Fund without the country's approval. Member countries agree not to propose a change of parity of their currency unless they consider it appropriate to correct a Fundamental disequilibrium. Changes shall be made only with the approval of the Fund subject to the provisions below.

3. The Fund shall approve a requested change in the par value of a member's currency if it is essential to correct a Fundamental disequilibrium. In particular, the Fund shall not reject a requested change necessary to restore equilibrium because of domestic social or political policies of the country applying for a change. In considering a requested change, the Fund shall take into consideration the extreme uncertainties prevailing at the

time the parities of currencies of member countries were initially agreed upon.

4. After consulting the Fund a member country may change the established parity of its currency provided the proposed change inclusive of any previous change since the establishment of the Fund does not exceed 10 per cent. In the case of application for a further change not covered by the above and not exceeding 10 per cent, the Fund shall give its decision within two days of receiving the application if the applicant so requests.

5. An agreed uniform change may be made in the gold value of member currencies, provided every member country having 10 per cent, or more of the aggregate quotas approves.

V. *CAPITAL TRANSACTIONS.*

1. A member country may not use the Fund's resources to meet a large or sustained outflow of capital and the Fund may require a member country to exercise control to prevent such use of the resources of the Fund. This provision is not intended to prevent the use of the Fund's resources for capital transactions of reasonable amount required for the expansion of exports or in the ordinary course of trade, banking and other business. Nor is it intended to prevent capital movements which are met out of a member country's own resources of gold and foreign exchange, provided such capital movements are in accordance with the purposes of the Fund.

2. Subject to VI, below, a member country may not use its control of capital movements to restrict payments for current transactions or to delay unduly the transfer of Funds in settlement of commitments.

VI. *APPORTIONMENT OF SCARCE CURRENCIES.*

1. When it becomes evident to the Fund that the demand for a member country's currency may soon exhaust the Fund's holdings of that currency, the Fund shall so inform member countries and propose an equitable method of apportioning the scarce currency. When a currency is thus declared scarce, the Fund shall issue a report embodying the causes of the scarcity and containing recommendations designed to bring it to an end.

2. A decision by the Fund to apportion a scarce currency shall operate as an authorization to a member country, after consultation with the Fund, temporarily to restrict the freedom of exchange operations in the affected currency and, in determining the manner of restricting the demand and

rationing the limited supply amongst its nationals, the member country shall have complete jurisdiction.

VII. MANAGEMENT.

1. The Fund shall be governed by a board on which each member will be represented, and by an executive committee. The executive committee shall consist of at least nine members including representatives of the five countries with the largest quotas.

2. The distribution of voting power on the board of directors and the executive committee shall be closely related to the quotas.

3. Subject to II (2) and IV (5), all matters shall be settled by a majority of votes.

4. The Fund shall publish at short intervals a statement of its position showing the extent of its holdings of member currencies and of gold and its transactions in gold.

VIII. WITHDRAWAL.

1. A member country may withdraw from the Fund by giving notice in writing.

2. The reciprocal obligations of the Fund and the country are to be liquidated within a reasonable time.

3. After a member country has given notice in writing of its withdrawal from the Fund, the Fund may not dispose of its holdings of the country's currency except in accordance with arrangements made under 2, above. After a country has given notice of withdrawal its use of the resources of the Fund is subject to the approval of the Fund.

IX. THE OBLIGATIONS OF MEMBER COUNTRIES.

1. Not to buy gold at a price which exceeds the agreed parity of its currency by more than a prescribed margin and not to sell gold at a price which falls below the agreed parity by more than a prescribed margin.

2. Not to allow exchange transactions in its market in currencies of other members at rates outside a prescribed range based on the agreed parities.

3. Not to impose restrictions on payments for current international transactions with other member countries (other than those involving capital transfers or in accordance with VI, above) or to engage in any discriminatory currency arrangements or multiple currency practices without the approval of the Fund.

X. TRANSITIONAL ARRANGEMENTS.

1. Since the Fund is not intended to provide facilities for relief or reconstruction or to deal with international indebtedness arising out of the war, the agreement of a member country to III (5) and IX (3), above, shall not become operative until it is satisfied as to the arrangements at its disposal to facilitate the settlement of the balance of payments differences during the early post-war transition period by means which will not unduly encumber its facilities with the Fund.

2. During this transition period member countries may maintain and adapt to changing circumstances exchange regulations of the character which have been in operation during the war, but they shall undertake to withdraw as soon as possible by progressive stages any restrictions which impede multilateral clearing on current account. In their exchange policy they shall pay continuous regard to the principles and objectives of the Fund; and they shall take all possible measures to develop commercial and financial relations with other member countries which will facilitate international payments and the maintenance of exchange stability.

3. The Fund may make representations to any member that conditions are favourable to the withdrawal of particular restrictions or for the general abandonment of restrictions inconsistent with IX (3), above. Not later than three years from the coming into force of the Fund any member still retaining any restrictions inconsistent with IX (3) shall consult the Fund as to their further retention.

4. In its relations with member countries the Fund shall recognize that the transition period is one of change and adjustment and in deciding on its attitude to proposals presented by members it shall give the member country the benefit of any reasonable doubt.

THE FINAL ACT

FINAL ACT

(22 July 1944)

The Governments of Australia, Belgium, Bolivia, Brazil, Canada, Chile, China, Colombia, Costa Rica, Cuba, Czechoslovakia, Dominican Republic, Ecuador, Egypt, El Salvador, Ethiopia; the French Delegation; the Governments of Greece, Guatemala, Haiti, Honduras, Iceland, India, Iran, Iraq, Liberia, Luxembourg, Mexico, Netherlands, New Zealand, Nicaragua, Norway, Panama, Paraguay, Peru, Philippine Commonwealth, Poland, Union of South Africa, Union of Soviet Socialist Republics, United Kingdom, United States of America, Uruguay, Venezuela, and Yugoslavia;

Having accepted the invitation extended to them by the Government of the United States of America to be represented at a United Nations Monetary and Financial Conference;

Appointed their respective delegates, who are listed below by countries in the order of alphabetical precedence:

AUSTRALIA

LESLIE G. MELVILLE, Economic Adviser to the Commonwealth Bank of Australia; *Chairman of the Delegation*

JAMES B. BRIGDEN, Financial Counselor, Australian Legation, Washington

FREDERICK H. WHEELER, Commonwealth Department of the Treasury

ARTHUR H. TANGE, Commonwealth Department of External Affairs

BELGIUM

CAMILLE GUTT, Minister of Finance and Economic Affairs; *Chairman of the Delegation*

GEORGES THEUNIS, Minister of State; Ambassador at Large on special mission in the United States; Governor of the National Bank of Belgium

BARON HERVÉ DE GRUBEN, Counselor, Belgian Embassy, Washington

BARON RENÉ BOEL, Counselor of the Belgian Government

BOLIVIA

RENÉ BALLIVÁN, Financial Counselor, Bolivian Embassy, Washington; *Chairman of the Delegation*

BRAZIL

ARTHUR DE SOUZA COSTA, Minister of Finance; *Chairman of the Delegation*

FRANCISCO ALVES DOS SANTOS-FILHO, Director of Foreign Exchange of the Bank of Brazil

VALENTIM BOUÇAS, Commission of Control of the Washington Agreements and Economic and Financial Council

EUGENIO GUDIN, Economic and Financial Council and Economic Planning Committee

OCTÁVIO BULHÕES, Chief, Division of Economic and Financial Studies, Ministry of Finance

VICTOR AZEVEDO BASTIAN, Director, Banco da Provincia do Rio Grande do Sul

CANADA

J. L. ILSLEY, Minister of Finance; *Chairman of the Delegation*

L. S. ST. LAURENT, Minister of Justice

D. C. ABBOTT, Parliamentary Assistant to the Minister of Finance

LIONEL CHEVRIER, Parliamentary Assistant to the Minister of Munitions and Supply

J. A. BLANCHETTE, Member of Parliament

W. A. TUCKER, Member of Parliament

W. C. CLARK, Deputy Minister of Finance

G. F. TOWERS, Governor, Bank of Canada

W. A. MACKINTOSH, Special Assistant to the Deputy Minister of Finance

L. RASMINSKY, Chairman (alternate), Foreign Exchange Control Board

A. F. W. PLUMPTRE, Financial Attaché, Canadian Embassy, Washington

J. J. DEUTSCH, Special Assistant to the Under Secretary of State of External
Affairs

CHILE

LUIS ALAMOS BARROS, Director, Central Bank of Chile; *Chairman of the
Delegation*

GERMÁN RIESCO, General Representative of the Chilean Line,
New York

ARTURO MASCHKE TORNERO, General Manager, Central Bank
of Chile

FERNANDO MARDONES RESTAT, Assistant General Manager, Chilean
Nitrate and Iodine Sales Corporation

CHINA

HSIANG-HSI K'UNG, Vice President of Executive Yuan and concurrently
Minister of Finance; Governor of the Central Bank of China; *Chairman of
the Delegation*

TINGFU F. TSIANG, Chief Political Secretary of Executive Yuan;
former Chinese Ambassador to the Union of Soviet Socialist
Republics

PING-WEN KUO, Vice Minister of Finance

VICTOR HOO, Administrative Vice Minister of Foreign Affairs

YEE-CHUN KOO, Vice Minister of Finance

KUO-CHING LI, Adviser to the Ministry of Finance

TE-MOU HSI, Representative of the Ministry of Finance in Washington;
Director, the Central Bank of China and Bank of China

TSU-YEE PEI, Director, Bank of China

TS-LIANG SOONG, General Manager, Manufacturers Bank of China;
Director, the Central Bank of China, Bank of China, and Bank of
Communications

COLOMBIA

CARLOS LLERAS RESTREPO, former Minister of Finance and Comptroller
General; *Chairman of the Delegation*

MIGUEL LÓPEZ PUMAREJO, former Ambassador to the United States;
Manager, Caja de Crédito Agrario, Industrial y Minero

VICTOR DUGAND, Banker

COSTA RICA

FRANCISCO DE P. GUTIÉRREZ ROSS, Ambassador to the United States; former Minister of Finance and Commerce; *Chairman of the Delegation*

LUIS DEMETRIO TINOCO CASTRO, Dean, Faculty of Economic Sciences, University of Costa Rica; former Minister of Finance and Commerce; former Minister of Public Education

FERNANDO MADRIGAL A., Member of Board of Directors, Chamber of Commerce of Costa Rica

CUBA

E. I. MONTOULIEU, Minister of Finance; *Chairman of the Delegation*

CZECHOSLOVAKIA

LADISLAV FEIERABEND, Minister of Finance; *Chairman of the Delegation*

JAN MLÁDEK, Ministry of Finance; *Deputy Chairman of the Delegation*

ANTONÍN BASCH, Department of Economics, Columbia University

JOSEF HANČ, Director of the Czechoslovak Economic Service in the United States of America

ERVIN HEXNER, Professor of Economics and Political Science, University of North Carolina

DOMINICAN REPUBLIC

ANSELMO COPELlO, Ambassador to the United States; *Chairman of the Delegation*

J. R. RODRIGUEZ, Minister Counselor, Embassy of the Dominican Republic, Washington

ECUADOR

ESTEBAN F. CARBO, Financial Counselor, Ecuadoran Embassy, Washington; *Chairman of the Delegation*

SIXTO E. DURÁN BALLÉN, Minister Counselor, Ecuadoran Embassy, Washington

EGYPT

SANT LACKANY BEY; *Chairman of the Delegation*

MAHMOUD SALEH EL FALAKY

AHMED SELIM

EL SALVADOR

AGUSTÍN ALFARO MORAN; *Chairman of the Delegation*
RAÚL GAMERO
VÍCTOR MANUEL VALDES

ETHIOPIA

BLATTA EPHREM TEWELDE MEDHEN, Minister to the United States;
Chairman of the Delegation
GEORGE A. BLOWERS, Governor, State Bank of Ethiopia

FRENCH DELEGATION

PIERRE MENDÈS FRANCE, Commissioner of Finance; *Chairman of the
Delegation*
ANDRÉ ISTEL, Technical Counselor to the Department of Finance *Assistant
Delegates*
JEAN DE LARGENTAYE, Finance Inspector
ROBERT MOSSÉ, Professor of Economics
RAOUL AGLION, Legal Counselor
ANDRÉ PAUL MAURY

GREECE

KYRIAKOS VARVARESSOS, Governor of the Bank of Greece; Ambassador
Extraordinary for Economic and Financial Matters; *Chairman of the
Delegation*
ALEXANDER ARGYROPOULOS, Minister Resident; Director, Economic
and Commercial Division, Ministry of Foreign Affairs
ATHANASE SBAROUNIS, Director General, Ministry of Finance

GUATEMALA

MANUEL NORIEGA MORALES, Postgraduate Student in Economic
Sciences, Harvard University; *Chairman of the Delegation*

HAITI

ANDRÉ LIAUTAUD, Ambassador to the United States; *Chairman of the
Delegation*
PIERRE CHAUVET, Under Secretary of State for Finance

HONDURAS

JULIÁN R. CÁCERES, Ambassador to the United States; *Chairman of the Delegation*

ICELAND

MAGNÚS SIGURDSSON, Manager, National Bank of Iceland; *Chairman of the Delegation*
ÁSGEIR ÁSGEIRSSON, Manager, Fishery Bank of Iceland
SVANBJÖRN FRÍMANNSSON, Chairman, State Commerce Board

INDIA

SIR JEREMY RAISMAN, Member for Finance, Government of India; *Chairman of the Delegation*
SIR THEODORE GREGORY, Economic Adviser to the Government of India
SIR CHINTAMAN D. DESHMUKH, Governor, Reserve Bank of India
SIR SHANMUKHAM CHETTY
A. D. SHROFF, Director, Tata Sons, Ltd.

IRAN

ABOL HASSAN EBTEHAJ, Governor of National Bank of Iran; *Chairman of the Delegation*
A. A. DAFTARY, Counselor, Iranian Legation, Washington
HOSSEIN NAVAB, Consul General, New York
TAGHI NASSR, Iranian Trade and Economic Commissioner, New York

IRAQ

IBRAHIM KAMAL, Senator and former Minister of Finance; *Chairman of the Delegation*
LIONEL M. SWAN, Adviser to the Ministry of Finance
IBRAHIM AL-KABIR, Accountant General, Ministry of Finance
CLAUDE E. LOOMBE, Comptroller of Exchange and Currency Officer

LIBERIA

WILLIAM E. DENNIS, Secretary of the Treasury; *Chairman of the Delegation*
JAMES F. COOPER, former Secretary of the Treasury
WALTER F. WALKER, Consul General, New York

LUXEMBOURG

HUGUES LE GALLAIS, Minister to the United States; *Chairman of the Delegation*

MEXICO

EDUARDO SUÁREZ, Minister of Finance; *Chairman of the Delegation*
ANTONIO ESPINOSA DE LOS MONTEROS, Executive President of Nacional Financiera; Director of Banco de México
RODRIGO GÓMEZ, Manager of Banco de México
DANIEL COSÍO VILLEGAS, Chief of the Department of Economic Studies, Banco de México

NETHERLANDS

J. W. BEYEN, Financial Adviser to the Netherlands Government; *Chairman of the Delegation*
D. CRENA DE IONGH, President of the Board for the Netherlands Indies, Surinam, and Curaçao in the United States
H. RIEMENS, Financial Attaché, Netherlands Embassy, Washington; Financial Member of the Netherlands Economic, Financial, and Shipping Mission in the United States
A. H. PHILIPSE, Member of the Netherlands Economic, Financial, and Shipping Mission in the United States

NEW ZEALAND

WALTER NASH, Minister of Finance; Minister to the United States; *Chairman of the Delegation*
BERNARD CARL ASHWIN, Secretary to the Treasury
EDWARD C. FUSSELL, Deputy Governor, Reserve Bank of New Zealand
ALAN G. B. FISHER, Counselor, New Zealand Legation, Washington

NICARAGUA

GUILLERMO SEVILLA SACASA, Ambassador to the United States; *Chairman of the Delegation*
LEÓN DEBAYLE, former Ambassador to the United States
J. JESÚS SÁNCHEZ ROIG, former Minister of Finance; Vice Chairman, Board of Directors, National Bank of Nicaragua

NORWAY

WILHELM KEILHAU, Director, Bank of Norway, p. t., London; *Chairman of the Delegation*

OLE COLBJORNSEN, Financial Counselor, Norwegian Embassy, Washington

ARNE SKAUG, Commercial Counselor, Norwegian Embassy, Washington

PANAMA

GUILLERMO ARANGO, President, Investors Service Corporation of Panama; *Chairman of the Delegation*

NARCISO E. GARAY, First Secretary, Panamanian Embassy, Washington

PARAGUAY

CELSO R. VELÁZQUEZ, Ambassador to the United States; *Chairman of the Delegation*

NESTOR M. CAMPOS ROS, First Secretary, Paraguayan Embassy, Washington

PERU

PEDRO BELTRÁN, Ambassador-designate to the United States; *Chairman of the Delegation*

MANUEL B. LLOSA, Second Vice President of the Chamber of Deputies; Deputy from Cerro de Pasco

ANDRÉS F. DASSO, Senator from Lima

ALBERTO ALVAREZ CALDERÓN, Senator from Lima

JUVENAL MONGE, Deputy from Cuzco

JUAN CHÁVEZ, Minister, Commercial Counselor, Peruvian Embassy, Washington

PHILIPPINE COMMONWEALTH

COLONEL ANDRÉS SORIANO, Secretary of Finance of the Philippine Commonwealth; *Chairman of the Delegation*

JAIME HERNANDEZ, Auditor General of the Philippine Commonwealth

JOSEPH H. FOLEY, Manager, Philippine National Bank, New York Agency, Philippine Commonwealth

POLAND

LUDWIK GROSFELD, Minister of Finance; *Chairman of the Delegation*

LEON BARAŃSKI, Director General Bank of Poland

ZYGMUNT KARPIŃSKI, Director, Bank of Poland
STANISŁAW KIRKOR, Director, Ministry of Finance
JANUSZ ZÓŁTOWSKI, Financial Counselor, Polish Embassy, Washington

UNION OF SOUTH AFRICA

S. F. N. GIE, Minister to the United States; *Chairman of the Delegation*
J. E. HOLLOWAY, Secretary for Finance; *Co-delegate*
M. H. DE KOCK, Deputy Governor of South African [Reserve] Bank;
Co-delegate

UNION OF SOVIET SOCIALIST REPUBLICS

M. S. STEPANOV, Deputy People's Commissar of Foreign Trade; *Chairman of
the Delegation*
P. A. MALETIN, Deputy People's Commissar of Finance
N. F. CHECHULIN, Assistant Chairman of the State Bank
I. D. ZLOBIN, Chief, Monetary Division of the People's Commissariat of
Finance
A. A. ARUTIUNIAN, Professor; Doctor of Economics; Expert-Consultant of
the People's Commissariat for Foreign Affairs
A. P. MOROZOV, Member of the Collegium; Chief, Monetary Division of
the People's Commissariat for Foreign Trade

UNITED KINGDOM

LORD KEYNES; *Chairman of the Delegation*
ROBERT H. BRAND, United Kingdom Treasury Representative in Washington
SIR WILFRED EADY, United Kingdom Treasury
NIGEL BRUCE RONALD, Foreign Office
DENNIS H. ROBERTSON, United Kingdom Treasury
LIONEL ROBBINS, War Cabinet Offices
REDEVERS OPIE, Counselor, British Embassy, Washington

UNITED STATES OF AMERICA

HENRY MORGENTHAU, JR., Secretary of the Treasury; *Chairman of the
Delegation*
FRED M. VINSON, Director, Office of Economic Stabilization; *Vice Chairman
of the Delegation*
DEAN ACHESON, Assistant Secretary of State
EDWARD E. BROWN, President, First National Bank of Chicago

LEO T. CROWLEY, Administrator, Foreign Economic Administration

MARRINER S. ECCLES, Chairman, Board of Governors of the Federal
Reserve System

MABEL NEWCOMER, Professor of Economics, Vassar College

BRENT SPENCE, House of Representatives; Chairman, Committee on
Banking and Currency

CHARLES W. TOBEY, United States Senate; Member, Committee on
Banking and Currency

ROBERT F. WAGNER, United States Senate; Chairman, Committee on
Banking and Currency

HARRY D. WHITE, Assistant to the Secretary of the Treasury

JESSE P. WOLCOTT, House of Representatives; Member, Committee on
Banking and Currency

URUGUAY

MARIO LA GAMMA ACEVEDO, Expert, Ministry of Finance; *Chairman of the
Delegation*

HUGO GARCÍA, Financial Attaché, Uruguayan Embassy, Washington

VENEZUELA

RODOLFO ROJAS, Minister of the Treasury; *Chairman of the Delegation*

ALFONSO ESPINOSA, President, Permanent Committee of Finance,
Chamber of Deputies

CRISTÓBAL L. MENDOZA, former Minister of the Treasury; Legal Adviser
to the Central Bank of Venezuela

JOSÉ JOAQUÍN GONZÁLEZ GORRONDONA, President, Office of Import
Control; Director, Central Bank of Venezuela

YUGOSLAVIA

VLADIMIR RYBÁŘ, Counselor of the Yugoslav Embassy, Washington;
Chairman of the Delegation

Who met at Bretton Woods, New Hampshire, on July 1, 1944, under the
Temporary Presidency of The Honorable Henry Morgenthau, Jr., Chairman
of the Delegation of the United States of America.

The Honorable Henrik de Kauffmann, Danish Minister at Washington,
attended the Inaugural Plenary Session in response to an invitation of the
Government of the United States to be present in a personal capacity.

The Conference, on the proposal of its Committee on Credentials, extended a similar invitation for the remaining sessions of the Conference.

The Economic, Financial, and Transit Department of the League of Nations, the International Labor Office, the United Nations Interim Commission on Food and Agriculture, and the United Nations Relief and Rehabilitation Administration were each represented by one observer at the Inaugural Plenary Session. Their representation was in response to an invitation of the Government of the United States, and either the observers or their alternates attended the subsequent sessions in accordance with the resolution presented by the Committee on Credentials and adopted by the Conference. The observers and their alternates are listed below:

Economic, Financial, and Transit Department of the League of Nations

ALEXANDER LOVEDAY,   Director
RAGNAR NURSKE;   *Alternate International Labor Office*
EDWARD J. PHELAN,   Acting Director
C. WILFRED JENKS,   Legal Adviser; *and* E. J. RICHES, Acting Chief, Economic and Statistical Section; *Alternates United Nations Interim Commission on Food and Agriculture*
EDWARD TWENTYMAN,   Delegate from the United Kingdom *United Nations Relief and Rehabilitation Administration*
A. H. FELLER,   General Counsel; *or* MIECZYSLAW SOKOLOWSKI, Financial Adviser

Warren Kelchner, Chief of the Division of International Conferences, Department of State of the United States, was designated, with the approval of the President of the United States, as Secretary General of the Conference; Frank Coe, Assistant Administrator, Foreign Economic Administration of the United States, as Technical Secretary General; and Philip C. Jessup, Professor of International Law at Columbia University, New York, New York, as Assistant Secretary General.

The Honorable Henry Morgenthau, Jr., Chairman of the Delegation of the United States of America, was elected permanent President of the Conference at the Inaugural Plenary Session held on July 1, 1944.

M. S. Stepanov, the Chairman of the Delegation of the Union of Soviet Socialist Republics; Arthur de Souza Costa, the Chairman of the Delegation of Brazil; Camille Gutt, the Chairman of the Delegation of Belgium; and

Leslie G. Melville, the Chairman of the Delegation of Australia, were elected Vice Presidents of the Conference. The Temporary President appointed the following members of the General Committees constituted by the Conference:

COMMITTEE ON CREDENTIALS

E. I. MONTOULIEU (Cuba), *Chairman*
J. W. BEYEN (Netherlands)
S. F. N. GIE (South Africa)
WILLIAM E. DENNIS (Liberia)
WILHELM KEILHAU (Norway)

COMMITTEE ON RULES AND REGULATIONS

HSIANG-HSI K'UNG (China), *Chairman*
GUILLERMO SEVILLA SACASA (Nicaragua)
LUDWIK GROSFELD (Poland)
LESLIE G. MELVILLE (Australia)
IBRAHIM KAMAL (Iraq)

COMMITTEE ON NOMINATIONS

WALTER NASH (New Zealand), *Chairman*
HUGUES LE GALLAIS (Luxembourg)
JULIÁN R. CÁCERES (Honduras)
MAGNÚS SIGURDSSON (Iceland)
PEDRO BELTRÁN (Peru)

In accordance with the regulations adopted at the Second Plenary Session, held on July 3, 1944, the Conference elected a Steering Committee which was composed of the following Chairmen of Delegations:

HENRY MORGENTHAU, JR. (U.S.A.), *Chairman*
CAMILLE GUTT (Belgium)
ARTHUR DE SOUZA COSTA (Brazil)
J. L. ILSLEY (Canada)
HSIANG-HSI K'UNG (China)
CARLOS LLERAS RESTREPO (Colombia)
PIERRE MENDÈS FRANCE (French Delegation)
ABOL HASSAN EBTEHAJ (Iran)
EDUARDO SUÁREZ (Mexico)

M. S. STEPANOV (U.S.S.R.)
LORD KEYNES (U.K.)

On July 21, 1944, the Coordinating Committee was constituted with the following membership:

FRED M. VINSON (U.S.A), Chairman
ARTHUR DE SOUZA COSTA (Brazil)
PING-WEN KUO (China)
ROBERT MOSSÉ (French Delegation)
EDUARDO SUÁREZ (Mexico)
A. A. ARUTIUNIAN (U.S.S.R)
LIONEL ROBBINS (U.K.)

The Conference was divided into three Technical Commissions. The officers of these Commissions and of their respective Committees, as elected by the Conference, are listed below:

COMMISSION I
International Monetary Fund

Chairman: HARRY D. WHITE (U.S.A)
Vice Chairman: RODOLFO ROJAS (Venezuela)
Reporting Delegate: L. RASMINSKY (Canada)
Secretary: LEROY D. STINEBOWER
Assistant Secretary: ELEANOR LANSING DULLES

COMMITTEE 1—Purposes, Policies, and Quotas of the Fund
Chairman: TINGFU F. TSIANG (China)
Reporting Delegate: KYRIAKOS VARVARESSOS (Greece)
Secretary: WILLIAM ADAMS BROWN, JR.

COMMITTEE 2—Operations of the Fund
Chairman: P. A. MALETIN (U.S.S.R)
Vice Chairman: W. A. MACKINTOSH (Canada)
Reporting Delegate: ROBERT MOSSÉ (French Delegation)
Secretary: KARL BOPP
Assistant Secretary: ALICE BOURNEUF

COMMITTEE 3—Organization and Management
Chairman: ARTHUR DE SOUZA COSTA (Brazil)
Reporting Delegate: ERVIN HEXNER (Czechoslovakia)

Secretary: MALCOLM BRYAN
Assistant Secretary: H. J. BITTERMANN

COMMITTEE 4—Form and Status of the Fund
Chairman: MANUEL B. LLOSA (Peru)
Reporting Delegate: WILHELM KEILHAU (Norway)
Secretary: COLONEL CHARLES H. DYSON
Assistant Secretary: LAUREN CASADAY

COMMISSION II
Bank for Reconstruction and Development

Chairman: LORD KEYNES (U.K.)
Vice Chairman: LUIS ALAMOS BARROS (Chile)
Reporting Delegate: GEORGES THEUNIS (Belgium)
Secretary: ARTHUR UPGREN
Secretary: ARTHUR SMITHIES
Assistant Secretary: RUTH RUSSELL

COMMITTEE 1—Purposes, Policies, and Capital of the Bank
Chairman: J. W. BEYEN (Netherlands)
Reporting Delegate: J. RAFAEL OREAMUNO (Costa Rica)
Secretary: J. P. YOUNG
Assistant Secretary: JANET SUNDELSON

COMMITTEE 2—Operations of the Bank
Chairman: E. I. MONTOULIEU (Cuba)
Reporting Delegate: JAMES B. BRIGDEN (Australia)
Secretary: H. J. BITTERMANN
Assistant Secretary: RUTH RUSSELL

COMMITTEE 3—Organization and Management
Chairman: MIGUEL LÓPEZ PUMAREJO (Colombia)
Reporting Delegate: M. H. DE KOCK (South Africa)
Secretary: MORDECAI EZEKIEL
Assistant Secretary: CAPTAIN WILLIAM L. ULLMANN

COMMITTEE 4—Form and Status of the Bank
Chairman: SIR CHINTAMAN D. DESHMUKH (India)
Reporting Delegate: LEON BARAŃSKI (Poland)
Secretary: HENRY EDMINSTON

Assistant Secretary: COLONEL CHARLES H. DYSON

COMMISSION III
Other Means of International Financial Cooperation

Chairman: EDUARDO SUÁREZ (Mexico)
Vice Chairman: MAHMOUD SALEH EL FALAKY (Egypt)
Reporting Delegate: ALAN G. B. FISHER (New Zealand)
Secretary: ORVIS SCHMIDT

The Final Plenary Session was held on July 22, 1944. As a result of the deliberations, as recorded in the minutes and reports of the respective Commissions and their Committees and of the Plenary Sessions, the following instruments were drawn up:

INTERNATIONAL MONETARY FUND

Articles of Agreement of the International Monetary Fund, which are attached hereto as Annex A.

INTERNATIONAL BANK FOR RECONSTRUCTION AND DEVELOPMENT

Articles of Agreement of the International Bank for Reconstruction and Development, which are attached hereto as Annex B.

Summary of the Agreements in Annex A and Annex B, which is attached hereto as Annex C. The following resolutions, statement, and recommendations were adopted:

I
PREPARATION OF THE FINAL ACT
The United Nations Monetary and Financial Conference

RESOLVES:

That the Secretariat be authorized to prepare the Final Act in accordance with the suggestions proposed by the Secretary General in *Journal* No. 19, July 19, 1944;

That the Final Act contain the definitive texts of the conclusions approved by the Conference in plenary session, and that no changes be made therein at the Closing Plenary Session;

That the Coordinating Committee review the text and, if approved, submit it to the Final Plenary Session.

II

PUBLICATION OF DOCUMENTATION
The United Nations Monetary and Financial Conference

RESOLVES:

That the Government of the United States of America be authorized to publish the Final Act of this Conference; the Reports of the Commissions; the Minutes of the Public Plenary Sessions; and to make available for publication such additional documents in connection with the work of this Conference as in its judgment may be considered in the public interest.

III

NOTIFICATION OF SIGNATURES AND CUSTODY OF DEPOSITS
The United Nations Monetary and Financial Conference

RESOLVES:

To request the Government of the United States of America

(1) as depository of the Articles of Agreement of the International Monetary Fund, to inform the Governments of all countries whose names are set forth in Schedule A of the Articles of Agreement of the International Monetary Fund, and all Governments whose membership is approved in accordance with Article II, Section 2, of all signatures of the Articles of Agreement; and

(2) to receive and to hold in a special deposit account gold or United States dollars transmitted to it in accordance with Article XX, Section 2 (d), of the Articles of Agreement of the International Monetary Fund, and to transmit such funds to the Board of Governors of the Fund when the initial meeting has been called.

IV

STATEMENT REGARDING SILVER

The problems confronting some nations as a result of the wide fluctuation in the value of silver were the subject of serious discussion in Commission III. Due to the shortage of time, the magnitude of the other problems on the agenda, and other limiting considerations, it was impossible to give sufficient attention to this problem at this time in order to make definite recommendations. However, it was the sense of Commission III that the subject should merit further study by the interested nations.

V

LIQUIDATION OF THE BANK FOR INTERNATIONAL SETTLEMENTS
The United Nations Monetary and Financial Conference

RECOMMENDS:

The liquidation of the Bank for International Settlements at the earliest possible moment.

VI

ENEMY ASSETS AND LOOTED PROPERTY

Whereas, in anticipation of their impending defeat, enemy leaders, enemy nationals and their collaborators are transferring assets to and through neutral countries in order to conceal them and to perpetuate their influence, power, and ability to plan future aggrandizement and world domination, thus jeopardizing the efforts of the United Nations to establish and permanently maintain peaceful international relations;

Whereas, enemy countries and their nationals have taken the property of occupied countries and their nationals by open looting and plunder, by forcing transfers under duress, as well as by subtle and complex devices, often operated through the agency of their puppet governments, to give the cloak of legality to their robbery and to secure ownership and control of enterprises in the post-war period;

Whereas, enemy countries and their nationals have also, through sales and other methods of transfer, run the chain of their ownership and control through occupied and neutral countries, thus making the problem of disclosure and disentanglement one of international character;

Whereas, the United Nations have declared their intention to do their utmost to defeat the methods of dispossession practiced by the enemy, have reserved their right to declare invalid any transfers of property belonging to persons within occupied territory, and have taken measures to protect and safeguard property, within their respective jurisdictions, owned by occupied countries and their nationals, as well as to prevent the disposal of looted property in United Nations markets; therefore

The United Nations Monetary and Financial Conference

1. Takes note of and fully supports steps taken by the United Nations for the purpose of:

(a) uncovering, segregating, controlling, and making appropriate disposition of enemy assets;

(b) preventing the liquidation of property looted by the enemy, locating and tracing ownership and control of such looted property, and taking appropriate measures with a view to restoration to its lawful owners;

2. RECOMMENDS:

That all Governments of countries represented at this Conference take action consistent with their relations with the countries at war to call upon the Governments of neutral countries

(a) to take immediate measures to prevent any disposition or transfer within territories subject to their jurisdiction of any

(1) assets belonging to the Government or any individuals or institutions within those United Nations occupied by the enemy; and

(2) looted gold, currency, art objects, securities, other evidences of ownership in financial or business enterprises, and of other assets looted by the enemy;

as well as to uncover, segregate and hold at the disposition of the post-liberation authorities in the appropriate country any such assets within territory subject to their jurisdiction;

(b) to take immediate measures to prevent the concealment by fraudulent means or otherwise within countries subject to their jurisdiction of any

(1) assets belonging to, or alleged to belong to, the Government of and individuals or institutions within enemy countries;

(2) assets belonging to, or alleged to belong to, enemy leaders, their associates and collaborators; and to facilitate their ultimate delivery to the post-armistice authorities.

VII
INTERNATIONAL ECONOMIC PROBLEMS

Whereas, in Article I of the Articles of Agreement of the International Monetary Fund it is stated that one of the principal purposes of the Fund is to facilitate the expansion and balanced growth of international trade, and to contribute thereby to the promotion and maintenance of high levels of employment and real income and to the development of the productive resources of all members as primary objectives of economic policy;

Whereas, it is recognized that the complete attainment of this and other purposes and objectives stated in the Agreement cannot be achieved through the instrumentality of the Fund alone; therefore

The United Nations Monetary and Financial Conference

RECOMMENDS:

To the participating Governments that, in addition to implementing the specific monetary and financial measures which were the subject of this Conference, they seek, with a view to creating in the field of international economic relations conditions necessary for the attainment of the purposes of the Fund and of the broader primary objectives of economic policy, to reach agreement as soon as possible on ways and means whereby they may best:

(1) reduce obstacles to international trade and in other ways promote mutually advantageous international commercial relations;

(2) bring about the orderly marketing of staple commodities at prices fair to the producer and consumer alike;

(3) deal with the special problems of international concern which will arise from the cessation of production for war purposes; and

(4) facilitate by cooperative effort the harmonization of national policies of Member States designed to promote and maintain high levels of employment and progressively rising standards of living.

VIII
The United Nations Monetary and Financial Conference

RESOLVES:

1. To express its gratitude to the President of the United States, Franklin D. Roosevelt, for his initiative in convening the present Conference and for its preparation;

2. To express to its President, The Honorable Henry Morgenthau, Jr., its deep appreciation for the admirable manner in which he has guided the Conference;

3. To express to the Officers and Staff of the Secretariat its appreciation for their untiring services and diligent efforts in contributing to the attainment of the objectives of the Conference.

IN WITNESS WHEREOF, the following delegates sign the present Final Act. DONE at Bretton Woods, New Hampshire, on the twenty-second day of July, nineteen hundred and forty-four, in the English language, the original to be deposited in the archives of the Department of State of the United States, and certified copies thereof to be furnished by the Government of the United States of America to each of the Governments and Authorities represented at the Conference.

For AUSTRALIA:
L. G. Melville
For purpose of certification

For BELGIUM:
Gutt

For BOLIVIA:
R. Ballivian

For BRAZIL:
A. de Sza. Costa

For CANADA:
W. A. Mackintosh

For CHILE:
Luis Alamos

For CHINA:
K'ung Hsiang Hsi [SEAL]

For COLOMBIA:
Carlos Lleras Restrepo

For COSTA RICA:
Luis D. Tinoco C.

For CUBA:
E. I. Montoulieu

For CZECHOSLOVAKIA:
L. Feierabend

For THE DOMINICAN REPUBLIC:
A. Copello

For ECUADOR:
E. F. Carbo

For EGYPT:
S. Lackany

For EL SALVADOR:
Ag. Alfaro

For ETHIOPIA:
Ephrem T. Medhen

For THE FRENCH DELEGATION:
Mendès France

For GREECE:
K. Varvaressos

For GUATEMALA:
M. Noriega M.

For HAITI:
A. Liautaud

For HONDURAS:
Julián R. Cáceres

For ICELAND:
Magnús Sigurdsson

For INDIA:
A. J. Raisman

For IRAN:
Dr. Taghi Nassr

For IRAQ:
Ibrahim Kamal

For LIBERIA:
William E. Dennis

For LUXEMBOURG:
Hugues LeGallais

For MEXICO:
Eduardo Suárez

For THE NETHERLANDS:
J. W. Beyen

For NEW ZEALAND:
E. C. Fussell

For NICARAGUA:
Guillermo Sevilla Sacasa

For NORWAY:
Wilhelm Keilhau

For PANAMA:
A. G. Arango

For PARAGUAY:
N. Campos Ros

For PERU:
P. G. Beltrán

For THE PHILIPPINE
COMMONWEALTH:
A. Soriano

For POLAND:
Ludwik Grosfeld

For THE UNION OF SOUTH
AFRICA:
S. F. N. Gie

For THE UNION OF SOVIET
SOCIALIST REPUBLICS:
M. S. Stepanov

For THE UNITED KINGDOM:
Keynes

For THE UNITED STATES OF
AMERICA:
Henry Morgenthau Jr.

For URUGUAY:
Mario La Gamma

For VENEZUELA:

The Venezuelan Delegation wishes to express that its signing of this Act does not imply any recommendation to its Government as to the acceptance of the documents herein contained. The Venezuelan Delegation shall present to its Government these documents for their careful examination within the broad spirit of collaboration that has always guided the acts of our Government.
Rodolfo Rojas

For YUGOSLAVIA:
Dr. Vladimir Rybář

[SEAL]
Warren Kelchner
Secretary General

SPEECH BY LORD KEYNES ON THE INTERNATIONAL
MONETARY FUND DEBATE. HOUSE OF LORDS
May 23, 1944.

My Lords, it is almost exactly a year since the proposals for a Clearing Union were discussed in your Lordships' House. I hope to persuade your Lordships that the year has not been ill-spent. There were, it is true, certain features of elegance, clarity and logic in the Clearing Union plan which have disappeared. And this, by me at least, is to be much regretted. As a result, however, there is no longer any need for a new-fangled international monetary unit. Your Lordships will remember how little any of us liked the names proposed—bancor, unitas, dolphin, bezant, daric and heaven knows what. Some of your Lordships were good enough to join in the search for something better. I recall a story of a country parish in the last century where they were accustomed to give their children Biblical names—Amos, Ezekiel, Obadiah and so forth. Needing a name for a dog, after a long and vain search of the Scriptures they called the dog "Moreover." We hit on no such happy solution, with the result that it has been the dog that died. The loss of the dog we need not too much regret, though I still think that it was a more thoroughbred animal than what has now come out from a mixed marriage of ideas. Yet, perhaps, as sometimes occurs, this dog of mixed origin is a sturdier and more serviceable animal and will prove not less loyal and faithful to the purposes for which it has been bred.

I commend the new plan to your Lordships as being, in some important respects (to which I will return later), a considerable improvement on either of its parents. I like this new plan and I believe that it will work to our advantage. Your Lordships will not wish me to enter into too much technical detail. I can best occupy the time available by examining the major benefits this country may hope to gain from the plan; and whether there are adequate safeguards against possible disadvantages. We shall emerge from this war, having won a more solid victory over our enemies, a more enduring friendship from our Allies, and a deeper respect from the world at large, than perhaps at any time in our history. The victory, the friendship, and the respect will have been won, because, in spite of faint-hearted preparations, we have sacrificed every precaution for the future in the interests of immediate strength with a fanatical single-mindedness which has had few parallels. But the full price of this has still to be paid. I wish that this was more generally appreciated in the country than it is. In thus waging the war without counting the ultimate cost we—and we alone of the United Nations—have burdened ourselves with a weight of deferred indebtedness to other countries beneath which we shall stagger. We have already given to the common cause all, and more than all, that we can afford. It follows that we must examine any financial plan to make sure that it will help us to carry our burdens and not add to them. No one is more deeply convinced of this than I am. I make no complaint, therefore, that those to whom the details of the scheme are new and difficult, should scrutinise them with anxious concern.

What, then, are these major advantages that I hope from the plan to the advantage of this country? First, it is clearly recognised and agreed that, during the post-war transitional period of uncertain duration, we are entitled to retain any of those war-time restrictions, and special arrange-ments with the sterling area and others which are helpful to us, without being open to the charge of acting contrary to any general engagements into which we have entered. Having this assurance, we can make our plans for the most difficult days which will follow the war, knowing where we stand and without risk of giving grounds of offence. This is a great gain—and one of the respects in which the new plan is much superior to either of its predecessors, which did not clearly set forth any similar safeguards.

Second, when this period is over and we are again strong enough to live year by year on our own resources, we can look forward to trading in a world of national currencies which are inter-convertible. For a great commercial nation like ourselves this is indispensable for full prosperity. Sterling itself, in due course, must obviously become, once again, generally convertible. For, without this, London must necessarily lose its international position, and the arrangements in particular of the sterling area would fall to pieces. To suppose that a system of bilateral and barter agreements, with no one who owns sterling knowing just what he can do with it—to suppose that this is the best way of encouraging the Dominions to centre their financial systems on London, seems to me pretty near frenzy. As a technique of little Englandism, adopted as a last resort when all else has failed us, with this small country driven to autarchy, keeping itself to itself in a harsh and unfriendly world, it might make more sense. But those who talk this way, in the expectation that the rest of the Commonwealth will throw in their lot on these lines and cut their free commercial relations with the rest of the world, can have very little idea how this Empire has grown or by what means it can be sustained.

So far from an international plan endangering the long tradition by which most Empire countries, and many other countries, too, have centred their financial systems in London, the plan is, in my judgment, an indispensable means of maintaining this tradition. With our own resources so greatly impaired and encumbered, it is only if sterling is firmly placed in an international setting that the necessary confidence in it can be sustained. Indeed, even during the transitional period, It will be our policy, I hope, steadily to develop the field within which sterling is freely available as rapidly as we can manage. Now if our own goal is, as it surely must be, the general inter-convertibility of sterling with other currencies, it must obviously be to our trading advantage that the same obtains elsewhere, so that we can sell our exports in one country and freely spend the proceeds in any other. It is a great gain to us in particular, that other countries in the world should agree to refrain from those discriminatory exchange practices which we ourselves have never adopted in times of peace but from which in the recent past our traders have suffered greatly at the hands of others. My noble friend Lord Addison has asked whether such an arrangement could be operated in such a way that certain markets might be closed to British exports. I can firmly assure him that none of the monetary proposals will do so provided that, if we find ourselves with currencies in a foreign country which we do not choose to spend in that country, we can then freely remit them somewhere else to buy goods in another country.

There is no compulsion on us, and if we choose to come to a particular bargain in the country where we have resources, then that is entirely at our discretion.

Third, the wheels of trade are to be oiled by what is, in effect, a great addition to the world's stock of monetary reserves, distributed, moreover, in a reasonable way. The quotas are not so large as under the Clearing Union, and Lord Addison drew attention to that. But they are substantial and can be increased subsequently if the need is shown. The aggregate for the world is put provisionally at £2,500,000,000. Our own share of this—for ourselves and the Crown Colonies which, I may mention, are treated for all purposes as a part of the British monetary system (in itself a useful acknowledgement)—is £325,000,000, a sum which may easily double, or more than double, the reserves which we shall otherwise hold at the end of the transitional period. The separate quotas of the rest of the sterling area will make a further large addition to this. Who is so confident of the future that he will wish to throw away so comfortable a supplementary aid in time of trouble? Do the critics think it preferable, if the winds of the trade cycle blow, to diminish our demand for imports by increasing unemployment at home, rather than meet the emergency out of this Fund which will be expressly provided for such temporary purposes?

I emphasise that such is the purpose of the quotas. They are not intended as daily food for us or any other country to live upon during the reconstruction or afterwards. Provision for that belongs to another chapter of international co-operation, upon which we shall embark shortly unless you discourage us unduly about this one. The quotas for drawing on the Fund's resources are an iron ration to tide over temporary emergencies of one kind or another. Perhaps this is the best reply I can make to Lord Addison's doubts whether our quota is large enough. It is obviously not large enough for us to live upon during the reconstruction period. But this is not its purpose. Pending further experience, it is, in my judgment, large enough for the purposes for which it is intended.

There is another advantage to which I would draw your Lordships' special attention. A proper share of responsibility for maintaining equilibrium in the balance of international payments is squarely placed on the creditor countries. This is one of the major improvements in the new plan. The Americans, who are the most likely to be affected by this, have, of their own free will and honest purpose, offered us a far-reaching formula of protection against a recurrence of the main cause of deflation during the inter-war years—namely, the draining of reserves out of the rest of the world to pay a country which was obstinately lending and exporting on a scale immensely greater than it was lending and importing. Under Clause VI of the plan a country engages itself, in effect, to prevent such a situation from arising again, by promising, should it fail, to release other countries from any obligation to take its exports, or, if taken, to pay for them. I cannot imagine that this sanction would ever be allowed to come into effect. If by no other means, than by lending, the creditor country will always have to find a way to square the account on imperative grounds of its own self-interest. For it will no longer be entitled to square the account by squeezing gold out of the rest of us. Here we have a voluntary undertaking, genuinely offered in the spirit both of a good neighbour and, I should add, of enlightened self-interest, not to allow a repetition of a chain of events which between the wars did more than any other single factor to destroy the world's economic balance and to prepare a seed-bed for foul growths. This is a tremendous extension of international co-operation to good ends. I pray your Lordships to pay heed to its importance.

Fifth, the plan sets up an international institution with substantial rights and duties to preserve orderly arrangements in matters such as exchange rates which are two-ended and affect both parties alike, which can also serve as a place of regular discussion between responsible authorities to find ways to escape those many unforeseeable dangers which the future holds. The noble Lord, Lord Addison, asks how the Fund is to be managed. Admittedly this is not yet worked out in the necessary detail and it was right that he should stress the point. But three points which may help him are fairly clear. This is an organisation between Governments, in which Central Banks only appear as the instrument and agent of their Government. The voting power of the British Commonwealth and that of the United States are expected to be approximately equal. The management will be in three tiers—a body of expert, whole-time officials who will be responsible for the routine; a small board of management which will make all decisions of policy subject to any over-riding instructions from the Assembly, an Assembly of all the member Governments meeting less often and retaining a supervisory, but not an executive, control. That is perhaps even a little better than appears.

Here are five advantages of major importance. The proposals go far beyond what, even a short time ago, anyone could have conceived of as a possible basis of general international agreement. What alternative is open to us which gives comparable aid, or better, more hopeful opportunities for the future? I have considerable confidence that something very like this plan will be in fact adopted, if only on account of the plain demerits of the alternative of rejection. You can talk against this plan, so long as it is a matter of talking—saying in the same breath that it goes too far and that it does not go far enough, that it is too rigid to be safe and that it is too loose to be worth anything. But it would require great fool-hardiness to reject it, much more fool-hardiness than is to be found in this wise, intuitive country.

Therefore, for these manifold and substantial benefits I commend the monetary proposals to your Lordships. Nevertheless, before you will give them your confidence, you will wish to consider whether, in return, we are surrendering anything which is vital for the ordering of our domestic affairs in the manner we intend for the future. My Lords, the experience of the years before the war has led most of us, though some of us late in the day, to certain firm conclusions. Three, in particular, are highly relevant to this discussion. We are determined that, in future, the external value of sterling shall conform to its internal value as set by our own domestic policies, and not the other way round. Secondly, we intend to retain control of our domestic rate of interest, so that we can keep it as low as suits our own purposes, without interference from the ebb and flow of international capital movements or flights of hot money. Thirdly, whilst we intend to prevent inflation at home, we will not accept deflation at the dictate of influences from outside. In other words, we abjure the instruments of bank rate and credit contraction operating through the increase of unemployment as a means of forcing our domestic economy into line with external factors.

Have those responsible for the monetary proposals been sufficiently careful to preserve these principles from the possibility of interference? I hope your Lordships will trust me not to have turned my back on all I have fought for. To establish those three principles which I have just stated has been my main task for the last twenty years. Sometimes almost alone, in popular articles in the Press, in pamphlets, in dozens of letters to The Times, in text books, in enormous and obscure treatises I have spent my strength to persuade my countrymen and the world at large to change their traditional doctrines and, by taking better thought, to remove the curse of unemployment. Was it not I, when many of to-day's iconoclasts were still worshippers of the Calf, who wrote that "Gold is a barbarous relic"? Am I so faithless, so forgetful, so senile that, at the very moment of the triumph of these ideas when, with gathering momentum, Governments, Parliaments, banks, the Press, the public, and even economists, have at last accepted the new doctrines, I go off to help forge new chains to hold us fast in the old dungeon? I trust, my Lords, that you will not believe it.

Let me take first the less prominent of the two issues which arise in this connexion—namely, our power to control the domestic rate of interest so as to secure cheap money. Not merely as a feature of the transition, but as a permanent arrangement, the plan accords to every member Government the explicit right to control all capital movements. What used to be a heresy is now endorsed as orthodox. In my own judgment, countries which avail themselves of this right may find it necessary to scrutinise all transactions, so as to prevent evasion of capital regulations. Provided that the innocent, current transactions are let through, there is nothing in the plan to prevent this. In fact, it is encouraged. It follows that our right to control the domestic capital market is secured on firmer foundations than ever before, and is formally accepted as a proper part of agreed international arrangements.

The question, however, which has recently been given chief prominence is whether we are in any sense returning to the disabilities of the former gold standard, relief from which we have rightly learnt to prise so highly. If I have any authority to pronounce on what is and what is not the essence and meaning of a gold standard, I should say that this plan is the exact opposite of it. The plan in its relation to gold is, indeed, very close to proposals which I advocated in vain as the right alternative when I was bitterly opposing this country's return to gold. The gold standard, as I understand it, means a system under which the external value of a national currency is rigidly tied to a fixed quantity of gold which can only honourably be broken under force majeure; and it involves a financial policy which compels the internal value of the domestic currency to conform to this external value as fixed in terms of gold. On the other hand, the use of gold merely as a convenient common denominator by means of which the relative values of national currencies—these being free to change—are expressed from time to time, is obviously quite another matter.

My noble friend Lord Addison asks who fixes the value of gold. If he means, as I assume he does, the sterling value of gold, it is we ourselves who fix it initially in consultation with the Fund; and this value is subject to change at any time on our initiative, changes in excess of 10 per cent requiring the approval of the Fund, which must not withhold approval if our domestic equilibrium requires it. There must be some price for gold; and so long as gold is used as a monetary reserve it is most advisable that the current rates of exchange and the relative values of gold in different currencies should correspond. The only alternative to this would be the complete demonetisation of gold. I am not aware that anyone has proposed that. For it is only common sense as things are to-day to continue to make use of gold and its prestige as a means of settling international accounts. To demonetise gold would obviously be highly objectionable to the British Commonwealth and to Russia as the main producers, and to the United States and the Western Allies as the main holders of it. Surely no one disputes that? On the other hand, in this country we have already de-throned gold as the fixed standard of value. The plan not merely confirms the dethronement but approves it by expressly providing that it is the duty of the Fund to alter the gold value of any currency if it is shown that this will be serviceable to equilibrium.

In fact, the plan introduces in this respect an epoch-making innovation in an international instrument, the object of which is to lay down sound and orthodox principles. For instead of maintaining the principle that the internal value of a national currency should conform to a prescribed de jure external value, it provides that its external value should be altered if necessary so as to conform to whatever de facto internal value results from domestic policies, which themselves shall be immune from criticism by the Fund. Indeed, it is made the duty of the Fund to approve changes which will have this effect. That is why I say that these proposals are the exact opposite of the gold standard. They lay down by international agreement the essence of the new doctrine, far removed from the old orthodoxy. If they do so in terms as inoffensive as possible to the former faith, need we complain?

No, my Lords, in recommending these proposals I do not blot a page already written. I am trying to help write a new page. Public opinion is now converted to a new model, and I believe a much improved model, of domestic policy. That battle is all but won. Yet a not less difficult task still remains—namely, to organise an international setting within which the new domestic policies can occupy a comfortable place. Therefore, it is above all as providing an international framework for the new ideas and the new techniques associated with the policy of full employment that these proposals are not least to be welcomed.

Last week my noble friend Lord Bennett asked what assumptions the experts might be making about other phases of international agreement. I do not believe that the soundness of these foundations depends very much on the details of the superstructure. If the rest of the issues to be discussed are wisely settled, the task of the Monetary Fund will be rendered easier. But if we gain less assistance from other measures than we now hope, an agreed machinery of adjustment on the monetary side will be all the more necessary. I am certain that this is not a case of putting the cart before the horse. I think it most unlikely that fuller knowledge about future commercial policy would in itself make it necessary to alter any clause whatever in the proposals now before your Lordships' House. But if the noble Viscount meant that these proposals need supplementing in other directions, no one could agree with him more than I do. In particular, it is urgent that we should seek agreement about setting up an international investment institution to provide funds for reconstruction and afterwards. It is precisely because there is so much to do in the way of international collaboration in the economic field that it would be so disastrous to discourage this first attempt, or to meet it in a carping, suspicious or cynical mood.

The noble Lord, Lord Addison, has called the attention of your Lordships to the striking statement made by Mr. Hull in connexion with the National Foreign Trade Week in the United States, and I am very glad that he did so. This statement is important as showing that the policy of the United States Administration on various issues of political and economic preparation forms a connected whole. I am certain that the people of this country are of the same mind as Mr. Hull, and I have complete confidence that he on his side will seek to implement the details with disinterestedness and generosity. If the experts of the American and British Treasuries have pursued the monetary discussions with more ardour, with a clearer purpose and, I think, with more success so far than has yet proved possible with other associated matters, need we restrain them? If, however, there is a general feeling, as I think that there is, that discussion on other matters should be expedited, so that we may have a complete picture before us, I hope that your Lordships will enforce this conclusion in no uncertain terms. I myself have never supposed that in the final outcome the monetary proposals should stand by themselves.

It is on this note of emphasizing the importance of furthering all genuine efforts directed towards international agreement in the economic field that I should wish to end my contribution to this debate. The proposals which are before your Lordships are the result of the collaboration of many minds and the fruit of the collective wisdom of the experts of many nations. I have spent many days and weeks in the past year in the company of experts of this country, of the Dominions, of our European Allies and of the United States; and in the light of some past experience I affirm that these discussions have been without exception a model of what such gatherings should be—objective, understanding, without waste of time or expense of temper. I dare to speak for the much abused so-called experts. I even venture sometimes to prefer them, without intending any disrespect, to politicians. The common love of truth, bred of a scientific habit of mind, is the closest of bonds between the representatives of divers nations.

I wish I could draw back the veil of anonymity and give their due to the individuals of the most notable group with which I have ever been associated, covering half the nations of the world, who from prolonged and difficult consultations, each with their own interests to protect, have emerged, as we all of us know and feel in our hearts, a band of brothers. I should like to pay a particular tribute to the representatives of the United States Treasury and the State Department and the Federal Reserve Board in Washington, whose genuine and ready consideration for the difficulties of others, and whose idealistic and unflagging pursuit of a better international order, made possible so great a measure of agreement. I at any rate have come out from a year thus spent greatly encouraged, encouraged beyond all previous hope and expectation, about the possibility of just and honourable and practical economic arrangements between nations.

Do not discourage us. Perhaps we are laying the first brick, though it may be a colourless one, in a great edifice. If indeed it is our purpose to draw back from international co-operation and to pursue an altogether different order of ideas, the sooner that this is made clear the better; but that, I believe, is the policy of only a small minority, and for my part I am convinced that we cannot on those terms remain a Great Power and the mother of a Commonwealth. If, on the other hand, such is not our purpose, let us clear our minds of excessive doubts and suspicions and go forward cautiously, by all means, but with the intention of reaching agreement.

BRETTON WOODS AND INTERNATIONAL COOPERATION

HENRY MORGENTHAU, JR., Secretary of the Treasury

T HE United Nations won a great if unheralded victory at the Bretton Woods Monetary and Financial Conference. For they took the first, the most vital and the most difficult step toward putting into effect the sort of international economic program which will be necessary for preserving the peace and creating favorable conditions for world prosperity.

International agreements in the monetary and financial field are admittedly hard to reach, since they lie at the very heart of matters affecting the whole complex system of economic relations among nations. It is a familiar fact that in all countries sectional interests are often in conflict with the broader national interests and that these narrow interests are sometimes sufficiently strong to shape international economic policy. It was, therefore, a special source of satisfaction to all the participants in the Conference that agreements were reached covering so wide a range of international monetary and financial problems. This was largely due to long and careful preparation preceding the Conference during which we secured general recognition of the principle of international monetary and financial coöperation.

The Conference of 44 nations prepared Articles of Agreement for establishing the International Monetary Fund and the International Bank for Reconstruction and Development to provide the means for consultation and collaboration on international monetary and investment problems. These agreements demonstrate that the United Nations have the willingness and the ability to unite on the most difficult economic issues, issues on which comprehensive agreement had never before been reached even among countries with essentially similar political and economic institutions. The victory was thus all the greater in that the Bretton Woods Agreements were prepared by countries of differing degrees of economic development, with very far from similar economic systems, and will operate not merely in the immediate postwar years, as will UNRRA, but in the longer period ahead.

The hope that the United Nations will not prove a merely temporary wartime coalition which will disintegrate after military victory has thus received substantial reinforcement. No matter what pattern future organs of international coöperation may assume—and the pattern may be diverse and varied to correspond with the great variety of problems to be met— Bretton Woods proved that if the determination to coöperate for peace as well as for war is present, adequate and suitable instruments can be devised in every sphere where international action is needed. In that sense, Bretton Woods was an unmistakable warning to the Axis that the United Nations cannot be divided either by military force or by the diplomatic intrigues of our enemies. It gave an unequivocal assurance to the soldiers of the United Nations that the sacrifices they are making to stamp out forever the causes of war are not being made in vain. And lastly it was a sign to the civilians on whose labors the war efforts of all the United Nations depend that such labors are bearing fruit in the councils of peace no less than those of war.

I have indicated that at Bretton Woods the United Nations took the first and hardest step toward the adoption of the kind of economic program necessary for world stability and prosperity. It was only the first step because the Articles of Agreement for the establishment of the Fund and the Bank still have to be ratified by each of the participants in accordance with legal and constitutional requirements and procedures. I would be the last to claim that the process is likely to be a simple or an easy one. Yet, so far as the action to be taken by the United States is concerned, I have sufficient faith in the common sense of the American people to believe that they have learned the painful lesson that the best way to guard our national interests is through effective international coöperation. We know that much remains to be done in other fields. But, despite their highly technical nature, the Fund and the Bank are the best starting point for international economic coöperation, because lack of agreement in these spheres would bedevil all other world economic relations.

Highly technical questions have one great advantage from the political point of view—their very intricacy should raise them above merely partisan considerations. My optimism is partly based on the belief that the Bretton Woods proposals will be discussed on an objective basis and that such differences of opinion as may emerge will not follow party lines. The American delegation was non-partisan in composition and was thoroughly united on all major questions. Republicans and Democrats alike had an equal voice in shaping its decisions, and there is good reason to expect that the precedent followed before and during the Conference will be continued and that the next stage of ratification will be conducted on the same high plane. In the light of my experience as chairman of the American delegation, I believe that men of broad vision in both parties will rise to the challenge and the opportunity to initiate the historical pattern of international economic coöperation that world peace demands. The challenge and opportunity are all the greater because our course of action will largely determine the course of action of many other members of the United Nations. "As America goes, so goes the world" may be an exaggeration. But it is a pardonable exaggeration in a world made one by time and fate, in which America's strength and potentialities are perhaps more clearly realized by the rest of the world than by the American people itself. I should therefore like to emphasize as strongly as possible that a tremendous responsibility rests on our government and people in connection with the ratification of the Bretton Woods Agreements. For our action will be rightly or wrongly interpreted as a sure and infallible index of our intentions with respect to the shape of things to come.

II

The fate of the Treaty of Versailles adds to the significance of the course we adopt on the Bretton Woods proposals. As the President has pointed out, the Allied leaders are acquainted with our constitutional processes as they affect our dealings with foreign powers. If there are any Americans who would utilize the division of powers to defeat the ends sought by the vast majority of Americans, they are not likely to succeed if the issues are clearly and unambiguously presented to the Congress and the people. We must always keep in mind that other nations are anxiously asking whether the United States has the desire and ability to coöperate effectively in establishing world peace. If we fail to ratify the Bretton Woods Agreements, they will be convinced that the American people either do not desire to coöperate or that they do not know how to achieve coöperation. They would then have little alternative but to seek a solution for their pressing political and economic problems on the old familiar lines, lines which will inexorably involve playing the old game of power politics with even greater intensity than before because the problems with which they will be confronted will be so much more acute. And power politics would be as disastrous to prosperity as to peace.

One important reason for the sharp decline in international trade in the 1930's and the spread of depression from country to country was the growth of the twin evils of international economic aggression and monetary disorder. The decade of the 1930's was almost unique in the multiplicity of ingenious schemes that were devised by some countries, notably Germany, to exploit their creditors, their customers, and their competitors in their international trade and financial relations. It is necessary only to recall the use of exchange controls, competitive currency depreciation, multiple currency practices, blocked balances, bilateral clearing arrangements and the host of other restrictive and discriminatory devices to find the causes for the inadequate recovery in international trade in the decade before the war. These monetary devices were measures of international economic aggression, and they were the logical concomitant of a policy directed toward war and conquest.

The postwar international economic problems may well be more difficult than those of the 1930's, and unless we coöperate to solve these problems, we may be faced with a resumption and intensification of monetary disorder and economic aggression in the postwar period. There is no need to enlarge on the consequences of such a development. It is a bleak prospect, yet it is one we must understand. In some countries it will present itself as the only practical alternative if the rest of the world should be unable to count on effective American participation in a rounded and coherent program covering international political and economic relations. If that should come to pass, we will have to frame our own future to fit a world in which war will never be a remote contingency and in which economic barriers and restrictions will be the rule in a contracting economic universe. On the other hand, if we ratify the Bretton Woods Agreements, we will be showing the rest of the world not only that we can coöperate for winning the war, not only that we are capable of formulating a program for fulfilling our common aspirations, but that we intend to enforce and implement such a program in every relevant sphere of action. Ratification would thus strengthen all the forward-looking elements in every country who wish to translate their craving for peace into deeds and will be a resounding answer to the pessimists who feel that peace is unattainable.

The institution of an international security organization on the lines agreed on at Dumbarton Oaks constitutes a history-making accomplishment of which we may well be proud. Here is an organization for maintaining peace and political security which for the first time has teeth in it. But it is our duty to keep to a minimum the tensions to which that organization will be subjected and to deal with the economic causes of aggression before the stage is reached where more far-reaching measures would be necessary. International monetary and financial coöperation is indispensable for the maintenance of economic stability; and economic stability, in turn, is indispensable to the maintenance of political stability. Therefore, a program for international economic coöperation of which Bretton Woods is the first step must accompany the program for political and military security toward which the United Nations are moving. Bretton Woods is the model in the economic sphere of what Dumbarton Oaks is in the political. They reinforce and supplement each other. Political and economic security from aggression are indivisible, and a sound program for peace must achieve both.

III

As I have already said, agreement on international monetary and banking policy is only the first step toward the achievement of a constructive economic program through which world stability can be maintained and within which the horizon of prosperity can be expanded. Other measures, both national and international, will be required to round out the program.

Domestic economic stability is, of course, intimately bound up with international stability. But international stability by itself will not ensure domestic stability. It will be incumbent on us to adopt the kind of domestic program which will make possible the attainment and maintenance of high levels of employment with rising standards of living. I have sufficient faith in our economic system and the institutions of free enterprise and individual initiative to hope that this goal will be achieved. Needless to say, its achievement will be greatly facilitated by the promise of international monetary stability held forth by the Bretton Woods Agreements, just as the achievement of international monetary stability will be facilitated by a high level of prosperity in the United States. This is merely another illustration of the thesis that we are an integral part of the world economy and that the relations between the parts and the whole are intimate and mutual. High levels of employment in the United States strengthen economic and political stability throughout the world, which in turn reinforce American domestic prosperity.

In addition, international collaboration in the sphere of commercial policy, control of cartels, and possibly in the supply of primary commodities and labor standards will be needed if the basic causes of economic friction and aggression are to be abolished. The Fund and the Bank are not intended to cover these fields, which will, of course, be subjects for further discussion among the United Nations. The great objective of the Fund and the Bank is to provide the monetary and financial foundation without which agreement in these other important fields would be either impossible to attain or meaningless if attained. For no economic agreements among nations could survive discriminatory exchange practices, severe and repeated competitive currency depreciation, tight permanent exchange controls, and the like. In fact, it is not too much to say that when nations are pursuing competitive exchange policies—whether their purpose is aggressive or merely defensive is immaterial—reciprocal trade agreements cannot be made. Thus no reciprocal trade agreement with Germany in the period from 1933 to 1939, say, would have been worth the paper it was written on for the simple reason that all its purposes and effects would have been completely nullified by the exchange policy which the Germans pursued in those years.

This consideration applies with still greater force to agreements for protecting producers of primary commodities or for raising labor standards. How, for example, can we protect the American farmer in the world markets if a sizable wheat-producing country can resort to monetary action which places the wheat producers in that country in a preferred position with respect to American wheat exporters? If the American farmer is to continue to export wheat and to receive a fair price in dollars for the wheat he sells at home, he must know that the world price of wheat in terms of his own currency will not be seriously disturbed by large exchange fluctuations in the principal wheat exporting and importing countries.

And how can we obtain agreement protecting our own high labor standards if we do not participate in expansion of international long-term investment? For if the economically less advanced countries are to raise their labor standards they must increase their productivity, and to increase their productivity they need capital for modern machinery and processes. Unless adequate provision is made for a resumption and expansion of international investment by private investors on sound lines, the less developed countries will have no alternative but to meet all their capital requirements themselves. The process of industrialization would then inevitably become more painful both to themselves and to the rest of the world, since they would have little choice but to control their imports rigorously and to compete as intensively as possible for their share of the world market, ruthlessly exploiting their own cheap labor, and undercutting countries with higher labor standards in the process. Instead of tending to raise their labor standards to our high level, this would tend to pull our labor standards down to theirs.

These instances are corollaries of the broader proposition that world stability and prosperity demand the expansion and growth of international trade and investment. In a contracting market each country will fight to maintain its foothold and will not be too fastidious as to the weapons it uses in the fight. An expanding market does not eliminate competition, but while competition assumes cutthroat and destructive forms in a contracting market, it tends to have socially beneficent effects in an expanding one.

IV

The Bretton Woods Agreements are thus the most vital step in the path of realizing effective international economic coöperation. Without monetary coöperation, international economic coöperation in other spheres will at best be short-lived; and it may not be too much to add that without monetary coöperation, international coöperation in non-economic spheres may be short-lived also. The Bretton Woods Agreements are also the most difficult step in international economic coöperation because while we were not exploring entirely uncharted seas, while precedents for monetary and financial collaboration for specific purposes existed, the scope and content of the collaboration proposed at Bretton Woods are so much broader and fuller that problems with infinitely more complications had to be solved. Our own stabilization fund has in the past entered into a number of arrangements with other governments and Central Banks to promote stability in exchange relationships between the United States and other countries. And such arrangements, while *bilateral* in character, undoubtedly made a definite contribution to orderly international monetary relations. An even broader form of *multilateral* coöperation through consultation with respect to contemplated changes in exchange rates was achieved by the Tripartite Declaration of September 1936 among France, Great Britain and the United States, to which Belgium, Holland and Switzerland subsequently adhered. But without minimizing the significance of such monetary arrangements, and particularly of the Tripartite Accord, it is proper to note that because of their limited and improvised character, and also because of the conditions in which they were made, they could not cope with the range of problems the Fund and Bank are designed to handle.

Take, for example, the question of the relative international economic positions of the United States and England to which so much attention has been devoted in discussions of postwar trade possibilities. England was formerly a creditor nation and has now become a debtor. Previously she was able to turn her unfavorable trade balance into a favorable, or at least a compensated, balance of payments by receipts of interest and dividends on foreign investments and by receipts for current banking, insurance and shipping services. After the war she will have to expand her exports. Otherwise she will have to run down her foreign investment still further or resort to new borrowing, or she will have to curtail her imports which would lower her living standards and sharply restrict world trade. The United States has become a creditor country with the prospect of increasing exports, provided our customers are in a position to find the dollars which they need to pay for the goods and services they want to buy from us. Other countries cannot find the necessary dollars to pay for our exports unless we are willing to increase our own imports, our tourist and other expenditures abroad, or unless we are willing to become a creditor country on a greater scale, or both.

The measures for international coöperation on monetary and investment problems required to meet the needs of the United States and England must obviously be flexible in character and broad in scope. This was one of the outstanding accomplishments of Bretton Woods, an accomplishment which was easier to achieve because of the spirit of mutual understanding with which the American and British delegations faced their problems, and because of the extended British and American technical discussions during the two years prior to the Conference. I believe that the economic interests of the United States and Great Britain are not irreconcilable, that the world is large enough to provide an expanding market for the exports of both, and that, given the good will which has characterized the discussion of our common economic and financial problems in the past, no problem involving our two countries need remain unsolved. Quite obviously, the solution will be much less difficult in a world in which international trade is expanding and in which an adequate volume of sound and productive international investment is undertaken by private investors. That is precisely how the Fund and the Bank can contribute to the adjustment of international accounts.

V

But that is only part of the picture. At Bretton Woods, countries in very different stages of economic evolution joined in working out common instruments of monetary and investment policy. China and India are predominantly agrarian countries with low levels of industrialization and low standards of living. Naturally, they desire to raise both. The United States and England are countries with high levels of industrialization and high standards of living, which just as naturally desire to maintain and if possible raise both. Unless some framework which will make the desires of both sets of countries mutually compatible is established, economic and monetary conflicts between the less and more developed countries will almost certainly ensue. Nothing would be more menacing to world security than to have the less developed countries, comprising more than half the population of the world, ranged in economic battle against the less populous but industrially more advanced nations of the west.

The Bretton Woods approach is based on the realization that it is to the economic and political advantage of countries such as India and China, and also of countries such as England and the United States, that the industrialization and betterment of living conditions in the former be achieved with the aid and encouragement of the latter. For the process of industrialization, without which improvement of living standards is unattainable, can be most efficiently accomplished by an increasing volume of imports of machinery and equipment. And what could be more natural than for India and China to import such goods from England and the United States with their vastly expanded capacity for producing such goods? The harmony of economic interests in international trade between the more and less developed countries is a doctrine which has long been preached by economists, but it is a doctrine which has often not been honored in observance. The United Nations Monetary and Financial Conference made a big advance toward translating this theoretically sound maxim into practice.

Again, there is a clear line of demarcation between those countries ravaged by war and the countries fortunate enough because of their geographic situation to have escaped invasion, bombing and looting by the enemy. Nowhere was what I should like to call the Bretton Woods spirit more clearly manifest than in the Conference's determinations to give special attention and consideration to the problems of countries in the first category. It was shared no less by the countries whose territories had not been damaged by Axis operations than by the immediate victims of totalitarian aggression. The reconstruction of the devastated countries of Europe and Asia is essential if normal international trade relations are to be resumed promptly. These countries are vitally important to the export and import trade of the western hemisphere. That is why all the American Republics gave wholehearted support to the provision that the Bank is to facilitate economic reconstruction. I should like to single out for special mention Russia's splendid demonstration of the sincerity of her intentions to participate in world economic reconstruction by raising her subscription to the Bank from 9 million dollars to 1.2 billion dollars on the last day of the Conference.

Finally, countries with widely divergent economic systems participated in preparing the Agreements for the Fund and the Bank. The United States is as indubitably a capitalist country as Russia is a socialist one. Yet both agree not only on the desirability of promoting monetary stability and international investment but on the means required to realize these ends. And this for a very simple and satisfactory reason—it is to the advantage of each to do so. As an impenitent adherent of the capitalist system, which in the crucible of war has once again shown its ability to deliver the goods, I am firmly convinced that capitalist and socialist societies can coexist, as long as neither resorts to destructive practices and as long as both abide by the rules of international economic fair play. Perhaps it is not too much to claim for the International Monetary Fund that it prescribes the standards in the field of monetary policy which it is hoped all countries, whatever their political and economic systems, will follow.

Despite these difficulties, the Bretton Woods Conference had to succeed because there is no other method of dealing with international monetary and financial problems than through international coöperation. There is no satisfactory alternative. There has been a suggestion that these were questions that could be solved by the United States and England, perhaps with the aid in later years of a few so-called key countries. But this approach takes no account of the realities of the postwar situation. The establishment of an exclusive Anglo-American condominium would not be the appropriate means of dealing with international monetary problems. In the absence of effective international action, unstable exchange rates are much more likely to occur in other countries than in Britain. In fact, unless there is a *general* environment of stable and orderly exchange rates with expanding trade and adequate investment, the adjustment of the British balance of payments after the war will be immeasurably more difficult. The problem of exchange stability is a general problem. Our own exporters of agricultural and industrial goods need more assurance than the stability of the dollar-sterling rate of exchange provides. They want to know that the price and quantity of their exports will not be suddenly reduced by depreciation in the countries to which they export or in the countries with whose exports they compete.

I doubt that the 42 other United and Associated Nations, who have been fighting and working with us during the war, would take kindly to what might be regarded as dictatorship of the world's finances by two countries. There is a vague promise in this alternative that other countries might in time be added to the select group whose coöperation was regarded as desirable. But even these countries would be expected to coöperate by attaching themselves to a dollar bloc or a sterling bloc. If we should exclude the greater part of the world from coöperation on these problems and postpone for ten years agreement on stability and order in exchange rates, we should find that the world had become irrevocably committed to fluctuating exchange rates, exchange controls and bilateral clearing arrangements. Once firmly established, it would not be possible to obtain the general abandonment of these restrictive and discriminatory measures. Beyond that, there would seem to be considerable danger—political as well as economic—in setting up a world divided into two blocs. Such a division of the world would not only deprive us of the general advantages of multilateral trade but would inevitably lead to conflict between the two groups. The fact is that the problems considered at Bretton Woods are international problems, common to all countries, that can be dealt with only through broad international coöperation.

The above are only the most striking examples of the range of issues before the Conference. Each country has its own peculiar position in the world economy which no other country duplicates. Naturally each country wants to safeguard and, if possible, strengthen this position. The representatives of all countries always had this consideration in mind in weighing the merits of the proposals for the Fund and the Bank. Yet the very fact that so broad an agreement was reached is the best proof that the United Nations have all learned that we are one world community in which the prosperity of each is bound up with the prosperity of all. Because this is a point on which I feel so deeply, I should like to quote from my speech to the final session of the Conference on July 22:

There is a curious notion that the protection of national interest and the development of international coöperation are conflicting philosophies—that somehow or other men of different nations cannot work together without sacrificing the interests of their particular nation. There has been talk of this sort—and from people who ought to know better—concerning the international coöperative nature of the undertaking just completed at Bretton Woods.

I am perfectly certain that no delegation to this Conference has lost sight for a moment of the particular national interest it was sent here to represent. The American delegation, which I have the honor of leading, has been, at all times, conscious of its primary obligation—the protection of American interests. And the other representatives here have been no less loyal or devoted to the welfare of their own people.

Yet none of us has found any incompatibility between devotion to our own country and joint action. Indeed, we have found on the contrary that the only genuine safeguard for our national interests lies in international coöperation.

VI

Attention should also be called to two resolutions of special significance passed by the Conference. The first recommends the earliest possible liquidation of the Bank for International Settlements. Whether rightly or wrongly, this institution has become inextricably identified with appeasement and collaboration. It is fitting that a United Nations Monetary and Financial Conference should record its unqualified stand on an existing financial organization which, to say the least, did not promote the ends we are seeking. Further, the Conference did not wish considerations of power politics to enter into the functioning of the instruments it fashioned. It is specifically stated that the Fund and the Bank should not be affected by political factors in their operations or in their recommendations to member countries. The Conference wanted to avoid linking the Fund and the Bank in any way with the Bank for International Settlements. It might be said that the best way to deal with the problem was to ignore it. But that was not the feeling of the countries that have suffered from enemy occupation. Such a passive attitude would in itself have constituted appeasement of the Axis, and the root-and-branch recommendation is in much better accord with the determination of the United Nations to tolerate no institution that does not serve in the struggle for freedom and democracy.

The second resolution was designed to ensure the restoration to their rightful owners of property looted by Germany, Japan and their satellites. It supports the steps already taken by the United Nations and calls on the governments of neutral countries to facilitate the process of restoration. It is part of the United Nations program that the Axis and its Allies and agents should not be allowed to get away with any loot this time. This resolution implements that program and contributes to the strengthening of international law concerning international theft and banditry.

If I have dwelt at some length on the significance of the Bretton Woods program for international coöperation, it is because the subject has received less than its due attention and merit in the press, which has confined its discussions to the more purely monetary and financial aspects of the Conference. Its long-run political implications may be no less far-reaching than its economic achievements. For it is in our power to transform the Bretton Woods Agreements into an epoch-making precedent, a beacon of world progress.

LORD KEYNES'S SPEECH AT INAUGURAL MEETING OF
GOVERNORS OF FUND AND BANK
Savannah, 9 March 1946

M r Secretary Vinson, Governors, Alternates, Advisers—and Observers. Like several others here present, I have been intimately concerned with what will, I think, always be known as the Bretton Woods plans. The gestation has been long; the lusty twins are seriously overdue; they will have put on, I hope, as a result, a weight and strength which will do credit to their mixed and collective parentage. At any rate it is a privilege I would not have readily forgone to be present at the hour of birth, in some capacity whether as Governor or governess, along with the midwives, nurses, doctors and parsons ready to christen (and I shall always hold to the view that the christening has been badly done and that the names of the twins should have been reversed).

Hidden behind veils or beards of Spanish moss, I do not doubt that the usual fairies will be putting in an appearance at the christening, carrying appropriate gifts. What gifts and blessings are likely to be most serviceable to the twins, whom (rightly or wrongly) we have decided to call Master Fund and Miss Bank?

The first fairy should bring, I suggest, a Joseph's coat, a many-coloured raiment to be worn by these children as a perpetual reminder that they belong to the whole world and that their sole allegiance is to the general good, without fear or favour to any particular interest. Pious words exceedingly difficult to fulfil. There is scarcely any enduringly successful experience yet of an international body which has fulfilled the hopes of its progenitors. Either an institution has become diverted to be the instrument of a limited group, or it has been a puppet of sawdust through which the breath of life does not blow. Every incident and adjunct of our new-born institutions must be best calculated to emphasise and maintain their truly international character and purpose.

The second fairy, being up-to-date, will bring perhaps a box of mixed vitamins, A, B, C, D and all the rest of the alphabet. The children may faithfully wear their many-coloured raiment, yet themselves show pale, delicate faces. Energy and a fearless spirit, which does not shelve and avoid difficult issues, but welcomes them and is determined to solve them, is what we must demand from our nurslings.

The third fairy perhaps, much older and not nearly so up-to-date, may, like the Pope with his cardinals, close the lips of the children with her hand and then open them again, invoking a spirit of wisdom, patience and grave discretion, so that, as they grow up, they will be the respected and safe recipient of confidences, of troubles and of perplexities, a reliable and prudent support to those who need them in all times of difficulty. If these institutions are to win the full confidence of the suspicious world, it must not only be, but appear, that their approach to every problem is absolutely objective and oecumenical, without prejudice or favour.

I am asking and hoping, you will see, a great deal.

I hope that Mr Kelchner has not made any mistake and that there is no malicious fairy, no Carabosse, whom he has overlooked and forgotten to ask to the party. For if so the curses which that bad fairy will pronounce will, I feel sure, run as follows:—'You two brats shall grow up politicians; your every thought and act shall have an *arrière-pensée*; everything you determine shall not be for its own sake or on its own merits but because of something else.'

If this should happen, then the best that could befall—and that is how it might turn out—would be for the children to fall into an eternal slumber, never to waken or be heard of again in the courts and markets of Mankind.

Well, ladies and gentlemen, fairies or no fairies, this looks like being a very pleasant party and a happy christening and let the omens be good.

PRESS CONFERENCE BY CHARLES DE GAULLE, SEEKING THE ABOLITION OF THE GOLD EXCHANGE STANDARD AND A RETURN TO THE GOLD STANDARD

February 4, 1965

Question: Mr. President, by converting a portion of its dollar holdings into gold, France has elicited certain reactions which have brought out the defects in the present monetary system. Do you advocate a reform in this system, and if so, how?

Question: My question, Mr. President, fits in with the preceding one. Can you specify your policy on foreign investments in France, and especially on American investments?

Answer: I shall try to explain my thoughts on these points.

As the Western European States, destroyed and ruined by the wars, recover their substance, their relative situation following their debilitation appears inadequate, even abusive and dangerous. Moreover, nothing in this statement implies that they, particularly France, are in any way unfriendly toward other countries, especially toward America. For the fact that these States wish, more each day, to act independently in every field of international relations is due merely to the nature of things. This is true of the monetary relations which have been practiced in the world since the ordeals undergone by Europe made it lose its equilibrium. I refer—is this not clear?—to the system which appeared following the first World War and which was established after the second.

We know that, starting with the Genoa Conference in 1922, this system had given two currencies, the pound and the dollar, the privilege of being held automatically as gold equivalents for all foreign payments, while the others were not. Later on, since the pound had been devalued in 1931 and the dollar in 1933, this extraordinary advantage could have seemed to be compromised. But America surmounted its great crisis. After that, the Second World War ruined the currencies in Europe by unleashing inflation there. As nearly all the world gold reserves were then held by the United States which, as the world supplier, had been able to maintain the value of its own currency, it could seem natural for other States to include dollars or gold without distinction in their exchange reserves and for foreign balances of payments to be settled by transfers of American credits or currencies as well as gold. All the more so because America experienced no difficulty in settling its debts in gold if it was asked to do so. This international monetary system, this "gold exchange standard," has consequently been accepted in practice since that time.

However, today it no longer seems to conform to reality, and it suddenly presents disadvantages which are increasingly encumbering it. Since the problem can be considered in the desired conditions of calm and objectivity—for there is nothing urgent or alarming about the present situation—this is the time to do so.

The conditions which formerly were able to give rise to the "gold exchange standard" have changed. The currencies of the Western European States are today restored, to the extent that the total gold reserves of the Six today equal those of the Americans. They would even exceed them if the Six decided to convert all their dollar holdings into gold. This means that the custom of ascribing a superior value to the dollar as an international currency no longer rests on its initial foundation—I mean America's possession of the largest share of the world's gold. But, in addition, the fact that many States in principle accept dollars on the same basis as gold so as to offset, if need be, the deficits in their favor in the American balance of payments, leads the United States to indebt itself abroad at no cost. Indeed, what it owes abroad, it pays for, at least partially, with dollars which it alone can issue, instead of paying entirely with gold, which has a real value, which must be earned to be possessed, and which cannot be transferred to others without risks and sacrifice. This unilateral facility which is granted to America is serving to cloud the idea that the dollar is an impartial and international medium of exchange, when it is a means of credit belonging to one State.

Obviously, this situation has other consequences, particularly the fact that the United States—since it is not required, at least entirely, to settle its payments deficits in gold according to the former rule which required States to take the measures, sometimes severe ones, necessary to correct their imbalances—suffered a deficit each year. Not because its total commercial exchanges were unfavorable, quite the contrary. Its exports of goods always exceed its imports. But this is also the case for dollars, for which outflows always exceed inflows. In other words, capital was created in America, by means of what must be called inflation, which in the form of dollar loans granted to States or to individuals, is exported outside. As, even in the United States, the increase in fiduciary currency which results as a side effect makes investments at home less profitable, there is a growing tendency in the United States to invest abroad. The result for certain countries is a sort of expropriation of some of their business firms.

Assuredly, such a practice has greatly facilitated, and further encourages to some extent, the manifold and substantial aid that the United States furnishes to numerous countries for their development, and from which we ourselves once benefited in large measure. But circumstances are such today that it is possible to wonder how far the difficulties would go if the States which hold dollars sooner or later reached the point where they wanted to convert them into gold. Even if such a widespread movement would never occur, the fact is that there is to a certain extent a fundamental imbalance.

For all these reasons, France recommends that the system be changed; we know that she did so, notably during the monetary conference in Tokyo. Given the world-wide upset that a crisis occurring in this domain would probably cause, we have, indeed, every reason to hope that in time the means for avoiding it will be taken. Therefore, we consider that international exchanges must be established, as was the case before the great world-wide disasters, on an unquestionable monetary basis which does not bear the mark of any individual country.

What basis? Actually, it is difficult to envision in this regard any other criterion, any other standard than gold. Yes, gold, which does not change in nature, which can be made either into bars, ingots or coins, which has no nationality, which is considered, in all places and at all times, the immutable and fiduciary value *par excellence*. Furthermore, despite all that it was possible to imagine, say, write or do in the midst of major events, it is a fact that even today no currency has any value except by direct or indirect relation to gold, real or supposed. Doubtless, no one would think of dictating to any country how to manage its domestic affairs. But the supreme law, the golden rule—and indeed it is pertinent to say it—that must be enforced and honored again in international economic relations, is the duty to balance, from one monetary area to another, by effective inflows and outflows of gold, the balance of payments resulting from their exchanges.

Certainly, the termination of the gold exchange standard without rude jolts, the reinstitution of the gold standard, the supplementary and transitional measures which could be indispensable, particularly for organizing international credit on this new basis, will have to be deliberately concerted among the States, especially those whose economic and financial capability gives them special responsibilities. Moreover, the frameworks already exist in which such studies and negotiations would normally be carried out. The International Monetary Fund, set up to guarantee, as much as it is possible, currency solidarity, would offer all States an appropriate meeting ground once it was no longer a matter of perpetuating the gold exchange standard, but of replacing it. The Group of Ten, which includes, alongside the United States and Great Britain, on the one hand France, Germany, Italy, the Netherlands and Belgium, and on the other Japan, Sweden and Canada, would prepare the necessary proposals. Lastly, it would be up to the six States, which seem to be on the way toward achieving a European Economic Community, to formulate between them, and to advocate outside, the solid system which common sense recommends and which is in keeping with the reappearing power of our old continent.

France, for her part, is ready to take an active share in the vast reform henceforth imposed in the interest of the entire world.

ADDRESS TO THE NATION BY RICHARD NIXON OUTLINING A NEW ECONOMIC POLICY: "THE CHALLENGE OF PEACE."

August 15, 1971

Good evening:

I have addressed the Nation a number of times over the past 2 years on the problems of ending a war. Because of the progress we have made toward achieving that goal, this Sunday evening is an appropriate time for us to turn our attention to the challenges of peace.

America today has the best opportunity in this century to achieve two of its greatest ideals: to bring about a full generation of peace, and to create a new prosperity without war.

This not only requires bold leadership ready to take bold action—it calls forth the greatness in a great people.

Prosperity without war requires action on three fronts: We must create more and better jobs; we must stop the rise in the cost of living; we must protect the dollar from the attacks of international money speculators.

We are going to take that action—not timidly, not half-heartedly, and not in piecemeal fashion. We are going to move forward to the new prosperity without war as befits a great people—all together, and along a broad front.

The time has come for a new economic policy for the United States. Its targets are unemployment, inflation, and international speculation. And this is how we are going to attack those targets.

First, on the subject of jobs. We all know why we have an unemployment problem. Two million workers have been released from the Armed Forces and defense plants because of our success in winding down the war in Vietnam. Putting those people back to work is one of the challenges of peace, and we have begun to make progress. Our unemployment rate today is below the average of the 4 peacetime years of the 1960's.

But we can and we must do better than that.

The time has come for American industry, which has produced more jobs at higher real wages than any other industrial system in history, to embark on a bold program of new investment in production for peace.

To give that system a powerful new stimulus, I shall ask the Congress, when it reconvenes after its summer recess, to consider as its first priority the enactment of the Job Development Act of 1971.

I will propose to provide the strongest short term incentive in our history to invest in new machinery and equipment that will create new jobs for Americans: a 10 percent Job Development Credit for 1 year, effective as of today, with a 5 percent credit after August 15, 1972. This tax credit for investment in new equipment will not only generate new jobs; it will raise productivity; it will make our goods more competitive in the years ahead.

Second, I will propose to repeal the 7 percent excise tax on automobiles, effective today. This will mean a reduction in price of about $200 per car. I shall insist that the American auto industry pass this tax reduction on to the nearly 8 million customers who are buying automobiles this year. Lower prices will mean that more people will be able to afford new cars, and every additional 100,000 cars sold means 25,000 new jobs.

Third, I propose to speed up the personal income tax exemptions scheduled for January 1, 1973, to January 1, 1972—so that taxpayers can deduct an extra $50 for each exemption 1 year earlier than planned. This increase in consumer spending power will provide a strong boost to the economy in general and to employment in particular.

The tax reductions I am recommending, together with this broad upturn of the economy which has taken place in the first half of this year, will move us strongly forward toward a goal this Nation has not reached since 1956, 15 years ago: prosperity with full employment in peacetime.

Looking to the future, I have directed the Secretary of the Treasury to recommend to the Congress in January new tax proposals for stimulating research and development of new industries and new techniques to help provide the 20 million new jobs that America needs for the young people who will be coming into the job market in the next decade.

To offset the loss of revenue from these tax cuts which directly stimulate new jobs, I have ordered today a $4.7 billion cut in Federal spending.

Tax cuts to stimulate employment must be matched by spending cuts to restrain inflation. To check the rise in the cost of Government, I have ordered a postponement of pay raises and a 5 percent cut in Government personnel.

I have ordered a 10 percent cut in foreign economic aid.

In addition, since the Congress has already delayed action on two of the great initiatives of this Administration, I will ask Congress to amend my proposals to postpone the implementation of revenue sharing for 3 months and welfare reform for 1 year.

In this way, I am reordering our budget priorities so as to concentrate more on achieving our goal of full employment.

The second indispensable element of the new prosperity is to stop the rise in the cost of living.

One of the cruelest legacies of the artificial prosperity produced by war is inflation. Inflation robs every American, every one of you. The 20 million who are retired and living on fixed incomes—they are particularly hard hit. Homemakers find it harder than ever to balance the family budget. And 80 million American wage earners have been on a treadmill. For example, in the 4 war years between 1965 and 1969, your wage increases were completely eaten up by price increases. Your paychecks were higher, but you were no better off.

We have made progress against the rise in the cost of living. From the high point of 6 percent a year in 1969, the rise in consumer prices has been cut to 4 percent in the first half of 1971. But just as is the case in our fight against unemployment, we can and we must do better than that.

The time has come for decisive action—action that will break the vicious circle of spiraling prices and costs.

I am today ordering a freeze on all prices and wages throughout the United States for a period of 90 days. In addition, I call upon corporations to extend the wage-price freeze to all dividends.

I have today appointed a Cost of Living Council within the Government. I have directed this Council to work with leaders of labor and business to set up the proper mechanism for achieving continued price and wage stability after the 90-day freeze is over.

Let me emphasize two characteristics of this action: First, it is temporary. To put the strong, vigorous American economy into a permanent straitjacket would lock in unfairness; it would stifle the expansion of our free enterprise system. And second, while the wage-price freeze will be backed by Government sanctions, if necessary, it will not be accompanied by the establishment of a huge price control bureaucracy. I am relying on the voluntary cooperation of all Americans—each one of you: workers, employers, consumers—to make this freeze work.

Working together, we will break the back of inflation, and we will do it without the mandatory wage and price controls that crush economic and personal freedom.

The third indispensable element in building the new prosperity is closely related to creating new jobs and halting inflation. We must protect the position of the American dollar as a pillar of monetary stability around the world.

In the past 7 years, there has been an average of one international monetary crisis every year. Now who gains from these crises? Not the workingman; not the investor; not the real producers of wealth. The gainers are the international money speculators. Because they thrive on crises, they help to create them.

In recent weeks, the speculators have been waging an all-out war on the American dollar. The strength of a nation's currency is based on the strength of that nation's economy—and the American economy is by far the strongest in the world. Accordingly, I have directed the Secretary of the Treasury to take the action necessary to defend the dollar against the speculators.

I have directed Secretary Connally to suspend temporarily the convertibility of the dollar into gold or other reserve assets, except in amounts and conditions determined to be in the interest of monetary stability and in the best interests of the United States.

Now, what is this action—which is very technical—what does it mean for you? Let me lay to rest the bugaboo of what is called devaluation.

If you want to buy a foreign car or take a trip abroad, market conditions may cause your dollar to buy slightly less. But if you are among the overwhelming majority of Americans who buy American-made products in America, your dollar will be worth just as much tomorrow as it is today.

The effect of this action, in other words, will be to stabilize the dollar.

Now, this action will not win us any friends among the international money traders. But our primary concern is with the American workers, and with fair competition around the world.

To our friends abroad, including the many responsible members of the international banking community who are dedicated to stability and the flow of trade, I give this assurance: The United States has always been, and will continue to be, a forward-looking and trustworthy trading partner. In full cooperation with the International Monetary Fund and those who trade with us, we will press for the necessary reforms to set up an urgently needed new international monetary system. Stability and equal treatment is in everybody's best interest. I am determined that the American dollar must never again be a hostage in the hands of international speculators.

I am taking one further step to protect the dollar, to improve our balance of payments, and to increase jobs for Americans. As a temporary measure, I am today imposing an additional tax of 10 percent on goods imported into the United States. This is a better solution for international trade than direct controls on the amount of imports.

This import tax is a temporary action. It isn't directed against any other country. It is an action to make certain that American products will not be at a disadvantage because of unfair exchange rates. When the unfair treatment is ended, the import tax will end as well.

As a result of these actions, the product of American labor will be more competitive, and the unfair edge that some of our foreign competition has will be removed. This is a major reason why our trade balance has eroded over the past 15 years.

At the end of World War II the economies of the major industrial nations of Europe and Asia were shattered. To help them get on their feet and to protect their freedom, the United States has provided over the past 25 years $143 billion in foreign aid. That was the right thing for us to do.

Today, largely with our help, they have regained their vitality. They have become our strong competitors, and we welcome their success. But now that other nations are economically strong, the time has come for them to bear their fair share of the burden of defending freedom around the world. The time has come for exchange rates to be set straight and for the major nations to compete as equals. There is no longer any need for the United States to compete with one hand tied behind her back.

The range of actions I have taken and proposed tonight—on the job front, on the inflation front, on the monetary front—is the most comprehensive new economic policy to be undertaken in this Nation in four decades.

We are fortunate to live in a nation with an economic system capable of producing for its people the highest standard of living in the world; a system flexible enough to change its ways dramatically when circumstances call for change; and, most important, a system resourceful enough to produce prosperity with freedom and opportunity unmatched in the history of nations.

The purposes of the Government actions I have announced tonight are to lay the basis for renewed confidence, to make it possible for us to compete fairly with the rest of the world, to open the door to new prosperity.

But government, with all of its powers, does not hold the key to the success of a people. That key, my fellow Americans, is in your hands.

A nation, like a person, has to have a certain inner drive in order to succeed. In economic affairs, that inner drive is called the competitive spirit.

Every action I have taken tonight is designed to nurture and stimulate that competitive spirit, to help us snap out of the self-doubt, the self-disparagement that saps our energy and erodes our confidence in ourselves.

Whether this Nation stays number one in the world's economy or resigns itself to second, third, or fourth place; whether we as a people have faith in ourselves, or lose that faith; whether we hold fast to the strength that makes peace and freedom possible in this world, or lose our grip—all that depends on you, on your competitive spirit, your sense of personal destiny, your pride in your country and in yourself.

We can be certain of this: As the threat of war recedes, the challenge of peaceful competition in the world will greatly increase.

We welcome competition, because America is at her greatest when she is called on to compete.

As there always have been in our history, there will be voices urging us to shrink from that challenge of competition, to build a protective wall around ourselves, to crawl into a shell as the rest of the world moves ahead.

Two hundred years ago a man wrote in his diary these words: "Many thinking people believe America has seen its best days." That was written in 1775, just before the American Revolution—the dawn of the most exciting era in the history of man. And today we hear the echoes of those voices, preaching a gospel of gloom and defeat, saying the same thing: "We have seen our best days."

I say, let Americans reply: "Our best days lie ahead."

As we move into a generation of peace, as we blaze the trail toward the new prosperity, I say to every American: Let us raise our spirits. Let us raise our sights. Let all of us contribute all we can to this great and good country that has contributed so much to the progress of mankind.

Let us invest in our Nation's future, and let us revitalize that faith in ourselves that built a great nation in the past and that will shape the world of the future.

Thank you and good evening.

Glossary

ADJUSTMENT RESPONSIBILITIES (SYMMETRIC AND ASYMMETRIC) Loans of the
International Monetary Fund (IMF) are made on condition that the
recipient country adjust its policies to ensure repayment. The Keynes
Plan would have instituted symmetric adjustment responsibilities. That
is, it would have apportioned the burden of adjusting the balance of
payments on both debtors and countries running surpluses. The
agreement adopted at Bretton Woods placed the burden of adjustment
asymmetrically on the debtors. Conditionality usually requires the
burden of balancing payments to be shared between nations.

ATLANTIC CHARTER Joint declaration by the heads of state of the United States
and the United Kingdom in 1941 outlining a common policy in hope
of a better future for the world. The Atlantic Charter was the document
that inspired the formation of the United Nations and the General
Agreement on Tariffs and Trade (GATT). The charter proposed to
increase international collaboration in the postwar world to lower trade
barriers, improve labor standards, and promote social welfare.

BANCOR The bancor was an international monetary unit proposed by
Keynes for the purpose of clearing multilateral balance-of-payments
transactions. These transactions were to be overseen by the International
Clearing Union, which would have played a role similar to the Bank for
International Settlements in the 1930s. Keynes's proposal was opposed
by the United States and was not included in the Bretton Woods
Agreements.

BANK FOR INTERNATIONAL SETTLEMENTS Seated in Basel, Switzerland, the Bank
for International Settlements was established in 1930 to handle reparations payments imposed on Germany after the First World War, but it
quickly developed into an agency for multilateral clearing among central
banks.

BEVERIDGE REPORT Report published by the British government in 1942 that would become the blueprint for the Labour Party's postwar welfare state. It recommended the creation of the National Health Service as well as a deepening of the social insurance system.

COMBINED FOOD BOARD A bilateral agency created by the British and the US governments during World War II to manage food and the distribution of food resources.

COMPOSITE RESERVE UNIT (CRU) Part of the Bernstein Plan to pool national currency reserves in a reserve settlements account. Each G10 member would subscribe an amount of its own currency to a pool and receive in exchange a corresponding amount of CRUs. The value of the CRU would be a weighted average of the G10 currencies. CRUs could be used as equivalent to gold.

CONDITIONALITY (REQUIRED ADJUSTMENT) See Adjustment Responsibilities.

CONVERTIBILITY The ability to convert currency into gold or, more generally, to any liquid asset that it may be pegged to.

CURRENCY PAR VALUE Members of the Bretton Woods system were required to declare a target value for their currency in terms of gold or dollars and commit to keeping their currency close to that "par" value.

CURRENCY PEG A currency is said to be pegged to a commodity (such as gold) if the currency has a fixed exchange rate with that commodity over time. A currency can also be pegged to another currency or to a basket of other currencies.

CURRENCY WAR A situation in which a country devalues its currency in order to improve its terms of trade, and other countries retaliate with similar devaluations.

DOLLAR "GLUT" During the 1960s the United States ran a balance-of-payments deficit that led to a buildup of dollar reserves in central banks in Europe and Japan and a growing fear that the United States would not be able to maintain the convertibility of dollars into gold.

DOLLAR-GOLD SYSTEM The dollar-gold system refers to the ability to convert US dollars into gold and vice versa. Although in theory it made little difference whether countries held dollars or gold, from the inception of the Bretton Woods system countries mainly held dollars.

DUMBARTON OAKS CONFERENCE A conference hosted in 1944 by the US government in Washington, DC, at which representatives of the United States, the United Kingdom, the Soviet Union, and China planned the structure of a new world organization to be called the United Nations.

ECONOMIC COOPERATION ACT The Economic Cooperation Act, enacted by the US Congress in 1948, created the Marshall Plan. Its purpose was to help the European countries expand their economies, restore their export capacities, and achieve political stability after World War II.

EUROPEAN CURRENCY UNIT (ECU) The European Currency Unit was first proposed by the French in 1971 as a European unit of account pegged to gold. The Bretton Woods system was breaking down, and the French hoped that the ECU might substitute for the dollar in international transactions. In 1979 the European Economic Community adopted the ECU as its unit of account, with its value pegged to a basket of European currencies. In 1999 the ECU was replaced by the euro.

EUROPEAN PAYMENTS UNION (EPU) The European Payments Union was established in 1952 in order to clear transactions among member states without relying on US dollars, which were then in short supply relative to demand. The EPU operated through the Bank for International Settlements.

EXCHANGE CONTROLS Restrictions or complete bans on the exchange of foreign into domestic currency or vice versa. Governments adopt exchange controls in order to stabilize the value of their currencies and prevent the depletion of their stocks of gold or of currencies, like dollars, used as international reserves.

EXCHANGE RATE POLICY Exchange rate policy is a specific type of monetary policy. It aims to control exchange rates by changing the interest rate (to affect the demand for the currency) or buying and selling currency (to affect the supply).

FISCAL POLICY Fiscal policy is the use of taxation and government spending to control the business cycle.

FIXED CURRENCY PARITY SYSTEM The same as a fixed exchange rate system, but this term is more commonly used to refer to maintaining a constant par value vis-à-vis a commodity (for example, gold).

FIXED EXCHANGE RATES A regime under which the central bank uses monetary policy to keep the exchange rate between the domestic and foreign currencies fixed (pegged).

FLOATING EXCHANGE RATES A regime under which the exchange rate between a domestic currency and a foreign currency is allowed to fluctuate. In a floating exchange rate system the central bank may still use monetary policy but with the aim of controlling inflation or the business cycle, not to fix the exchange rate.

FOOD AND AGRICULTURE ORGANIZATION OF THE UNITED NATIONS (FAO) A special organization of the UN, founded in 1945 to ameliorate food scarcities around the world. The "want of food" was seen as a major problem that needed to be overcome to achieve other economic development goals.

GENERAL AGREEMENT ON TARIFFS AND TRADE (GATT) The General Agreement on Tariffs and Trade was a multilateral agreement joined in 1947 by twenty-three nations with the aim of reducing tariff barriers around the world. Members of GATT treated each other as most-favored nations. No member could grant a nonmember state a lower tariff than that offered to GATT members. GATT became part of the World Trade Organization (WTO) in 1995.

GOLD CONVERTIBILITY The ability to exchange currency into gold (mostly used for currency that is pegged to gold).

GOLD EXCHANGE STANDARD A more flexible version of the gold standard in which countries do not have to hold gold reserves in order to maintain the value of their currency in gold but may instead hold bills of exchange in currencies convertible into gold.

GOLD POOL A gold reserve created by the United States and seven European central banks in 1961 to stabilize the London price of gold at $35 dollars an ounce.

GOLD QUOTA Payments that member nations had to make to the International Monetary Fund (IMF) that were proportional to the size of their economies. Each member faced a borrowing constraint that was a multiple of its gold quota.

GRAND ALLIANCE The name given to the alliance formed by the United Kingdom, China, the United States, and the Soviet Union to defeat Germany and Japan in World War II.

HOT SPRINGS CONFERENCE The first of a series of conferences to plan for the postwar economic order. It was held in Hot Springs, Virginia, in the spring of 1943 and addressed nutritional standards, improved methods of farming, and trade policy. The efforts spurred by this conference led ultimately to the creation of the Food and Agriculture Organization of the United Nations (FAO).

IMPERIAL PREFERENCE OR IMPERIAL TRADE PREFERENCE A policy whereby members of the British Empire granted each other favorable tariffs and trade quotas.

INTERNATIONAL CLEARING UNION (ICU) The International Clearing Union was an organization proposed by Keynes on the model of the Bank for International Settlements. It would clear transactions denominated in bancors, an international monetary unit that Keynes also proposed.

INTERNATIONAL RESERVE CURRENCY An international reserve currency is a currency that is held by many nations in order to meet payment obligations to each other. Countries elect to hold currencies with very stable values as reserve currencies to limit exchange rate risk.

LEND-LEASE A US program during World War II to lend weapons and heavy machinery to Allied forces in Europe and Asia as well as to supply them with food and energy resources. In return the United States obtained leases on army and naval bases in these countries.

LENDER OF LAST RESORT An institution, usually a central bank, that supplies credit or loan guarantees when no other economic actor is able or willing to do so. By providing loans to a failing bank or other large enterprise, the lender of last resort may be able to prevent a bank run or another type of systemic crisis.

MAASTRICHT TREATY Treaty signed in 1992 by the twelve members of the European Economic Community to replace the Treaty of Rome. The treaty created the European Union and provided for the formation of a European Central Bank and the introduction of a common currency (the euro).

MARSHALL PLAN The Marshall Plan, created by the Economic Cooperation Act of 1948, was an effort to aid economic recovery in Western Europe after World War II. The US government provided approximately $13 billion in grants and loans to Western European countries between 1948 and 1952, including former Axis powers as well as the Allied nations.

MONETARY POLICY Monetary policy manages the supply of money to control inflation and the business cycle.

NEW INTERNATIONAL ECONOMIC ORDER (NIEO) A proposal made by developing countries during the 1970s to replace Bretton Woods with a system that would be more supportive of their own state-led development strategies.

ORGANIZATION FOR ECONOMIC COOPERATION AND DEVELOPMENT (OECD) The OEEC (Organization of European Economic Cooperation) was established in 1948 to further economic cooperation and the implementation of the Marshall Plan. It later was reformed and renamed OECD. The headquarters is in Paris.

PHILLIPS CURVE An observed inverse relationship between unemployment and inflation, which suggests that the government could use its fiscal policy tools to lower the unemployment rate at the cost of increasing inflation.

PRICE-SPECIE FLOW MECHANISM The mechanism that was supposed to solve the problem of trade imbalances under the gold standard. If a country had a positive trade balance, gold would flow in to pay for exports. The gold inflows would cause prices in the country to rise, making its exports more expensive until the trade surplus was eliminated.

QUOTA SYSTEM A system in which the volume of imports is regulated by limiting the quantity of a good that can enter from a specific country during a given time period.

SMITHSONIAN AGREEMENT An agreement negotiated in 1971 among the major European nations, Japan, and the United States that attempted to save the gold-exchange standard by revaluing the dollar from $35 to $38 per ounce of gold, pegging other currencies to the dollar, and allowing exchange rates to fluctuate within wider bands than the Bretton Woods accords had originally permitted.

SPECIAL DRAWING RIGHTS (SDR) An international unit of account (similar to Keynes's bancor) first created by the International Monetary Fund (IMF) in 1969 to provide an increased pool of reserves to support international transactions. The IMF sets the value of SDRs on the basis of a basket of important currencies.

STERLING AREA The set of countries that pegged their currency to the British pound sterling instead of gold, mainly members of the British Empire and British Commonwealth and countries that traded heavily with the United Kingdom (in the 1930s it included countries like Portugal, Denmark, and Sweden).

TERMS OF TRADE Terms of trade are the ratio of the price of the goods a country exports to the price of the goods it imports. This ratio is a measure of the purchasing power of a country in world markets.

TREATY OF ROME Signed in 1957 by six countries (France, Germany, Italy, the Netherlands, Belgium, and Luxembourg), it established the European Economic Community, a customs union that expanded trade within Europe by reducing tariff barriers among member countries. The Treaty of Rome was replaced in 1992 by the Maastricht Treaty, which established the European Union.

TRIFFIN DILEMMA Named after Robert Triffin, an economist who pointed out a fundamental problem with the dollar's role in the Bretton Woods system. The limited supply of gold in conjunction with the growth in international trade would lead to an increase in demand for dollars as foreign exchange reserves. This increase in demand would lead the United States to run trade deficits that would ultimately undermine confidence in the dollar as a reserve asset.

TRIPARTITE AGREEMENT A 1936 agreement made by Britain, France, and the United States to end the currency wars of the 1930s. The three countries committed themselves to maintain the relative values of their currencies and to coordinate any future devaluations that proved necessary.

Contributors

ANDREW BAILEY is the chief executive officer of the Financial Conduct Authority, as well as a member of the Prudential Regulation Committee, the Financial Policy Committee, and the Board of the Financial Conduct Authority in the United Kingdom.

GORDON BANNERMAN teaches business history in the Business Department at the University of Guelph-Humber, Ontario, Canada.

MICHAEL D. BORDO is professor of economics and director of the Center for Monetary and Financial History at Rutgers University, New Brunswick, New Jersey.

JAMES M. BOUGHTON is a Senior Fellow at the Centre for International Governance Innovation (CIGI) and a former historian of the IMF.

OLIVIA BRIFFAULT graduated with a BA from Yale University in 2017, where she majored in French and economics. She now works in New York City in sales and trading.

SELWYN CORNISH is Honorary Associate Professor in the Research School of Economics at Australian National University. He is the official historian of the Reserve Bank of Australia.

MARTIN DAUNTON is Emeritus Professor of Economic History and Emeritus Master and Honorary Fellow of Trinity Hall at Cambridge University.

BARRY EICHENGREEN is George C. Pardee and Helen N. Pardee Professor of Economics and Political Science at the University of California, Berkeley.

JEFFRY FRIEDEN is professor of government at Harvard University.

MICHAEL GRAETZ is the Wilbur H. Friedman Professor of Tax Law and the Columbia Alumni Professor of Tax Law at Columbia Law School. He is also the Justus S. Hotchkiss Professor of Law Emeritus and Professional Lecturer, Yale Law School.

ERIC HELLEINER is a professor in the Department of Political Science at the University of Waterloo, Ontario, Canada.

DOUGLAS A. IRWIN is the John French Professor of Economics at Dartmouth College.

HAROLD JAMES is the Claude and Lore Kelly Professor in European Studies, professor of history and international affairs, and the director of the Program in Contemporary European Politics and Society at Princeton University.

NAOMI LAMOREAUX is Stanley B. Resor Professor of Economics and History at Yale University and a research associate at the National Bureau of Economic Research.

FRANCES MCCALL ROSENBLUTH is the Damon Wells Professor of Political Science at Yale University.

CHERYL SCHONHARDT-BAILEY is professor in political science in the Government Department of the London School of Economics and Political Science.

KURT SCHULER is Senior Fellow in Financial History at the Center for Financial Stability in New York.

IAN SHAPIRO is Sterling Professor of Political Science at Yale University, where he also serves as Henry R. Luce Director of the MacMillan Center for International and Area Studies.

JAMES SUNDQUIST is a second-year PhD student studying international political economy at Yale University.

Credits

Articles of Agreement of the International Monetary Fund, July 22, 1944. Source: International Monetary Fund.

Articles of Agreement of the International Bank for Reconstruction and Development, July 22, 1944. Source: World Bank.

Preliminary Draft Outline of a Proposal for an International Stabilization Fund for the United and Associated Nations (Revised July 10, 1943). Source: U.S. Department of the Treasury.

Department of State Publication No. 2866, *Proceedings and Documents of the United Nations Monetary and Financial Conference, Bretton Woods, New Hampshire, July 1–22, 1944* (Washington: Government Printing Office, 1948), vol. ii, p. 1536

Proposals for an International Clearing Union (April 1943). London: HM Stationery Office, Cmd. 6437, 8 April 1943. Great Britain. *Treasury proposals for an international clearing union : presented by the Chancellor of the Exchequer to Parliament by command of His Majesty, April 1943.* H.M.S.O, London, 1943.

Suggestions Regarding International Monetary Relations (May 1943). Republished with permission of the International Monetary Fund, from *The International Monetary Fund 1945–1965. Twenty Years of International Monetary Cooperation*, J. Keith Horsefield [Ed.], Vol. III, 1969.

The Employment Agreement. National Archives of Australia A989, 44/735/55/4/1.

Joint Statement by Experts on the Establishment of an International Monetary Fund (April 1944). Source: U.S. Department of the Treasury.

Final Act (Text). Source: U.S. Department of State. Department of State (Ed.). United Nations Monetary and Financial Conference: Bretton Woods, Final act and related documents, New Hampshire, July 1 to July 22, 1944. Washington: United States Government Printing Office, 1944. 121 p.

Speech by Lord Keynes on the International Monetary Fund debate: House of Lords, May 23, 1944. Source: House of Lords, Deb 23 May 1944 vol 131 cc834–83.

Henry Morgenthau, "Bretton Woods and International Cooperation," *Foreign Affairs* 23(1)(1945), p. 190. Republished with permission of The Council on Foreign Relations, Inc., from *Foreign Affairs*, Vol. 3, No. 2, 1945.

Lord Keynes's Speech at Inaugural Meeting of Governors of Fund and Bank, Savannah, 9 March 1946. John Maynard Keynes, *The Collected Writings of John Maynard Keynes, Vol 26. Activities*, 1941–46, 1980, © The Royal Economic Society, published by Cambridge University Press, reproduced with permission.

Press Conference by Charles de Gaulle, Seeking the Abolition of the Gold Exchange Standard and a Return to the Gold Standard, February 4, 1965. Source: *Major Addresses, Statements, and Press Conferences of General Charles de Gaulle, March 17, 1964–May 16, 1967*, French Embassy, Press and Information Division, 1967.

Address to the Nation by Richard Nixon Outlining a New Economic Policy: "The Challenge of Peace." August 15, 1971. Source: Public Papers of the Presidents of the United States, Pub. Paper 264, Richard Nixon, 1971.

Index

Note: An italicized page number indicates a figure.